Mysterium Magnum

Volume Two

Mysterium Magnum

An exposition of
The First Book of Moses
called

GENESIS

written Anno 1623 by

Jacob Boehme

translated by
John Sparrow

[Volume Two]

Hermetica

San Rafael, Ca

Third, facsimile edition
Hermetica, 2007

For information, address:
Hermetica, P.O. Box 151011
San Rafael, California 94915, USA

ISBN-13: 978-1-59731-214-1
(Vol 1: pbk.: alk. paper)
ISBN-13: 978-1-59731-216-8
(Vol 1: hardcover: alk. paper)
ISBN-13: 978-1-59731-215-8
(Vol 2: pbk.: alk. paper)
ISBN-13: 978-1-59731-217-2
(Vol 1: hardcover: alk. paper)

Mysterium Magnum
VOLUME TWO

The Forty-Fourth Chapter

How *Lot* departed out of Sodom, and of the Terrible Overthrow of this whole Region in *Ham's* Generation; of the circumstances thereof, and how it was effected

1. WHEN, as the wrath of the judgment was now set on fire, and the day appeared, that the sun shone bright, and every man thought, all is in peace and quiet, there is no danger, The Angels commanded Lot to make haste, and said, Arise, take thy wife, and thy two daughters, which are here; lest thou also perish in the iniquity of this city. And while Lot lingered, the men took him, and his wife, and his two daughters, by the hand (the Lord being merciful to him), and they brought him forth, and set him without the city (Gen. xix. 15, 16).

2. The internal figure stands thus: The spirit in Moses setteth the figure so clearly, that a man may easily take it; for he saith, *When the morning came*, and the sun was risen, *they took him by the hand, and brought him, and his wife, and his two daughters, forth out of the city*. And now as the figure was externally, in the arisen light of the day and the sun, so it was also internally, in God's truth and judgment.

3. Namely, in the truth the figure was internally thus: In Lot, and his two daughters, the light of the understanding concerning the Messiah was arisen in God's truth; which Lot's daughters knew very well; that it [viz. the light of the sun of righteousness] in God's truth had moved itself in their father Lot; from which cause afterwards, when they were gone out from Sodom, and the night approached, they made their father drink sweet wine to the full, and lay with him, that they might receive seed, viz. the holy seed from him. For the spirit, both in Lot and his daughters, did also signify thus much, in their risen light, and shewed it to them.

4. And now as the sun was externally risen, and it seemed to be a very lovely pleasant day, so also internally, in God's truth, the sun of the Covenant, viz. the holy Sun-Day, was risen according to the probation in their essence, for they were now passed through the judgment. And likewise on the contrary, the sun of the dark world's

property, viz. the working of God's anger, was risen now in the children of Sodom, and forced mightily into God's righteousness. Therefore the angels bade Lot make haste; for the sun of anger was already risen, and had apprehended the children of iniquity.

5. Like as the holy sun in God's truth (which had apprehended Lot and his daughters in the essence of faith) took Lot and his daughters by the hand, and brought them forth from them; so likewise the wrath had already taken the children of Sodom by the hand of their essence, and brought them into the judgment of execution. And we will signify and apply (O Babel) this figure unto the time of thy seal: mark and observe it, ye daughters, children of Lot: it concerns you.

6. When God will punish a land, he first sends them messengers, and exhorts them to repentance, and declares unto them his grace. Soon after he sends them the angel of righteousness, who trieth and sifteth them whether they be capable of the grace that is tendered unto them; and sets judgment before them, with threats of their ruin; denouncing great war and plagues upon them to blot and root them out if they will not return and repent; and sheweth them also by his messengers the light and way of righteousness; and suffers them to run on in the light that is tendered to them, till they be weary and glutted with it, and hold it only for a common customary thing, and a history, and again become a Sodom.

7. And then he sends them both angels together, to wit, the angel of righteousness, and the angel of truth; and first threateneth them severely, and exhorts them, and sets the judgment before them; but when they grow[1] wholly a Sodom, he leaveth off from the outward figure, and lets them fill up their measure; and then it seems as if the sun were risen upon their Sodom, and now it should be good and prosperous. But even then saith the angel of truth in his children, Hasten and go out, the punishment and ruin is at hand.

8. Thus we declare unto thee, Babel, that God hath already long since sent thee messengers, and with the declaration of the Gospel hath tendered thee his grace; and therewith also hath mightily threatened to punish thee with ruin. But thou hast made only a contentious disputing Babel of the light of the Gospel, and art now the well-fatted Sodom.

9. And know for certain, that the Lord for a farewell hath now sent thee two angels, one hath the truth in him, and bids Lot with his

[1] Are.

HOW LOT DEPARTED OUT OF SODOM

daughters to go out from Sodom; and the other hath the severe judgment, and hath now at last sifted thee, and turned thy inward signature outwards, and set it before the Lord; and thy murderous[1] cry is come up before the presence of the Most High; and it is exceeding great; he hath sent his angel to destroy thee, and to overturn the cities.

10. Thy signature wherewith thou art now outwardly marked is the great covetousness and envy, together with thy ammunition-money; and the great wrathful severity of thy oppression of the poor and miserable, in that thy covetousness hath served itself so high, that it desires to devour all into itself, whence thy great enhancement of man's necessaries[2] is risen.

11. But thou sayest, Now it is a good and a prosperous time; the sun is risen upon me, and shineth on my purse, so that I can fill it as I please; it is a good and a fine time for me; it shall now be a good and a golden time, sure enough; I shall certainly enjoy it, and arise in high power and authority, and be respected.

12. But hear now, what at present the sound of the trumpet declareth. It saith, Go out from Sodom; the sun is risen in love and anger, this we will not hide from you. The angel of truth hath now already taken Lot's daughters, with the father, and his wife, by the hand; and bids them go; it is time; this thou shalt soon see by woeful experience.

13. For the angel of anger hath also taken thee into judgment, and therefore thou art so wrathful, covetous, murderous, and wicked. Do but behold thyself, whether we speak truth. Thou gettest thyself much to spend in thy signature; and thou hast indeed a storehouse full of provision in the abyss: He that can see, let him see; in whom there is but the least inkling of the trumpet's sound, let him go out of Sodom: there is no longer any tarrying.

14. And Moses speaketh further: *And when he had brought Lot forth, he said, Escape for thy life; look not behind thee, and stay not also in this whole plain; escape unto the mountain, lest thou be consumed. But Lot said unto him, Oh, not so, my Lord: Behold now, seeing thy servant hath found grace in thy sight, be pleased to magnify thy mercy which thou hast shewn unto me, in that thou hast saved my life; I cannot escape to the mountain, lest some evil take me, and I die: Behold, there is a city very near, unto which I may flee, it is a little*

---

[1] Thy Cain like crying ruin upon others.
[2] The scarcity and dearness of commodities, and all oppression ariseth from the covetousness and pride of man, who seeks to maintain it by the sword.

one: Oh, let me escape thither (is it not a little one?) and my soul shall live. And he said unto him, See, I have accepted thee concerning this thing, that I should not overturn the city for which thou hast spoken. Haste thee, escape thither; for I can do nothing till thou be come thither. Therefore the name of the city was called Zoar. And the sun was risen upon the earth when Lot came into Zoar (Gen. xix. 17–23).

The inward figure stands thus:

15. The spirit of truth had moved the spirit in the Covenant in Lot, and taken him by his spiritual hand, and brought him forth out of the judgment; understand, the soul of Lot, in which the Word of Promise in the Covenant had opened itself according to the spiritual property, into which also the now sent voice of truth and judgment did force, and defended Lot from and in the judgment.

16. For with the judgment the first Principle, viz. the soul's centre, was sifted and proved through all the properties of the eternal nature. Into this the Lord's hand, viz. the angel of the Lord, did put itself, with the grace of Christ's Covenant in Abraham, and drew Lot out of the judgment, and from the children of Sodom. Therefore the angel said, Deliver thyself, and look not behind thee into judgment, viz. into the enkindled wrath, lest the same take thee. As happened to Lot's wife, who turned her desire back again to see and behold what the wrath of the Lord should be.

17. As Adam and Lucifer also did the like, who would essentially behold and prove God's, viz. the eternal nature's, wrath, which yet is a consuming fire, and forthwith proveth spirit, and body; and if it reacheth anything of which it is capable, it devoureth it into itself.

18. Now the soul of Lot trembled and stood in fear before the angel of the judgment, viz. before God's righteousness; and entreated his truth, that he would be pleased to magnify his mercy in the Covenant towards him, lest the turba should take hold of him; and it is a very excellent example, how God taketh his children, in the time of punishment and judgment, into his love, defendeth them, and brings them forth from great destruction; as he did here unto Lot, and also unto the upright children in the final destruction of Jerusalem.

19. Also the angel of vengeance said: I can do nothing, until thou be come thither. Oh! thou wonderful God, who can hinder thee? But this is even thus to be understood: the spirit of his love in the Covenant had set or established itself with the truth, in Lot, and kept off the anger that it could not burn until Lot came out.

HOW LOT DEPARTED OUT OF SODOM

20. And we see that oftentimes the children of God are able to withhold great plagues and punishment of God [from coming down on a people]; there is even such a might in them, that God's anger is able to do nothing, and is as it were impotent where they are present. Also they are a might and power against hell and the devil; for such a thing is true real faith, that it can withhold and overpower God in his anger.

21. Therefore the Lord said to Lot, I cannot do anything, until thou be gone out. And he spared also the little city called Pella, or Zoar (viz. a diversion or turning away of the anger) for Lot's sake; for when he came thither the turba must be extinguished, as the name, in the uncompacted tongue of sense, doth express it.

22. *And then the Lord rained upon Sodom and upon Gomorrah brimstone and fire from the Lord out of heaven; and overthrew the cities, and all the plain; and all the inhabitants of the cities, and all whatsoever grew upon the ground. And his wife looked back, and she became a pillar of salt* (Gen. xix. 24-26).

23. This is now the figure of the kingdom of Christ, who had opened himself to Abraham in the love, how he would sit in judgment over the world; and how the might and dominions is given unto him of God, that he should destroy the devil's kingdom upon the earth, and give all wicked men unto the anger of God to be devoured. For when he had manifested himself to Abraham, and confirmed the Covenant of righteousness, he then sent these two angels, viz. God's truth and judgment, to Sodom, to blot out and destroy the children of Ham, viz. the malicious, vile, rebellious, half-devil's-men; that so the devil's kingdom might be lessened, and not grow so great upon the earth, and hinder his kingdom.

The inward figure stands thus:

24. It rained brimstone and fire from the Lord from heaven, saith Moses: This was not the inward hellish fire, which at the end of days shall purge the floor; otherwise the four elements would have been changed: it was only a figure of the future. The original of the brimstone and fire was generated in turba magna in the third Principle: it was only a sword of vengeance. The inward fire consumes earth and stones, and all elements: but this was only [such] a fire as is generated in the tempest in turba magna in the *egest*,[1] which the

[1] Or, excrement.

constellation casteth forth from itself, which is a *materia* thereunto. Although it be no palpable matter of substance, yet it is a spiritual substance, in which Mercurius doth enkindle itself in the Salniter, viz. in the fire-crack, where then also the flagrat or fire-crack doth fix itself into a substance or essence, which is brimstone.

25. For the three [first properties], viz. Sulphur, Mercurius, and the Salt-sharpness, are in the original (as they are yet a spirit) only one thing. But when Mercurius, viz. the sound of the formed Word, doth move itself in the Principle, viz. in its first original by an opposition or contrary aspect, then he is terrified in himself: that is, the motion stirreth the original of the heat and cold, viz. the original of the first Principle according to the cold and hot fire; which is the beginning of the contrariety and horror; from whence the fire-flash or salnitral flagrat doth arise; where also the three first, viz. the heat, the cold, and the sound, do each impress and introduce itself into a peculiar substance in the flagrat, viz. the heat into brimstone, and the cold into a saltish property, and Mercurius into a watery property. And yet they were not wholly separated, and each of them of another or sundry substance by itself, but fixed together according to one property.

26. The like also we are here to understand concerning the brimstone-fire: the wrath of the first Principle, viz. God's anger according to the eternal nature, did behold the outward nature in the third Principle with an aspect,[1] which is called turba magna, being a turba in the soul of the outward world in the spirit of nature, whence the outward nature doth inflame and enkindle itself; and the three first [properties][2] do fix themselves into a substance, viz. into Brimstone, Salt, and into a Mercurial poisonful water, in which the flagrat or flash of the fire did enkindle and impress itself; and so being enkindled did rain upon Sodom and Gomorrah, and upon the plain of the country, and destroyed all. This is it which is said, *The Lord rained brimstone and fire from the Lord out of heaven.*

27. Not that this matter of the brimstone and fire came from the inward heaven; but the wrath came forth from the inward into the outward [Principle], so that the outward, in the might of the inward, did impress and enkindle itself out of the properties of the inward. And this is a real type of the inward dark world: if the same nature doth move itself, then it is even so in spiritual property, which God calleth his wrath and anger, and a consuming fire; for if this inward

---

[1] Or, darting flash.   [2] The prime Ternary of nature.

HOW LOT DEPARTED OUT OF SODOM

spiritual dark world did move itself, the outward world, with the four elements, would forthwith be swallowed up in this same spirit-fire; which shall come to pass at the end of days.

28. And here we have a figure of this in Lot's wife, who was turned into a pillar of salt: that the three first [properties] had moved themselves; for she, after that she had looked back into the turba, was apprehended or taken in the salt's spirit in its impression; which denoteth, that she was most of that very property,[1] viz. covetous in the desire, in which she also was taken and apprehended in the sifting [probation] of the angel.

29. And though the angel had defended her from the fire-wrath, yet she was taken in the wrath of nature of her own peculiar property; viz. the turba magna laid hold of the body, viz. the substance of the third Principle, and changed it into its own peculiar property, viz. into the might of the first, which was chiefly predominant in her body, according to which property also she was apprehended in the turba.

30. And we ought not to account this a strange thing; for we have very much hereof in the Scripture. Let us look upon Uzza, who was apprehended and smitten by the Ark of the Covenant, when he did only touch the same, when the wrath of God was moved[2] but in the sound. Let us see also, how it seized on the Philistines, when they had the Ark of the Covenant with them. Also how it devoured Chorah, Dathan, and Abiram, by Moses in the wilderness. All these have but one original; but each is peculiarly manifest in its own [matter and manner] according as the turba is enkindled among the three first [properties].

31. But if Lot's wife had apprehended and laid hold of the word of truth and mercy in the message of the angel, it had well protected her. But she did not believe what the angel said, and very like she loved her temporal goods, all which she must forsake, and looked back again, and earnestly longed after the temporal, and the turba of time did also apprehend her; so that she, according to the substance of the body, must remain in the first matter (out of which God had extracted the limus of the earth, and formed it into a spiritual living image) until the Lord shall again transmute the same substance into a spiritual essence.

32. And it was done to the end that man should yet see what he is

---

[1] Or, that property was most predominant in her.
[2] That is, awakened and stirred up, and not atoned.

according to the outward body, if God withdraweth his spirit therefrom; and that he requireth the ground of the heart, and not only a mouth-hypocrisy [and flatteries of a seeming holy devout lip-labour], that a man should only comfort himself with the grace tendered [feeding himself with an outward apprehension or application thereof], and receive the same only as a free gift of grace from without, and yet remain an evil beast in the spirit and will.

33. As the present Babylonical Christendom doth, which also with Lot's wife receiveth the grace only externally [or by a strange imaginary imputation], and comforts itself with the grace, but remaineth in the heart in selfhood, and the lust of the flesh, unconverted; and hath turned its eyes only towards Sodom, but with the mouth it is gone out of Sodom, and the body is yet at Sodom, and looketh with Lot's wife only upon covetousness, and temporal pleasure, and will not go with the heart out of Sodom.

34. Therefore the angel of the wonders saith, Thou art sifted, and apprehended[1] in the turba, thou art [guilty, and] capable of the brimstone-fire: thy verbal hypocrisy, in that thou sayest that thou art gone out of Babel, and Sodom, doth not at all avail thee; thou art wholly captivated with Lot's wife in the three first; seeing thou hungerest only after the three first; and usest the spirit of Christ [only] for an external covering, and wilt not hear in thee what now the Lord speaketh; but hearest only what the Antichrist speaketh in his pride, covetousness, envy, and anger, how thou mayest please thy earthly mortal idol, Mausim [and Mammon], viz. self-love, self-will, self-sense.

35. Thou seekest and honourest only the external idol-god, viz. silver, and gold, copper, and the fullness of the belly to thy luxurious, sumptuous, and stately Sodomitical pleasure. And this idol is also sifted for thy sake, and is made nigh and far off unto thee, and thou understandest not what it means. Thou sayest, There is no danger, and it may well be helped and amended; we may contrive it well enough to a good use. But thou knowest not what is thereby signed and signified.

The most inward figure of Lot's wife being turned into a pillar of Salt, is this:

36. When these two angels came from Abraham, viz. from the spirit of Christ, unto Sodom to Lot, and he bowed himself before the

---
[1] Taken or captivated.

Lord unto the earth, and entreated these angels to turn in unto him; they entered according to the divine property essentially in unto him, in manner as they came in unto Abraham with the ens of faith. Even so it was here: for it was but one Covenant. But in Abraham, the seed to Christ's person was named, and not in Lot; as Moses declareth very sufficiently.

37. Lot's faith took the ens from the angel, who brought the same to him from Abraham's faith's-ens; for of one (viz. of him who did move and manifest himself in Abraham) they must all be sanctified. Now Lot, by the administration of the angel (understand formed angels, sent out of the divine property, out of Christ's ens and word), was sanctified as a proxime line,[1] or branch on the ens of Abraham.

38. And seeing Lot's daughters were capable of this sanctification, and not the mother, the mother must go again into the first matter; and Lot must copulate with his two daughters in the blessed seed; for they were capable of it, and none else in the world. For two potent generations were to arise from thence, viz. the Moabites, and the Ammonites, a great people, as the spirit in Moses doth also speak very covertly and hiddenly concerning Lot's daughters; that the one said unto the other, Lo! there is not a man on the earth to come in unto us after the manner of men; come let us give our father sweet wine to drink; and then we will lie with him; that so he may not know it, and we may preserve seed of our father: for the mother was not capable of this holy seed, seeing she was captivated and taken in the probation[2] in the turba.

39. Now reason would object, and say, Wherefore did not the daughters of Lot marry with Abraham's generation; why would they lie with their father, contrary to the right and law of nature, and of all nations? Answer: This might not be, for the seed of Christ was called in Abraham; but now there lay two other lines in the seed of Christ, as near affinities, which should be born of Abraham's faith, viz. of Christ: As Abraham's faith was born out of JEHOVA, out of the name Jesus, so these two lines of affinity were in the tree of wonders, which should spring forth from God's truth and righteousness, and be brought into the love of Jesus. This manifestation the angels brought unto and into Lot, which opening and manifestation did spring forth in Lot's seed.

40. But seeing his two daughters did also stand in this judgment, and were apprehended in the same spirit which opened itself in Lot,

---

[1] Or, line of affinity.   [2] Or sifting trial.

and received also the same properties as their father, it must be so. And it was so permitted of God, that these two sons, Ammon and Moab, must be born of two sisters of one seed; for they were to be two nations, proceeding from two lines of nature, yet from one root.

41. But in that the spirit in Moses doth so cover it and saith, The two daughters caused their father to drink sweet wine, that he did not know what he did, and so were gotten with child of their father in the father's drunkenness (which yet seems to be wonderfully strange without God's work), the same is thus to be understood: Not that it did not so come to pass: it did so come to pass, as the text in Moses declareth; but this was a work of the Spirit of God, and hereby also he covereth the external shame.

42. For the outward work is only a shame in God's sight, and also in the sight of all people, but the inward work, in its figure, must be so. And it is the true figure, that the Man, Christ, viz. God's Son, should be born through a shame, which also was a shame before God. But so he took our shame and reproach upon himself, and hung it as a curse upon the tree of the cross, and offered it up unto the righteousness of God; so likewise both these lines must be covered with a shame, that they both might be sanctified only and alone under Christ's shame on the cross; and they should not dare to say, that they were pure before God and nature. For the Scripture saith, He hath shut them up all under sin, that he might have mercy upon all (Rom. xi. 32).

43. And that this was truly and certainly a work of God, appears in this: that on the same day the mother was turned into a pillar of salt, and Sodom was destroyed, doubtless with all their household stuff and goods. That yet that same night they set about this work, whereas they continued all night in a cave of the mountain by Zoar [so that we may well think], no natural fleshly instigation did provoke them thereunto.

44. But it must be, that the father should be drunk, that the human understanding might not do it; but that it might be God's work. Also, that the soul of Lot might not be turbated in the tincture of the seed, with the shame of the daughters. It must be done, therefore, as it were in man's drunkenness, and misunderstanding, lest the nations should make a right or custom thereof: For the daughters of Lot were also as 'twere drunk in the spirit, so that the spirit might do what he would, and they were only an instrument.

45. And that they did understand that the father was sanctified,

HOW LOT DEPARTED OUT OF SODOM

and they willingly would conceive of the holy seed, appears, in that they said, There was not a man upon the earth who could come in unto them after the manner of mankind; and therefore they would lie with their father, that they might preserve seed. There were indeed many upon the earth, but none was capable of this seed, but these his daughters. This, the spirit in them gave them to understand.

46. Therefore we ought narrowly to observe what it means, when the spirit in Moses draweth a veil before his face, that it doth not appear wholly pure before God: and yet for the unavoidableness' sake it must be so.

47. And in the deeds of God we ought not to judge according to reason; for reason looketh only upon the outward, and understands nothing of the inward. It knows nothing of the root of this tree; and of its boughs and branches, from whence each branch or people must take its unavoidable rise and original.

The Forty-Fifth Chapter

How God led *Abraham* very wonderfully, and how he always stood by him in Temptation, and defended him: What we are to understand hereby

1. ABRAHAM must be only as a pilgrim upon the earth, and travel from one place unto another, and dwell in tents;[1] and was everywhere tried, and tempted. His wife Sarah was twice taken from him; but wonderfully protected and preserved of God; as once by Pharaoh, in Egypt, and then by Abimelech, King of Gerar; but both times protected by God.

2. And now that Abraham, viz. the stock and beginning of the conceived ens of faith, in which Christ was understood, must thus wander from one place to another, and could have no abiding place upon the earth, and moreover must stand in fear and temptation: the same is the true type of Christendom upon the earth; how the same should not be bound unto any certain place; not unto any people that God did choose thereto in a peculiar manner; but that Christ was given, with his Gospel of the kingdom of God, to all nations.

3. And how he would wander with his knowledge from one people to another; and have no where any constant abiding place with a people, but be among the nations with his children upon the earth, only as a sojourner or stranger; and how they would continually try to destroy Christendom[2] among the nations, and cast reproach upon it, as they would sinfully reproach Sarah, Abraham's wife.

4. And how the Christians should be continually tempted and exercised of the nations, and plagued with contention and war. Also, how Christ would go with his Gospel from one people to another, when they should be weary and glutted with the same, and hold it only for a custom and a common ordinary thing; and so they would grow wholly blind in it, and make only a fine devout lip-labour[3] thereof, and suppose to find out Christ by their acute disputations and arguments.

[1] Gen. xx. [2] The true Christians.
[3] A work of prating and fair spoken discourse.

HOW GOD LED ABRAHAM VERY WONDERFULLY

5. And then he would depart with the understanding and spirit from them, and come unto another people, which also would be only fleshly, and account and look upon Christ externally, as a mere man; as Pharaoh and this king Abimelech looked upon Abraham, and his wife; and desired to have carnal knowledge of Sarah, by reason of her beauty; which did signify and denote, that they would put on Christ in the flesh in an outward bestial manner, but not in power and spirit.

6. As it is here to be seen in Abimelech, and also in Pharaoh, that when they desired to know Sarah carnally, that the Lord came in among them with punishments, and plagues, and shewed them his angry countenance, shut them up, and dismayed them, as if he bound them with the chains of his might; and made their women barren, and terrified them with visions and presages; as he did to this Abimelech, and threatened him with death in the dream; and made known unto him that Abraham was a man of God; and how he was blessed of God.

7. Through which means God brought the nations to the faith; [for] when he came unto a fleshly unbelieving people, then he shewed himself in power and wonders, which the carnal nations seeing, did convert themselves, and turn unto God.

8. Thus Abraham must be a type of Christ's kingdom upon the earth; and go up and down from one people to another, whereupon the people which he left, did yet boast themselves of Abraham, and called themselves after his name, but were only historical children, brought forth of strange women without Abraham's faith and spirit.

9. Thus also it hath fallen out in Christendom, when they have been weary of[1] the spirit of Christ; and made only a prating business thereof, the spirit of Christ hath then departed, and hidden itself from them; and then these people have indeed stood yet in the history, and boasted themselves to be Christians, but have been indeed only the children of the bond-woman, viz. of Hagar; and the sons of mockery, who, with disputing and wrangling about Christ's name and will, have mocked, scorned, reviled, contemned, reproached, and branded each other for heretics; and mere Ishmaelites have risen of them.

10. As it is as plain as the day, that now men go from the scorning and reproaching each other, to the sword of murder; and will wholly slay and root out Christ [in his members], and set the Babylonical tower in Christ's stead, whereby a man shall be able in self-will and

[1] Negligent of.

power to climb into heaven; so that a man need not enter in through the mortifying of the old evil man, but may be able to come in, after a fine hypocritical way with the selfhood of the evil man; or indeed as outwardly adopted children covered with Christ's purple mantle; where yet the will of self is unmortified, and cannot truly come to God.

11. Now as these people were afterwards judged, when Abraham departed from them, they being only mockers of the children of Abraham, as may be seen in Pharaoh, and the heathen also, especially in the land of Canaan: so likewise it hath happened to the Christians, that these nations which continued only under the name of Christ, and yet were only heathenish in the heart, were always judged and banished by such heathenish people. As may be seen by Asia, Egypt, and Greece, and many other nations besides, how God hath pulled off the mantle of Christ from them, as verbal hypocrites and mockers of Christ, and given them a darkened heart and understanding of the kingdom of Christ, and cast away their candlestick, that they could no longer say, We are Christians, and belong unto Christ, but Turks, and barbarous people, begotten of the wild tree of nature.

12. Thus Christ must here in this world wander only as a light from one people to another, *For a testimony unto all people* (Matt. xxiv. 14). And unto thee, O Germany,[1] it is now shewn (and also to those nations of whom thou art born with the name of Christ), in that thou hast for a long time walked under the mantle of Christ with a heathenish heart, and boasted of the adoption, but lived only in the iniquity of the flesh: That thy judgment is nigh at hand.

13. For the angel of the judgment calleth aloud to the residue of Abraham's children in Christ, Go out of Sodom: Abraham in Christ is gone away from you; ye have no more of Christ than an empty breath; and a disputing verbal lip-labour; a mockery, whereby one brother doth contemn, scorn, and mock another for Christ's knowledge' sake, and only killeth Christ in his members. The city, Jerusalem and Babylon, wherein thou hast gloried [and proudly perked up thyself in thy devout hypocrisy] shall go to ruin. Amen.

14. Lo, a star shineth from the East and North, which shall blindfold thee, and break down thy walled towers and strongholds in Jerusalem and Babylon. For thou art called no longer, Jerusalem, but Babel; and the children which sit in the shadow of the night, and which lie imprisoned in Babel, shall be delivered; and come forth, and

---

[1] And to thee also, O England.

HOW GOD LED ABRAHAM VERY WONDERFULLY

enter into the city of God, which he hath set open to all nations and tongues of the earth, that his glory may be known: A light for all nations [or people].

15. The figure of Abraham, Sarah, and Abimelech (Gen. xx) is an emphatical type of Christendom, how they should be weak in their own power, and be delivered by God alone; as Abraham was of a faint and timorous spirit, when he was to go among these nations, and prayed his Sarah, that she would say of him, that he was her brother; that so they might not slay him, for her sake. To signify, that a Christian in his own strength is not able to do anything, or to take unto himself therein the spirit of Christ; who gives courage; but he must go only naked among his enemies; and not at all rely on himself and his knowledge, but merely and only upon God's grace.

16. For he himself cannot stand, Christ alone in him must be his sole courage, and steadfast perseverance. As Abraham here, in his own abilities, was full of doubt before Pharaoh and Abimelech, and continually fearful of his life, and must see only when and how God would shield him and his Sarah. And this history is excellently, elegantly and exactly written of Esdras,[1] in the vision of the spirit of Christ concerning Christ's kingdom, as if the spirit had on purpose figured this history concerning Christ's kingdom, for it aimeth directly thereat.

17. But the outward man understands nothing of the kingdom of Christ. As we may see in Sarah, when she conceived and brought forth Isaac: she said, the Lord hath made me to laugh, the people will laugh at this, that the very aged Sarah should give a child suck. She did not yet understand the type[2] of Christ; but the spirit of Christ in her understood it; and not the natural man in selfhood, but the will which was resigned and given up to God, the same alone did apprehend the Covenant, and the spirit of Christ.

18. But reason, viz. the self-full will, did not perceive anything thereof, it was only matter of mirth and laughter to it; for it looked only upon itself, what it was. As Abraham's will of self-ownhood looked only on itself, and was afraid and dismayed; and yet in him there was the great might over all powers and principalities; but it did not belong to the human ownhood.

19. For Christ in his children doth not belong to the human ownhood, viz. to the self-will; neither doth he appropriate or give in himself to it; but unto the humble, resigned will; to that he doth

[1] Note, Esdras.   [2] Image.

incline and appropriate himself; and sometimes he doth also defend the own will thereby.

20. For the own self-will is of the nature of this world, born of flesh and blood. But the resigned will dieth to the world, and is brought forth to life in God. Thus also we are to understand in Abraham and in all Christians a twofold will, viz. one of this world, which always stands in fear; and then, according to the second Principle, viz. the kingdom of heaven, the poor captive soul's will, which diveth and immerseth itself into God's mercy, in hope.

The Forty-Sixth Chapter

Of *Isaac's* Birth, and the Casting Out of *Ishmael*, with his Mother, *Hagar*. What thereby is signified

1. THE Spirit in Moses[1] setteth the figure of man's regeneration in its process so exactly and orderly together in the history of Abraham, that a man may even lay hold of it, much more see it; how he doth set the natural man in self, and in Christ, so punctually by each other, and points even with the finger at the figure. For when God had destroyed Sodom and Gomorrah, and that plain over against which Abraham dwelt, and brought forth Lot, then Abraham journeyed from thence towards the south; shewing that when the kingdom of Christ should be despoiled[2] in any place, that then Christ would depart thence.

2. And he lived under the king Abimelech, and sojourned as a stranger at Gerar. In these two names, viz. Abimelech, and Gerar, the figure stands plain in the generation or formation of the Word, without any interpretation or exposition; wherefore the spirit in Moses wrote down this history; and from whence he looketh as through an exact perspective. For Abimelech denoteth the man of ingenious and discreet reason, viz. the true man, but without Christ, only in the creature, as he is created. Gerar betokeneth the strong austere life of nature, wherein the understanding must dwell, which nature is corrupted, and from that corruption casteth or darteth temptations and oppositions continually into the life's understanding, or reason-light; so that the life stands in a constant contrariety, and is incessantly sifted, winnowed and proved, which is the cross of the children of God; that they see, that while they live in themselves in self-reason, they can do nothing else but go astray, slip and err. As may be seen here in Abraham, when God led him away from the borders of the Sodomites he went towards the south, unto king Abimelech.

The inward figure of this stands thus:

3. When God had manifested himself to Abraham, and set forth the figure of Christ and his kingdom, and also the power of judgment

[1] Gen. xxi.   [2] Corrupt.

upon the whole earth, then God hid himself again from Abraham; and then Abraham went towards the south country; that is, into his reason, viz. into man's own understanding; and dwelt at Gerar, that is, in the corrupt nature; which manifests itself plainly, in his carriage towards Abimelech, where he, in the fear of nature, in the temptation, did deny his wife, and said that she was not his wife; that so he might but preserve himself by the subtlety of reason. And we see here also, how that that very thing, by which he thought in reason to keep himself from mischief, must reprove and teach him; as we see how Abimelech reproved him in that he had denied his wife, with whom he had almost sinned, if the Lord had not warned him; and the exposition is this:

4. If we see a man whom the Spirit of God driveth, and by whom he oftentimes speaketh, we must not so take it up, and think that he is something more than other men: as Abraham was no more than others in his own reason. The self-reason in them is as wavering, dubious and imperfect as in other men, and that what they know and teach of God, is not their own propriety. As we see here in Abraham, how he out of fear did not spare his Sarah [but denied her out of a timorous conjecture]; though Abimelech had taken her away from him to be his concubine, that so he [Abraham] might but live, and it might be well with him for her sake.

5. Thus God proveth his children, that they might see that they, in their own ability, are no more than all other sinful men; and that men should not so set by them and hold them for a god. Thus oftentimes God permits them to go astray and err, and yet then he rebukes them also by those whom they ought to teach, as we see here in Abimelech; how he must reprove Abraham, and make him ashamed, that he would not spare his wife for a small fear's sake, but would deny her.

6. And although it doth fall out, that sometimes we see such a man whom God driveth to err, yet we ought not therefore presently wholly to reject him and set him at nought, and think that he is wholly without God, as the world doth; but think that God doth thus set his children under the cross to prove them; that they should learn to know themselves. And then the sun ariseth again upon them, as here it did upon Abraham, when God had suffered him to go unto Gerar; that is, into his natural rational life, wherein he committed a great offence before Abimelech. A twofold sun did afterwards arise and shine on him, viz. one was, that Abimelech did acknowledge him,

OF ISAAC'S BIRTH

and learned to fear the Lord; and gave the land for a possession unto Abraham. He gave him also gifts for rebuke; as the reproof of the saints is, that men should fear at God's reproof. Thus the sun of king Abimelech's favour arose upon him. And then the other sun which shone on him was, that Sarah conceived; and a branch sprang forth unto him out of the line of the Covenant, from the divine sun's power, and Isaac was born unto him.

7. And that we may understand the very truth: we see how always the cross stands by the children of God; and Adam and Christ are continually set by each other; as here Abimelech and Abraham; and Ishmael and Isaac; and also the man of right reason, and the corrupt nature against reason; which incessantly sifts and tries reason. As we may see it here in Hagar and Sarah, which also were set one against another, that one did exercise the other; as Hagar in the property of corrupt nature, viz. in Adam's life; and Sarah, in Christ's person; so that Hagar did exercise and prove the natural Sarah; that she pressed forth out of the reason [or carnal wisdom[1] of the flesh] into God.

8. And we have here (in Sarah and her maid Hagar, with her son Ishmael, and with Isaac, Sarah's son; how Sarah cast out the bondwoman, with her son; which seemed grievous to Abraham, and yet was right in the sight of God), such an excellent mirror, as we find not the like again in the Bible; shewing how Christ and the natural man dwell by one another;[2] and how the natural man, with Ishmael and his mother, must be wholly cast out from the right of inheritance, and self-will; [from this we see] that the natural own-will is no heir of God.

9. And when the resigned will hath wholly cast him out,[3] then the poor nature of man sitteth in its rejected will in fear and trembling, and utterly despairs of life. As here, Hagar with her son Ishmael; when she was cast out from Abraham, she wandered in the wilderness of Beer-sheba, that is, in the brokenness of her heart; and looked upon herself as one wholly forsaken [and as one quite spent and faint] and despaired of her own and her son's life. For she had lost the inheritance, and the favour of her mistress also, and all her goods; and there was neither water nor bread for to preserve life, and they were as given up to death. For she went and sat a stone's cast from the child, because she would not see him die; and when she had even wholly given up

---

[1] Or, natural carnal wisdom.
[2] Sojourn together.
[3] Understand, the self-assuming will of nature, which seeks to be master in man.

herself to die, then the angel came again unto her, and called her, and comforted her, and shewed her also a fountain; and told her that she should not be so afraid of death, her son must yet become a great nation.

The inward figure of this is thus:

10. When Isaac, that is, Christ, is born in the convert, then the spiritual new-born will rejecteth its own evil nature; it contemneth it, and condemneth it to death; casteth it out also from itself, with its son, the mocker, viz. the false interpreter [and perverter of the truth]; as if it would even burst the same in the mind; so very a hateful enemy the new-born spiritual will becomes to the natural will in its evil qualities, viz. to Ishmael, the son of the natural will, who is only a mocker, scoffer, pharisaical censurer, liar, backbiter and unrighteous.

11. And when the new-born will hath thus cast out the evil nature with its wicked children from itself, then the poor forsaken nature stands in great distress, trembling and desertion. For the internal holy soul doth forsake it; and then it even gives up itself wholly to death; and wandereth in itself in the wilderness; and looketh upon itself as a foolish and simple one, who is every one's by-word and laughing stock.

12. And then when the nature doth willingly give itself thereunto, that it also will now die wholly to its selfness, and despairs wholly on itself, as a poor forsaken woman, that is deprived of all the worldly glory, riches, beauty, and the pleasure of the outward life also; being wholly cast out from its former desire; and almost quite forlorn, so that the own desire begins to faint and quail within itself. Then comes the angel of God to the nature, and comforts it, and bids it not to despair; and gives it also water to drink, that is, some faithful upright man [or some inward ray and beam of light from the new birth of Christ in the heart] which comforts it in its forsaken condition; and helps to nourish and cherish it, and tells it that it shall not die, but become a great nation; but not in its innate and inbred heritage, viz. in the evil self-will, but in Beer-sheba; that is, in the true contrition in the wilderness, viz. in the valley of tears in the desertion; that is, the poor nature must work in this forsakenness, and in its present banishment and exile [from the sensible and full enjoyment of Paradise] bring forth much fruit, which fruit the angel brings again into Abraham's tent, to be a sojourner of Christ.

13. That is (we must understand) when Christ is born in man, he

OF ISAAC'S BIRTH

rejecteth the vanity of nature, with the will which worketh and desireth vanity, and maketh the natural will to be servant, whereas before it was lord and master. But nature standeth in the wilderness, in the vanity of death, encompassed with sin; and now it must work and bring forth fruit, and yet it looketh upon itself as wholly impotent; and as one wholly cast out from the inward spiritual will of Christ; and in itself it seems as one foolish, and contemned of the world; and every way beaten off from its own will. And then it begins even to sink and quail in itself; and to leave off from its own will; and all things are of small esteem with it: That which before did rejoice it, that now is against it; and it stands always as if it should die; it hopeth, and doubteth; that is, it hopeth amendment, that it might yet once be delivered from the scornful contempt, and be set again into the honour of its selfhood; but it drieth up also its well of water; and God's anger appears in its sight; that is, all its friends depart from it, with whom before, in its temporal goods and prosperity, it had pleasure, respect and honour; so that it looks upon itself as continually a-dying.

14. And when this comes to pass, then it is right in the way to Beer-sheba; and wandereth in the wilderness; for it knows not what it shall do; it is everyone's scorn; whatsoever it looks upon, rebukes it for a fool, in that its power is taken from it; that it must now forego the beauty, riches and honour of the world, and all whatsoever might advance and prefer it in temporals; and yet it would fain have them; but yet it is drawn from them by the inward man in Christ's spirit, and reproved[1] in these temporals for unrighteous and abominable.

15. And then indeed it enters right into Beer-sheba, viz. into the contrition of the heart, and sets reason by the empty water-pot of Hagar; and goeth a stone's cast from its son Ishmael, viz. from the own desire of nature; and stands and compels also the thoughts of nature; and will not give any thing any longer to its own children, viz. to the senses and cogitations of the mind; but casteth them away (as children that now must die) a stone's cast, that is, a while from itself, that it might not see the death of its children. So wholly doth Hagar, viz. the nature with its son, give up itself to the mind for the mortification of the selfhood of the own will; sits also and mourns in itself in Beer-sheba, viz. in the broken and contrite heart; and wholly despairs of its reason; would fain die, that it might be but freed from the miserable forlorn condition.

[1] Blamed or upbraided.

16. And then, when it is thus prepared that it quite despairs of itself, and gives up itself wholly into the death of selfhood; then cometh the angel of God to Hagar, that is, to the poor forsaken and dying nature, and saith, *What aileth thee, Hagar? fear not; for God hath heard the voice of the lad, where he lieth. Arise, take up the lad, and hold him in thy hand, for I will make him a great nation. And then God openeth the eyes of Hagar,* viz. of nature, *and she sees a well of water, and then filleth her bottle with water, and gives the lad drink,* who grows in the desert, and is a good archer, and dwells even in the wilderness of Paran, and must take an Egyptian wife.

The inward exceeding precious and worthy figure
of this stands thus:

17. When man hath put on Christ in faith, and is entered into right true repentance, and hath in his mind forsaken the whole world, even all its honour, goods, and things temporal; then the poor nature of man doth thus stand in the mortification of self, as is above-mentioned concerning Hagar and her son. For it desireth also to die, even to the senses and cogitations of the mind, and to enter wholly into resignation.

18. And when it stands thus in the thoughts of death, having given up its will and cogitations into mortification, then the inward voice of God's Word manifests itself in the mind and senses.[1] And even there the divine Word heareth the voice of the child's crying, viz. the troubled disconsolate mind in its thoughts;[2] for it soundeth therein in the divine voice; and saith in the divine voice to nature, viz. to Hagar, What aileth thee, thou troubled and perplexed nature? fear not, God hath heard the voice of the lad, viz. of thy thoughts, which thou hast offered up in the desire to God: Arise, that is, lift up thyself to God in this resignation; and stand up in the voice which hath graciously heard thee, and looked upon thee, and take thy cogitations, viz. thy son, by the hand of faith; and guide and govern the [powers of the] mind; they shall not die, but live, and go; for I will make them a great nation; that is, to a great divine understanding and capacity in divine Mysteries; and God openeth unto nature the fountain of living water; so that it receiveth, into the bottle of its essence in itself, of God's well-spring, and therewith it gives the lad, viz. the senses [or powers of the mind] drink.

---

[1] Thoughts, meditations.   [2] Cogitations, meditations.

OF ISAAC'S BIRTH

19. And then God is with this lad of the thoughts, and he groweth great in the wilderness, that is, in the corrupt nature; the right, discreet and intellectual child groweth great in the spirit of the Lord, and becomes an archer; that is, an archer of the Lord, and his brethren; who shoots the birds of prey, and the wild beasts; understand, he shooteth down out of his spirit, with the holy spirit, the evil beasts and birds in his brethren; he teacheth them, and reproveth them with divine arrows.

20. But he must dwell in the wilderness of Paran, viz. in the corrupt flesh; and in the wilderness amongst ungodly people, and there he must be an archer of God; and his mother, viz. nature, gives him an Egyptian woman, that is, nature layeth a fleshly woman by the noble mind born in Christ's spirit, with which the noble new-born mind must sit in wedlock, and be plagued with this idolatrous fleshly woman. Understand it thus:

21. This Egyptian woman is his flesh and blood, with reason, wherein the idol Mausim, viz. the Babylonical whore sitteth, where the devil hath his pulpit, which, to the precious mind, is the cross of Christ, where the woman's seed, viz. the spirit of Christ, must incessantly bruise the Serpent's head, viz. the devil's introduced desire in this whore of Babylon.

22. This whore is now the exercise and probation of the spiritual cogitations or senses in the Christian mind; but this whore doth not hurt the children of Christ; indeed it hath a false lust, and is a very wedded harlot, which shall not see the kingdom of God; but it must yet serve for good to the children of God; for by it the cross of Christ is laid upon the precious mind, so that the mind must continue in humility, and not say, I am righteous, I am holy. No! no! the holiness is not this child's own; but it is God's mercy, who hath heard the crying of the lad, viz. of the poor forsaken mind. Thus the noble holy mind, viz. the new man, born in Christ's spirit, must be wedded with this Egyptian, evil, malicious, idolatrous, whorish, ungodly woman, which is neither able to do, will, nor think any good,[1] and bear with it the foul shame and reproach, so long till the unclean idolatrous whore dieth. And then this lad is led of the angel into Isaac's tent, viz. into Christ's flesh and blood.

23. And this is the very real figure of the spirit in Moses, wherefore he hath so punctually and emphatically deciphered this figure; for the spirit in Moses aimeth so directly and fully at the mortifying of man's

---

[1] *Note.*—How we cannot so much as think a good thought.

selfhood; and plainly speaketh, that the self-will must be cast out from God; and where Christ is born, there the same is brought to pass; as here, when Isaac, the type of Christ, was born of the free woman, then the son of the bond-woman must be cast out. For in Isaac the seed which should inherit the kingdom of God was to be called; it should not proceed out of the self-full nature, of the flesh and will of man, but out of God's will; out of the mortified will of our nature, which dieth to its selfhood, and despairs of itself, a Christian must be born. That is, Ishmael, viz. the poor sinner (when he becomes an enemy to sin, repents of it, and wills it no more) shall be born in God's mercy; indeed nature must and shall be there, even with its evil earthly flesh, but Christ is brought forth from thence, as a fair blossom out of the wild earth, as a [pleasant] fruit out of the kernel.

24. A very excellent figure the spirit in Moses doth present unto us, in Abraham and Sarah, when Sarah would cast out the son of the bond-woman from the inheritance; so that the son of the bond-woman should not be heir with the free. *The same seemed unjust to Abraham, seeing the lad was of his seed, and his own son. But God said to him, Let it not be grievous in thy sight because of the lad, and because of the bond-woman; in all that Sarah hath said unto thee, hearken to her voice; for in Isaac shall thy seed be called.*

The inward precious figure of this is thus:

25. When a man is born again in Christ's spirit, as it was here with Abraham, then he thinks sometimes that he is wholly new, and knows not himself yet aright; and that he hath the whorish Egyptian bond-woman, with her scoffing son of vanity, in his arms. And now, when it happeneth that oftentimes the mocker, viz. Ishmael, the son of the bond-woman, doth break forth out of him, yea, even wholly without his will and purpose, that Sarah (that is, honest minds, to whom God doth make it known) do reprove him; nay, and is oftentimes reproved of the evil, so that it is plainly declared to him that this mocker should be cast out, this, Abraham, viz. the man, will by no means brook. He will be uncontrolled; and yet he doth not know, that he in this time of his earthly life stands in the judgment of God; that his words and works must be daily proved and judged. He will often go in a way of justification, and maintain his own cause, and will be praised; and in the mean time forgets the Egyptian bond-woman in his arms, and her scoffing son, who sometimes peeps forth in his words with evil interpretations, wrong meanings, and evil surmises, and covers itself

OF ISAAC'S BIRTH

finely under a glozing mantle of glistering hypocrisy. This now the free woman casts out, that is, the spirit of Christ casts it out by other people's mouths; and yet this seems to be unrighteous to the man; seeing the word is born of his body, and arisen out of his very mind.

26. But the Lord speaketh in the spirit of the humility of Christ: Let it not seem grievous in thy sight, that people do find fault with thy words, and reject thy labour. Hearken to Sarah, viz. to the divine voice; and do thou thyself cast out from thee whatsoever thou hast at any time spoken or meant evilly, wrongfully or partially. For in Isaac, that is, in thy deepest humility, thy seed shall be called; where, in thy words and works, the spirit of God worketh in love; and not in thy natural selfness and peculiar ownhood of reason, wherein the son of the bond-woman speaketh and worketh.

27. And the children of God ought well to consider this figure, and think, that whatsoever is spoken and done from favour, affection, and partial siding, be it either towards honest or dishonest men, the same proceeds from the son of the bond-woman, which must go into judgment to be tried; and must be judged of men, viz. of the evil and of the good. It must be cast forth among a company of evil and good tongues; where every one passeth his sentence and judgment thereupon: God judgeth upon the earth externally by men, both by the evil and by the good.

28. This now must seem so very grievous and heinous to Abraham, viz. to man, when his words and works are judged and proved, and [he must] think, that his divine seed must be brought forth only in the love and humility, and that whatsoever he speaketh, judgeth, or doth from partiality or favour, doth belong again unto judgment, where it must be proved and purged: as Hagar with her son Ishmael was. And then, when it is judged, that is, cast out by the people, then comes the angel of God, and speaketh to the natural man, that he should not despair in this judgment, but take it in good part, and be content that his words and works are judged.

29. Therefore we say, as the Lord hath given us to know it, that whosoever will read and understand aright the history of the Old Testament, he must set before him two types, viz. externally Adam, viz. the earthly man, and internally Christ, and change both these into One; and so he may understand all whatsoever Moses and the prophets have spoken in the spirit.

30. He must not be so blind as to look upon it as the Jews and Babel do, who make only of this history, conclusions of reason in

respect of the Election of God; as if God had thus chosen to himself only one sundry and peculiar nation or sort of people to be his children. The Election of God passeth upon the figure only, shewing what [kind of] people should bear the figure of the inward kingdom of Christ in the outward, in which people God would set forth and manifest the kingdom of Christ externally. The Jews have had only a mirror and type hereof externally, and so likewise the Christians, who looked upon Christ in the flesh as a mere pure man.

31. These figures have remained very speechless to the world, even to this last time; and that, from the purpose of God, seeing man is such a piece of mere vanity and flesh; and so soon weary of the pearls, and afterwards comes to trample them under foot. Therefore God hath dealt with man in types and parables; as Christ also did when he came upon the earth: He spake all these mysteries in parables, for man's unworthiness' sake.

32. But now at present there is great cause (as all the prophets have prophesied thereof) that the same should be made manifest. And the cause is this: that in this last trumpet's sound the mystery of the kingdom of God shall be finished (Rev. x. 7); and the bride of Christ, viz. the wise virgins, shall be prepared, who shall meet the Lord in his appearance. And it betokens the day of Christ's coming, when he will appear with the holy city, the New Jerusalem, and bring home his bride. Therefore the mystery of the kingdom of God must first be unfolded and explained out of its types, and become wholly manifest.

33. And this will be the fall of the fleshly sinful man, in that the man of sin must be made manifest; as St. Paul plainly prophesieth thereof (2 Thess. ii. 3-8), that the child of perdition shall be revealed to all nations, speeches, tongues; and the beast with the whore shall go into the bottomless pit. That is, when the kingdom of Christ becomes wholly manifest, then the beast, and the whore of flesh, viz. the false bond-woman, with her scoffing son, stands in great shame, and is judged of everyone, as a whore in the cage, that everyone scorns and scoffs at.

34. As indeed hitherto men have reviled Christ in the outward image of simplicity in his children and members, in which, reason hath seen and known no more, than Hagar and Ishmael in their miserable banishment; under which, notwithstanding, the voice of the angel hath been; which they have scorned and mocked in the foolish plain simplicity under the veil, and have set up the mocker, Ishmael, in Christ's stead; which hath been only an Antichrist. Now,

OF ISAAC'S BIRTH

this mocker and Antichrist shall be revealed under this trumpet's sound; and be cast out of[1] the children of God into the abyss, which Babel shall see in a short time: Declareth the spirit of the wonders of God.

35. We see all an excellent figure of this in Abimelech, that, when God will manifest himself to a people, how he terrifies them in the midst of their sins, and appeareth to them in anger; as to Abimelech in the vision; and to Moses in the bush of fire; and also to Israel upon the Mount Sinai, also in the fire; and also to Elias in the fire and wind. Where always the rebuke of God's wrath is fore-signified, how God doth bruise the hearts of men that they may fear and tremble before him; as here, Abimelech, when the Lord appeared to him by night in a vision, and threatened him by reason of Sarah, he was astonished, and told the same in the ears of his people, and the people were sore afraid, and Abimelech called Abraham, and made a covenant with him.

36. This is an excellent figure [and pregnantly intimates] how God terrifieth the enemies, and comforts poor dejected nature when it quails for fear; and turns its fear into joy. And how the miserable and afflicted, if he be honest, is at last drawn out of misery and affliction; and how at last his enemies (who before he thought to be his enemies) must serve him and advance him. So wonderfully doth God lead his children, if they do but endure temptation and continue under the cross of Christ in humility, and not look upon self-revenge, but put on patience in hope, and persevere steadfast in the faith. At last all a man's adversaries must see and acknowledge that God is with the man, and that the world hath dealt wrongfully and unrighteously with him.

37. Also this is an excellent emphatical figure how Abraham (when God would punish Abimelech) did pray unto God for Abimelech, and made reconciliation, that God did bless Abimelech. And this whole history stands in the figure of Christ, and holds forth how Adam and Christ are together; how Christ is come into the self-assumed kingly ownhood or selfness of man, and terrifieth sin and death; and how the poor corrupt nature doth turn itself, in the horror and acknowledgment of sin, to God, as here Abimelech turned unto Abraham; and how it then giveth the kingdom of nature for a possession unto Christ. And the inward figure in the spirit of Moses (who was the type and figure of Christ, who yet pointeth, out of the father's property, upon the Son, in the flesh, viz. in the humanity) can be understood no otherwise, than even thus: It is the true ground.

[1] Or, by.

The Forty-Seventh Chapter

Of the Covenant of *Abimelech* and *Abraham*, shewing what the same is, in the spiritual figure; and what the Spirit in *Moses*, under his veil, doth here point at

A VERY PRECIOUS AND EXCELLENT GATE TO THE CHILDREN OF GOD IN BEER-SHEBA

1. COURTEOUS and friendly Reader, know, that if a man should write many hundred books of the history of Abraham, yet he could not sufficiently express the abundant richness which lieth hid under this figure. But we will afford a little service to the children of God in their weakness, and somewhat unveil this figure, seeing otherwise it is not to be understood by the natural man; and yet the Lord doth thus lead us in grace [to the understanding thereof]. Therefore I shall here lend and give him the hand thereto. Observe it well: there is couched under it a peerless matchless pearl, which shall here stand open, and yet also continue hidden, which cannot be purchased with the goods of the whole world. It is hidden unto reason.

The outward figure in the Text of Moses stands thus:

2. And it came to pass at that time, that Abimelech, and Phichol the chief captain of his host spake unto Abraham, saying, God is with thee in all that thou doest: Now therefore swear unto me here by God that thou wilt not deal unfaithfully[1] with me, nor with my children, nor grand-children: but according to the kindness which I have done unto thee, thou shalt also do unto me, and to the land wherein thou art a stranger. And Abraham said, I will swear. And Abraham reproved Abimelech because of a well of water, which Abimelech's servants had violently taken away. And Abimelech answered, I know not who hath done this thing: neither didst thou tell me, neither yet heard I of it, but to-day. And Abraham took sheep and oxen, and gave them unto Abimelech; and both of them made a covenant together. And Abraham set seven ewe lambs of the flock by themselves. And

[1] Unkindly [falsely].

OF THE COVENANT OF ABIMELECH AND ABRAHAM

Abimelech said unto Abraham, What mean these seven ewe lambs which thou hast set apart by themselves? And he answered, Seven lambs thou shalt take of my hand, that they may be a witness unto me, that I have digged this well. Whereupon he called that place Beer-sheba; because they there sware both of them. And thus they made a covenant at Beer-sheba: then Abimelech rose up, and Phichol the chief captain of his host; and they returned into the land of the Philistines. And Abraham planted trees in Beer-sheba, and preached there of the name of the Lord, the eternal God; and was for a long time a stranger in the land of the Philistines (Gen. xxi. 22 et seq.). This figure seems outwardly, as if Abimelech was afraid of Abraham; seeing God had given him to understand in a vision, that Abraham was a prince of God; thereupon he desired a covenant and oath from Abraham, lest he should root out him and his posterity.

3. But the spirit of Christ under the veil of Moses hath ciphered out before him far another figure, wherewith he alludes and prophesieth; for under all the acts of Abraham which the spirit of Moses hath written down, we are to understand a twofold figure, viz. externally a history relating something done; and under that same history, the spirit of Christ in the Covenant doth so aptly and exactly set its figure, as if he played therewith.

4. For the place here mentioned is even the same whither Hagar fled with Ishmael; it is even the same Beer-sheba, and the same fountain of water signified, which the angel shewed Hagar; which Abraham, that is, Christ, digged; where afterwards Christendom preached of[1] the name of the Lord, the eternal God, in Christ, by this well of water in Beer-sheba.

5. And the covenant between Abimelech and Abraham, is the Covenant of Christ with the humanity, where Abraham, that is, Christ, sware that he would not destroy the humanity; as he also said when he came into the flesh; that *he was not come into this world to condemn the world, but to save the world* (John iii. 17), that is, to bless and keep Covenant.

The inward holy figure stands thus:

6. Abimelech and Phichol, who spake with Abraham concerning the covenant, the spirit doth here represent in the type of God the Father, and then also of nature. King Abimelech points at the Father

---

[1] Or, called on.

in the soul's property, and Phichol, his field-captain, points at nature, viz. God's officer. Both these approach to the type of Christ, viz. to Abraham. For mankind was given to this Christ: he should be a Prince of God in and over the humanity.

7. Now nature had brought itself out of the Father's property into false lust, (understand in the human nature), for it desired to manifest Sarah, viz. the free woman, (understand the heavenly virgin-like matrix), in the earthly bestial property, which came to pass in Adam when he brought his female property into a bestial lust. Now the spirit here in Moses doth hint at this figure, and representeth, under King Abimelech, Adam in the Father's property and nature.

8. As Adam lusted to manifest himself with his female property, viz. with the mother of the holy birth in the earthly bestial mother, or to prove, try and taste in the tincture of Venus the root or the ground of the third Principle; so here, King Abimelech in the same nature (understand the masculine out of the Father's property) did lust after the mother of the Covenant which was now moved in Sarah, to know the same. Which the holy God would not have, and therefore came unto Abimelech, and terrified this nature of lust, and threatened punishment and destruction to it.

9. Now understand in King Abimelech the soul out of the Father's property; and by Phichol understand the outward nature, viz. the third Principle, which is the field-captain or servant of the king, viz. of the soul; and by Abraham understand Christ in the humanity, or in the ens of the faith of the Covenant, as the spirit signifieth and sets forth pregnantly by way of allusion in this figure.

10. God the Father bringeth the poor soul, viz. the king of the human property, unto Christ, after that it had given itself to lust with its servant, viz. the body of nature; and now the soul speaketh to Abraham in the figure of Christ, Wherefore didst thou not tell me that God was in Sarah, viz. in this image? wherefore didst thou not say unto me that she was thy wife? understand, Christ's wife, which is called the woman's seed in this mother, for I had almost heinously offended towards her.

11. Understand, the soul of Adam knew not Christ in its heavenly matrix in the tincture of Venus. It thought that it was the fair pleasant child; therefore it went with this holy tincture into self-full lust. But now when God shewed the soul this holy tincture in the Covenant, then the soul said, I did not know it; viz. that this female property, as it was in me, was God's wife, who bringeth forth by it;

OF THE COVENANT OF ABIMELECH AND ABRAHAM

and spake by the field-captain, viz. by the outward nature to Abraham in Christ: Take now thy wife, viz. the heavenly matrix in me; for, lo! God is with thee in all that thou dost. That is, I will restore again unto thee whatsoever I have taken into my self-possession, viz. the matrix of the divine world's property, which is closed up in me, and now awakened in thee; take it, it is thy wife. And when Abraham, understand Christ, took the same (Gen. xx. 17) then all the women and maids of Abimelech, and his servants, understand the daughters of Eve, were healed in the heavenly matrix through Christ's wife, viz. through Sarah in the Covenant, that they again might bring forth God's children.

12. Now the soul in the Father's property spake to Abraham in Christ, seeing (Matt. xxviii. 18) all power over the humanity was given unto him, Swear unto me by God, that thou wilt not shew any unkindness[1] to me, nor my children, nor my nephews; but according to the kindness that I have done unto thee, do thou also unto me, and to the land wherein thou art a stranger. That is, as if God the Father in the soul should speak with Christ his Son, to whom he had given the whole humanity[2] for a peculiar possession, and say thus: Seeing I have given thee the power in the human property which is mine, to be thy own, swear now unto me by God; that is, deeply bind thyself therewith into an essential oath, or one eternal covenant; that thou wilt not shew any unkindness to my nature in the human property, nor to the children, viz. to the branches which spring forth anew out of their property; nor to their nephews, or grand-children; that is, to those children who spring out from the wild property, where oftentimes a wicked husband or a wicked wife are joined together, the one being ungodly, and the other honest; but according to the kindness which I have done unto thee, even unto thy image, (in that I have restored unto thee again this heavenly matrix, which in Adam was captivated in my wrath, and disappeared from thy image, in my anger), thou shalt do likewise to me; and unto the land, that is, unto the outward man, wherein God's children bear the heavenly image; that is, unto the land wherein thou sojournest.

13. For Christ is a stranger in our earthly humanity, and our earthly humanity doth oftentimes make our children or grand-children strangers to God: There the Father of nature in the soul's property said unto Christ, he was a stranger in our land; as Christ also said, that *his kingdom was not of this world*, that is, of the earthly man.

[1] Or, unfaithfulness.   [2] That is, all mankind.

But Christ should shew kindness in this strange land, (understand the strange humanity), and not reject the children which should be born therein, as the Father had done to his image of the heavenly humanity, which disappeared in Adam. This, Christ should swear unto God; as he also sweareth in the prophet Ezekiel, *As true as I live, I will not* (or have no delight in) *the death of the wicked or sinner, but rather that he should turn and live* (Ezek. xxxiii. 11): for Abraham in Christ, viz. in the figure, said, I will swear, that is, I will do it.

14. And Abraham reproved Abimelech because of the well of water which the servants of Abimelech had taken away by force. That is, Christ reproved the soul, that the soul's servants, viz. the essence of nature, had taken away the well-spring of the essence from the heavenly corporality, viz. Christ's body in Adam, whereupon the heavenly image died or disappeared. For Christ's holy fountain of water sprang up in the soul's fiery essence, but the soul's essence had taken this fountain of divine sweetness into its own self-full power, and changed the same in itself to another property.

15. And Abimelech, that is, the soul, answered, I wot not who hath done this. That is, I did not know that the devil had deceived me, that the false lust was arisen in the very essence of my nature; and who hath done this hurt. Also, thou didst not tell it unto me; that is, thou didst not declare unto me that thy image was in me; that this holy divine fountain was thine, which my servants, viz. my essences, have taken it to selfhood.[1] Moreover, I heard not of it, but to-day; that is, thou hast not revealed to me that this fountain is thy seat, save to-day only; that is, to-day, where thou dost again manifest thyself in me in Adam with a Covenant of Grace, where now I heard thy voice in me.

16. And Abraham took sheep, and oxen, and gave them to Abimelech, and they both made a covenant with each other. That is, then Christ took his sheep, that is, children; and his oxen are the Gentiles: the sheep are the children in whom the Covenant was manifested, viz. the Jews, and gave them to the Father; and made between Christ's spirit and humanity, and between the Jews and the Gentiles, an eternal Covenant, that it should be one humanity and not two.

17. And Abraham set seven lambs apart by themselves. These seven lambs are the seven properties of the natural humanity of Christ, which he did manifest in our humanity. And in that the spirit

[1] Turned it to a selfish ownhood.

OF THE COVENANT OF ABIMELECH AND ABRAHAM

saith, *by themselves*, signifieth that *Christ*, in his humanity of the seven properties, *is a distinct person*; so that we men (viz. Jews and Gentiles, who come to his grace) ought *not* to say, *we are Christ*, but we are his *house* in which he dwells: the power of the holy fountain of water is his; *we are only branches* on his tree: *he is* with the seven lambs of the divine property *apart in us*;[1] they belong not to man's selfhood.

18. Only in the right resignation Christ and man is wholly one; when man's will wills nothing any more without Christ, but gives up itself wholly in Christ: then it is dead to self, and Christ alone liveth in it; also it doth signify that his creatural person, with the seven properties of the humanity, shall dwell among us as a distinct person, as eternal high priest.

19. *And Abimelech said, What mean these seven lambs which thou hast set by themselves?* That is, God the Father made an allusion, through the essence of the soul in this figure, with Christ's figure in Abraham, and said, What mean thy seven properties of our divine nature by themselves? Wherefore, seeing thou shouldst regenerate mankind, and dwell in them, wilt thou also set forth thy seven properties of our divine nature in a distinct human person? And Christ answered in the figure of Abraham, *Thou shalt take seven lambs from my hand, that they may be an eternal testimony unto me, that I have digged this well.* That is to say, Christ speaketh to his Father in man's person, Thou shalt take the figure or the image of my seven properties of the human creature for an everlasting testimony, that I, in my suffering and death, have again digged the well-spring of eternal life in the human property; that man's new-digged fountain of life is mine.

20. And the spirit in Moses speaketh wholly under a veil; therefore, or from hence, the place was called Beer-sheba: this is, the very precious place where God the Father and his Son in the humanity sware both of them together. The place was called Beer-sheba, viz. a bruising of death by the will of him that liveth and seeth in the disappeared humanity, where, in Christ's humanity (which he assumed from us men), death was bruised, and broken in pieces; and the well-spring of love did flow forth again out of the living God in our bruised humanity of the heavenly part into the soul's creatural fountain. Now the spirit of Moses speaks here very pregnantly, that the place was called Beer-sheba, where the testimony of this oath (viz. a fountain of grace) was established.

21. And the place of God at Beer-sheba is shewn to us poor men,

---

[1] Or, by himself.

where God the Father hath made an everlasting Covenant with us in Christ Jesus, viz. in the penitent contrite soul. When the poor soul in this precious Covenant and oath doth wholly give up itself to repentance, with a broken and contrite heart; then the oath of God in the Covenant of Jesus Christ stands open to it in Beer-sheba, viz. in the soul's contrition; where God in Christ Jesus hath sworn that he will not destroy the poor soul, and its children and grand-children; nor do any hurt to this land of the soul, viz. to the body of the humanity.

22. Thus now we ought steadfastly to trust our dear Immanuel, Jesus Christ, who hath sworn a precious oath to his Father, in our soul's property, that he will not turn away his mercy and love from us. We should but come to him in Beer-sheba, and receive the oath as our own; that is, with contrite penitent hearts.

23. And Moses saith further: *When this was done, then Abimelech arose, and Phichol his field-captain, and they returned into the land of the Philistines.* That is to say, when God the Father had given over the humanity to his Son, Jesus Christ, with this Covenant and oath, then he went with his regiment [or host], viz. with Phichol, that is, with the outward nature, again into the land of the Philistines; that is, into the dominion or regiment of the outward and inward nature, which is Philistrean,[1] that is, inclined to good and evil. This denotes that the poor soul, although it hath taken on it the Covenant and oath of God, and sworn with Christ to God, yet it must in this lifetime dwell in the earthly body, viz. under the heathenish Philistrean[2] essence of the flesh; which is a constant adversary to this King Abimelech, viz. to the poor soul, and only forsaketh the Covenant and oath; and brings itself, in its Philistrean,[2] selfish, lustful concupiscence and desires, into selfhood, as into its own land.

24. And hereby it is signified to the poor Christians, that they must lodge and lie with the new birth in this Philistrean land[3] or house of flesh, as mere strangers, and cannot be wholly freed in this lifetime. For Phichol, the field-captain of the soul, viz. nature, must have its rule and work in this time, in evil and good, and be a hard cross, and continual temptation to the precious image of Christ, viz. to the new birth; by which cross the noble and dear tree of pearl is moved, stirred, and caused to spring and grow. As a tree which comes out of the earth must grow in heat and cold, in wind, rain and snow, so also must the precious little tree of Jesus Christ, which is a stranger with Abraham in Beer-sheba, viz. in the earthly cottage.

---

[1] Or, Philistineal. [2] Or, Philistine. [3] Philistine Land.

OF THE COVENANT OF ABIMELECH AND ABRAHAM

25. And the spirit in Moses speaketh further, saying, *Abraham planted trees at Beer-sheba, and there preached of the name of the Lord, the ever-living God. And was a stranger in the land of the Philistines a long time.* This is as much as if he should have said: The spirit of Christ in Abraham (when the soul hath received the Covenant and oath, that it is contrite in true repentance) doth plant trees in Beer-sheba; that is, it bringeth forth heavenly branches in this penitent heart in the strange land, the earthly man; and preacheth, from these new branches, of the name of the eternal God, and dwelleth a long time, viz. the time of the whole earthly life, in this Philistrean[1] cottage.

26. And this is a real figure of the poor penitent sinner, which in Christ's spirit becomes a new creature according to the inward man; shewing how he must enter into repentance, and plant, out of Christ's spirit, the little tree of Christ in his contrite and truly broken mind; and dwell also with this little pearl-tree of Christ among a company of wicked men in a strange land, viz. in the evil corrupt flesh and blood; and there teach of the name of God, and instruct the heathenish and Philistrean[1] children, that they, in his preaching, may come to him in Beer-sheba, that is, into true and unfeigned repentance.

27. Thus very exactly doth the spirit in Moses play here with the type of Christ under an external history in a simple child-like form; and shews us how we must continually stand in temptation, trials, danger and opposition; and how God doth thus wonderfully deliver his children, that even those of whom they are afraid, and do also wish them no good, must at last make a covenant of peace with them in their conscience. And also how the poor soul, by reason of great fears and horror, hath no rest in itself, unless that it come through earnest repentance in Christ to God, and make a covenant with Christ in God, so that the poor dejected conscience and nature be comforted. Without this there is mere distress, anguish, horror, unsettlement; as happened to Abimelech when he was enkindled in false lust towards Sarah: then God terrified his conscience, that he went to Abraham and humbled himself before him; and with great recompense and gifts made a covenant with him. Thus also it goeth with the children of Christ, when they endure temptation and continue steadfast in the faith; then at last their enemies must be ashamed, and return back, as it is to be seen here in this figure.

[1] Philistine.

The Forty-Eighth Chapter

How God Tried *Abraham*, and set forth the Figure of Christ's Offering in his Suffering and Death[1]

1. AFTER that the spirit in Moses had deciphered the figure of the Covenant of God, established in Christ Jesus with his children, shewing how we poor children of Eve should and must depart out of this earthly will of selfness, and be born in Christ with a new will and life; he here now sets forth the figure, how the same should and must be brought to pass: How Christ must again offer up our soul and humanity to his Father, even as he also was to be cast as an offering into the fire of God's anger, and wholly die in the wrath of God to the human soul's selfness and own will, and yet spring forth powerfully with the divine only will of God, through death and the anger of God, and break in pieces and make a scorn of death which held the humanity captive. And so bring the human soul again to God his Father into the only eternal divine will, and *deliver up again the kingdom unto him* (1 Cor. xv. 24), which he had given him in the humanity, so that afterwards, and to all eternity, *God might be all in all* (1 Cor. xv. 28), and the creature might not live any more to its own will, but sound only as an instrument of a divine tune, in a divine harmony, and the whole human tree might be only one in all its boughs and branches.

2. The spirit in Moses doth set forth this figure very clearly, even to the end of all his writings, and playeth under the outward figure with the inward, which shall remain for ever. I will therefore set down this figure of Abraham's temptation in respect of his son Isaac, likewise in the spiritual figure, and shew what is thereby to be understood. For although the learned have expounded it, that God tempted Abraham, to see if he would continue steadfast in the faith upon him, yet it hath far another meaning and interpretation; for God knows well aforehand what man will do; also man cannot, without his grace, stand in the temptation, as may be seen here in Abraham, when he denied his wife before King Abimelech, as he came into Gerar.

3. Abraham is here represented in Adam's stead, and his son Isaac is represented in Christ's humanity, and the voice which came to

[1] Gen. xxii.

HOW GOD TRIED ABRAHAM

Abraham is God the Father's. These three stand here in the figure of the process of the work of man's redemption; shewing how Abraham, that is, Adam, should offer up his person[1] in Isaac, that is, in Christ, to the voice of God in the fire of God, that so the humanity might be proved in the fire of God.

4. Now the voice of God spake to Abraham, and said, *Abraham! And he answered, Here am I.* That is, God called to Adam in Abraham, viz. to all men, and said: *Take thy own son Isaac, whom thou lovest, and go into the land of Moriah; and offer him there for a burnt offering upon a mountain which I will tell thee of* (Gen. xxii. 1, 2). Here the spirit looketh with Isaac upon Christ, for in Isaac lay the Covenant, and the ens of Abraham's faith, out of which Christ should come. Now said the voice of God to Adam in Abraham, Take thy son, whom thou lovest, and offer him for a burnt offering upon the mountain which I shall tell thee of. That is, the Jews, viz. Adam's children, should offer Christ for a burnt offering; that is, the divine ens should give in itself into Adam's ens, which the children of Adam should offer up one with another in the fire of God; and it betokens, that every man, when he hath received the ens of faith, must offer up himself wholly unto God, and die to his own will in the fire of God; and in the divine ens of faith be born anew through the offering in the fire of God.

5. For said the spirit in Moses: *Thy son whom thou lovest,* viz. thy own will, which hath brought itself into self-love. This self-will must be offered up to God, that it may leave the own selfish will in the fire of God, and wholly give over its ownhood, and no more will and live to itself, but to God. And it rightly points out, how Christ *in our human will,* (which [human will] had broken off or *turned itself in Adam* from God), should again wholly offer and give up himself in Adam's person to God his Father; and how the wrath of God should devour the will, viz. the will wherein Adam had introduced himself into selfhood.

6. In which devoration of the fire of anger the love-ens, in the word of faith, of divine power, viz. the true man created in Adam, must be formed, and also preserved in this devouring fire; as gold or silver in the crucible, where the copper, and all that is impure, purgeth[2] from it, and only the gold or silver subsists in the fire. So likewise the human assumed ownhood, together with the assumed ens of the serpent and beast; and all whatsoever subsists not in the divine fire, must be consumed in the offering. And that we might have again, in Christ's person, a wholly pure entrance and open fountain of grace,

---

[1] Text, image.   [2] Evaporates.

Christ must offer up our human will of self to his Father, and resign it up to him wholly, and that, upon the mount Moriah; that is, in his death, where he, for (2 Cor. v. 15) all, and in all, should die to the human selfhood. Even as when the stock of a tree dieth, then also all its branches in it do die;[1] and as the tree doth renew its youthful growth, it also introduceth its new power and strength into its branches; which indeed is not possible to the outward nature, but in God it is very possible, as may be seen in the dry rod of Aaron, which was dead to its sap and life, and yet in one night sprang forth afresh, and bare fair almonds.

7. Now said God: *Upon the mountain which I shall shew thee*. That is, it must not be done according to Adam's will; also it must not be done in us according to our will, as if we should prescribe to ourselves where and how we would offer up ourselves in Christ to the Father, as Babel doth. No, but upon the mountain; that is, on the place, in the property, and in the death, as the Lord appoints, orders, and sends it to us. We must be only obedient with Abraham, and give up ourselves willingly thereunto, when he will have us offer unto himself; not whip, beat, and plague ourselves, but only sink with our will into him, and wait till the Lord shews us the place, where and how he will have us offer unto him. We must give up unto him our whole heart and will, with body and soul, and commit it to him what he will further do with us; where he, in the type[2] of Jesus Christ, will offer us according to the body. And when the Lord calleth us to the offering with his cross, or will offer us up to the temporal death, then we should say with Abraham: *Lo! here am I, Lord. Do what thou pleasest.*

8. *And Abraham rose up early in the morning, and saddled[3] his ass, and took with him two young men, and Isaac his son, and clave wood for the burnt offering, and rose up, and went unto the place of which God had told him* (Gen. xxii. 3).

This figure stands thus:

When the voice of God calleth us, then we should with Abraham go presently: for *early in the morning* signifieth here, when the voice breaks forth as the dawning of the day; when God *in us* calleth us. When man hath a thought come into him, saying, Thou shouldst return, amend, and truly repent; *then* it is time. He must forthwith girt his ass, viz. the bestial man with power. Although he [the bestial

---
[1] *Note.*—How Christ's death was effectual to all men.
[2] Image, or likeness.   [3] Text, girt.

man] cries, Stay yet a while, it is time enough tomorrow; yet it should be done presently, in the first look of the will to God. For this is the hind which is hunted early in the morning, as the prophetical spirit prophesieth: for Christ must girt this ass early, with the voice of God, and go to the offering.

9. And the two young men which Abraham took along with him do betoken, the soul from the first Principle, and the soul of this world, viz. the outward spirit of the outward life. These must go with Isaac, that is with Christ in the old Abraham, that is, Adam, to the offering of God; and Abraham, that is, the man Adam in his children, must himself cleave the wood upon which the offering must be burnt; that is, when he confesseth Christ then he cleaves the hearts of the wicked, who run with him to the death and the offering of God. For Adam in his humanity clave God's love and anger; and now also Abraham must cleave the wood for the offering; for Christ should also cleave death and life asunder, and offer up himself upon the cloven wood of death and life, unto God's anger.

10. *And on the third day Abraham lifted up his eyes, and saw the place afar off* (Gen. xxii. 4). Here the spirit pointeth at the sleep of Adam, wherein he slept to the angelical world; and on the third day after his falling asleep, when as now the woman was made out of him, and the fall effected, he saw Christ, viz. the place of God in the Covenant afar off. Also herein is included the resurrection of Christ on the third day, where he saw his place (where he would and should offer and give up man to God his Father), viz. the Last Judgment, and the final offering, afar off. Also it signifieth, that Abraham in the spirit saw the offering of Christ afar off, viz. above two thousand years then to come. And that the spirit saith, *Abraham lifted up his eyes on the third day, and saw the place,* is nothing else but that Christ did again lift up on the third day our human eyes out of the grave, from the dead, unto God; and also that it was yet afar off in the days of Abraham: Thus the spirit doth allude with the outward figure at that which was and is to come.

11. *And Abraham said unto the two young men which he took with him, Abide you here with the ass; and I and the lad will go yonder and worship, and come again to you* (Gen. xxii. 5).

The figure of it internally stands thus:

The two young men must tarry there with the ass, and not go at this time unto the offering, only Abraham and Isaac must perform that; that is, we poor children of Eve must abide with the first and third Principles of our life, this our time with the ass, viz. with the outward body here in this world. But Christ in Isaac, and Abraham in Adam, must go forth to the offering; that is, Christ stood in Abraham's, viz. Adam's, person, and also in his heavenly humanity; who should alone go, and offer up the offering of his body to the anger-fire of his Father, and worship for us, unto God his Father. Therefore he said he would go yonder, that is, when he should offer up his life he would go yonder, that is, to God, and worship for us, unto God.

12. This points at his ascension according to the humanity, when he had finished the sacrifice he went thither,[1] and worshipped in our assumed humanity, unto God his Father; that is, our assumed soul, in divine power and property, doth pray and intercede for our weaknesses and ignorances, unto and before God. Therefore saith Abraham, We will go yonder and worship; that is, we, God, and man, and when we have worshipped we will come again to you; that is, we poor children of Eve must in the mean while tarry with the ass, until the time of its offering and prayer be out; and then he comes again unto us; when we have finished the course of the outward assinine life.

13. Also it intimates very pregnantly, that he (when the time of the offering in prayer is out) will certainly come again unto us, from the place whither he is gone, and dwell visibly with the creatural humanity among us; as the two angels said unto the men of Israel, *Ye shall see this Jesus come again in like manner as he is ascended*;[2] which time is now near; and his voice to prepare the bride hath already sounded; and therefore hold not this for an uncertain fiction. The Morning Star and Messenger of the Annunciation is appeared.

14. *And Abraham took the wood of the burnt offering, and laid it upon Isaac his son; and he took the fire in his hand, and the knife; and they went both of them together* (Gen. xxii. 6).

The inward figure stands thus:

Adam had divided and rent asunder God's love, and anger, in himself, and brought himself with the creatural life into the anger, which had amassed the earthly vanity to itself: Now the spirit of Moses doth here point at this figure, how Christ should take our introduced sin upon himself, and carry it to the burnt offering.

15. And Abraham took the knife, and the fire: Abraham denoteth

---

[1] Yonder, or to that place. [2] *Note.*—Jesus's coming again. Acts i. 11.

HOW GOD TRIED ABRAHAM

Adam, who took the fire of God's anger into himself; and the knife signifieth death, that Christ should be killed, and offered up in Abraham's, that is, in Adam's, anger-fire, to the Father; and it clearly denotes that Abraham, that is, Adam, should do it to Christ; for Christ should be offered up of man: seeing the man Adam had taken on himself the fuel (viz. the sin) for the offering; therefore also man, viz. the Jews, must offer it up to the anger of God, that so man might be atoned by man, understand by the humanity of Christ.

16. *And Isaac spake unto Abraham his father, and said, My father: and Abraham answered, Here am I, my son. And he said, Lo! here is the fire and the wood: but where is the lamb for the burnt offering? And Abraham said, My son, God will provide himself a lamb for the burnt offering: and so they went both of them together* (Gen. xxii. 7, 8).

The precious figure is thus:

The spirit here playeth in Christ's person, who was come in great humility into Adam's humanity, and presents himself to his father in Adam's essence, with his heavenly humanity, and saith: Behold, my father! here I have taken on me the sin and death in the humanity; here is now the fire of thy anger, viz. the divided life's forms of man's property, selfhood and own will; in this now I have the fuel, wherein thy fire of anger burneth: Here now I have the wood, viz. the sins of all men; and also thy fire to the offering; where is now the lamb,[1] viz. the patient lamb which shall be offered up in this fire? And Abraham answered from his strong faith's ens: My son, God will provide himself a lamb for the burnt offering; and they went both of them together.

17. Here Christ doth in Isaac's figure present himself in our assumed humanity to his Father; and saith, Where is now the lamb for the true peace offering? But the faith of Abraham had apprehended the patient lamb, which lay in Isaac, viz. the heavenly humanity, which God would open in the ens of faith in our disappeared and also heavenly humanity, and said: God would provide himself a lamb for the right burnt offering. And hereby he secretly points at the heavenly humanity, which God would introduce into Christ's humanity, viz. into our humanity, which should be the patient lamb that God would provide for himself, which Abraham had already apprehended in faith, and hints at.

[1] Text, sheep.

18. And that the spirit of Moses saith, They went both of them together (understand, unto the offering), betokens our Adamical humanity, and Christ's heavenly supernatural humanity of divine essentiality, that both these should go together to the offering of God; as Christ offered on the cross his heavenly humanity in our humanity to the Father; and with the heavenly reconciled ours, captivated in the anger of God, and preserved it in the fire of God's anger, as the gold is preserved of the tincture, in the fire.

19. *And when they came to the place of which God had told him; Abraham built there an altar, and laid the wood in order upon it; and bound Isaac his son, and laid him on the altar upon the wood. And Abraham stretched forth his hand, and took the knife to slay his son* (Gen. xxii. 9, 10). This is now the right earnestness, viz. the figure how God would bind his Son by Adam's children, viz. by Abraham's children, the Jews; that is, he would bind our sin, and lay it upon the wood; that is, hang it on the cross; viz. on the figure of the holy Trinity, which was become in man a wooden earthly cross: whereas before, the life's cross, viz. the figure of the Deity, was spiritual and holy in Adam; but in the earthly lust it had made itself earthly, and as 'twere wooden. Thus also the death, viz. the dying of the holy cross in man must be again offered up to God upon a wooden earthly cross; and be again changed out of the earthly death into the holy spiritual figure.

20. Christ should not be slain, but hung up on the cross, pierced through in his hands and feet. For the anger of God was awakened in the conversation and works of our hands and feet; and therefore also Isaac, in the figure of Christ, must not be slain; and also not burnt; for he was not the right one, but only the figure in our humanity; for he could not accomplish this offering in its powers. And it denotes that we are indeed bound with Christ, and laid upon the wood, and also must die for Christ's sake. But with our death we cannot attain this offering, as Isaac also could not effect that; but the ens of faith in Abraham and Isaac, out of which Christ arose, the same did effect it; and can yet now in these days effect it in the Christians in Christ in his humanity in us.

21. And as Isaac was represented in Christ's figure, as if he were to be the sacrifice, even so every true Christian must with Isaac enter into Christ's figure. He must willingly resign himself into Christ's death; and bind his sin with the will in the spirit of Christ, and offer it upon the altar of Christ; and with a full and free will die wholly to sin. Then cometh the voice of God, as it came to Abraham, and to Hagar

HOW GOD TRIED ABRAHAM

in the wilderness of Beer-sheba, and saith, Do not anything to nature, viz. thy son: now I know thou believest God.

22. But it must come so far with the penitent sinner, as here it did with Abraham and Isaac, where Isaac was laid, ready bound upon the wood, and Abraham took the knife to slay him. There must be a very real sincere earnestness in this matter. The sinful man must bind the sin with all his thoughts and mind, and give himself wholly into the process; that he will now die unto sin, and offer it up in faith and confidence to God, in Christ's death. He must take the knife with Abraham into the hand; that is, he must wholly take and fasten into his mind to do the work of earnest repentance in dying to sin. It must come to the real and effectual practice, and not only come before the altar and say, *I am a sinner, God hath offered Christ for me*, and yet keep the sinful will; but he must bind sin in Christ's death, and lay himself wholly with all power and strength on the burnt-offering's altar upon the wood.

23. The evil earthly will must be bound, and resigned up with earnestness, and cast upon God's altar in Christ's death; and be also offered up in Christ's dying; and not only comfort the sinful man, and flatter it with Christ's death, saying, God takes away sin from us in Christ's satisfaction and merit; we need only comfort ourselves therewith, and apply it from without to ourselves. No, no; but we also ourselves must die to sin in Christ's death, and put on Christ's offering in his death; and as an obedient Isaac we must cast ourselves on God's mercy, in the spirit and will of Christ, and arise in Christ, in and with him, that God may justify us from the altar of sin-offering, with Isaac, in Christ, which is the true offering in the figure of Isaac.

24. Not as Babel teacheth. There must be an entire and sincere earnestness, and not only a comforting [and applying promises of consolation], but we must with Abraham obey God, and then we put on Christ's suffering and death; and Christ's death avails only *in* us, and here 'tis truly said, *Ye are saved by grace, in Christ's merit*. The will of self attains it not, but that which entereth into Christ's death, and dieth; it must come to the death and mortification of the own self-will: the soul's will must be an utter destroying enemy to sin in the flesh, viz. to the lust of the flesh; there must be an opposite enmity between them, else Christ's death is not at all profitable to any.[1]

25. And Moses saith, *The angel of the Lord called unto him out of heaven, and said, Abraham, Abraham* (Gen. xxii. 11): that is, when man

[1] *Note.*—To whom Christ's death is not profitable.

resigneth up his will wholly, and willingly desireth to obey the voice of the Lord, having given himself into Christ's suffering, death, and reproach, that he now will in the cross and suffering hold still, and steadfast to God, under Christ's red banner,[1] then God calleth man with a double[2] voice; as here he did Abraham, where God said unto him, *Abraham, Abraham.* That is, he calleth to him in his own voice in his word, and also in the voice of the human essence; that is, he openeth to him the divine hearing in himself, so that he heareth God from without in his word of his servants, and also from within in his own life's word, viz. in the sensual voice, which was divided in Babel by the children of Nimrod, and formed into the spirits of letters, where the mental tongue was then compacted. Here it ariseth again in the uncompacted sensual tongue, so that man heareth what the Lord speaketh in him. Of which Babel knoweth nothing, nor can know, nor will know; but climbeth up continually in the compacted tongue on the tower of Babel into a heaven of human selfhood; and hath put Christ's garment outwardly upon itself; but it hath not the twofold voice; therefore also it doth not hear when God calleth Abraham.

26. And Abraham answered, *Here am I. And he* [the angel] *said, Lay not thine hand upon the lad, neither do thou any thing unto him: for now I know that thou fearest God, and hast not spared thy only son for my sake* (Gen. xxii. 12). That is thus: when man hath wholly resigned up his self, viz. his own will or son, and put it wholly to the mortification in Christ's death, then the nature of man falls into sadness; for it hath lost its right [its own law and will]. Then saith the spirit of God by the soul, Do nothing to thy nature; now I know that it is given up and resigned to me, and that the soul hath now an assurance[3] of confidence in God; and is fully bold even to leave the outward life, for God's sake, and give over its will to me in obedience. As here Abraham had fully resigned up his will unto God; he would now do whatsoever God commanded him.

27. And as Abraham did not spare his son, and would have given him up unto death; so also God did not spare his Son, and gave him to death for us. Even so should we also not spare even our own will, but rather be willing to leave all whatsoever the own will hath taken possession of, and delights in, and willingly die to all temporals for God's sake; let it be principality, dominion or kingdom, temporal honour, or goods, or whatsoever it may be that is our dearly beloved son. All this a Christian must give over, and resign up in the mind;

---

[1] Ensign.   [2] Twofold.   [3] Plerophory.

HOW GOD TRIED ABRAHAM

and account and esteem himself only a servant therein; yea, esteem his outward life not for his own; but in his mind depart from and forsake every creature. And then he lieth bound upon the wood of the burnt-offering's altar, and waiteth for the voice of God from heaven, which calleth to him; and becomes the voice and mouth of his life. And this is truly with Abraham, to believe God, where God believes in man; and then God saith, Now I know that thou fearest God, and puttest thy trust in him alone, for the human will sinketh into the most pure being of God.

28. *And Abraham lifted up his eyes, and looked, and lo! a ram was hung in a thicket by his horns: and he went and took the ram, and offered him up for a burnt offering in the stead of his son. And Abraham called the name of the place*, The Lord[1] seeth; *as it is said to this day*, Upon the mount where the Lord seeth (Gen. xxii. 13, 14). This is the golden figure which sheweth that the killing, death and dying, doth not reach the true man, but only the ram with his horns, which sticketh in the flesh and blood in the thorns of sin. And it chiefly denotes that the true human soul[2] in Christ and his children shall not die in this burnt offering of God; but after that it hath resigned up the will of self, then God openeth its eyes, that it seeth the ram behind it, viz. it spieth the will of the wild evil flesh, and learns to know it, which will sticketh with its pushing beast's horns in the thorny thicket of the devil, in flesh and blood, viz. in the desire of the vanity of the world in self-full lust. This the resigned soul seeth, and offereth it up for a burnt offering in the stead of the true nature; for in this burnt offering the right nature is delivered from the ram of the flesh. The horns are the injections, oppositions and assaults of the devil, and the thicket of thorns is the Serpent's ens, which the lust of Adam hath introduced.

29. Thus we must understand in this figure, that the whole man in Christ's person should not be given to the anger of God, as if the Adamical man should be wholly consumed and devoured by it. No; but the wild ram only; the enmity, the opposite will, the property of apostacy and rebellion; but the life's essence should remain for ever. The same Adam, which God created unto Paradise, the same shall remain eternally; but the division or dissonant disunion of the life's forms, in that they are rent asunder and brought into the property of selfhood, whence strife and enmity is arisen in man; [I say] this evil ram; viz. this introduced infection, vain desire, and adverse will, must be offered up in Christ in the fire of God's anger; this was the beast

---

[1] Jehovah-jireh.   [2] Text, souls-man.

for the burnt offering. The Lamb of God in Adam shall not be consumed in the fire; but it must only shed its blood; it must immerse and sink itself wholly, with the human nature, into the One, viz. into the Eternal Nothing, without all nature; and then this place is called, *Here the Lord seeth*; that is, when the ram is offered, then this place is afterwards the temple of God, where the Lord seeth.

30. And the spirit of Moses speaketh very hiddenly hereof, and saith, *Hence it is said still to this day: Upon the mount where the Lord seeth.* The mount is the life's nature, where the Lord hath seen, not only in Abraham and Isaac, but he seeth in Christ's spirit, yet, at this day upon this mount in the children of God. When the ram is offered up, then the Spirit of God seeth through nature, as the sun through-shineth a glass, or as a fire through-heats an iron.

31. Therefore a man ought not to be so foolish as to torment his whole life in his repentance and conversion, and to offer it up in the fire of death, without God's command; but he must sacrifice only the sin, and self-love of vanity; he must offer up only the ram, and not do any violence or mischief to nature; not, strike, whip and beat it; or creep into a corner, and suffer the body to starve for hunger. No, he must not, out of his own purpose, give the image of God to death; but the ram he must. He merits not anything by plaguing, martyring and torturing himself; for God hath bestowed his heart to that end, to redeem us from pain and torment.

32. When the soul with the right nature hath tamed itself from the ram of the flesh, then it must sacrifice the ram to the death of Christ; but it must remain steadfast in great humility and resignation in God; and not any further afflict and rack itself, either with doubts, or with any other external inflicted tortures; and also give nature its necessary nourishment, and not enfeeble and distemper itself; for it is the temple and the image of God. But it must daily and continually mortify the ram in the flesh, viz. the selfish lust of the evil flesh, and the will to the selfhood [or ownhood] of this world; and although the flesh be disquieted, seeing it must forsake what it fain would have, yet the true nature and the soul must not give heed to it. Also it must not take care for the sake of the flesh, where that should have its maintenance, but commit it to God, and go on in his calling as a day-labourer in the service of his Lord and Master, and let God take care for the ram, and give it what he please.

33. *And the angel of the Lord called unto Abraham out of heaven the second time, and said, By myself have I sworn, saith the Lord, because thou hast*

HOW GOD TRIED ABRAHAM

done this thing, and hast not spared thy only son, that I will bless and multiply thy seed as the stars of the heaven, and as the sand that is upon the seashore; and thy seed shall possess the gate of his enemies; and through thy seed shall all the nations of the earth be blessed; because thou hast obeyed my voice. And so Abraham returned to his young men, and they rose up and went together to Beer-sheba, and dwelt there (Gen. xxii. 15–19). This is now the seal of faith: when man hath wholly given himself up to God, then God sweareth unto the humanity by himself, that he will bless man; that his life's essence shall thenceforward spread forth itself in his power, and grow unto a great tree of divine essence in the wisdom, whose fruit and knowledge shall be infinite and innumerable. As he sware unto Abraham, that out of his body or life's essence many nations should arise; also how his life's essence should possess the gates of the enemies, viz. of the devil, and death, as here he gives a full and pregnant hint concerning Christ and his Christendom; how they should destroy the devil's kingdom, and break down his gate in man: This the faith in God's children is able to do.

34. For so soon as the judgment of the earthly man hath been held in the penitent man, so that the soul rejecteth the will of the evil flesh, viz. the will of the animal soul, and brings it into judgment to the condemnation of death, and resigns itself up wholly unto God; then God sweareth in Christ Jesus this oath unto the soul, and sets it to be a prince over the enemies, viz. over the proud and haughty devils, even to judge them, and obtains full power over them, and drives them out.

35. After these things Moses mentioneth how the blessing of Abraham did spread forth itself, and he maketh a relation of his brother Nahor, how Milcah bare unto him eight sons; from whom great nations did arise, viz. the Assyrians; who indeed did not spring forth out of the ens of faith, viz. in the line of Christ, as Abraham, but out of the natural Adam, upon whom also the blessing of Abraham did light.[1] For the history is so exactly deciphered that a man may see, that God hath not only chosen the natural line of Christ, proceeding from Abraham and Isaac, but also the lines of nature in the Adamical tree, which he would also bring together, and manifest himself to them, and they who would believe in God should be engrafted into the line of Christ; that is, those who should be capable of the divine ens in the voice of the Lord, whose will should direct itself to God.

36. As we may see again in this figure, how God hath not rejected

---
[1] Passed or went.

the kingdom of nature in man, but that he in Christ will deliver it out of the anguish and enmity; and that a man should and must continue in the kingdom of nature; as Abraham when he had finished this offering, he went with his son and two young men to Beer-sheba, and dwelt there. By which the spirit of Moses signifieth, that when Abraham had performed this calling in the figure of Christ before the Lord, he returned again unto his natural affairs, viz. unto the doing of this world's business. He went to Beer-sheba, that is, into the toil and labour whereinto Adam hath brought us, where a child of God in the cloven and broken nature, viz. in Beer-sheba, must work in God, with teaching, and praying, and also in nature, with the labour of the hand to maintain the outward man, and follow the wonders of the outward world in the formed word, and help to form, manifest and bring them forth in figure, to the contemplation of the wisdom of God.

37. Also hereby is hinted very clearly, that a child of God in this world's being doth not stand daily and hourly in the operation of the spiritual figure, that his spirit can see and know that [only]; but also in the natural, where the Spirit of God goes also along working in the work of nature, and manifests itself in another property in him. As it may be seen here in Abraham, and all the saints, that God did sometimes manifest himself to them in the figure of Christ, and sometimes again in the cross, and labour, in the temptation and contrariety of the nature of the corrupt Adam; so that they have lived in weakness and infirmities, as all Adam's children [have done and do].

38. And we ought not to look upon and consider this figure concerning Abraham, in all that the spirit of Moses and Esdras[1] hath written down, but as a type of Christ and Adam, viz. of the kingdom of Christ, and the kingdom of nature; that hereby God hath represented the figure of Christ and his Christendom, how he would again redeem and deliver them from the great toil and labour.

39. Wherewith also the kingdom of darkness in the pain and torment is continually represented, and how the same doth pant and reach after man, and how man doth stand here [in this life], as in a field, and grows; on whom sometimes the sun of divine love doth glimpse and shine, and sometimes again God's wrath and anger; and how man must be purged, tried and purified. And the chiefest and most especial point herein is this: that a man must give up and resign himself to God, in faith and full assurance, and hold still unto him, and let him work in him as he please; and how also he must learn to

---

[1] Text, Esra. *Note.*—Concerning Esdras.

bend and bow his own nature, and lead it towards God; that it, in all things may desire to be God's instrument and servant, and desire and will to work nothing but what belongs to the divine manifestation in the wonders of nature, for the contemplation of God's wisdom; and on the contrary reject the own-will of the devil, and all desire to selfhood.

40. And we should not look upon the written history of Moses concerning the patriarchs, so blindly as the Jews and Babel do; as if they were only a mere history. No; the same is not only full of the types of Christ and Adam, viz. of the old, and the new man, but there are also secret and mysterious intimations and prophecies concerning the hidden spiritual world, shewing what shall be after this time.

41. Reason must know, that the Spirit of God hath not laboured in the work only to set forth the histories of the ancients, which for the most part seem but simple and childlike. No; they are set forth for a type and information.

42. The Spirit of God hath represented the greatest wonders therein, which he would accomplish in man; and that, in a plain, simple and childlike manner, that so the pride of the devil, and the subtlety or wisdom of reason might be confounded and made foolish thereby.

43. For we must know, that the greatest power and virtue, together with the wonders, doth lie in the humility and lowliness; and how God is so near unto all things, and yet nothing apprehends him, unless it stand still unto him, and give up the own-will; and then he worketh through all, as the sun [worketh] through the whole world.

The Forty-Ninth Chapter

Of the Death of *Sarah*, and the hereditary Sepulchre of *Abraham*: What is understood and signified thereby[1]

1. THE spirit in Moses hath set before him the whole figure of man, by Abraham, shewing what his condition should be in this world; and what hereafter should become of him. For after he had first spoken of the beginning, viz. of the stock of the human tree, shewing whence it did spring, he afterwards declares its boughs and branches, together with its power and virtue, and mentioneth how this tree is corrupted in its power and essence; and that God hath bestowed the highest tincture upon it to tincture it again, and renew it; and how the poison in the essence of the tree is to be resisted.[2]

2. Here he doth now very wonderfully signify how this tree hath stood in the corrupt property in a strange field, and rooted itself with the root into a strange or alienate ownhood, wherein the root was not native; and how the root of the human tree must forsake the strange field, together with the strange introduced essence; and wholly give itself freely out of its life's will and desire.

3. Also hereby is signified, how the place whence the human root did spring, is between the holy spiritual world, and this earthly corrupt world; and that man's propriety, from whence he is sprung, doth stand in a double cave,[3] viz. in two Principles; and how he must be buried in this twofold pit, as a kernel which is sown into the ground; and how also [this cave of Machpelah] this twofold pit, is man's propriety, of which essence or substance he himself is, essentially.

4. The figure of this we see here in Abraham, that when he conversed in this outward world; he possessed upon the earth no land of his own, but went from one place unto another, and was everywhere a stranger. But when his Sarah died, then he would have a burying place for a certain possession for his wife, himself also, and his children; and moreover, he would not have it for nothing, but buy it; all which

---

[1] Gen. xxiii.
[2] Or, hath been withstood.
[3] Our Text hath it, The Cave of Machpelah, which here, in the German version is rendered a double cave, or a twofold pit.

is a very wonderful typification, and not only a bare history, as the Jews have held it to be, before whose eyes the veil of Moses is hung. But we will here also set forth the inward figure with the outward, and see what the spirit in Moses doth here signify.

5. Moses saith, *Sarah died at Hebron, in the head city*[1] *in the land of Canaan* (Gen. xxiii. 2). This may very well thus be: but the spirit hath his figure under it; for he looks upon the centre, where the death of the saints is; and where the true man must die, as namely, in the head city, Hebron, that is, in the formed word; where he hath introduced the ownhood and selfish lust into the formed word of his life's property; and set himself up into a self-full dominion and regiment, as into a head city, where the self-will hath framed and contrived to itself a city, or propriety in the formed word, and built it up for its own peculiar land of possession; where he indeed supposeth he is a god, or something of his own, that he may do with and how he please. Now this self-will must die in the head city, viz. in the formed ens of the word in its centre, viz. in the city of its ownhood.

6. And this city, Hebron, lieth right over against Mamre, viz. between the eternal and the temporal nature; where [the cave of Machpelah] the twofold pit is, viz. the kingdom of God, and [the kingdom] of nature; for in this twofold pit, Abraham would bury his Sarah, and have the pit for his own.

7. That is to say, when the children of the saints in Hebron, viz. in the city of human ownhood, do die unto the self-full outward natural life or selfhood, then the true resigned life will no longer stand in a strange field or strange essence, but in its own, from whence it is originally arisen. But seeing it hath lost this same life's field in Adam, and rooted itself into a strange field, viz. into the Serpent's field of falsehood, the life cannot take unto itself again, of due right, the first true field, but it must buy it. This is even the figure, that Christ hath bought it for his blood of the heavenly essentiality (for the holy tincture), understand [he hath thus purchased it] of the eternal nature, wherein God's anger, viz. the wrath of God in the centre of nature, was manifest, and had devoured this field in the human property into itself as its own. For out of the centre of nature the Word of the human property was brought into a formation: this, the children of self had taken into possession; therefore saith the spirit, the children of Heth had this field for their own possession.

8. This signifieth, that God's children must wholly forsake the

---

[1] Our Text, Kirjath-arba.

nature-right in this field of the formed life or word; for they have lost the natural right in it; but in Christ they must buy it again of the Father of nature: They must take Christ for their ransom; and give the Father four hundred shekels of silver for the same. And these are the four centres in the spiritual body's property, which are born in the holy tincture, viz. in Christ's property.

9. The first shekel is the true magical fire; the second is the light or love-desire; the third is the holy sound of the mental tongue; the fourth is the formed or conceived ens out of the other properties, where the holy life is formed, and stands in an essence. This is the pure silver without any spot or foulness; under which the spirit of Moses points, that Abraham, in Christ, hath given to the children of Heth, viz. to Ephron; understand to the Father, or the Father's property, [for his cave of Machpelah] for his twofold pit, viz. for the centre of the Father's nature according to eternity, and for the centre of the temporal nature; in both which the divine lubet[1] hath brought itself out of the property of both centres, into an ens, and into the creature of the humanity; which human creature hath broken itself off from the universal being, and put itself into a selfishness; therefore it must be again rooted into the universal. For which end it must be tinctured with the most holy ens, and engrafted in; which the spirit doth here compare to pure silver, and so secretly intimates in the figure.

10. When Abraham conversed upon the earth he desired to buy no field for his own possession. But now, when he was to bury his Sarah, he would have the sepulchre hereditary and peculiar; *and bowed himself before the children of the land* (Gen. xxiii. 7); and entreated them for it; whereas they would freely have given him the field, and bowed themselves before him. But the spirit of Moses hath its figure here; for he hath represented man to him in a very perfect model; for which cause also he playeth in the process in the figure; shewing that the children which belong unto Christ must bow themselves before God the Father, from whom all beings do originally come; that he would sell unto them the twofold pit,[2] viz. the kingdom of nature, and the kingdom of grace, in Christ's blood, for the same, with the four centres of humility and the love-birth, the Father takes for payment.

11. And that the children of Heth and Ephron would freely give it to Abraham, and yet at last, upon the desire of Abraham, took money for the same, intimates unto us, that God the Father hath indeed freely

---

[1] Or, good will and pleasure.
[2] The Cave of Machpelah, the double valley.

OF THE DEATH OF SARAH

given us the kingdom of grace; for he gave it freely to Christ his Son, in our humanity; but Christ would have it for a natural due right; therefore he offereth his humility to his Father, that he would be pleased to take his payment for it, viz. his human property, of him; as here Abraham did in Christ's figure. Although he could have taken the field, yet he would not; for the cave[1] of Machpelah should not be taken, but dearly purchased with the most precious substance. God took the earnest or ransom of Christ for his cave[1] of Machpelah, for payment. Therefore Abraham must stand in Christ's figure; for the body must be buried in the cave[1] of Machpelah, viz. in the eternal and temporal nature, viz. in the formed compacted Word, if so be it shall arise again in the motion in the voice of this same Word, and subsist in its image which it first had.

12. For Moses saith, *Hebron is situate in the land of Canaan* (Gen. xxiii. 2), which God promised to give unto Abraham. And understand by Canaan the holy crystalline world or earth, viz. the city of God; which shall hereafter be manifest; wherein Hebron lieth, viz. the head city of the land; whereby externally the outward world with its figure is set forth; and internally the holy eternal land of Canaan.

13. And we see very clearly what the spirit of Moses meaneth in its figure; for first it representeth by Isaac Christ's figure with his offering and death; and presently thereupon it sets forth also man's own death, and where man must die, namely, in his city, Hebron, the city of human self; and whereinto he must be buried and put, namely, into the twofold pit, viz. into the kingdom of God, and [into the kingdom of] this world. And it is therefore called a twofold cave, because there are two mansions, viz. a twofold continent of life in two Principles, whence man did originally arise. But if he be buried in the will of his selfhood in the Serpent's desire, then he doth not reach this twofold cave; and though he should be therein, yet he liveth only in the apostate essence in the ownhood of the devil, viz. in the introduced Serpent's ens in the dark world's property, which is manifest and predominant in the Serpent's ens.

14. The chiefest piece in this figure is, that the spirit of Moses doth point at the twofold life; how this world hath a twofold life and essence, which he intimates by the twofold cave wherein Abraham would have his burying place. To signify that his twofold humanity, viz. one out of the divine ens, out of the eternity and [the] heavenly spiritual essentiality; and the other which is out of the time, even out

[1] Twofold pit.

of this world's being and substance, should be buried and put into an eternal sepulchre, where the substance of the twofold body shall lie in its original mother; and leave the own-will in this eternal grave in death, that so the Spirit of God might alone live, rule and will in the spirit of the creature, viz. in the soul: and the life of man might be only his instrument, wherewith he might work and will how and what he please.

15. For so it must be, that the human will might be brought again into the only will of the Deity, and [the] eternity; for, in the beginning, when God breathed the soul into the flesh, it was in the eternal living Word (John i), and God's Spirit did form it into a likeness of the Deity, viz. into a creatural soul. Which soul had turned itself away from the only eternal Word of God into a selfhood, that so it might be manifest in evil and good, and rule in the unlikeness or distemperature.

16. This unlikeness or distemperature should be buried or put again into the likeness or temperature, viz. into the essence out of which the soul and body did arise. That is, each essence's property should return again into its mother: and the mother is a twofold cave, viz. the inward spiritual and divine kingdom, and the outward visible, sensible, palpable kingdom of the external world, wherein Abraham would have his burying place.

17. For the outward kingdom remains for ever, for it is produced out of the eternal, as a model, platform or visible image of the inward spiritual kingdom. But the dominion in the stars and four elements doth not remain for ever in such ownhood or propriety; but only one element [remains], wherein the four are understood, but in equal accord and harmony, in just and equal weight, number and measure, in one only love-will; where the ascending, domineering, stirring might of the divided figure, four elements, doth no longer rule, but the soft, meek and still humility, in a pleasant, lovely, delightful air[1] [or still, harmonious sound].

18. The compacted property of the Word, in the soul of the outward world, viz. in the ownhood or selfness of the third Principle, doth cease; the outward spirit of the world is changed into the inward, that the inward might rule and govern wholly through the outward (which at present the great motion of the enkindled might of the dark world doth withhold), and carry in its dominion; in which [dark world's property, which is now so predominant] the devil is an aspiring, assaulting prince. And all things work and tend to the Great

---

[1] Musical air.

OF THE DEATH OF SARAH

Severation; that so the properties of the three Principles might each become creatural in themselves, to which end the eternity hath brought itself into a Fiat, or desire, to the formation of the essence, viz. of the Grand Mystery;[1] that thus one might be manifest in the other; the evil in the good, and the good in the evil; and each thing might have its own seat and habitation.

[1] Mysterii Magni.

The Fiftieth Chapter

Of *Abraham's* sending forth his Servant to take a wife for his Son *Isaac*: what we are to understand under this figure

1. ABRAHAM strongly engageth his servant, who was the chief ruler in his family government, and laid an oath upon him, that he should not take a wife unto his son of the daughters of the Canaanites, among whom he dwelt, but go unto his kindred, and to his father's house, and take him a wife (Gen. xxiv. 2, 3). Reason doth look upon this figure in a mean and simple manner, as if Abraham did hate and abominate this people among whom he dwelt, because of their evil conversation; but the Spirit of God in Moses who hath thus noted down this figure, hath his secret and mysterious meanings couched herein; and playeth with the whole written history of the first book of Moses,[1] as with a most pleasant interlude; and pointeth continually by the outward act of the external man upon the spiritual figure of the spiritual eternal man, in the kingdom of Christ.

2. The servant must swear unto Abraham an oath, that he would take a wife unto his son out of his family, stock and kindred. Wherefore did Abraham lay an oath upon him, whereas the servant must obey his master without taking an oath; and Isaac would not have taken a wife contrary to his father's mind and will? But the spirit of Moses doth look here into the internal figure: Isaac stands here in the figure of Christ; and Abraham's servant stands in the figure of nature; and the Canaanites do stand in the figure of the introduced Serpent's ens, out of which the rebellious, selfish will of man's selfhood is arisen, viz. in the figure of the bestial man, which shall not inherit the kingdom of God. These three the spirit of Moses doth set before him in the type, and thereby points at the true man which shall subsist eternally.

The inward figure is thus:

3. Abraham requires his servant, who was the chief in his whole family. Abraham here betokens God the Father; and the servant, by whom he governeth, betokens nature. Nature must here in its might

[1] Genesis.

and strength swear unto God, that is, deeply engage and essentially bind itself, that it will not take unto Isaac, that is, to the Christians, viz. to God's children, a wife, that is, a matrix, of the Canaanites, viz. of the Serpent's ens; or associate with it to the propagation of the Serpent's ens; that it will not assume the poison of the dark world's property unto it, viz. the Canaanitish property, and introduce it into the children of Christ for their wife, viz. into the tincture of Venus, which is the true female matrix in men and women; but that it will join the true Adamical man, which God had created in his image (viz. the true human essence proceeding from the first original tree out of the first root, viz. from Abraham's stock, who betokens Adam) unto the ens of Christ, viz. to the true Isaac in the children of Christ.

4. Understand this thus: Adam hath introduced into our flesh and soul the ens of the Serpent and the devil, which nature hath taken into soul and body; and hath begotten and brought forth therein a selfish, rebellious will, which is disobedient unto God.

5. But now, seeing that God had again introduced the holy ens of his holy word into Isaac, which Abraham apprehended in the desire of faith, and represented the same here in Isaac, with a new twig springing forth out of the corrupt tree of the human property, and born out of Christ's spirit, thereupon nature, viz. God's officer, must here deeply engage itself to God, and swear that it will no more take the Serpent's ens for a wife, viz. for its beloved companion and yoke-fellow (understand [that it will not take its comfort] out of the poisonful Serpentine property of the introduced iniquity of the adverse opposite will). But God's officer, viz. nature, must take essence and substance out of Abraham's true climate, where Abraham's home was, in Adam, viz. out of the right human essence; and bring the same to Isaac, viz. to Christ's members in their heavenly spiritual holy ens of faith, as a spiritual woman, with whom the true man taketh delight in himself, with the heavenly matrix, in pure desire of love, and loveth his own nature in God's love, and not in the Canaanitish selfish Serpent's ens, in the apostate, rebellious, ungodly will; that so the new birth might be holy in its virginity as to the inward man.

6. For man, in his essence or being, doth stand in a twofold essence, viz. in the natural and [in the] supernatural; in the divine ens of the formed Word, and in the natural ens of the centre of nature in the Fiat, viz. in the divine desire; in which desire nature, and the bright-burning world, do take their original; which bright-flaming nature should not any more take the false lust of the bestial Serpent's

property into itself: of which the spirit here doth prophesy in the inward figure.

7. *And Abraham's servant said, How, if the woman will not follow me, shall I bring thy son again unto the land from whence thou camest* (Gen. xxiv. 5)? The meaning hereof in the inward understanding is this: Nature speaketh to God, and saith, How, if the right human ens will not follow me, seeing it hath a cleaving affection to the Serpent's poison, shall I then bring thy son, viz. the holy heavenly ens, again into the land, viz. into the place from whence it came, along with me? That is, when God betrusteth the officer of nature with his holy ens, to bring the same into the human property, and to take the human ens for a wife of the heavenly man, then saith nature, viz. God's officer, How then, if the woman (understand the human ens) will not follow me and come with this Isaac, that is, with the ens of Christ, into the true human land, viz. into the true Adamical paradisical tree, shall I bring thy son again, viz. thy holy ens, into the place of God?

8. *And Abraham said, Beware thou that thou dost not bring my son thither again. The Lord God of heaven, which took me from my father's house, and from the land of my kindred, and that spake unto me, and swear also unto me, saying, Unto thy seed I will give this land; he shall send his angel before thee, and thou shalt there take a wife unto my son. But if the woman will not follow thee, then thou art clear from the oath: only bring not my son thither again. And then the servant put his hand under the thigh of Abraham his master, and sware unto him concerning this matter* (Gen. xxiv. 6–9).

9. The inward meaning is thus: God saith to his officer, nature, Have a care, that thou dost not go according to thy reason, and conceive another will, and bring my holy ens again thither from whence it is come, for it must dwell in man. The God of heaven, who hath taken the human ens from the eternal Word, from his eternal native country, which is the house of the eternal Father, who hath promised man the land of Canaan according to the paradisical property, and moreover hath sworn to him, he shall send his angel before thee; that so thou mayest take a wife unto my son there, even where the angel, viz. the divine will, shall guide and direct thee. That is, when God will betroth and bind himself with his Word and power in his children, with an eternal marriage, then he sendeth his angel before, viz. his will, into the human ens; that the same doth convert and turn itself to God.

10. The nature of the mind must not in its will of reason take upon

it to lord and master it, and doubt at what God will do, when the office or charge of a servant is laid upon it; it must not make itself its looking-glass, and doubt, when it seeth that the soul lieth captivated in the ens of the Serpent; it must not think with itself, I shall not here arrive [with a prosperous success] with my divine message; but it must leave that to God, and discharge its message according to God's command, and commit it to God, how he will bring the woman, viz. the human spirit, and betroth and join it with the son Isaac, that is, with Christ, in the divine ens.

11. But if the woman will not follow thee, then thou art clear of the oath; that is, if the human will, when I send my will before thee in man, will not follow thee, then the messenger, viz. God's officer, with the sent heaven's ens, is clear. Only, bring not my son thither again; that is, bring not the heavenly ens again into that essence out of which it is come; but stand still therewith, and hear whereunto God shall direct and incline thee; for the rain from heaven shall not ascend up again empty without fruit. So likewise God's word and command shall not return home empty, but work and bring forth fruit in its formed wisdom.

12. If one man will not, then the same word falls upon another which is capable of it. Therefore nature, viz. the messenger, officer, advocate or petitioner of the heavenly message, must not bring the word with the divine ens back again into that place, viz. into the inward divine voice. For what God once speaketh forth by his Word in power, that shall and must stand in a divine form, to the divine contemplation. Nature must go forward as a messenger his way, and declare that the Lord hath given Isaac all his goods; that is, he hath given to Christ all his goods; and desires now a wife, viz. man, who should give himself in marriage with Isaac in Christ.

13. *And the servant laid his hand under the thigh of Abraham his master, and sware unto him concerning this matter* (Gen. xxiv. 9). That is, when God put his holy word with the heavenly ens or essence,[1] viz. with the formed wisdom, into the natural ens of Mary, as into God's servant, and God and man became one person, then the human nature sware under the thigh of the Father's eternal nature unto God,[2] that it would obey God, and henceforward go forth, and seek the human wife, and marry it to the divine ens. All which is to be understood in Christ's person, who in his assumed humanity, as Abraham's, or God his Father's, servant, in the natural property, should go forth with his

---

[1] Did dive, immerse, or baptise.   [2] Or, in God.

word and seek this woman, viz. his bride and spouse, which the angel of the Lord, viz. God's will, should bring unto him.

14. *And the servant took ten camels of the camels of his master, and departed; and had with him all sorts of his master's goods: and arose and went to Mesopotamia, the city of Nahor* (Gen. xxiv. 10). Here now the spirit looks upon the process of God; and intimates, how God sent his angel or messenger, Gabriel, with the voice of nature to the human nature in Nahor, viz. to Adam's nature in the ens of Mary; in which voice the living holy word was hidden with the heavenly living ens; and gave also the Father's nature ten camels; that is, the ten forms of the three Principles to the natural and supernatural fire-life. Namely, seven forms of the centre of nature, and three forms of the three distinctions of the Principles; all which are God's camels whereby he beareth and carrieth all things.

15. And the goods of the Lord are the formed wisdom of the great wonders and powers. All these, God's officer took along with him, when he had the divine word in himself, and introduced the same into the human natural ens, even into the ens of Mary; or awakened, opened or manifested the same therein; as a man might express the great deeds and works of God; whereas indeed the outward, compacted, bound-up, sensual tongue, cannot give words sufficient enough to the deep mental understanding.

16. For here the spirit of Moses doth take the angel's message along with Isaac's figure, and playeth externally in the figure, with Isaac and Rebecca, as Christ's figure; and inwardly he playeth with Mary, as Adam's essence, and with Christ's, as the virginlike divine ens.

17. And the spirit of Moses saith further, *And the servant caused the camels to kneel down without the city by a well of water at evening time, even about the time that women use to go out to draw water* (Gen. xxiv. 11). This signifieth and noteth out internally, how the mystery of the nature of the three Principles, being the bearers or carriers of the formed wisdom of God, hath laid itself down by the divine fountain without the city. The city betokens the hidden mysteries of the divine holy ens of the formed wisdom; about which, the nature of the three Principles[1] hath laid itself; for nature is external, and a carrier of the mysteries of God: it lieth by the wellspring of God, viz. by the birth of the holy Trinity.

---

[1] Or, the three Principles of nature.

OF ISAAC TAKING A WIFE

The outward figure is thus explained:

18. At evening: that is, in the last days of the world, or towards the evening time in man. When the eternal night draws near, then God bringeth his bearer,[1] viz. the will of the Father's nature, which lieth down by the fountain of the divine property in man, and will there give his camels, viz. his will, drink. Like as towards the evening, that is, in the last time, he did lay his will to the human nature in the ens of Mary, by the true wellspring of the Covenant, and there gave the human nature drink.

19. And as the servant of Abraham, standing by the well of water in Mesopotamia, did purpose and endeavour to fulfil his master's will, and yet did not look upon himself [and cast about in his reason] how it should be, but commended his cause to God, to do as he would please, and only set a lot before him, that he might see what way God would lead and direct him; even so also the spirit of Moses doth here play in the figure of Christ. For nature in the ens or seed of Mary was the servant of God, which pitched down before the ens of the Covenant, as an instrument of God, and gave God the honour, and committed it unto him, how he would bring it to the holy virginity in the holy ens of the Covenant in Mary; as here Abraham's servant commended it to God, when he came before the fountain, how he would lead him and whither, or what he should do; that God might bring him to the true virgin, whom God would give his master's son.

20. So likewise it was not effected by and from the purpose, understanding or power of nature, that nature was brought to the holy ens in the Covenant, and married the divine Virgin in the ens of the Word of God. Nature understood nothing of it, how it should be brought to pass, or what it should do to purchase or accomplish the same. It knew not the holy virginity in the Covenant. But when God's command did sound or speak unto it, by the angel Gabriel, then it gave God the honour, and committed it to him what he would do and work through it; that God might espouse it to the virgin of wisdom. As here Abraham's servant prayed unto God, that he would bring to the fountain of water the right virgin which God had chosen for him.

21. For by the well of God nature shall know what kind of virgin shall come and give the camels, or the bearer, nature, drink. As Rebecca came forth by God's instigation, and gave the camels of Abraham's servants drink, so likewise the divine virginity in the ens

---

[1] Or, carrier.

MYSTERIUM MAGNUM

of Mary came and gave the essence in the seed of Mary, drink; and took the human nature for a spouse and consort.

22. And the human nature in the Covenant, in the seed of Abraham, in his ens of faith (when he apprehended the word of promise in the faith, which was his righteousness), had the fair golden-forehead-jewel[1] in itself, and the two bracelets, which it hung on the word of God, which moved itself in the angel's message in Mary, where then the ens of faith was espoused or married with the now-moving voice; which motion beset and embraced nature; as here Abraham's servant, when he saw that God had brought to him the true virgin, he drew forth the free gift of his master, Abraham, and hung it on the virgin.

23. Thus also nature, in the Covenant, in the seed of Mary, did put the fair jewel (which God promised Adam in Paradise, and opened in Abraham, which Abraham apprehended in the spirit and faith), upon the voice of God, viz. on the living moving word of God, which sounded in the angel's message, in Abraham's ens of faith; and herewith also, itself.

24. For Abraham had laid hold on the word of the Covenant in faith, so that it was formed into an ens, but not wholly into the humanity; and this ens was the fair jewel, which nature bare as a hidden treasure in itself, until the limit of the Covenant, even towards the evening of the world; and then God's living voice sounded into nature in the seed of the woman. And so nature, viz. God's servant, gave forth the hidden pearl, and hung it on the forehead of the virgin-like love of Jesus, which was moved in the angel's message; and came now to the fountain to draw forth the shut-up virginity, in man, from the divine ens. And there it obtained its bridegroom, viz. the soul of man, with the Father's jewels and great goods: With this the spirit of Moses doth here play, and holds forth a secret intimation under the outward act.

25. Abraham's servant made him a lot, to know the virgin by, which was this: *She that should come and give him, and all his servants and camels drink, that even she should be the right one* (Gen. xxiv. 14). Thus also God hath planted this lot, and put it into the nature of the soul and the right humanity: that the virgin, which should refresh the soul with the true humanity out of God's love-fountain, the same the soul should desire for its eternal spouse.

26. As it came to pass in Mary, when the angel greeted her, he

---

[1] Or, ear-rings.

OF ISAAC TAKING A WIFE

refreshed the soul, and also her seed of the soul's nature, proceeding from the woman's tincture, whereby this soul's essence brought its desire towards the sweet spring-water of the fountain of Jesus, and drank of this water of the love of Jesus; whereby and wherein it was married to the sweet love of Jesus, in Jehova. So that in this seed of Mary, in the limit of the Covenant, a manly virgin of God was conceived; which is Christ Jesus in our humanity, and in the divine ens in the power of the word of God; a formed God, according to the creature; but according to the divine voice, God all in all. Understand, a formed God according to the human property, viz. a visible image of the Deity, and therein the whole invisible immense God in Trinity in essence.

27. This whole figure stands in the process of the new birth, and shews how it should come to pass. For Abraham in his faith stands in the figure of Adam, viz. in God the Father's figure; who created him in his very image and likeness. And Isaac his son stands in the figure of the humanity of Christ, viz. in the Son's figure.

28. God the Father hath given all his goods, understand, of the formed Word, viz. all created and procreated beings, in the place of this world, unto his Son, who manifested himself in the divine Image of the humanity; even as Abraham gave all his goods to Isaac, who was the type of Christ.

29. And as Abraham would take a wife unto his son Isaac of his kindred, and sent out his chief officer to take a wife unto his son, and yet did not beforehand name the same unto him, and tell him who she should be; but bade him go only to his father's house, and to his kindred, and see what woman God would bring unto him for his son Isaac to take; so likewise God hath sent his officer (who ruleth chief in his whole house, that is, dominion, which is the voice of his revealed Word) into the world, to the right Adamical man, and not to the Canaanitish Serpent's ens; but to the disappeared virginlike image of God, and to the living soul, which is of God the Father's house, that is, property; and looks out, about a virgin, for a wife to his Son, Jesus Christ; that is, he woos for the heavenly virginity in man, which disappeared in Adam; for this virgin God's officer of nature doth woo, by his servants which he sendeth forth, and bids them make suit for this virginity, for a wife to his Son; and join it with him in marriage.

30. And as Abraham did not name aforehand the virgin unto his officer, but commanded him to go unto his father's house, and there look up unto God, and see where he should bid him make suit, and

take that virgin which God should choose and bring unto him; so likewise God hath sent his officer, viz. his holy word, by his servants, into the world to the true man; not to the Serpent-beasts, for these hear not God's word; they have no hearing in them thereto; like as the Canaanites in the Serpent's ens were even wholly bestial, and half dead as to the divine hearing, by reason of their iniquity and self will.

31. And he causeth his servants, viz. officers, to sit down by the fountain of his holy word; with command, that they should in their office and charge committed unto them, call upon God, and pray, and teach his word, until God draweth the virgin's heart, and brings her to the fountain of his word, to draw water out of the wellspring of God's word.

32. And when this virgin, understand the inward divine image, which was obscured in Adam, draws water in the fountain of the divine word, then the officer, Abraham's servant, viz. the Father's will, speaketh in the soul, saying, Give me to drink of thy sweet water of the eternal virginity; and the precious virgin saith to the will of God, Drink, my Lord; I will also draw [water] for thy camels. Understand by the camels the essences of the human nature proceeding from the Father's property; and by the virgin, understand the nature and property of the light in the love, viz. the essence of the divine ens of the angelical world, which disappeared in Adam, and now cometh again to draw water for its bridegroom the soul.

33. And now when the officer, viz. God's will, with his camels, viz. the essences of nature, is refreshed with drink by the virgin; then the forth-sent will of the Father, in the essence of nature, giveth thanks unto the true Deity; that God hath brought this virgin unto him; that he should take this virgin of the love and humanity of Jesus Christ for a wife.

34. And forthwith the will of God the Father, taketh the precious jewels which God did incorporate into Adam's soul, even into the light of his life, in Paradise, with the precious name Jesus; yea, which jewels were incorporated in the centre of the soul *before the foundation of the world was laid* (Eph. i. 4), which have been wholly hidden to the soul; which jewels are the holy fire of the hidden love-desire, and hangeth the same on the noble virgin of the heavenly world's essence; as a golden ear-ring[1] of half a shekel weight.

35. This golden jewel [or ear-ring of half a shekel weight] is the new heavenly essentiality which came down or proceeded from

---
[1] Or, jewel for the forehead.

OF ISAAC TAKING A WIFE

heaven; as Christ said, *That he was come from heaven* (John iii. 13); there he means the ens proceeding or coming from thence, which was the half-holy humanity, viz. the holy ens in the word, which did unite itself to the disappeared heavenly ens in the humanity; so that this golden jewel of half a shekel weight belongs to the divine sound or word, which cometh into the humanity, and is hung upon the heavenly virginity in man.

36. And now when the marriage is celebrated, and the virginlike ens betrothed to this holy ens, so that the virginity receiveth this jewel proffered unto it; then it is a whole shekel of gold; half of the Deity, and half of the humanity.

37. And the two bracelets, which Abraham's servants, viz. the will of the Father in the soul's nature, putteth on the virgin, which are of ten shekels weight of gold, they are the ten forms of the holy fire which are hung with the new introduced humanity of Jesus Christ, his divine ens, on the disappeared virginity; whereby it again receiveth its true life.

38. And when this virgin hath thus received this jewel and bracelets, then it rejoiceth, and runneth to her brother Laban, viz. to the third Principle of the outward humanity, proceeding from the limus of the earth; that is, to the outward soul; and telleth this unto him; that is, when the virgin's image doth receive the ens of Christ, viz. this fair and precious jewel of half a shekel, together with the holy fire of the word, then it penetrates, with its voice of the divine essence, through the outward man (viz. its brother), and declareth the divine power; whereby the outward man (understand the third Principle) is glad, and exceedingly rejoiceth with the virgin of the inward man, and runneth also unto the fountain of the word of God, and prayeth God that he would be pleased to come in unto him with his word. As here Laban prayed Abraham's servant to come in to him; which Abraham's servant, viz. God's will, doth willingly, and turns in unto the outward man.

39. As Abraham's servant did, thus doth the human nature likewise, when it heareth the voice of Christ sounding in the inward man, and seeth the ornament which the holy Spirit hath put on the virgin's image. Then Laban, viz. the brother of the inward image, doth earnestly entreat the will of God to come in.

40. And when the will of God (here typified by Abraham's servant) is come in unto Bethuel and Laban, viz. into the third Principle of the humanity, then the officer of God, viz. the word of God which cometh

into man, saith, *I will not eat of thy food* (understand of the outward life's essence) *except I obtain my errand*: that thou givest my master, viz. my master's son (that is, the humanity of Jesus Christ) thy sister, viz. the heavenly virginity, to wife. And he relateth the mission or errand of God to the human nature; that is, he openeth to it the divine understanding, so that even the natural man doth learn to understand the will of God, in which, before, it was blind.

41. And then the poor nature with the soul gives up itself into God's will. And then thus speak Laban and Bethuel, This cometh from the Lord; we shall not speak anything against it; behold, here is thy place, do with me and with my inward [ground] as thou pleasest. Here is Rebecca, viz. the formed word of the heavenly property; take it, and marry it to thy master's son, viz. to the humanity of Jesus Christ, according to thy good-liking, as the Lord hath spoken.

42. We see here very exactly how the spirit of Moses doth speak in the figure, for he sets Laban, viz. Bethuel's son, before the father; viz. the outward soul before the inward fire-soul, the air-soul before the right fire-soul; albeit they are not two, but one, yet they are understood in two Principles. For the fire-soul gives answer through the air-soul; the fire-soul useth the uncompacted tongue, but the air-soul useth the compacted formed language.

43. Therefore the spirit of Moses doth set Laban, Rebecca's brother, first, as if the business were done by Laban. To signify, that when God's officer, viz. the will of God, in the drawing of the Father, doth come into man, and seeketh a lodging, and the virgin, then the outward spirit of man must give its promise; for it is turned away from God and the true resignation: Now it must again give its will wholly and fully into God's will.

44. And when it comes to pass that the outward soul, with the inward fire-soul, doth wholly consent unto this holy match, and give up itself to God, then the will of God, viz. the officer, in the drawing of the Father, doth bow himself again towards the true Deity; that is, he cometh again unto its seat and place, and brings forth out of Abraham's treasure (that is, out of God the Father's treasury of his formed wisdom) the silver and golden jewels, and hangeth them on Rebecca, viz. the heavenly virginity.

45. For these jewels do not belong to Laban, or Bethuel (understand to the outward, or inward fire-soul) while it is here in this earthly life, but to the true virgin, Rebecca, proceeding from the divine ens of the formed holy Word, according to the angelical world's

OF ISAAC TAKING A WIFE

property; viz. according to the second Principle, viz. the inward spiritual new man, which is, with Rebecca, married to the right Isaac, Christ. And therefore the spirit of Moses sets down how Abraham's servant gave Rebecca the golden ear-ring and bracelets, with silver and golden jewels, and raiment; but unto Laban, viz. unto Rebecca's brother, and her mother also, he gave spices[1] (Gen. xxiv. 53).

46. O thou wonderful God! how plainly dost thou set forth the great mysteries! The silver and golden jewels are the treasure of the divine wisdom in the word of life, which treasure the divine Word brings along with it to the right virginity, which died in Adam, and is again brought in Christ to its beloved; and giveth it wholly and peculiarly for the ornament of the banquet. And the raiment is the new humanity, wherewith she cometh before her bridegroom; and the spices, which were given to Laban and the mother, are the power and virtues of the Holy Spirit, which are freely given to the fire-soul and the air-soul, by the coming in of the tender humanity of Jesus Christ.

47. For the outward soul is not in this life time (seeing yet the earthly body adheres unto it) clothed with the new raiment; neither is the silver and golden jewel of the humanity of Jesus Christ given in this life time wholly unto the peculiar possession and power of the fire-soul; but the spices only, that is, the virtue and pleasant aspect of the Holy Spirit; for the fire-soul might become proud and haughty again, if it should have this virgin in its own power, as Lucifer and Adam did. Therefore the fire-soul must here in this life time remain in its Principle; and in the air-soul, viz. in the third Principle, where the earthly evil man liveth, it must take on it the cross of Christ.

48. But virgin Rebecca, or Sophia, with her bridegroom, Christ, remain in their own, viz. in the second Principle, in heaven; for St Paul saith, *Our conversation is in heaven* (Phil. iii. 20); understand, the conversation of the virgin [Sophia], where she, with her beloved, Christ, stands in wedlock; and Christ and virgin Sophia are one person: understand the true manly virgin of God, which Adam was before his Eve when he was man and woman, and yet neither of them, but a virgin of God.

49. And now, when these nuptials are celebrated, then Abraham's servant, with all his servants, sits down with his obtained bride, and with father and mother at the table, and eat together the marriage feast (Gen. xxiv. 54). That is, when man, understand the inward virginlike spiritual man, is married to Christ, then God eateth of

---

[1] Our text, precious things.

man's will and words; and again man eateth of God's will and words. There they sit at one feast, and then 'tis truly said and applied, *Whosoever heareth you, he heareth me.* Whosoever heareth these men to teach and speak of God, he heareth God speak, for they speak in the power of the Holy Spirit's spices, and eat together of the great Supper of Christ.

50. O, what a very glorious and sumptuous feast is there kept, where this wedding day is celebrated in man! which no Canaanitish serpent-man is worthy to know, or taste of; yea, he doth not experimentally taste of it to all eternity; neither knows he what meat or food is there eaten; also what internal joy is there, where Christ and virgin Sophia are bride and bridegroom; and the inward and outward soul sit by the bride, and eat with her of this feast; which we leave to the consideration of the children of Christ, who have been at this wedding feast: No man else in this world understands it: none knows anything thereof, but the right Laban and Bethuel.

51. But this bridal doth not last continually, but when Abraham's servant had obtained the virgin, and celebrated this feast and wedding day with the father and mother, and Laban; and had continued there all night, he arose up early in the morning, and said, *Let me go unto my master.*

The inward figure stands thus:

52. When Christ hath married himself with virgin Sophia, viz. with the inward humanity, soon after, the voice of God soundeth in the soul, and saith, *I will go away from thee with the virgin,* and it is continually as if he would force away and depart from man. Then the poor soul must make continual prayers and supplications, that he would be pleased to tarry still longer with it; but the voice oftentimes sounds, *Hinder me not, I must go, or make my journey, to my master,* thou art vain, evil and sinful, I may not tarry with thee any longer.

53. And then the poor soul calleth virgin Rebecca, viz. Christ with his bride, and puts him in mind of his precious word and promise, in that *He hath promised to remain with us even to the end of the world, and to make his abode in us* (Matt. xxviii. 20). And thus one day upon another it is delayed, and yet Christ goeth with his bride into his native country, viz. into the second Principle, but the marriage is celebrated in all the three Principles.

54. A very excellent figure we have in this also: That when Rebecca went home with Abraham's servant, and Isaac met her in the

OF ISAAC TAKING A WIFE

field, and she asked Abraham's servant what man that was, and he told her that it was his master, Isaac, how she lighted off the camel, and put a veil before her eyes, and was ashamed; and how Isaac took her and carried her into his mother's tent (Gen. xxiv. 61 et seq.).

The inward figure is this:

55. When the inward disappeared humanity doth again obtain the precious jewel, and is quickened in the spirit of Christ, and discovers its beloved Christ in itself, then it falls down into the deepest humility before the holiness of God, and is ashamed that it hath lain so long captive in the bestial man, and that it was a queen, but hath lost its kingdom in Adam; then it veileth its own face before God's glorious clarity, and humbleth itself. But Christ taketh her into his arms, and leads her into his mother's tent, viz. into the heavenly world's essence, from whence he is come with his heavenly essence, and there she becomes his wife; and thus Isaac is truly comforted for his mother, viz. for the disappeared matrix in the tincture of Venus which died in Adam, and which he again doth now obtain in virginlike chastity for his spouse: as here the history concerning Isaac soundeth.

56. And we seriously admonish the reader not to contemn, scorn or deride at our exposition, it is the true ground. For when Isaac met his bride, he came from the well Lahai-roi [from the fountain of the living and seeing one], as Moses saith (Gen. xxiv. 62). If any desire to understand our meaning and knowledge, he must then make towards this fountain, that so he may be received with Rebecca; and then he will see from what spirit this pen hath written, and in what number and voice[1] it is arisen.

57. If any here see nothing, he may well blame himself for blind, and no man else. The Jews, and Turks, and also Babel, may here open their eyes wide, and look upon the figures of the Old Testament aright: they will even find them so.

[1] Seal, vial or trumpet.

The Fifty-First Chapter

How *Abraham* took another wife, of whom he begat six Sons to which he gave gifts; and unto his Son *Isaac* he gave all his goods; but the others he sent away from his Son *Isaac* while he yet lived; and also how he died, and was buried by his Sons, *Ishmael* and *Isaac*; what hereby is signified unto us

1. MOSES saith, *Abraham took a wife, and her name was Keturah, and she bare unto him Zimran, Jokshan, Medan, Midian, Ishbak and Shuah* (Gen. xxv. 1, 2), from whom sprang forth six generations. But of Sarah Abraham begat only one son, at which the whole history pointeth; but of Keturah he begat six sons, concerning whom no peculiar or especial thing is mentioned, but only their families or generations.

This is thus to be understood in the inward figure:

Abraham and his Sarah must be first old, before he begat Isaac, to signify that Christ should be manifested in the flesh in the old age of the world.

2. Isaac was begotten and conceived of Abraham's nature, and of the ens of faith in an old and almost dead matrix, as to the human nature, that so the divine ens might have the pre-eminence. But when Sarah died, Abraham took unto him Keturah, and soon begat of her six sons. Keturah doth in its name express the centre of nature. When we form the sensual uncompacted spirits of the letters in this word Keturah, then we understand that Keturah is a formed matrix of nature; which signifieth to us, that Abraham, after he had begotten the type of Christ in the ens of faith, should now beget his own likeness as to Adam's nature, out of the six properties of the natural spirit's life, and also set forth and represent his own natural likeness; and therefore he must also have such a vessel thereunto.

3. Sarah must bring forth but one son: to signify that the kingdom

HOW ABRAHAM TOOK ANOTHER WIFE

of mankind is given but to one; and that they all do belong to this one; and should in him become the same only one, as branches on one tree; which [one] should be Christ in all.

4. But here Abraham did now with Keturah beget six sons, according to the six properties of the formed nature, of the operation of the six days' works; and Isaac, that is, Christ, is the seventh, viz. the day of rest, or Sabbath, wherein the six sons should enter into rest; even as the six days of the creation, understand the six properties of the centre of nature (viz. the working spirit-life), do rest in the seventh: Thus the Spirit of God doth represent the figure in Abraham.

5. And we have here a very excellent figure against the reason-wise, who say, That whosoever is not born by nature in the ens of faith [that is, naturally, as it were, begotten of the seed of the woman, which works only by a particular election of God, as they feign] the same is hardened, and cannot attain to the adoption of God, he is not drawn by God, that he should come to the new birth. This figure quite strikes down their fiction, and shews the true ground; and first, it sets forth Isaac, viz. Christ, and declareth plainly that to him alone the kingdom of God is hereditary and peculiar, and that no man can have it any more for or from the right of nature; and how we are altogether cast out from thence with Adam, and have lost the same; as the children of Keturah were all cast out from the inheritance of Abraham's goods, and Isaac alone did inherit them.

6. And he sets down hereby, how Adam's children were also begotten of Abraham, and how he gave them gifts of his goods (Gen. xxv. 6); betokening how free gifts were given to Adam's natural children, out of God the Father's, and Christ's, goods; as Abraham's goods were given them of grace as a free gift.

7. For Abraham did not cast out his natural children from him without gifts: so likewise God did not cast Adam out of Paradise without his free gift;[1] he first gave him the Bruiser of the Serpent in the Word of the Covenant; and afterwards he cast Adam from the childlike inheritance of the natural right; and yet he received him again in the free donation; as Abraham also did not here reject his children and cast them out from the childship, but from the natural right of his goods; yet they were dear unto him in the childship. Therefore he freely gave them gifts of his goods, and thereby he signifieth to us, that the kingdom of heaven doth indeed belong only unto Christ, viz. to the true Isaac. But as he freely of grace gave the

---

[1] *Note.*—Where the free grace of God was given to mankind.

Covenant to Adam, and as Abraham gave gifts out of Isaac's right to the sons of the concubines, so God the Father doth still to this day give Adam's, and Abraham's, natural children the Covenant and heritage of Christ, as a free gift of grace.

8. And as Abraham's natural children were not disinherited from the Covenant, but only from his goods; so likewise no man is disinherited from the Covenant of God, established in Adam and Abraham. Every man receiveth the free-given Covenant in the womb, in which free-given Covenant he hath power to turn in unto Christ's goods.

9. But he hath not the goods in the right of nature, to take the same at or by his own will, but as a free gift. He shall and must resign himself up unto the Covenant, as a servant, wholly giving up his own natural will in the Covenant, and forsake the will to the right of nature, and become wholly the Covenant's own; so that he doth not any longer introduce his own natural will into the Covenant and free gift, but give up his will to the Covenant. And then the free gift standeth in the place of the own-will; and the nature of Adam liveth in the free gift, and also enjoyeth the inheritance; but not in the self-will, but in the true resignation, where the will of the Covenant becomes man's will.

10. For the will of the Covenant inheriteth the sonship in the right of nature, but the will of the natural selfness is cast out from it, the same must die unto the assuming ownhood; and when it is brought so to pass, it ariseth in the Covenant in Christ, and possesseth the free gift in the right of grace. Christ hath manifested himself in the Covenant in Adam's freely-given gift in the human nature, and is become the life and will of the Covenant, and fulfilled the same.

11. But now this free-given Covenant which God bestowed on Adam lieth in all men, for as sin passed as a birthright from one upon all, so also the Covenant and the free gift of grace passeth from one upon all. Every man hath Christ in him; but the own-will doth not apprehend Christ, but it crucifieth him, and will not die to its selfness, that so it might enter into Christ's death, and arise in the Covenant in the will of Christ.

12. The own-will desireth only to be an outwardly assumed or adopted son of grace, and yet it is cast out from the presence of God, as Abraham cast out his natural children from his goods, and disinherited them, and gave the goods only to Isaac; so likewise the kingdom of God belongs only to the will of the Covenant.

13. Which indeed lieth in all men; but no man can receive or see the kingdom of God, unless he become the child of the Covenant, so that he forsake the natural forth-proceeded will, and put on the will of Christ in the Covenant; so that his will in the Covenant be born anew in Christ; and then he is a branch on the vine of Christ (John xv. 5), and receiveth Christ's spirit, will, and life; and becomes, as to the Covenant, Christus [or one anointed]. And thus Christ then dwelleth in Adam, and Adam in Christ; and this is that which the spirit of Moses doth represent in this figure.

14. But that Abraham did send the children of his Adamical nature away out of his house with gifts, and did not keep them with him as sojourners, betokens that the external man will, while it is in this life, live in the will of self upon the earth, and that it cannot wholly put off the same according to the earthly man; but this same earthly self-will is cast out of the holiness of God, viz. from the kingdom of heaven.

15. And although the free gift of the Covenant lieth hid in him, yet the outward earthly man is cast out from Paradise and the Covenant of God, and shall not inherit the kingdom of heaven, but he only shall inherit it who is born of the free gift of the Covenant. Not Adam, but Christ in his members; not the Serpent's ens, and the selfish, rebellious, Ishmaelitish, scoffing, false will, but the will of the Covenant in Ishmael's circumcision, where the mocker is cut off from the Covenant; and Ishmael then becomes Isaac's brother.

16. The own, self-made, gross, earthly Adam, who by his own lust hath made himself a beast, and received and taken in the devil's desire and will, into the selfly assumed beast, the same cannot be or remain in the image of Christ. He is cast out from thence, and walketh in the world of vanity, and his own lust, so that he is not capable of the free gift in the Covenant.

17. But the right Adamical man, which God made out of the matrix of the earth, out of which the earth had its original, in the same is the Covenant and the free gift; even as a tincture in the gross lead, which doth swallow up in itself the grossness, viz. the gross Saturn in its own desire, and mortifieth the Saturnine will, and advanceth or sublimeth its own (understand the tincture's will and propriety) in the lead, whereby the lead is changed into gold.

18. Thus likewise we are to understand, that the gross Saturnine self-will, proceeding from the dark world's property in man, cannot dwell in God's house: it is without, in the corrupt world; God hath cast it forth out of Paradise; as Abraham cast out his natural Adamical

children from Isaac's goods. So also our earthly man as to its assumed grossness and ownhood is not at all fit for, or profitable unto, the kingdom of heaven. It is only the axe wherewith the carpenter builds in this life time, in heaven he hath no need of this axe, for he shall not need build him a house for his propriety, but Christ, viz. the formed Word of God, is his house.

19. For as Abraham cast out of his house the sons of his concubines with gifts, so likewise the Adamical man is cast out from God, whom Christ, viz. the Father's free gift, receiveth again unto himself. For when Christ was come into our humanity God suffered him to be hung upon the cross, and be put to death; but received him again in his free favour, and set him at the right hand of the power of God in heaven, and our humanity also with and in him; but the human self-will must die on the cross.

20. Thus likewise the spirit of Moses doth here signify in the figure, concerning Abraham and his natural children, that the outward natural man shall not dwell in the ens of Christ, for he is cast out of Paradise in Adam; therefore also he cannot be received according to his bestial selfish propriety unto the possession of Isaac's goods; that is, unto the ens of faith, viz. in Christ; and albeit Christ, viz. the free gift of the Father, doth dwell in the inward true man which God created in Adam, yet the gross beast, viz. the earthliness and vanity, shall and must in every respect be cast away from Christ. Yea, every man who desireth to be a Christian must cast out from himself the earthly will, which longeth and breatheth after vanity and self-lust.

21. As Abraham (in this figure) did not spare his own children, but cast them out, so likewise a Christian must not spare or forbear his children, viz. his own lust and vain desire, and all whatsoever doth hang or depend thereon; but daily and hourly cast them out by the understanding, out of the true Temple of Christ, viz. out of God's free gift, and crucify the old Adam. Else, if it be not thus effected, the old self-willed Adam crucifieth Christ in him, and so Christ indeed must hang on the cross, and be put to death.

22. Also this figure (concerning Abraham's casting out his natural children) doth signify that, when Christ, viz. the true Isaac, came into the flesh, viz. into the humanity, Abraham's natural children, viz. the Jews, should, under the kingdom of Christ, be cast out from the natural goods, viz. from all dominion, from country and kingdom; and their rule and dominion should cease. For the dominion belongs only unto Christ, viz. to Christendom; for Christ brought an eternal

kingdom with him: the goods were all his; as Abraham's goods belonged to Isaac.

23. And although it hath not dominion over all, as Isaac had possession and rule of that only which his father left him; for the natural children of Abraham, born of Keturah, became afterwards heathen, and ruled over the outward goods as children of the outward nature: yet Abraham's children, who were in the Covenant under circumcision, must, when Christ did manifest himself, be cast out: To signify that the earthly man also, viz. self in the Serpent's ens which is on the children of the Covenant, must be cast away from God.

24. Thus in Abraham and his son Isaac the figure of the kingdom of Christ was represented. But when Christ came into the flesh, God put away the figure; and took from the external children of Isaac the outward goods of the land, Canaan: To intimate, that now the holy land of Canaan is become manifest: where Isaac's children shall take possession of the true promised inheritance in Christ, and no longer have the figure only, but the essence of the figure, viz. the perfect substance, and now forsake the outward goods with the figure, and put on Christ in the flesh.

25. But that the Jews, viz. Isaac's and Abraham's children, viz. the children in Christ's figure, did not all turn unto Christ when he did manifest himself in the flesh, hath this meaning: God gave them the law of nature; where, in the law, the government of nature was understood externally, and internally Christ, viz. the Covenant, and the promised free gift of God in Paradise. So that the law of nature was to be Christ's sojourner, and the true man also was to live under the law of nature in a right rationality, and yet bring his own nature into Christ's house. And thus the figure of the law must continue among some of Abraham's children, viz. amongst some of the Jews, to signify that the law is Christ's sojourner.

26. Understand, that the nature of man shall remain, for it is not so rejected of God, as if clean another new man should arise out of the old; but [the new man] shall arise out of Adam's nature and property, and out of God's, in Christ's nature and property; so that man is become an Adam-Christ, and Christ a Christ-Adam; a Man-God, and a God-Man. And therefore the figure continued still among the Jews; and for this cause they were not all converted to Christ; that so nature might keep its figure and due right; for it shall deliver up its children under the law, viz. the figure of Christ, to God the Father, in Christ. But its figure shall be proved in the fire of God, so that it shall

be known who hath been the true child of the natural law in the figure of Christ, that hath been born in the spirit in the law out of the figure of Christ, and who hath not.

27. It is not he that hath the words and title of the law, that is a Jew, born in the figure and in the law; but he who is born of the promise in Abraham's faith. He that liveth in the figure of Christ, viz. in the law in profession, and practiseth (with mouth and heart) the same, the law of God in Christ's figure hath comprehended, and will bring him into the fulfilling of the figure.

28. For it doth not depend alone on man's knowing, that Christ hath given himself into the law, and is become the fulfilling in the law, as the titular Christian boasteth; but it depends on God's order,[1] on the mercy of God. Whosoever hath been a true Jew, and hath put on Abraham's faith in the law, he hath put on the ens of Christ, which Abraham conceived or apprehended; which ens of faith the humanity of Christ hath fulfilled; and it is hidden to him what it is, for he worketh in the office of nature in the law of God, which Christ hath taken into himself and fulfilled; so that he serveth God in the office of nature, and the office of nature serveth Christ, for it is become Christ's own propriety.

29. For unto him all power is given both in heaven and on earth (Matt. xxviii. 18), under which power the office of nature also is, in the law. For God, in the spirit of Christ, is even the selfsame who gave the law and the office of nature to do righteousness; together with the figure of the kingdom of Christ, with the ens of faith, to Abraham and Moses; and he is also the very same who fulfilled the faith, and the law.

30. Thus the Jew worketh in his faith in Christ's office, viz. in the law, wherewith Christ governeth in nature; and hath put on Christ in the Covenant, and in the ens of faith in Christ's figure, which Christ hath fulfilled.

31. For the Christian who confesseth Christ in the flesh, worketh in his faith in the flesh of Christ, and hath, in his faith, the law of nature, viz. God's officer, to do uprightly. For Christ ruleth in the law of God (which he hath fulfilled and made a servant) in his children, and killeth the law of sin through the fulfilling of his love in his blood and death; both in them who live in the dominion of his law, and also in them who live in the dominion of his conquest, as the Christians do.

---

[1] Ordinance.

HOW ABRAHAM TOOK ANOTHER WIFE

32. For the faith which presseth or cometh in unto God in the law, in the figure, in the Covenant, the same cometh unto God in the ens of Abraham's faith, out of which Christ was born. And he that cometh in unto God in the fulfilling of the same, doth come or press into God in the humanity of Christ, viz. in the whole process of his suffering, death, and resurrection.

33. A Christian is Christ in the inward humanity; and a Jew is Christ in the figure, and in the office of his law, viz. according to nature. But now Adam in his nature and Christ in the divine nature are but one person, one only tree. Who now is here that judgeth (Rom. viii. 34)?

34. St Paul saith, *There is no respect of persons before God. For as many as have sinned without law shall also perish without law: and they who have sinned in the law shall be judged by the law. For not the hearers of the law are just before God, but the doers of the law shall be justified. For when the Gentiles, which have not the law, do by nature the things contained in the law, these, having not the law, are a law unto themselves: Which shew that the work of the law is written in their hearts, their conscience also bearing witness to them, and their thoughts within themselves either accusing or excusing each other* (Rom. ii. 11–15). That is, or signifieth, thus much:

35. When the Gentiles do apprehend Christ, then they do apprehend the law of nature to do uprightly, for Christ is the beginning, and the fulfilling, of the law. But the Jews have the law. Now whosoever transgresseth and sinneth (either the Jew in the law of nature, or the Gentile who acknowledgeth Christ in the law of the fulfilling), each shall be punished or judged in his law; viz. the Jew in the law of God the Father in Christ, and the Christian in the law of the Gospel, viz. in the law of the accomplishment.

36. For here is no respect of name, in that one saith, I am a Jew, the other, I am a Christian. The name maketh no difference in the adoption of God, but the spirit in the heart to do uprightly, to obey God. They all come in the grace under the obedience of Christ unto God; both the Jew and the Christian.

37. For without Christ there is neither law nor Gospel; Christ is the righteousness which availeth before God in the law, so that man, without Christ, hath no God. Now let him run either in the law or Gospel, if he runneth in the desire to obey God, then he runneth in the law of the accomplishment; for Christ is the only obedience which availeth before God, both in the law and Gospel. All men who give up themselves in obedience unto God, they are received in Christ's

obedience, viz. in the fulfilling of the obedience, the Jew and the Christian, and so likewise the heathen who hath neither the law nor Gospel.

38. For if the Gentile desires to obey the only God, and yet knoweth him not according to the essence of his manifestation, but presseth into the obedience of God, then he is a law unto himself; and declareth indeed that God hath written his law in him, which he hath fulfilled in his Son, as Paul saith. For he who knoweth the law and Gospel, knoweth the same only as a gift of the Giver, who hath given him the knowledge; but he that doth not know it, and yet desireth the power of the law and Gospel, in him God in Christ knows what he pleaseth.

39. For grace doth not lie only in knowing, that one knoweth the grace in Christ; but it lieth in the pressing into that grace, and in the mercy of God. One presseth into mercy in the law, the other in the Gospel, and the third without the law, and without the knowledge of the Gospel; he that hath neither, but hangs on the grace of God, the same is freely given without his knowledge of it.

40. Even as the branch on the tree doth not know whence the stock doth introduce the sap and power into it, it only longeth and gaspeth after the power and virtue of the root, and draweth with its desire the sap into itself; even so likewise many an ignorant man doth long after his eternal mother, out of whom he is arisen with Adam, and cometh in his ignorance [or unknowing condition] again unto the free gift of grace which God freely bestowed on Adam in his fall. For the Covenant and grace passed from Adam upon all originally or by way of inheritance, even as sin passed from one upon all: whosoever desireth the grace of the only God, he obtaineth it in Christ, who is the grace itself.

41. The Jews will not believe the outward humanity of Christ, and do deny the same. But the Christians do believe it, and yet defile the same with ungodly conversation; and the one is as the other before God, except the children of faith among the Jews and Christians, whose defiled garment is washed in the blood of Christ.

42. We do not hereby confirm or speak for the unbelief of the Jews and Gentiles, that they should or might remain in blindness, for the time of their visitation is at hand,[1] that they shall see; but we hereby disclose and lay open the wicked Antichrist among the Jews and Christians, in that everyone boasteth of his name, and condemneth

---
[1] Text, born.

another: the Jew in the law, and the Christian in the Gospel, and the Heathen in his superstition.

43. Each of them will be God's child in his knowledge, and yet the disobedience and unbelief is as great among one people as among another; and they are in the knowledge, only as a figure before God, and none is saved by his knowledge alone. For, that I do believe and hold for a truth, that Christ was born, died and arose again from death for me, doth not make me a child of God; the devil knoweth it also, but it doth not avail him; I must put on Christ in the desire of faith, and enter into his obedience, into his incarnation, suffering and death, and arise again in him, and put on the obedience of Christ: then am I a Christian, and not before.

44. The judging, censuring and condemning others without God's command is only the Antichrist among the Jews, and among the Christians: Without God's mercy none cometh to the sonship: we must all enter in through the free mercy of God; the Jew, and the Christian, and the knower and he that knoweth not; our knowledge must be filled and abound with the love of Christ effectually, so that we love one another, else knowledge is not at all available. If I bring not my knowledge, with the desire, into the love of God wherewith he hath loved us in Christ, and love my neighbour in the love of God in Christ, with that love wherewith God generally loveth us, and loved us when we were his enemies, then have I not as yet the love of God dwelling in me.

45. But how will he love his brother, who contemneth him for his knowledge' sake? Did not God love us when we knew nothing of his love? If a man hath not this love of God in him, wherewith God loved us when we knew him not, why doth he boast then of God's sonship? If he be the child of God, then he hath the free love of God, wherewith he loveth all things: if he hath it not, he is not then as yet capable of the adoption. So now, if any one contemneth and condemneth his brother, who hath not as yet his knowledge, how can he boast of the love of God, wherewith God loved his enemies in Christ, wherewith Christ prayed for his enemies?

46. O thou false cold love of the titular Christendom! how doth the eternal truth strike thee in the face of thy conscience, in that thou dependest only on thy knowing, and contendest about the mere knowledge, and hast not love! Thou judgest thyself alone in thy judging others. One sect and company judgeth and condemneth another, and before God they are no other than the natural children of

Abraham, born of Keturah, one laying the blame upon another, that the father had cast them out from the inheritance. And yet they could not see what was the fault, namely, that it was by reason of the evil corrupt nature, which was not a true heir.

47. So likewise your judging and censuring others doth not entitle you to the goods of Christ: nay, the same is wholly cast out from the inheritance, both of the Jews, and also of the Christians, and also of the Turks. All your contention is nothing else but the mocker, Ishmael, who mocketh Christ in his members. Ye do all abuse the name of God with your judging, and condemn the manifold gifts of the Spirit of God among you, and judge only in self, and not according to the love of Christ.

48. Your judging [one another] is only the hurt and wound of the world, wherewith ye make the ignorant to err, and bring them to blaspheme. Ye teach them [the art of] censuring and condemning, and ye yourselves have not the true knowledge in the Spirit of God; ye do not teach yourselves, and yet ye will be teaching and judging others. And in this way and course ye are all, one with another, the disinherited children of Keturah; ye contend, bite and devour one another about Abraham's, viz. Christ's, goods, and yet ye have them not: if ye had them, then ye would have the love of Christ, which is the true goods.

49. No knowledge without the love of Christ is at all available to the sonship: it is only Babel, and fable; teaching, and yet effecting and doing nothing, save only honouring the idol Mäusim in itself. The knowledge of the high schools, and the knowledge of the devil, without the spirit of Christ in love, do both of them bring only contention and desolation.

50. If the devil had not known in self, then he had been [remained to this day] an angel; and if Adam had not desired the self-knowledge without God's love, he had continued in Paradise. If the high schools did not know the sharp acute disputing, they had continued in the simplicity of Christ, and had not brought the whole world, with their contention and disputings, into opinions, and judgings of one another, so that now there is nothing but contemning and condemning in Christendom, and all love and truth is extinct; and men have set and put salvation in opinions [in this or that way and form], and bound the Master to the servant, so that Antichrist domineereth over Christ, and yet pretends all for Christ; but indeed he thereby only honoureth and mindeth his Lucifer, and his belly-god Mäusim, as it is plainly to be seen.

HOW ABRAHAM TOOK ANOTHER WIFE

51. Now after that *Abraham had sent away all the children of the concubines from Isaac's goods, with gifts towards the east,* as Moses saith, they came into the east country, that is, into the dominion and government of nature, where the essence beginneth. *And Abraham died in a quiet age, when he was old and full of years, and was buried by his Sarah in the cave of Machpelah, which is before Mamre* (Gen. xxv. 6-9).

The inward figure is this:

52. Abraham's natural children of the concubines went towards the east: Here the spirit points at the figure of the whole man, when Christ hath manifested himself in man, and possessed his goods, as here Isaac. Then nature goeth into the east,[1] viz. into the Father's property, and worketh, according to the soul, in the first and third Principles; and Christ sitteth in the midst, viz. in the second Principle, and ruleth over that which nature in the Father's property doth form and fashion in the divine wisdom.

53. Therefore Moses saith here, that they went towards the east, and pointeth secretly in his figure at the property of man, signifying how nature doth possess the east,[2] viz. the beginning or rise of the dominion; even as Christ also said, that He was as a Vine-dresser who did glean. In God's kingdom, nature is Christ's servant, but in the kingdom of nature's self or propriety, Christ hath given himself with his humility to be a servant, and an assistant, and serveth the Father in his natural manifestation, and continually picketh up or gleaneth: what the Father formeth through nature, that the Wisdom bringeth into its treasure.

54. Therefore saith St Paul, that the Spirit of God is subject to the children of God, and goeth along with them in the *searching even into the depths of the Deity* (1 Cor. ii. 10). And when it comes thus far, then man is in a quiet old age, and then all things stand in order in him, viz. nature in the morning,[3] in the Father's property, and Christ in the evening,[4] in the humility. And then man hath enough of the outward evil sinful life; he longeth continually to enter with his essence into the cave of Machpelah,[5] viz. into the eternal mother, as it is before mentioned.

55. And when he hath brought his life's forms into the divine

---

[1] Text, beginning.   [2] Text, morning.   [3] East.
[4] West.
[5] That is, the twofold pit, as the Dutch translation hath it.

order, as here Abraham had set all things into order, then he giveth up himself wholly and fully in one essence into the eternal generatress, and with his own will he resigneth up himself into mortification and death, and is wholly tired and weary of the life of self, and so resteth in his God.

The Fifty-Second Chapter

Of the History of *Isaac*, and also of the Birth of *Esau* and *Jacob*, and what hath been acted concerning them; the meaning thereof is hinted to us in this Chapter

1. MOSES saith, *After the death of Abraham God blessed his son Isaac, and he dwelt by the well of the living and seeing*[1] (Gen. xxv. 11). Reason understands this externally of a place where Isaac dwelt, but the spirit looketh upon the figure of the life's form, shewing how the human nature and creature hath dwelt by the wellspring of the divine ens in the Covenant, which Abraham laid hold of in faith; viz. the soul of Isaac dwelt by the wellspring of the holy Trinity, in which the soul received its light, and saw, and knew the will of God; out of which wellspring the highest love of the Deity did manifest itself to the soul, and out of which fountain, afterwards, in the fullness of time, the holy name Jesus, out of Jehova, did manifest itself and espoused itself for a bride unto the soul.

2. The soul of Isaac dwelt by this fountain of the living and seeing, until the same fountain afterwards did pour forth, and open itself in the humanity of Christ in the soul. And then afterwards the soul dwelt in the fountain, when it was exalted in Christ's person to the right hand of God; and then the fountain of God did spring forth through the soul, where then it received the divine might as a prince of God, or as an image or express likeness of God, or as a formed word of the voice of God, through which voice God was made known and manifest.

3. So likewise our soul, when it forsaketh the earthly will of its assumed self, and apprehendeth the ens of Christ in the Covenant, and turns itself to God, then it dwelleth also by the fountain of the living and seeing, that is, by God's eye, which he hath again with Christ manifested and opened in the humanity. Indeed our soul doth not in this time of the earthly cottage dwell in the wellspring of God, as if it did apprehend the wellspring in self; but like as the sun through-shineth the glass, and yet the glass is not turned to be sun, but it

---

[1] Lahai-roi.

dwelleth by the lustre and virtue of the sun, and suffereth the sun to work and shine through it: even so is the soul in this time.

4. And further yet, As the sun doth give its tincture into the metalline ens, and the metalline ens giveth its desire into the sun's tincture, so that out of them both the fair and precious gold is generated, so likewise it is to be understood concerning the soul. The Deity inhabiteth[1] the soul, but the soul comprehends not the same, as to its creatural power; but the eye or light of God, with the holy love-tincture from the light's lustre, giveth itself into the desire of the soul.

5. For the desire of the soul is the Fiat,[2] which takes the power of the holy love-tincture into itself, and makes it essential; so that the divine tincture, proceeding from the desire of the true love-spring (viz. from the fountain of the living and seeing), and the soul's believing desire, do become one essence.

6. Understand, a spiritual essence. And this same spiritual essence is the inward new man, viz. a new house or habitation of the soul, in which it dwelleth according to the inward heavenly world; the name of which essence is *Sophia*, viz. the Bride of Christ, Christ's humanity; in which the glorious Jacob's Star of the dear and precious name, *Jesus*, is a shining light, whereby the soul seeth and knoweth God.

7. The soul is not changed into the Deity, viz. into [Lahai-roi] the fountain of the living and seeing, for it is the eternal and temporal nature's. But the Deity is not nature's, but the will to nature, and manifesteth itself through the soul's nature. As the fire manifesteth itself through the iron, where then the iron seems as if it were mere fire, and yet it keepeth its own nature, and the fire also its own, and the one doth only dwell in the other, and one is the manifestation of the other. The iron hath no power over the fire, only the fire giveth itself to the iron, and the iron giveth its ens to the fire, and so both are changed into one, and yet remain two essences: So likewise it is to be understood with the soul and the Deity.

8. And as the fiery property is different from the gross iron, and hath another source, so likewise the new spiritual humanity in the ens of Christ in the divine love-fire is far another essence than the earthly body; albeit the soul is understood in the fire, and in the light's lustre the body of Sophia; for the power or virtue of the light is the tincture or the beginning to the new spiritual body; which power, the soul's believing desire taketh, and formeth or bringeth it into an essence: that is, it makes it essential: it becomes an essence or spiritual body

---

[1] Or, dwelleth through the soul.   [2] Note what the Fiat is.

from the desire, which spiritual essence is the Temple of God, of which the Scripture speaketh.

9. But our Babylon will understand nothing hereof, but will be wholly blind therein; for she will not know how Christ is born in the faith *in us*, and how faith comes to essence; but she will downright make the half-Serpent man to be an assumed and adopted child of grace, and set it in God's Temple. But it avails not. Shall the devil sit at the right hand of God in the fountain of the living and seeing? He hath been once cast away from thence, he shall not any more possess the same: a beast is not Sophia: The Scripture saith, *Ye must be converted, and be born anew as children, else ye shall not see God* (Matt. xviii. 3).

10. The soul cannot see God, save only in its new-born image; only through and in virgin Sophia, in Jacob's Star, viz. in the name of Jesus, it seeth in Jehova, in the wellspring of the life of God. It is not itself this very fountain: it giveth only the fire to the manifestation of this fountain. But the fountain is understood in the light, viz. in the meekness of the light.

11. Now the soul's magic fire-source could not so be enkindled that a shining lustre of a light might arise in the soul's fire, if the divine love-desire, viz. the love ens, had not given itself into the soul's fire. The ens of Christ out of the divine love giveth itself into the soul's fire-source, which the soul's fire eateth into its fiery essence, and thereupon the life of the wrathfulness dieth, and the fair precious light is thence generated; for here Christ ariseth out of the consuming fire of the Father's property, according to his anger, from death, out of the fire of another life. Here the magical soul's fire becomes the precious Sophia's bridegroom, and here are man and wife; viz. both tinctures, of the fire and of the light, become one person, viz. an angel of God.

12. Here Lucifer loseth his throne, and the Serpent his viperous seed, and Christ sitteth at the right hand of God in man; and man then dwelleth truly by the fountain of the living and seeing. And this is that which the spirit of Moses sets forth by this figure concerning Isaac's habitation: if we would but once become seeing, and forsake the mere husk, and know ourselves aright, not according to the earthly beast, but according to the inward spiritual heavenly man.

13. As to the part of the bestial soul [of man], that attains not the precious image in this lifetime for propriety. The mortal soul, either from the stars or four elements, attains it not; only the inward soul, out of the eternal Word of God, out of the eternal nature, out of the formed Word, out of God's essence according to God's love and anger,

viz. out of the centre of the eternal nature, which hath its original out of the divine desire through the eternal Verbum Fiat,[1] whereby the divine lubet formeth and fashioneth the wisdom into a substance, to the contemplation of the Deity: This [soul is that which] is betrothed to Sophia.

14. The outward soul is now betrothed and espoused to the stars and four elements, to form and bring forth the wonders of God's formed wisdom, in figures, both in words and works. This outward soul obtains sometimes only a look from Sophia, for it hath the death and mortality in itself; but it shall after this time be changed again into the first image, which God created in Adam, and leave the Serpent's ens to the earth, which shall at the end of days be tried in the fire of God, where the Serpent's introduced desire shall evaporate from it; and then the whole image of God, out of all the three Principles, stands in one essence, and even then *God filleth all in all* (Eph. i. 23): This is here to be understood by this figure.

15. Further, the spirit of Moses describeth the *children of Ishmael*, and relates how *he begat twelve sons, from whom twelve princes arose in their generations*, and he sets down, at last, *He fell in the presence of all his brethren* (Gen. xxv. 16-18). Here he meaneth before Isaac's generation; and yet he waxed great in worldly dominion before them, and potent nations did arise from him; and Isaac with his children and posterity were only as pilgrims, and travelled up and down from one place to another, until they were at last redeemed from the Egyptian bondage, and possessed the promised land.

The inward figure.

16. Ishmael, in his twelve princes, typifieth the kingdom of the corrupt nature of man's property, which kingdom is twofold; viz. six numbers out of the inward life's figure, and six numbers out of the earthly outward life's figure; viz. the outward, visible, palpable man, and the inward, spiritual, soulish man. Both these have twelve numbers in the figure, whence twelve princes arose, according to the inward and outward nature's property. These the spirit of Moses puts in the figure and saith, that they fell in the presence of all their brethren; to signify that the twelve dominions of the inward and outward nature of the human property, in its corruption, fell before

---

[1] Word.

OF THE HISTORY OF ISAAC

the twelve dominions new born of the ens of faith in their corrupt self; for the devil had set his dominion and power into these properties.

17. But when the promised seed of faith was conceived in Abraham, it did suppress and beat down the devil's power in the dominion of man's self; and then happened the spiritual fall in Ishmael's line, wherein the devil, as a haughty prince, had set himself to bear the chief sway and domination; for Christ killeth the pride of the Serpent in man.

18. Now saith Moses, *Ishmael fell in the presence of all his brethren*. This was nothing else but a spiritual fall of the human selfness before God, for as to this world they were famous, renowned people, as their princely dominions do testify; whereas on the contrary Isaac's generation were a long time only strangers among the nations; which signifieth that Christ's kingdom and dominion is not in this world's nature; and yet the kingdoms of this world shall fall before Christ, and be in subjection to Christ.

19. Afterwards, the spirit of Moses describeth Isaac's children by Rebecca, and saith, that *she was barren, and Isaac intreated the Lord for his wife, and God was intreated of him; and Rebecca conceived with two sons, which strove together in the womb*. Here now the figure of the kingdom of nature, and also of the kingdom of Christ in the new birth, is clearly set forth: for Rebecca's two sons which she brought forth, viz. Esau and Jacob, point at two lines; viz. Esau proceeds from Abraham's own Adamical corrupt nature; and Jacob ariseth in the ens of faith, in which Abraham's faith's ens had incorporated itself into his Adamical nature, in which also the Covenant and the line of Christ stood, who should bruise the Serpent's head in the Adamical nature.

20. And here is deciphered and held forth how the two kingdoms in the two brothers, viz. the devil's kingdom in the corrupt nature of Esau, in Adam's own nature of the introduced Serpent's ens; and also the kingdom of Christ in Jacob in the ens of faith, did both strive together while they were children even in the womb; where then the kingdom of nature in Esau began to fall before the kingdom of Christ in Jacob; for here the woman's seed already bruised the head of the Serpent's ens, its might, in Esau; and the Serpent already stung the woman's seed, viz. the ens of faith in Jacob, on the heel, and therefore they struggled together in the womb.

21. Also we have here a very emphatical pregnant figure in Rebecca, in that she was shut up and could not be opened to conceive of Isaac's seed, until Isaac had intreated the Lord, that he would open

the withholdment[1] in the Covenant in Rebecca; where then the Lord was intreated in the Covenant concerning the barrenness of Rebecca, so that he did open the tincture in the woman's seed to this impregnation or conception.

The inward figure stands thus:

22. The seed of faith was in Isaac inherited from his father Abraham, but Rebecca had not this ens. Indeed she was in the Covenant, but the ens of faith was not in her in the essence, but only in the Covenant; and therefore her matrix was shut up, and was not capable of the ens of faith, so long, till Isaac immersed his believing desire into the Lord (understand into the centre of nature in Rebecca), so that the spirit of the Lord did move itself in the Covenant in Rebecca, and moved also the Covenant, together with her Adamical nature, so that the barrenness in her matrix was disclosed, both in the shut-up ens in the Covenant, and then likewise the Adamical matrix, whereupon she conceived two sons, of the property of two kingdoms.

23. And this is the meaning of the saying, *The Lord was intreated*, when Isaac brought his faith's desire, through the eternal and temporal nature, into the Lord; and therewith did earnestly press for his wife Rebecca, that the Lord would be pleased to open her through his prayer and faith's desire, that so she might be with child by him. Which faith's desire, together with the Adamical nature's desire, gave in themselves into the barrenness of the matrix in Rebecca, and opened her. Whereupon she conceived both natures' properties, from a twofold seed of Isaac.

24. Not that we are to think or understand that Jacob was wholly conceived of the ens of faith, but as well of the Adamical sinful nature as Esau; only, the kingdom of grace in the Covenant set forth its figure in the ens of faith in him; and in Esau the kingdom of nature, viz. the right corrupt Adamical nature did set forth its figure; not as a separation, sundry partition or rejection, but to signify that Christ should be conceived and born with his holy divine ens in the Adamical corrupt nature, and destroy death and the stronghold of sin, together with the self-raised desire to ownhood and propriety in self; and mortify the same with the love-desire in the divine ens, and ruinate the devil's rampant fort of prey, which he hath built up to himself therein; and change the wrath of God according to the eternal nature,

---

[1] Stop, or strong bar; barrenness.

OF THE HISTORY OF ISAAC

in the centre of the dark fiery-world's property, into divine love and joy, and tincture the Adamical nature with the holy tincture of the love-fire.

25. Therefore the corrupt Adamical nature in its type was represented in the womb in Esau, with the type of Christ in Jacob; and they both must be formed of one seed, to signify that Christ should give in himself to our corrupt nature, and redeem our corrupted right Adamical nature from corruption, and introduce it into his own holy nature in himself.

26. Also God did represent in Esau the figure of his wrath, and [of] the devil's might, who had possessed the kingdom of nature in man; and shews how he would fight, and exercise great enmity against the ens of faith and the kingdom of grace, which should deprive him of his strength.

27. Reason saith, Wherefore should God permit the devil to fight against the kingdom of his grace? Hear and hearken, thou very blind and altogether ignorant reason: Learn the A B C in the centre, how God's love, and the kingdom of grace and mercy, would not, nor could not, be manifest without strife and enmity; and then thou hast here no further question: Go forward into the centre of this book, and thou findest the ground.

28. And when the strife between the two kingdoms began in these children in the womb, so that they strove or spurned against each other, Rebecca became discontented and troubled at it, and said, *If it should be thus with me, wherefore am I with child? And she went to enquire of the Lord. And the Lord said unto her, Two nations are in thy womb, and two manner of people shall be separated from thy bowels; and one people shall be stronger than the other; and the greater shall serve the lesser* (Gen. xxv. 22, 23).

29. These two nations, which were conceived of one seed in Rebecca, are on one part the man of the Adamical selfish nature in selfness, viz. the original of man; and on the other part the new spiritual man, regenerated of the kingdom of grace in the Covenant. These came out of one seed: one out of the Adamical nature alone, and he was the greater [or elder], viz. the first man which God created in his image, which became corrupt and died as to God; the other came indeed out of the same Adamical nature, but the kingdom of grace in the ens of faith had given in itself unto it as a conqueror, and this was, as to the Adamical nature, the lesser [or younger], but God was manifest in him; therefore the greater (viz. the first Adamical man in

Esau's line) should serve and be subject to the lesser (who was the least according to the human property, but the greatest in God).

30. And yet we do not see that Esau was subject to Jacob; but it is the spiritual figure, shewing how the kingdom of nature in man should be broken by the children of God, and made subject to the kingdom of grace, viz. to the divine humility, and wholly dive itself into the divine humility, and be born anew of the humility. Thus the spirit of God shewed this by the answer to Rebecca, saying that it should be a striving or fighting kingdom, where indeed the first corrupt man, being the greater or elder in nature, should strive against the lesser, viz. the spirit of Christ in his lowliness and humility, and persecute him. But the Adamical man must at last be obedient and subject unto the humility of Christ, if he will be Abraham's child and heir; but if not, then he must be so long cast out from Abraham's and Christ's goods, till he doth humble himself and freely yield under Christ's humility, and forsake the ownhood of the greater and elder self and enmity, assumed in Adam.

31. By Rebecca's trouble, discontent, impatience and regret, in that she runneth to enquire of the Lord, wherefore the strife was in her, that the children did so struggle together, is signified thus much unto us: That when Christ doth manifest himself in the Adamical nature, then begins and ariseth the strife of both these kingdoms, viz. the devil's kingdom in God's anger in the Serpent's ens, and also Christ's kingdom. When Christ bruiseth the Serpent's head, then ariseth great disquietness in the mind, for the Serpent stingeth Christ, viz. the new birth, on the heel, and then ariseth this kicking and spurning, viz. a lamentable and woeful distress. And then saith reason in the mind, with Rebecca, If it should be thus with me, wherefore am I entered into the divine impregnation, into repentance? Am not I thereby come only into disquietness, and thereby become a fool to the world, and to my reason also? And then ariseth the combat, and Satan's bruising in the mind, with anguish and grief; and then the mind knows not whither to betake itself, but runneth into penitency, and asketh the Lord wherefore it goeth so with it.

32. And then the Lord shews him in his language that Christ now is in him in hell, and assaulteth the devil's strong rampant fort of prey. Whereupon there is such contest and disquietness in him; and shews him how his reason, and the Adamical nature, viz. the greater part of his life, must be broken, and dive itself wholly into resignation, into the deepest humility, into the process of Christ under his cross, and

OF THE HISTORY OF ISAAC

become a stranger to itself, yea, its own enemy, and go with the reason, and the greater Adamical will, into its Nothing.

33. And when this is done, then Esau, viz. the Adamical nature, is indeed born, and cometh forth always first. But Jacob, viz. the spirit of Christ, cometh soon after, and deprives Esau of the kingdom and power, and maketh nature a servant; and then Esau, viz. nature, must serve Jacob, viz. the spirit of Christ. Then it is even here as the Son said unto the Father: *Father, the men were thine, and thou hast given them me* (John xvii. 6), *and I give unto them eternal life* (John x. 28).

34. Understand, nature is the Father's property, for it is the strength and might, viz. the fire-spirit. This fire-spirit was given to the light- or love-spirit in Christ, viz. to the holy name Jesus, which introduced itself in Abraham's believing desire into an ens, out of which Christ, and then the new man out of Christ, is born; unto whom the kingdom of nature in the Father's fire-property was given. And he wholly gave his love ens for food unto the Father's fire-source, viz. to the fiery soul in the Father's nature: and even there Christ, with love, took possession of the Father's fire-strength, and changed it into the glory of the triumphant kingdom of joy: And thus also it is to be understood in the new birth of man.

35. And Moses saith further: *And now when the time came that Rebecca should be delivered, behold there were twins in her womb. And the first which came out was red, and all over rough like an hairy hide; and they called his name Esau. And presently after came his brother out, and his hand took hold on Esau's heel; and they called him Jacob* (Gen. xxv. 24-26). Here now stands the figure so lively and so clearly set forth, that even reason may see it: That which before was hinted at with words in the spiritual figure, that stands here in a lively personal figure. For Moses saith, *Esau came forth first, who was red, and had a rough skin.*

36. Red betokeneth the Father's nature in the fire: Rough betokens the earthly bestial nature, which Adam, with his lust, introduced into himself from the earthliness. His name is called *Esau* from the sensual language, from the property of the formation of his nature's property. The same in its formation in the language of nature stands thus: E. is the original *ex uno,* viz. *aus dem Einem* [out of the One]: and is the true angelical property created in Adam: *Sau*[1] is the formed beast or self lust, which hath enclosed and shut up the E., and obscured and slain the same in itself, that is, when it was extinct in it as to the light's fire; yet the *Sau,* viz. the outward bestial man who

---

[1] *Sau* signifieth sow, or the earthly swinish property.

had changed the E., viz. the angelical image, into a beast, did yet remain in its form. Therefore the spirit called his name *Esau*, viz. a formed or amassed image of lust, turned from its fine pureness into grossness, wherein notwithstanding the E. did still remain, but wholly encompassed and shut up with the *Sau*.

37. After this Esau cometh Jacob, viz. the type or image of Christ, conceived in the ens of faith, and holdeth Esau by the heel. This declareth that the Adamical image which God created shall and must be born first, for the same is it, which shall live for ever, *but not in its rough beast's hide*: for in that Jacob holds Esau, viz. the first man, by the heel, signifieth that the second Adam, viz. Christ, is born *after the first Adam*, and takes hold of him behind, and brings him back again from the course of his own self will, into the first mother, from whence nature is arisen, viz. to another new birth.

38. But that Esau goeth forward with his birth, and Jacob, by holding him by the heel, cannot withhold him, betokeneth that the earthly man in his selfness should go forward, and not go wholly in this lifetime back again into the mother of the new birth, but he would walk up and down with the bestial man through this time. For the beast shall not be new born, but [what shall be re-born is] the image of God, which was lost or perished in Adam.

39. And it further denotes, how Christ should take the true Adamical created man by his heel, that is, by the mind of his conversation, and put him back again into the first mother, whence he did arise; and how the spirit of Christ should follow after the earthly man in this lifetime. When as the devil would be the earthly man's chief guide in the anger of God, then Christ should come after him, and take the inward property of the poor, fallen and captivated man, viz. the poor corrupt mind of the soul, into his arms, and draw it back again out of the devil's nets and snares, as Christ said, That he was as a vine-dresser who gleaned. For in this lifetime the Adamical nature's image stands before, and the image of Christ [stands] behind; therefore the natural man must die, and Christ must arise and put himself forth eminently in him.

40. And it shews further, how the spirit of Christ in Jacob's line should take Esau in this lifetime by his heel, and hold and rebuke him; and by his children labour to hinder and suppress his evil conversation and wicked walkings. But the Esauitish generation would contemn, despise and only trample it underfoot; and lay about them as an evil, malicious, fiery beast. As it even so comes to pass, when God sends his

OF THE HISTORY OF ISAAC

prophets, that they must reprove and rebuke men; then they even spurn them away from them as dogs, and will by no means endure them. But Jacob, that is, the spirit of God, holds them yet by the heel, and makes them naked and bare, so long till Jacob's footstep or impression is known.

41. *Jacob* signifieth, in the formation of the name in the high tongue, a strong lubet or desire out of the mental tongue, viz. out of the name *JEHOVA*, brought into a compaction or ens; where the *I* takes the *A*, and exalts itself in the *A*, and takes the sensual tongue into the mental, viz. into the *COB*, so that the *O* is set for the centre of the word; where then the profound name of God is conceived or brought into the *O*, and therein it is rightly understood how the Father's nature, viz. the spirit of sense in *A*, *C* and *B*, doth form itself into the *I* and *O*, for *I* is the centre of the highest love, and *O* is the centre of the perceptive Word in the Deity, which is understood [to be] without or beyond all nature.

42. This the spirit hath understood in Isaac, therefore they call him *JACOB*, so long till this name was moved through the *I* in the ens of faith, so that the *I* opened the *C* and *B*, and put forth the formed or conceived ens in the *O*, seeing the *I* had formed itself with the *O* in nature, through nature as a holy blossom, and then the name was called *JESUS*: for the *I* brought itself again into the enclosed shut-up *Engels-Eigenschaft* (angel's property) in Adam's nature, and then the *A* was put into *E*: for the Father gave his nature in the humanity to the son, viz. to the *I*, and the Son made again thereout an *Engel* (angel) of it through the *I*. For the *I* entered into the deepest humility and lowliness. And then the figure stood thus *IE*, out of which the fiery love-spirit went forth, and made itself predominant; and set forth before it its character with the *S* and *V*, for the *S* is the character of the holy fire, and the *V* is the character of the efflux, issuing forth or emanation, out of the fire.

43. Thus the name Jacob was in the fullness of time in the ens of Mary changed into the name Jesus, which understanding hath been as dumb and dead both to the Jews and Christians; seeing no nation doth any more understand its own language, and contends only about the compaction of the formed nature of the outward name, and understanding. The mental tongue none will learn to understand, how the same hath formed, imprinted and ideafied[1] itself in the words and names in the sensual tongue; and yet the whole understanding lieth

---
[1] Formed and modelised.

therein, without opinions. If we were not so very blind and shut up in ignorance, suffering self in pride to rule and govern us, we should soon attain to the deepest understanding. But the Antichrist beareth the supremacy, therefore Esau alone ruleth in the understanding.

44. And Moses saith further, *And when the children were grown up, Esau was a cunning hunter, and a man of the field; and Jacob was a plain*[1] *man, and dwelt in tents. And Isaac loved Esau, and loved to eat of his venison: but Rebecca loved Jacob* (Gen. xxv. 27, 28). O thou wonderful God, how very simply and plainly are the greatest Mysteries typified and deciphered! Who can be able to understand, without thy spirit, from whence it was that the precious man Isaac, in the type of Christ, loved the natural man in Adam's corrupt image, Esau, more than Jacob, in the type of Christ in his figure? If thou hadst not in thy knowledge vouchsafed me to understand the same, I must be here even stark blind: But it is thy counsel, O Lord, that we know thee, and thy time is born, that thou revealest the secrets.

45. Moses saith, that *Esau was a hunter, and a man of the field, and the father loved to eat of his venison, and loved him above Jacob.* Here stands an external figure, as if Isaac loved Esau for his activeness, cunning skill or worldly exercise, and loved him more than Jacob. So wholly hath the Lord the heart of the wise and of his children in his hand, that his children must not in their will do what they please, and oftentimes well understand, but [must do] what God wills.

46. Also we herein see how oftentimes God withdraws the Mysteries from the most holy, that they must be even children in them; and although they bear the divine play in their hands, and 'tis their work and exercise, yet they must have a child-like heart in the understanding thereof, as it may be seen here in Isaac.

47. He loved Esau more than Jacob. Why so? The ens of Christ lay in him, which ruled him. For Christ should love his enemies, viz. the corrupt Esau, and his natural children; him he loved more than his divine nature; for he brought his divine nature into the death of the corrupt Adam, and loved Adam's corrupted nature[2] more than his holy ens, which he, for man's corrupt nature's sake, gave into the fire of God's anger, that so he might redeem it in his love. Of this, Isaac was here a figure in the image of Christ, who loved his hunter in his evil nature more than Jacob. He did not love his iniquity, but his

---

[1] Honest.
[2] Not his sin in the nature, but his poor undone nature by sin, which he by death freed from sin and death.

OF THE HISTORY OF ISAAC

child-like nature, to which he would do much good; as Christ loved us in our Adamical nature, and did us good. He did not love us according to the will of sin in us; as Isaac also did not therein love his son Esau, but [he loved him] according to the Father's nature and property, according to the child-like filial nature.

The inward figure stands thus:

48. When Isaac entreated the Lord, that his Rebecca might conceive, his natural desire, with the lubet[1] of the divine ens of faith, entered into Rebecca, whereby Rebecca was opened. And so the natural love of Isaac, which was environed with faith, was propagated in his seed, and opened itself in Esau. Isaac's love did not open itself in Esau as to his corrupt nature; [I say] not according to the kingdom of the nature of this world, but according to the Covenant, according to the second Principle, viz. according to God's kingdom, which the external nature in him had not as yet apprehended; as the divine ens in Abraham did open and manifest itself according to the second Principle, and not in the mortal corrupt Adamical nature of the outward world: The like also is here to be understood in the figure in Esau.

49. Not that Esau did receive the ens of Christ in the Covenant as Jacob [did], but [he received] his father's love-desire, in which the hidden Covenant stood unmoveable. Now there was thus a conjunction with his father's natural love (for every property loveth its own likeness, especially if the likeness be proceeded forth from the essence or thing loving), as Esau was conceived in Rebecca of his father through his love-desire.

50. And it even denotes that the divine ens in God's love in Isaac loved the miserable human nature, to redeem it. Therefore God manifested his love in Abraham's faith, and introduced the same into an ens; so that this same love, which God gave to redeem mankind, should love the human nature in its shut-up abandoned condition. As, in very truth, the true real Adamical nature ordained by God was shut up in Esau, and, on the contrary, the kingdom of the wrath had the outward dominion. Now to redeem this, the spirit in the Covenant, through Isaac's nature, loved his son Esau, viz. the filial nature, and not only because that he was a hunter of the creatures.

51. Yet here also by this hunter we are even to understand the

[1] Earnest longing.

same as is set down before concerning Nimrod, who was a mighty hunter before the Lord. For this whole description of the first book of Moses is God's spirit's figure, type or representation, where he playeth[1] with the kingdom of nature, and then also with Christ's kingdom; and he hath so portrayed, delineated and typified the acts of the holy Patriarchs under his figure, that we may clearly see in all the histories the glance or allusion of God's spirit, how he hath delineated and set forth to the life the kingdom of Christ, and the kingdom of nature, and also the devil's kingdom in the wrath of the eternal nature. And neither the Jews nor the Christians hitherto have had a right understanding of the same, which among the patriarchs was rightly understood in its true meaning.

52. But afterwards, when their children and posterity gave no heed unto the same, but disregarded the true understanding, and loved their evil nature more than the spirit in the Covenant, then the understanding was put out[2] among them; until they at last also lost the Book of the Law,[3] with the holy histories, and Esdras wrote for them again the figure and history, in the spirit of God; and that, very short, brief and exactly, according to the spiritual figure; in which they were more blind than seeing; as to this day their eyes are blinded; and that, because they abused the knowledge of the true God, and served the nature of this world, and honoured their evil will, above God. Therefore also God hath withdrawn himself from them, with his Mysteries; and hath suffered them to run up and down with the figure, as children full of ignorance; until the Gentiles' time, in the manifestation of grace (in which they also have only abused the time of grace, and the open seal, in their evil nature) doth also come to its end and limit: And then the figure shall be fully manifest in the essence *for a witness to all nations:*[4] *and after that, the Judgment* (Matt. xxiv. 14).

53. And the spirit of Moses saith further, *Jacob was a plain man, and dwelt in tents, and Rebecca loved Jacob* (Gen. xxv. 27, 28). Reason understands this figure [as] of a woman-like, motherly, natural love; but the spirit hath not written this figure for that, for Rebecca pressed earnestly, that Jacob might receive the blessing of Abraham and Isaac. She loved Jacob as to his original, which although she might not so well understand externally and rationally, yet the spirit in the

---
[1] Or, sets forth, as in a map. [2] Or, quenched.
[3] Esdras wrote the Book of the Law and Histories again after they were lost.
[4] Substantially declaring the very thing itself, unclothing it of its figures and parables.

OF THE HISTORY OF ISAAC

Covenant understood it in her, which moved her also to bear such a love towards Jacob; for there was also a conjunction between the mother and son.

54. For Rebecca was shut up and barren; but when Isaac did bring his prayer and earnest desire to God for her, then the ens in the Covenant gave itself into his faith in his desire, and so, forth in the opening of Rebecca into the conception; for herewith also the barren or shut-up mother was opened, so that her fruit, viz. Jacob, and she came into one degree of nature, and received one and the same love from Isaac's desire: for the ens of faith was conceived in the tincture of Venus in Rebecca. And as it is said of Mary, Christ's mother after the humanity, that *she was blessed among all women*, so also Rebecca did here receive the blessing from the divine ens; indeed not in the high degree as Mary, but yet according to the property of the Covenant. And hence it was that the love of the Covenant was manifest in her (as the ens of faith was also [manifest] in Jacob, wherein the love of God burned), so that she loved Jacob more than Esau. For the love-desire in the mother and son was from one original, and therefore her desire inclined itself more towards Jacob than Esau; and also because that the heavenly holy matrix [which had] disappeared in Adam, was moved in her image [which was] disappeared or dead as to the heavenly world's essence, which matrix afterwards was wholly opened in Mary. Now this matrix did long to receive the ens of Christ which was manifest in Jacob, which first was to be effected in Mary; and yet the spirit in the Covenant did take its love-sport and delight herewith [in Rebecca].

55. But that the spirit of Moses saith, *Jacob was a plain* [honest] *man, and remained in tents*, he understands thereby that the true Jacob in the ens of faith remained in the tents of the outward nature; that the ens of faith remained in his nature, which is only a tent thereto; that he did not give himself wholly to the tent, as Adam did, but he remained therein, in his Principle, till God, in the fullness of time, brought him forth in Christ's humanity through the tents of nature.

The Fifty-Third Chapter

How *Esau* contemned his Birthright, and sold it for a Mess of Lentil-Pottage: What we are to understand by this Figure

1. WHEN the spirit of Moses had set down the birth of Esau and Jacob, he proceeds to relate presently how the natural Adamical man would but little or nothing regard this high gift in the Covenant, and would seek only after the belly-filling of the earthly life, as Esau, who gave his birthright for pottage of lentil, that he might but serve his belly.

The figure of Moses stands thus:

2. *And Jacob sod pottage: and Esau came from the field, and he was faint. And Esau said to Jacob, Feed me, I pray thee, with that same red pottage; for I am faint: and hence his name was called Edom. But Jacob said, Sell me this day thy birthright. And Esau answered, Lo! I must even die: and what profit will this birthright be to me? And Jacob said, Swear to me this day; and he sware unto him: and so he sold his birthright to Jacob. Then Jacob gave Esau bread and pottage of lentils; and he did eat and drink, and rose up, and went his way: thus Esau despised his birthright* (Gen. xxv. 29–34).

This figure externally hath but a plain and childlike semblance; but yet it is a figure of the greatest Mysteries. For Esau betokens the first power of the natural, created Adam; and Jacob betokens the power of the other Adam, Christ; thus doth the spirit here play with the figure.

3. For Adam's nature came from the field, and was faint, and longed to eat of the pottage which Jacob had. Adam was a limus of the earth, and a limus of heaven; but seeing he died to the limus of heaven, the earthly nature had wearied him in its strife; and in this figure [of faint Adam] Esau here stood.

4. The red lentil pottage, which Jacob had, after which the faint Adam in Esau longed, was the ens of faith, viz. the ens of Christ. The Adamical nature in Esau, in its anguish and toilsome labour, in its corruption and misery, longed after this pottage, which was in Jacob; yet the earthly nature of Esau understood it not, but the soul's nature

HOW ESAU CONTEMNED HIS BIRTHRIGHT

[understood it], which also longed after Christ's ens, which was strange [or afar off, hidden] to reason.

5. Esau's soulish nature said to Jacob in its longing, Let me, I pray thee, taste of the red pottage, for I am weary and faint by reason of the driver or fomenter of the anxious birth; and from this longing or lust he was called *Edom*, which signifieth, in the compaction of the word, in the formation of the Tongue of Sense, as much as a dipping or immersing of the captivate angelical property into the pottage; as if there the soul's longing or lubet, in which the angel's character did yet stand (although captivated), did dip or plunge itself, with the desire, into the holy ens, and would take the holy ens in the divine pottage, viz. the heavenly essentiality into the lust of self: therefore the figure calls him in the High Tongue *Edom*.

6. For, the desire of Esau's soul said to the divine ens in Jacob, Give me thy taste into the essence of my creatural selfhood; but Jacob, that is, the spirit of Christ in the ens of faith, said, Sell me thy birthright for the pottage; that is, give me for it the soul's life's form, viz. the centre of the soul's nature, that so thy first birth,[1] viz. the soul's centre, may be my own; and then I will give thee the ens of God.

7. For Esau inherited the first soulish power from his father, and had the soul's centre for a natural due right; after this came the ens of Christ, as a divine free gift without a soulish centre. For the holy ens should receive the soulish centre from the Adamical nature. Now here the Adamical soulish nature did woo for the ens of Christ, and the spirit in Christ's ens wooed for the soulish nature; and the spirit of Christ in Jacob would not give the taste of the divine ens to the soul's nature in Esau, unless it did give him the fiery centre to the beginning of the soulish creature for a propriety; that is, unless it did wholly resign and give up itself in the natural selfness into God's will, and forsake the first birth of the creature, and esteem of itself, in its selfness, as dead; and give over the dominion and will of life to the spirit of Christ in this heavenly pottage.

8. But seeing Esau's reason did not understand this, he said to Jacob: Lo, I must even die, what then is this first birth to me: so very lightly did reason pass over it, and knew not what the poor soul stood in need of. But the spirit of Moses played here in the inward figure, and doth secretly hint hereby at what this externally signified.

9. And Jacob said, *Swear unto me this day.* That is, the life of Adam

[1] Or, birthright.

in Esau should freely give itself out of the fiery might, and wholly give itself up to the divine ens, and forsake the fiery right of ownhood; and it should do it this day, that is, from henceforward for ever. And this is said, to swear in God, viz. wholly, deeply and fully to cast, immerse, give up, and resign one's self into the divine power, and not resist upon pain of God's rejection.

10. And he sware unto him; and when as he had sworn he was called *Edom*. For the fiery soul's nature did dive and immerse itself into the lubet of the divine ens; whence this lentil pottage is said to be reddish. For here in this oath the fiery essence entered into the lubet of the divine ens; and thus the light's ens received the fire's ens. And the spirit of Moses playeth here in the figure, [alluding] how the soul's property in the fire's essence must wholly resign up and eternally immerse itself into the incarnation of Christ, in the divine light and love ens in the Covenant, viz. into the divine lubet; and how the light's ens would receive and take pity on the corrupted, miserable, fiery soul's nature, [and cause it to repent] and quit itself of its lust; and also how the poor soul would give up its natural right for this red pottage.

11. For this is even a figure, shewing how God the Father giveth his nature, viz. the soul, to his Son Christ, in the love ens, wholly for his own propriety, where the fiery right is made subject to the love in the light. For thus it goeth also in our new birth: the soul longeth after this pottage; but if it will taste it, it must give its birthright for it; and moreover it must swear to God this day, that is, for ever, to forsake and quit its nature's right: which the outward reason looketh upon as ridiculous and foolish, (I mean the children of the earthly lust), that when a man giveth honour, goods, and also the temporal life, for this pottage, they even call him a fool, as here they do Esau.

12. There is in this figure a twofold understanding, viz. inwardly it is the figure of Christ and Adam, as it is above mentioned; and outwardly it is the figure of the earthly man, shewing how carelessly and slightly he passeth over it, and selleth and gives away the heavenly substance to fill his carnal belly, and to satiate his lustful will. The poor soul indeed longeth in its essence after this red pottage, but the earthly reason desireth only a lentil pottage for the lusting belly; as the like also is here to be understood in Esau.

13. The soul of Esau longed after Jacob's heavenly ens; but the earthly Esau, according to the outward soul, minded only the

HOW ESAU CONTEMNED HIS BIRTHRIGHT

earthly power; the kingdom of nature was so very strong and earthly in him, that he neither understood nor regarded the eternal, but said, *What profit shall this birthright do unto me, seeing I must even die.* And he sat down, and did eat and drink the earthly food for the heavenly.

14. And Moses saith, that *when he had eat and drunk, he rose up and went away*; that is, he filled his belly with the pottage of lentils, and sold Jacob his nature-right, and went with the earthly man away from the divine enjoyment.

The inward divine figure is thus:

15. Abraham received the divine ens in his faith's desire, and the same was the stock and the root of Israel. But he was not Israel: for the kingdom of the corrupted nature, and the kingdom of grace, viz. the conceived ens of faith, were not as yet one in him. As when a kernel is sown into the earth, the kernel hath as yet no root upon which the stalk, branches and fruits should grow; but the kernel's power draws the essence of the earth into itself, and of both these, viz. of the kernel, and of the earth's power, grows the root, and then the stalk, and above again the manifold fruit.

16. The like also is here to be understood. The divine holy ens is not nature's; but the soul is nature's. Now if the divine ens shall be made manifest, then it must be done through a natural essence [or means], wherein the invisible may come into a visible essence.

17. The divine faith's ens which Abraham received was of the invisible spiritual property; the same desired to introduce itself through the human nature into a visible, substantial, creatural and natural essence, for a working life, wherein the holy light's natural ens, and the soul's fiery natural ens, might work and bring forth fruit in one essence.[1] For the Adamical nature was gone forth from the holy ens which was disappeared in it; and here now was the ground or foundation of the union. And as it is with the kernel in the ground, where the power in the kernel did mix itself with the ens of the earth, and afterwards leaves its shell and husk, when the earth's ens and the kernel's ens is changed into one ens, so likewise it is here to be understood.

18. Abraham received the divine faith's ens, wherein stood his justification. But his life's nature had not as yet laid hold of it to its own power and strength, for the divine essence doth not give itself

[1] In one substance or body.

into nature's own power: indeed it gives itself into the essence of nature, but the divine desire doth not incline and yield itself unto nature's own self-will, so that nature should have the predominancy: a similitude whereof we have in the corn which is sown into the earth.

19. The earthly nature cannot, in its own power, make another corn; and though it draweth the corn's ens into self, yet it bringeth forth only a stalk; in which stalk the corn's ens groweth up, and brings itself into a bloom, and again into corn,[1] whereunto the earthly nature, with its ens, must be only a servant.

20. And as the earthly nature of the earth doth always first shew its child visibly in the growth, and the corn's ens doth therein hide itself, the like also is to be understood here by Abraham. The Adamical nature in Abraham did first manifest itself with its fruit, and that was Ishmael; but the divine ens lay still hidden in his nature, and sprang forth with Isaac; and by Isaac the earthly and also the heavenly nature did again spring forth together, albeit in one seed.

21. But as the earthly ens in the stalk, and the corn's ens in the internal ground, do grow up in and with one another, and yet each sets forth its fruit, viz. the earth the stalk and the corn's mansion, and the corn or kernel the blooms and fruits, and yet the one without the other could not come to essence: the like also is here to be understood.

22. Abraham was the field into which God sowed his corn; Ishmael was the root, viz. the first birth; Isaac was the fruit which grew from the seed of God (understand out of the ens of grace); and Ishmael grew from the ens of nature out of the Father's property. For the ens of grace had given itself into the ens of nature. Now each did set forth its own figure: with Ishmael the kingdom of nature, and with Isaac the kingdom of grace [was represented]. Isaac was the twig which sprang up out of the field of faith, viz. in the line of Christ; and from him came Jacob, viz. the branch forth-spreading and displaying itself into a tree with many boughs and branches.

23. Not that we are to understand that Jacob did grow and spring forth only out of the kingdom of grace; for the kingdom of nature, in which Ishmael and Esau stood, was also his ground as to the creature, but the ens of faith had given itself thereinto, and tinctured nature, and advanced its power, viz. the line of the Covenant of God, in nature.

[1] Kernels, seeds.

HOW ESAU CONTEMNED HIS BIRTHRIGHT

24. As a blossom upon the stalk hath far a more pure subtle property than the stalk and root; and as out of the blossom first the fruit and a new seed proceedeth, viz. out of the subtle ens; so likewise in Jacob, the blossom of the kingdom of Israel first came forth; and no more in the division, as it is to be understood with Ishmael and Isaac, but both kingdoms together, viz. the kingdom of nature and the kingdom of grace, not any more each kingdom by itself or apart in the figure; but in the type of the new regeneration, shewing how God in his love had given himself again into man, viz. into the kingdom of nature, and how through his power the wicked ens of the Serpent (sown by the devil into the kingdom of nature) should be broken and killed.

25. Therefore God called Jacob, *Israel*, viz. a flourishing, forth-spreading tree of many boughs and branches; or, as it is understood in the formation of the word in the High Tongue, a flourishing or fresh springing of Paradise. Where the *I* gives itself into the root, to a new centre, and springeth forth powerfully through the root, with which the Word of the Covenant is understood in the name *JESUS*. For this *I* is the character of the *Unius*, viz. of the eternal One in the divine lubet, which Adam lost when he departed from the *I*, viz. from the only will of God, and entered into self, and into the various multiplicity of the properties in their disharmony, unequality and discord, to try, prove and taste good and evil, in the five senses.

26. This *I* brought itself of grace again into the divided, rent and torn properties of the Adamical human tree; and sprang forth through and with the Adamical tree; and hence he had his name, *Israel*; being as a great number and power of such branches, all which do spring and grow forth in the new tincture. In which also the ens of the corrupt nature grew up all along; even as the sun's and the earth's power do work and grow together in the fruit of the tree, and are always in contest one with another, until the fruit be ripe, and a new kernel for another fruit be produced and also ripe, and then the tree leaveth the fruit, and sows the new kernel for another young tree.

27. In this nature and manner also arose the strife and combat with Esau and Jacob in the womb; to signify that the corrupt nature with the Serpent's ens should be rejected and cast off; as the tree doth let fall its ripe fruit, and desireth only the kernel [to propagate its like]: so it was here when the ens of Christ did stir itself up in Jacob, then arose the strife and enmity. For the ens of Christ should rule; and the

wrath in the Serpent's ens, that would also rule; and hence came the contest about the dominion and kingdom. The ens of Christ set itself aloft in Jacob, and bruised the head of the essence of the Serpent's ens in Esau, and even there the Serpent stung Christ on the heel, and thence it came that both the children did strive and struggle together in the womb.

28. Not that we are to understand that Esau was wholly out of the Serpent's ens. No; he was of the right Adamical nature, from his father Isaac and Abraham; only, God did here set forth the figure of the kingdom of nature, which was poisoned in man, and then [he] also [set forth] the figure of the kingdom of grace; shewing that the natural man must forsake his own evil will, and therewith also wholly immerse and give up himself into the kingdom of grace. And the figure which was here represented in Esau was to shew that the evil[1] Adamical man did not at all avail [in God's sight, that it was not profitable for the kingdom of God, but] it was cast away and rejected from God, and that man must wholly forsake his natural right of selfness, and wholly give in himself into God's will.

[1] Jacob's evil nature was as rejected of God, as Esau's, only the figure was set in Esau; not that he was personally, and wholly from all eternity predestinated to damnation, as Babel falsely teacheth.

The Fifty-Fourth Chapter

How *Isaac*, by reason of the Famine, went down to *Abimelech*, King of the Philistines at Gerar; And how the Lord appeared there to him, and commanded him to stay there, and renewed there the Covenant of his Father with him: Of the meaning of this, in its Spiritual Figure[1]

1. THE twenty-sixth chapter of Genesis doth further relate the history touching Isaac; how God did so very wonderfully guide him, and renewed the Covenant of his father Abraham with him, and preserved and blessed him and his wife with him. For seeing the kingdom of grace in the Covenant of God was now manifested in him, the blessing of God did now spring forth effectually in his purpose through the kingdom of nature.

2. And, on the contrary, how the devil was an utter enraged enemy to this blessing, and desired to sift and search the kingdom of nature in Isaac, and in his wife Rebecca (in whom as yet the Serpent's ens lay in the earthly flesh) through the lust of King Abimelech.

3. And this again is a figure of Adam in Paradise, and also of Christ in the new regeneration; shewing how Adam went into King Abimelech's land, that is, into a strange kingdom, viz. into the four elements, where he hath denied his wife, viz. the matrix of the heavenly generatress in him, in that he introduced his lust into the bestial property.

4. As here Isaac did stand in fear of his life before King Abimelech, by reason of his wife, even so Adam, in his strange lust in the kingdom of the four elements and the stars, did also stand in fear before the strange king, viz. before the kingdom of this world, and denied his heavenly birth out of fear of the kingdom of this world; and gave his eternal will to the king of this world, that it might the better fare with him in his strange lust, as Isaac thought to do with his wife, who stood herewith in the figure of Adam.

[1] Gen. xxvi.

5. Which figure the divine imagination did represent unto itself in Isaac, and set down withal the Covenant of the new birth, viz. his promised truth, how he would lead and guide the children of his grace in the presence of the strange king, viz. in the kingdom of this world; and preserve them from[1] the lust and desire of this king, and would lay hold of this king with his power, and change his lust and desire, viz. the lust of the stars and four elements, into another will of the essential desire. So that the sharp and severe might of the astrum in flesh and blood should be changed into a covenant of peace, and do no hurt to the children of grace in the Covenant; but it should serve them to bring forth the blessing and fruits, that they might grow greatly, as here Isaac with King Abimelech stood surrounded in the mere blessing of God; and his possession of goods and cattle grew so great, that King Abimelech thought he would be too potent and mighty for him, and therefore commanded him to go out of his land.

6. Which is a figure of the new birth in the kingdom of nature; that if the inward spiritual man doth in divine power outgrow or overtop the kingdom of nature, then the kingdom of the outward nature in flesh and blood in the spirit of the world[2] is sore afraid and astonished at it, for it seeth and feeleth its ruin and decrease, and would fain preserve its ownhood and propriety in the outward life.

7. And then comes the spiritual man in the Covenant of the new birth, and reproveth King Abimelech, viz. the outward life in the spirit of the outward world, for the wells of water which the divine thoughts, viz. the servants of the new man, had digged in the soul's ground, viz. in the eternal centre. Because Abimelech with his servants, viz. the evil earthly thoughts, imaginations and senses, had filled them up with the vain lust of the flesh. This sets forth and represents the wells of water which Abraham's servants, viz. Abraham's faith's desire, had digged in the ens of faith; about which wells Abimelech's servants, viz. the desires of the flesh, have contended for, and continually filled them [up with earth]; which Isaac's servants do again open in the root of Israel, and at last dig up a well wherein they find of the living water; and there they did pitch their tent, which well signified Christ: for they called the place Beer-sheba, viz. an opening, or a contrition; which signifieth the repentance, breaking up, or contrition of the earthly will. In which repentance the water of life, viz. Christ, floweth forth.

[1] Before.   [2] In *spiritu mundi*, in the cosmic spirit.

HOW ISAAC WENT TO ABIMELECH

8. This whole twenty-sixth chapter of Genesis is a figure of the poor fallen man in the corrupt kingdom of nature, signifying how he doth swim therein, and how the poor soul is tossed to and fro therein, and seeketh itself in outward things, and labours to advance its strength and power, and yet finds nowhere any abiding place therein, but wandereth from one thing into another, and worketh now in this, and then in that, and soon in another, and seeketh rest, but findeth none; until it comes unto Beer-sheba, viz. into humility before God, and then the well of living water springs forth to it, out of God's Covenant.

9. Now although the words in this text of the twenty-sixth chapter do seem to treat only of external things, yet it is nothing else but the spirit in Moses alluding or playing, under the external history, with a spiritual figure of the kingdom of nature, and of the kingdom of Christ; for he begins and speaketh of a great famine which was come into the land, for which distress' sake Isaac went down to Abimelech, king of the Philistines, at Gerar.

The inward spiritual figure is this:

10. When God had created Adam, he came into the famine, viz. into the temptation, wherein the soul ought not to eat of the outward kingdom, but of the inward; but seeing it turned itself with its will into the outward kingdom, it did live in the famine, viz. in the hunger after the outward world's substance; and therefore it turned itself unto Abimelech, king of the Philistines, at Gerar; that is, to the corrupt kingdom in God's anger, viz. to the heathenish king, and was subject to it.

11. And then the Lord appeared unto it, as here he did to Isaac, and said, *Go not into Egypt* (that is, thou poor depraved soul, go not into the bestial lust), *but remain in the land which I shall tell thee of*; and be thou a stranger in this land; that is, remain in my Covenant, and be with the soul a stranger in this house of flesh, wherein the soul is not at home; *And lo, I will be with thee, and bless thee; for unto thee, and unto thy seed, I will give all these countries, and I will perform the oath which I sware unto Abraham thy father* (vv. 2, 3). That is:

12. Remain but steadfast in my will, and then I will give thee after this [lifetime] the kingdom of nature, according to its inward good ground, for possession and propriety; and I will perform and ratify my oath (viz. Jesus Christ, whom I promised thee in thy fall,

and whom I introduced into Abraham's faith) unto thee for ever; and *I will*, in the kingdom of nature, wherein thou must in this time stand, work, labour, toil, and be in need and distress, even *multiply thy seed as the stars in heaven*; and give thy seed all the wrought powers and works to an eternal propriety, *and through thy seed all the nations of the earth shall be blessed* (v. 4). That is:

13. Through thy ens of faith (which in Christ, viz. in the aim and limit of the Covenant, shall be manifested in the kingdom of thy nature and creatural property, and become man in thee) all nations, viz. the whole Adamical tree shall be blessed; and therefore, *because Abraham obeyed my voice, and kept my charge, commandments, ways, and laws* (v. 5). That is, Abraham hath received my working word into his soul's desire, and obeyed my voice in its operation; which divine operation is the command, law, and form. Out of which operation also God shewed Abraham, by the circumcision, the figure of the kingdom of Christ, that the same should cut off the sin and vanity; which figure God called his charge, law in the Covenant, and his statute.

14. The spirit of Moses doth now proceed further in the relation of this figure, and signifieth, under the outward history of King Abimelech, how that *Abimelech's servants and Isaac's servants contended about the wells of water, and that Abraham's and Isaac's servants digged the wells of water, which wells were continually stopped up by the envy and enmity of the Philistines* (vv. 18-21). By which figure the spirit secretly signifieth how the children of the saints, viz. the patriarchs Abraham and Isaac, have always digged in their ens of faith for the wellspring of life in the Covenant, and have also obtained the knowledge of the Messiah.

15. But these wells were continually covered and obscured by the devil in God's anger, and by their earthly reason, until they apprehended and laid hold of the promise of the Messiah in faith. And then they said we have digged a well, and have found of the water of life: the same, Isaac called Shebah,[1] and therein hinteth at the Sabbath, Christ, as he also forthwith saith, that thereupon the place was called Beer-sheba (vv. 32, 33), viz. a contrition, and breaking of the anger and envy of the devil in man's property; to signify that the Sabbath, Christ, viz. the spiritual wellspring, is truly called Beer-sheba, viz. a contrition of death, where the Sabbath introduceth itself into death, and brings forth the fountain of life through death.

16. At which fountain the children of God's Covenant did pitch

---

[1] Text, Saba.

HOW ISAAC WENT TO ABIMELECH

their tent, and waited upon the promise, until the same fountain was opened in the humanity, and flowed forth out of Christ's blood and death; of which the poor soul drank, and thereby was brought into the eternal Sabbath, where it was redeemed and freed from the strife of the Philistines, viz. from the contention of the anger of God and of the devil. As the history in this text doth clearly signify thus much in the High Tongue; which the spirit of Moses hath thus represented in the figure, and doth play with the description of this figure.

17. As indeed the whole Old Testament is a figure of the New, and the New a figure of the future eternal world, wherein the figure shall stand in divine power, and the spirit of God shall in eternity play with his deeds of wonder; to which end also he hath created man, and inspired[1] the power of his voice, viz. the living word, into him, that so he might be an image of the eternal Word, with which image the eternal spirit will play, and work wonders; that so there may be a joy and knowledge in the eternal wisdom.

18. Now when, as the spirit of Moses had pointed out the figure of Adam and Christ under a history, he proceeds, and further relates how it must go with the children of God in this time, shewing in what desire the poor soul in flesh and blood lieth captive, and is continually vexed and tormented, as here Isaac and Rebecca. For the text saith, *When Esau was forty years old he took to wife Judith the daughter of Beeri the Hittite, and Bashemath the daughter of Elon the Hittite, which were a grief of mind to Isaac and to Rebecca* (vv. 34, 35). And in this place he speaks no further of these wives, or their children; to signify that it is a figure, whereby he alludes at something else; which reason looks upon as very strange, and wonders that God should yet permit two evil women to be with holy Isaac, through his son Esau; with whom he and his fair, blessed Rebecca must live in trouble, vexation and opposition: so very secretly doth the spirit of Moses set forth his figure, that reason must even be blind in it.

The spiritual figure is thus:

19. The forty years of the age of Esau, or of Isaac after he begat Esau, signifieth, that Adam with his Eve, when as he was man and woman, and yet neither of them, did stand in Paradise forty days in the temptation or proba, and had joy with his fair Eve, viz. with his female[2] property in himself.

[1] Or, inspoken.   [2] Or, feminine.

20. But Abimelech, viz. the king of this world, had introduced his lust into this fair female[1] rose-garden, viz. into the tincture of Venus; understand, into the holy life of love in Adam; and stirred the centre of the soul's nature, whereupon Adam became lusting and longing to take to him in his property yet two wives, viz. the bestial wife, according to the beast-like property out of the four elements; and the astral [sidereal or starry] wife from the constellation [or astrum of this world]; which wicked woman did awaken in Adam's female property, which he took up to wife for his lust. As Esau did the wives of scorn and mockery, with whom he caused mere grief of mind, and lamentable perplexity to himself and his right female property: and we indeed do still suffer and endure the same, and must consume our time with them in misery and lamentation.

21. Further, this figure denoteth the forty years of Israel in the wilderness, when they did eat manna, and rejoiced with Rebecca under a strange king; where they lived in the kingdom of this world, and yet were led, preserved and nourished in the divine arm; and therefore they grew great before the world, as Isaac under king Abimelech. And when Israel, after forty years, pitched their tent at Beer-sheba, viz. in the promised land, they yet took these two wives to them in their fleshly lust; which caused mere grief of heart to them, for which two wives' sake they were sorely punished of God, and were at last for their sake, driven from Beer-sheba.

22. Thirdly, this figure denotes the hard combat of Christ in the wilderness, in Adam's stead, where Christ in our humanity took these two wives (which were manifest in Adam through his strange son, or will) unto his heavenly essentiality, and suffered them to hunger forty days, so that they must resign and give in their desire to the divine essence, and learn to eat heavenly manna. To signify that this earthly lust [in us], from the stars and four elements, should be broken in Christ's death, and cease.

23. Fourthly, it denotes the forty hours of Christ in the grave, where these two wives of unquietness in the human property were changed again into one eternal wife, viz. into the true Rebecca, and right Adamical Eve, which was in Adam before his Eve.

24. Fifthly, it points at the forty days of Christ after his resurrection, when the two wives of Adam and Esau were again changed into a manly virgin, when this virgin, viz. Christ in our male and female property, did rightly stand out the forty days of Adam in Paradise,

---

[1] Or, feminine.

HOW ISAAC WENT TO ABIMELECH

when he was tried; and therefore he set himself by divine might into the royal throne of ejected Lucifer, as a judge; and with these two wives in one virginity, and one only person or image, would rule over him,[1] as the causer of man's misery, seeing he was the great cause that Adam, viz. the image of God, did manifest, by his son of the new will, yet two wives in his virginity.

25. This, the spirit in Moses and Esdras[2] hath mystically and secretly hinted at under an outward figure, shewing how it should afterwards fall out. And although it is very likely that reason will not believe us, we care not for that, and it matters not much; seeing we have not disclosed this for its sake, but for the sake of the understanding children. However, we know very well in what vision we write [we know from what spirit's illumination and knowledge we have set down some glances of the great mysteries signified by this short divine history of Moses].

[1] Viz. Lucifer. [2] *Note* Esdras.

The Fifty-Fifth Chapter

Shewing what we are to understand by *Isaac's* blessing *Jacob*, unknowingly, when he was old and ready to die[1]

THE GATES OF THE GREAT MYSTERIES
OF THE WHOLE BIBLE

1. WHEN reason readeth this history of the twenty-seventh chapter of Genesis it hath a twofold conjecture upon the same: one is as if Rebecca [only] loved Jacob more than Esau, and therefore brought him by craft to obtain the blessing of his father; and again it conceives, that indeed it was from the appointment and providence of God, because Esau was not worthy of the blessing, and therefore it will take upon it wholly to condemn Esau, whereupon also it hath set the predestination; and yet it understands nothing at all of this wonderful figure.

2. Now, if we would rightly understand and interpret this figure, then we must set here in the figure the patriarch Isaac, in God the Father's stead, who alone can bless, who also blessed Isaac in Abraham's seed, that Isaac should again bless his seed in the Covenant's line.

3. And Esau was set in the place of the depraved nature, viz. in the kingdom of the corrupt nature in man's property, apprehended in the anger of God.

4. And Jacob we set in the new birth, in the humanity of Christ, which God the Father blessed instead of the depraved Adam, when he brought forth a new generation out of our humanity in this line.

5. And we see here how Adam hath fooled away and lost the blessing and divine unction, and how he was rejected in the earthly image, from God; and how he hath lost his right of the divine unction; as here Esau [had lost] the first birth, and also the blessing.

The inward spiritual figure stands thus:

6. *Isaac was old, and expected to die, and called Esau his first-born son, that he might bless him with the blessing of Abraham, and bade him go take*

---

[1] Gen. xxvii.

OF ISAAC'S BLESSING JACOB

some venison, and dress it for him, that he might eat gladly thereof, that his soul might be refreshed, and the blessing of the Lord might put forth itself in him, that he might bless Esau. And Esau went and did as his father would have him, that so he might be blessed (Gen. xxvii. 1-4). This, in the inward understanding in the figure, is thus:

7. When Isaac was ready to die, the blessing in God the Father's property moved itself in him, and would bless the natural seed of the Adamical nature, viz. the kingdom of nature, in Esau: For Isaac longed after venison, viz. after the kingdom of nature in the bestial property, viz. after the depraved Adamical man, as to the first creation.

8. For the Father's blessing would cast itself upon Adam, in whose stead Esau stood; but the heavenly ens was extinct in the first Adam, and therefore the natural man might not be helped and remedied only with a blessing; but there must be another serious earnestness: the blessing must become a substance, viz. man, in the kingdom of nature; of which [substantial blessing] the kingdom of nature was not capable, in its own power and might: as here Esau, in his kingdom of nature, was not capable of the Father's blessing.

9. For the kingdom of man's nature was so poisoned that it must be dissolved; therefore the blessing of God the Father turned itself upon the woman's tincture, viz. upon the Adamical female tincture, understand, the light's tincture. For the fiery tincture in Adam was awakened in the wrath, viz. in the kingdom of darkness, and was made an earthly image; and herein the heavenly was swallowed up and mortified. Now, the blessing would come to help this heavenly disappeared image, that so it might be quickened again in the blessing; and so the kingdom of nature with which it was incorporated should be blessed, tinctured and regenerated.

10. Seeing then two lines went forth in Abraham's and Isaac's seed, viz. in Ishmael and Esau, the right depraved Adamical image, and in Isaac and Jacob the line of the Covenant in the free given grace, the blessing of God the Father, which was manifested in Isaac, turned itself upon Jacob, viz. upon the line of Christ whom God hath anointed; that he should again anoint the first-born Esau, viz. the first Adamical depraved man; for the first Adam had lost his first birth given him out of the divine Word in the creation, and could not any more be blessed out of his centre.

11. For the soul's will was broken off from the eternal Word of divine holiness, and had given itself into the centre of the first

MYSTERIUM MAGNUM

Principle, viz. into the wrath of the eternal nature, into the severation of the speaking word, viz. into the opposition and contentious contrariety. Whence also Isaac blessed Esau with the word of strife, when he said unto him in the blessing, *Thou shalt live by thy sword, and break thy brother's yoke from off thy neck*. Signifying, that now the depraved nature in him was become a servant of God's anger, and should now bear and manage the combat which Adam had raised up in the life's properties, and be a servant of the same.

12. But that Isaac did not understand this thing, and would have blessed Esau with the blessing of the Covenant, and given him the sceptre in Zion, doth shew unto us that Isaac, and all the holy children of God (although they be born again of the new birth in the line of the Covenant and stand therein), do not apprehend and understand the internal ground of their essence, wherein the kingdom of God worketh and is in power, so as to be able to do anything thereby in self-will. But God turneth this internal ground of the place of God as he pleaseth; and the soul must see to what he [God] doth; as here Isaac must see to what the Lord had blessed by him.

13. For Isaac said to Esau, That he should make him ready savoury meat, such as he loved to eat; and then his soul would bless him (v. 4). But now this blessing stood in the line of the Covenant, in which, Christ should spring forth; not in the soul's might, but in God's might. For the soul of Isaac and of all the children of Adam were as yet, with the soul's root, on the band of God's anger, which anger this internal incorporated line of grace should destroy in Christ's death, and wholly incorporate and unite it into the line of the Covenant.

14. Therefore the soul's will in Isaac should not propagate the blessing of this Covenant's line, and give it to the kingdom of the soul-like[1] nature, viz. to the first-born, Esau, and first Adam; for the soul was a cause of the destruction: the fire's tincture received not the might and strength of the new virtue, for its might should be broken, viz. its proud Lucifer, who likewise is the very same; but the light's tincture (which disappeared in Adam when the fire's might introduced dark earthliness thereinto), which tincture sprang forth again afresh in this Covenant's line in the power of the inspoken and promised, incorporated Word of grace, the same had the might and power of the blessing.

15. The seed of the woman, viz. the light's tincture and virtue,

---
[1] Or soul's.

OF ISAAC'S BLESSING JACOB

should bruise the head of the fiery Serpent, and change the soul's fiery might into a meek love-fire. The fiery soul's will shall and must be wholly transmuted and turned into meekness.

16. As this disappeared light's tincture was brought from Adam into the woman, viz. into Eve, which when it was in Adam was his fair Paradisical rose-garden of peculiar love, wherein God was manifest, and seeing now the figure of the new birth was represented in Isaac's blessing, therefore also his wife, viz. the blessed Rebecca, must come, as one who also stood in the line of the Covenant; and set forth the right figure of Christ, viz. Jacob, in the place of the blessing. To signify that Christ should be manifested in this Covenant's line in the seed of the woman, viz. in the tincture of the light and the water, and assume the soul's nature from the power of the light, that so he might rule over the fiery nature of the soul, and change the same into the power of the light.

17. Now Rebecca, Isaac's wife, was here in this place a figure of the Virgin Mary, who brought forth Christ, viz. the blessed of God, who should bless Esau, and all the Adamical children. And it was so ordered by the Lord that Rebecca should so carry it, for she understood that the blessing, viz. the sceptre of Israel did rest in Jacob.

18. For seeing the sceptre in Zion lay in the seed of the woman, viz. in the virginity, the same sceptre was here also stirred in the seed of the woman; so that a woman must bring forth the Covenant's line to the place of God the Father's blessing, which was in Isaac; and the man's will, viz. the soul's natural fire-will, must come behind, and be a servant of God's wonders, and see what God hath done with him.

19. But that it appeareth to be as a deceit or cunning subtlety, in that Rebecca did so instruct and put on Jacob to take away the blessing from Esau, as if she loved Jacob far above Esau, therein reason hath blind eyes: For through the devil's cunning the curse came into the world; and through the divine cunning in the love the destruction of death and hell came again into the soul: the divine cunning killed the devil's cunning.

20. Understand it aright: All cunning ariseth from the lubet or desire. The devil's cunning arose from the false lubet or lust: so likewise God's lubet came again into the woman's seed (into which heavenly matrix the devil had insinuated his lust), and destroyed the devil's lust.

21. It was of God that Jacob obtained the blessing, wholly

contrary to the mind and will of reason. For he stood in the figure of Christ, and Esau stood in the figure of the depraved Adam.

22. Therefore Esau was a hairy or rugged man, signifying the monstrous bestial property, which Adam had awaked in the fall, through lust. Now when Adam's lust had brought itself to substance, then the flesh became gross and bestial. Thus the bestial part swallowed up the heavenly in itself, and death was manifested in the flesh. And we see here in this figure very clearly typified how it should be.

23. Isaac would bless the bestial man in Esau, this, God would not: the divine blessing belonged to Christ. But the depraved Adam could not be capable of receiving the blessing of God, unless Christ take this rugged bestial skin [or form] which Adam had put on; as here Jacob could not be blessed unless he had on him the hairy beast-like skin.

24. God the Father set before him our misery in his Covenant in Christ in our humanity which he assumed; for Christ must enter into our humanity, and walk in our hairy form, and destroy our death of the bestial property; as it is written, *He took on him our sickness; and laid on himself our grief* (Isa. liii. 4; Matt. viii. 17; 1 Pet. ii. 24).

25. For as Isaac took hold of his son Jacob in his hairy skin, and felt whether he was his first-born son to whom the blessing belonged, so God the Father reached into the essence of his Son, Christ, and felt whether the humanity of Christ were the first image created in Adam; whence the agony seized on him in the Mount of Olivet, that he sweat bloody sweat, of which Isaiah speaketh plainly, *He took on him our grief.*

26. And as Isaac found outwardly only Esau's skin on Jacob, and inwardly heard Jacob's voice, and yet blessed him instead of Esau, as if he were Esau; so likewise God the Father found our rugged human property on Christ, and yet inwardly he heard that the voice of God sounded in him; that the divine heavenly ens was within, under his assumed humanity. Therefore also his voice did, in his Baptism in Jordan, rest upon him, when he blessed our humanity, in that he said, *This is my beloved son, hear ye him.*

27. So likewise Isaac heard indeed the voice of Jacob under the hairy skin, and understood that it was not Esau; but the spirit in his blessing did yet forcibly pass upon him; for he proved in him the incorporated ground of the Covenant, viz. the line of the new humanity. For he said, *The voice is Jacob's voice, but the hands are the*

OF ISAAC'S BLESSING JACOB

hands of Esau (v. 22). In which the spirit intimates, that in Jacob, and all the children of God in flesh and blood, there is even the first depraved bestial Adamical man, with his hairy skin, which God doth not look upon; but only the divine voice, which is one spirit with God, doth inhabit in the inward soulish man.

28. And then we see in this figure that our beast's skin in flesh and blood, wherewith we do so pride ourselves and make devout shows before God, is only a deceit; as Jacob in this beast's hide stood as a deceiver before his father, and would blind his father with the beast's skin. So likewise the earthly man cometh in his bestial property before God, and desireth God's blessing: but he may not obtain it, unless he hath Jacob's, viz. Christ's, voice in him, under this beast's skin.

29. For, as Jacob was smooth and pure under this beast's skin, so must we be smooth, pure and holy in our inward ground[1] under this our beast's skin, if we will have the blessing of God to light and rest upon us. For we see very well in this figure that the blessing would not rest upon Esau, who had by nature a rugged hairy beast's skin in his essence, although he was the first-born to whom the blessing belonged by right of inheritance. For the first man was become depraved in his nature and had lost the inheritance of God. The blessing and the filial inheritance resteth only upon the Second New Adam.

30. Further, this figure denotes, that the new man in Christ should take away the sceptre and might from the devil, and also from the man of sin; and in this blessing rule over him in power, as Jacob was made lord over his enemies: This figure points wholly at Christ.

31. For as Jacob took a strange form on him, and came in strange attire before his father, and desired the blessing of him, and also obtained it; so Christ, viz. the eternal Word, took on him also a strange form, viz. our humanity, and brought the same before his Father to bless it.

32. And as *Isaac blessed his son Jacob with the dew of heaven, and the fatness of the earth, and with corn and wine* (v. 28); even so God the Father blessed our humanity, in Christ. For our humanity was also in its original out of the limus of the earth, and was nourished and brought up by the dew of heaven, even by corn and wine; this, God blessed to the new birth, and resurrection of the dead upon the life to come.

33. And as Isaac set Jacob to (v. 29) be lord over his brethren of

---
[1] Of the heart and soul.

the natural property; so God hath set the new birth in the blessing of Christ to be lord over the Adamical nature in flesh and blood; so that the new man, born of God's blessing, must rule over all the members of his natural body, and they must be subject to the new man.

34. And as Isaac set the curse between them, That whosoever should curse Jacob he should be accursed, and whosoever should bless him he should also be blessed (v. 29); so God hath set the curse upon the corrupt Adamical kingdom, that whosoever should not be found in the blessing of Christ, he must be eternally in the curse of God, but whosoever should bring his mind and will into this Jacob's, viz. Christ's, blessing, he should be eternally in the blessing.

35. Further, we see in this type how it goeth with the children of God; for when Isaac had blessed Jacob, then came Esau with his venison, and his father Isaac was astonished, and said, *Why, who art thou* (vv. 30–33)? And he was dismayed at it, that he had unknowingly blessed Jacob. Which typifieth how that the Adamical man understands nothing at all of God's ways; and how God doth oftentimes wonderfully lead him according to the inward ground, and that although he be carried on in the way of God, yet he looketh much at the outward reason, and often stumbleth at external rational things, at temporal orders and goods, and suffereth fear to surprise him; and would fain that the will of his reason be done: As here Isaac trembled exceeding when he saw that the will of his reason was broken.

36. And herein we acknowledge the misery and ignorance of the children of God, in that reason entereth into its own dominion, and will not wholly leave itself to God, and is astonished when it goeth otherwise than it hath imagined to itself.

37. And then we see how God at last doth break forth with his light in the understanding, and sheweth man his way, that he is satisfied; as he did here to Isaac, in that he said; *This Jacob is blessed, and he shall also remain blessed* (v. 33); for now Isaac understood God's will.

38. Further we see in this history how Esau weepeth lamentably before his father for the blessing, and saith to his father, *Bless me also my father; hast thou but one blessing? hast thou not reserved one blessing for me? But his father said, I have made him thy lord, and all his brethren I have given to him for servants, with corn and wine I have enriched him. What shall I do now unto thee, my son* (vv. 34–37)? This typifieth out the kingdom of Christ, shewing how God hath made it lord over the kingdom

OF ISAAC'S BLESSING JACOB

of nature, as Christ said, *All power both in heaven and upon earth is given to me of my father* (Matt. xxviii. 18).

39. Furthermore it denotes, that the corrupt Adamical nature in Esau and all men cannot receive the blessing, unless they first die unto their own self-right and will: as Esau could not be blessed of his father with the holy blessing. For he was the type of the corrupt Adam according to the kingdom of nature; so likewise the earthly nature cannot be capable of the holy Spirit in its essence; of which Paul said, *Flesh and blood shall not inherit the kingdom of God* (I Cor. xv. 50); unless it fall into the earth, and enter again into its first womb, as grain that is sown, and resign its nature to the first mother.

40. And then we see here how Isaac giveth his son Esau a temporal blessing, and intimates to him that the natural man is led by the spirit of this world. For to Jacob he said, *God give thee of the dew of heaven, and of the fatness of the earth, and of corn and wine abundance* (v. 28); but to Esau he said only, *Behold! thou wilt have a fat dwelling upon the earth, and of the dew of heaven from above; thou wilt live by thy sword, and serve thy brethren; and it will come to pass when thou shalt have the dominion, that thou wilt break his yoke from off thy neck* (vv. 39, 40).

41. And hereby he signifieth in what dominion the outward natural man is led, driven and nourished, and what his desire and endeavour should be; namely, he would be in his mind only a robber, murderer, and an evil malicious beast, that should desire to bear down all under it with power, force and murder.

42. For Isaac doth not say, *Live thou by thy sword*, but, *Thou wilt do it.* Namely, God's wrath in the kingdom of the corrupt nature, with the devil's will, will move thee thereunto; that thou wilt draw the fatness of the earth unto thyself, and wilt be ruled and driven by the stars above, and wilt in thy natural power drive away from thee the children of God, who rule in God's power. That is, when the holy Spirit in God's children doth reprove them by reason of their tyranny, they then kill and slay them, and tear the sword of the Holy Ghost from off their neck, as here Isaac said, *Thou wilt do it.*

43. As indeed Esau soon did, and would have killed Jacob, so that Jacob in God's blessing was fain to flee from him. And here he pulled off the yoke of the holy Spirit from his neck. And this prophecy of the patriarch is a figure, how the Esauites and tyrants, viz. the fleshly brethren of the Christians, would dwell among the Christians, and be born as to their natural brotherhood of the same parents; as Esau, and Jacob [were]; and yet they would persecute them with sword and

torments; and thrust them away, and yet stand themselves as [if they were the only true] Christians, and desire the blessing of God; as Esau stood and wept bitterly for the blessing, and he did not mind the kingdom of God, but that he might be a lord upon the earth over his brethren and other men; and might have riches, and fullness of the belly.

44. This Esau in his blessing is a true type of Antichrist, who draweth near to God with the lips, and gives himself to an external seeming service and worship of Christ; and sets himself forth as if he did it to God, and stands and makes mighty holy shows in his hypocrisy and glistering verbalities, sets forth himself with zeal and devotion, that so he might be honoured of man; and that his god [Mammon and] Mäusim may be fat, and doth even mourn and lament for malice, when men will not do that for him which he will have; when he cannot get enough of the belly-blessing, according to the will of his god Mäusim; and whosoever doth but reprove or touch him, and speaks to him of the blessing of God, him he will slay, and cannot endure a true servant of Christ under him.

45. Reason supposeth, that seeing Isaac said to Esau, Thou shalt live by thy sword, that God hath commanded him so to do, and here it props up [its murdering malice and bloodthirsty villainy], but it is far otherwise. God wills not any war; but the kingdom of nature in God's anger willeth it; and whosoever is born only of the kingdom of nature he liveth also to the same.

46. Therefore said Isaac, Thou wilt do it; as if he should have said, Thou, through thy anger wilt serve the anger of God, and wilt be a lord in the kingdom of nature in this world; even as the rich and wealthy ones do bring themselves into power and authority, and do it through the kingdom of nature, in the wrath.

47. And we see further, how that Esau did deadly hate his brother Jacob for the blessing's sake (v. 41), of which, notwithstanding, he was not capable, as to the kingdom of nature. To signify that the true children of Christ should for this blessing's sake be hated, persecuted and slain of the children in the kingdom of nature. And that, because the kingdom of grace shall rule over the kingdom of nature, and destroy the same at the end of days, and change it into its might; and therefore there is strife between both kingdoms.

48. For the children of Christ in this lifetime, as to the outward man, live in the kingdom of the depraved human nature, viz. in the kingdom of the Esauites, and are, as to the spirit, only strangers and

pilgrims therein. As Christ said, *My kingdom is not of this world*; and therefore the children of this world are enemies to them, and persecute them, as Esau his brother Jacob.

49. For where the kingdom of Christ begins to flourish, there presently the kingdom of the devil begins to storm and rage; and therefore, because the kingdom of Christ shall and will take away and ruin his might and princely throne; hence is the strife in this world between the children of Jacob, and Esau.

50. For as soon as Jacob had obtained the blessing, Esau purposed in his mind to kill Jacob (v. 41). Which is a figure of Christ, shewing how that God's anger would kill him in this blessing, in our assumed humanity, as to the kingdom of nature; and that the children of God also should be killed in God's anger, as to the kingdom of nature, and shed their blood into this murdering spirit; that thereby God's anger might be blotted out and changed into love.

The Fifty-Sixth Chapter

How *Isaac* and *Rebecca* sent away *Jacob* because of *Esau* into another Country; and how the Lord appeared to him in a Vision upon the Ladder, which reached even into heaven; and how *Esau* carried himself afterwards towards his Parents: What we are to understand by this figure

1. WHEN Jacob had received the blessing,[1] then he must depart from his native home, from father and mother, and flee from the wrath of Esau. This is now a figure of Christ, shewing how that he, after that he had assumed and anointed our humanity, should flee with our humanity out of its father's Adamical house again into the first Paradisical house.

2. And it further denotes that the children of Christ (after they have received the unction and blessing, and the new birth begins to spring forth in them, in the blessing), shall and must forthwith flee with their thoughts and mind from their father Adam's house of the depraved nature; and it shews that the devil and the world do soon hate them, and they must forthwith give themselves to the pilgrim's path of Christ, and live under the world's slavish yoke, in misery and oppression; in disfavour and disrespect. For God brings them forth with their thoughts and mind out of their father's house, viz. out of the desire in flesh and blood; so that they do nothing at all regard the pleasure of the world, and flee from it, as Jacob from his father's house.

3. And then we see how wonderfully God guideth his children, and defends them from their enemies, that the devil in God's anger cannot kill them, unless it be God's will. As he defended Jacob from the fury of Esau, and led him away from him. And we have here an excellent example in Jacob; in that he forsook his native home, also father and mother, for this blessing's sake, and loved God more than

---

[1] Gen. xxviii.

OF JACOB'S LADDER

all temporal goods, and willingly left all to Esau; that so he might but be the blessed of God.

4. And we see that when he had left the riches of the world in his father's house, the Lord appeared to him with the eternal goods, and shewed him a ladder, whereupon he could ascend into God's eternal kingdom: which ladder was no other than Christ, whom he had put on in the line of the Covenant. And here now the type was represented to him, shewing him what person Christ should be.

5. For this ladder (as to his apprehension) *was upon the earth, and the top of it reached into heaven; and thereon the angels of God did ascend and descend* (Gen. xxviii. 12). Which signifieth that God's eternal Word, with the power of heaven, viz. with the angelical divine world's essence, should descend or immerse itself into our essence, [which was] departed from God, and blind as to God; and assume our humanity; and so unite the heaven with the world *in* man; that the humanity, through this entrance of the Deity into the humanity, might have a ladder unto God.

6. And it shews that mankind should come through Christ's humanity into the society of the angels (*Matt. xxii. 30*). And this is clearly signified here, in that the angels of God do ascend and descend on this ladder. Also that the heaven in man should be again opened through this entrance of the divine essence into the humanity, and that the children of God should have the angels for companions in this world; which God shewed to Jacob, in that the angels came up and down to him on this ladder (*John i, 51*).

7. Which shall be a very great comfort to the children of God, who turn themselves from their father's house, viz. from this world's vanity, to this Jacob's ladder; for they shall certainly know that God's angels do come unto them upon this ladder to which they have turned themselves, and are willingly about them [to serve them].

8. For this ladder signifieth properly the pilgrim's path of Christ through this world into God's kingdom, in that the kingdom of the corrupt Adamical nature doth always yet cleave unto the children of God, and hinders them in flesh and blood in the spirit of this world; and therefore they must, according to the inward man in Christ's spirit, continually ascend up in much crosses and tribulation on this ladder, and follow Christ under his cross and red banner.

9. On the contrary, the world liveth in the pleasure of their father Adam's house, in scorn, jeering and mocking, in envy, spite and malice; whatsoever they can do to cross and vex these Jacob's children, that

they joy and take delight in, and laugh and fleer at them. As we have an example of it in Esau; how that he took, in contempt, disdain, and spite to his father and mother, Ishmaelitish wives, who were of the line of mockery or reviling, which were mere bitterness of spirit, and grief of heart, both to Isaac and Rebecca.

10. Where we clearly see that the devil hath his power in the kingdom of this world in the corrupt human property, and doth continually resist God's children, and vexeth and plagueth them, and fights with them for his kingdom, which he hath lost, and doth not willingly beteem it them.

11. And we see very finely how the Lord standeth above upon this ladder of the pilgrimage of Christ, as with Jacob; and without ceasing calleth the children of Christ, and comforteth them, that they should cheerfully ascend upon it. He will not leave them, but come to them and bless them, so that their seed and fruit shall grow, increase, and be as the dust upon the earth (Gen. xxviii. 14). That is, that they in their toil, labour and anxiety, shall spring up and flourish in the inward divine kingdom.

12. For, so much as the children of Christ go out from this world, and forsake it in their mind, so much they spring up in the inward kingdom of Christ; where then God standeth above upon this ladder, and continually inspireth or inspeaketh his blessing and power into them, so that they grow as branches on his vine (John xv. 5), which he hath planted (Ps. lxxx. 15) again in our humanity, in this Jacob's blessing, in Christ.

13. And we hereby clearly see that this whole type, from Abraham to Jacob, contains mere figures of the kingdom and person of Christ and his children. For here God reneweth the promised Covenant of Abraham concerning the seed of the woman, with Jacob also; that out of his seed (v. 14), as out of the line of the Covenant, He should come who should bless all nations. For which cause also Jacob was led from his father's house, God having set before him outwardly the kingdom of Christ in the figure; for whose sake he caused his wrath to cease from the children of unbelief, and did not destroy them, but afforded them time to repent; and so appeased his wrath in this type, which pointed at the fulfilling which was to come.

14. We have here also a firm ground and assurance that Christ hath truly taken upon him our Adamical soul and humanity in the body of Mary, and hath destroyed death, hell, and the anger of God in our humanity which he assumed, and hath set up this ladder of Jacob. For

OF JACOB'S LADDER

God said to Jacob, *Through thee and thy seed shall all the generations of the earth be blessed* (v. 14). Through thee, Jacob, through thine own seed, which is God and man, viz. the heavenly divine ens and substance, and the human ens and substance, in the power of the eternal Word.

15. In which Word the holy name Jesus, viz. the highest love of the Deity, hath unfolded and manifested itself in our humanity which he hath assumed; which sole love of God, in the name Jesus, hath overcome the wrath of the eternal nature in our souls [which is] from the Father's property in the anger; and hath changed it into the love of the divine joy; and hath broken the still death, which hath severed us from the life of God; and hath manifested the divine life of the highest holy tincture in the eternal speaking Word of the divine power, in death, and hath made death to be life; and so our soul, in this divine power, is together penetrated and pressed through death and the anger of God.

16. And it is in no wise to be so taken, as some say, that the substance wherein the Word is become man, proceeded not from Adam; but, as some erroneously say, the Virgin Mary proceeded not from mankind, she hath outwardly only taken upon her a human body from Anna, and is not of the seed of Jacob, but is an eternal virgin chosen by God for this purpose before the world was.

17. This text teacheth us otherwise, where God saith, *Through thee, and thy seed.* Not through a strange divine seed only, but through *thee and thy seed*, with the entrance of the divine substance. Christ should break death in Adam's soul and body, and destroy hell in Adam's soul and body, which was manifested or revealed in Paradise.

18. For here lay our sickness and misery, which Christ took upon him as a yoke. Christ sacrificed his Father's wrath, which was kindled in our humanity, and awakened his highest love in our human and his holy blood. His holy tincture entered into our human death, and tinctured our (in Adam) faded heavenly substantiality (which faded in Adam when he brought earthliness and the false will thereinto), and raised up our faded heavenly substance with his heavenly living substance, so that life sprang up through death: And this was signified by the dry rod of Aaron.

19. Therefore that is not the true meaning, as some say: Christ hath assumed a soul from the Word in the eternal Virgin Mary, so that Christ, as one come from God, and his soul in the humanity of Christ, hath one and the same beginning.

MYSTERIUM MAGNUM

20. They were indeed united in the incarnation or the becoming man, so that they are inseparable, but the true ens of the soul, which the Word assumed in the name Jesus, was of us men from the female tincture, viz. from the true Adamical soul, yet from the property of the light, which was severed from Adam [and put into the woman], that this property of the light might transmute or change the fiery masculine property again into the love and divine humility, and that the masculine and feminine property might be quite changed into one image again; as Adam was before his Eve, when he was neither man nor woman, but a masculine virgin.

21. Therefore Christ took his soul from a woman, viz. from a virgin, and yet was a man, so that he rightly stood in the Adamical image, and brought the averted severed properties of life, in which our will had broken itself off from God, again into the temperature and union, viz. into that ONE.

22. For Adam turned his will from the only will of God, and Jesus Christ took our soul again into the only will of God, and turned the will of our soul, in our humanity which he assumed, into the only will of God again.

23. But that the reader may be thoroughly and fundamentally informed what our soul, and what the Word that became man, is, compare one with the other. It is thus: Our soul, before the beginning of the human soul's[1] creature, was an ens of the Word of God, in the Word (John i), and yet it was inspired or inspoken from the speaking Word of God into the human image in a natural and creaturely life, and formed in an image of the eternal speaking Word. This creaturely life of the soul turned itself in Adam away from the divine speaking, into an own will and speaking, and was in this respect broken off from the most unsearchable substance, and separated from God.

24. Into this separated word, viz. into the soul, the only eternal divine speaking Word gave itself in again, and turned the will of the soul again into the eternal One, viz. into God's eternal speaking. Therefore the soul is indeed from the eternal Word; but Christ, viz. the highest love of the Deity, did not take a new soul out of the eternal speaking, but [he took] our soul, viz. the word which was once spoken or formed in Adam, viz. our human soul, into his love-speaking in the grace and union of the Deity.

25. God spake again, into our poor fallen soul in Paradise, immediately after the fall, the Covenant and root of his highest love and

[1] Soulish.

OF JACOB'S LADDER

grace, through the Word, as a centre of grace to conception, and to the new regeneration.

26. And in Abraham he manifested the Covenant, which Abraham laid hold on with his desire, and received it after a spiritual manner, as an ens to the tree, but it lay without substance in man, only as a spiritual form and model or idea of the powerful Word.

27. Which Word, in its spiritual figure in the Virgin Mary, was at the limit, viz. at the end of the spiritual form, where that same spiritual form of the Word of God was comprehended in a substantial ens; and therewith also in like manner our human substance as to the soul was comprised in the image of the Word, and as to the substance of the body in a human form;[1] and was a self-subsisting God-man.

28. This comprised spiritual image, which was the seed of faith which Abraham laid hold on in the faith, was invested on Isaac, and from Isaac on Jacob; and to Jacob God said, *Through thee and thy seed shall all the people of the earth be blessed* (v. 14); viz. through this seed of faith which Jacob had received from his father Isaac in this line of the Covenant; which line of faith had incorporated itself in the human property according to the inward ground of the second Principle, viz. in that image of the heavenly world's substance which was extinguished in Adam.

29. In which incorporated ground the limit of God's Covenant remained, in a spiritual form till Mary, and was propagated from man to man, as from Adam and Eve along to Mary; and there the Word of the divine power was moved, and essentially assumed our human flesh and blood, together with the soul, and quickened the extinguished heavenly ens in the seed of Mary as to our part; which manifestation penetrated and pressed also into Mary's heavenly substantiality, so that she became living as to that heavenly virginity which disappeared in Eve: and in this living virginity, viz. in Adam's heavenly matrix, God became man.

30. And this is the blessing of Mary above all other women (Luke i. 42), that she is the first from Adam in whom the heavenly matrix became opened, in which the dry rod of Aaron rightly budded, viz. the kingdom of God. She is the first in whom the hidden virtue was manifested, for in her the limit of the Covenant in the spiritual image or type was at an end; and in her it was fulfilled with[2] our humanity.

31. Nevertheless she is truly the daughter of Adam, Abraham, Isaac, and Jacob, both as to the humanity and as to the Covenant of

---

[1] Frame, or formation, building.   [2] In, or by.

the spiritual figure; and in her conception, when the inward incorporated image or type of the inspired or inspoken Covenant of grace, which was laid hold on in the faith, did assume our human property, then was the kingdom of Christ manifested in the flesh.

32. Wherein afterwards the faithful put on Christ in the flesh, in their faith, yet only as to that heavenly image which was extinguished in Adam, as Mary [did], where Christ embraceth the poor souls in his arms, and encompasseth them with the power of God, and infuseth and floweth in with his love into them; which love preserveth and defendeth them from the anger of God, from sin, death, the devil, and hell.

33. This is a brief summary of the true ground, what the spirit of God hath prefigured and typified by the patriarchs, in that he hath led them so wonderfully, and hath thus alluded with the figure of Christ how it would come to pass afterwards.

34. For Jacob was now the stock, out of which the great and wide tree of Israel should spread abroad in the dividing of its branches, as a genealogy; therefore must he go away from his father's house, and take wives of his father's genealogy, viz. of Abraham's brother's son, that the people Israel, viz. the line of the Covenant, might come of one stock.

35. Now, when *Jacob awaked from the dream* of the divine vision, where the Lord appeared to him and established the Covenant, *he said, Surely the Lord is in this place; and I knew it not. And he was afraid, and said, How holy is this place! here is no other than the house of God, here is the gate of heaven* (Gen. xxviii. 16, 17). This is a figure, shewing how it would go with God's children, when God was manifest in them, that they continue to be in fear and trembling, and suppose God is afar off and hath forsaken them.

36. For where God withdraws himself in man, there will always sin and the anger of God be first manifested in that man, so that he will acknowledge and tremble at his sin, and enter into repentance; then appeareth to him God's friendly countenance and comforteth him. For if the soul goeth forth from sin, then God's grace entereth into it; and then it saith, Surely the Lord was with me in my anxiety, and I knew it not; now I see that the Lord is with the troubled heart, which is troubled in a divine zeal or jealousy, There is the place of God, and the gate of heaven.

37. Further it signifies, how the highest love of God in this Covenant in Christ would be immersed into our humanity; and how the

OF JACOB'S LADDER

humanity of Christ would be conversant in trouble, in that he took upon him all our trouble and misery; and how the humanity of Christ would be astonished before the anger of God and hell. As was in the mount of Olives, where in his agony he sweat a bloody sweat (Luke xxii. 39-44), and Christ in his humanity said, *Father, if it be possible, let this cup pass from me* (Matt. xxvi. 39); where instantly the gates of God appeared and comforted the humanity. As here to Jacob, when he must in trouble depart from his father's house, in fear and trembling at his brother Esau, who lay in wait to murder him. All which is a figure concerning Christ, when God's anger in our humanity did lie in wait to murder him, that he would be in an agony, heaviness and distress; and how he would pray to his Father, and how his Father would comfort him; all which was done before he was crucified,[1] especially in the mount of Olives, in which place this figure of Jacob was fulfilled.

38. And as *Jacob took the stone which he had laid under his head, and set it up for a remembrance, and poured oil thereupon* (Gen. xxviii. 18), so hath Christ set up his anguish or agony for a remembrance to us poor men, and poured forth his oil of joy and victory upon it in our troubled terrified hearts; and of that same stone[2] hath erected his Church for a continual remembrance; of all which this type of Jacob was a prefiguration.

39. Which Jacob signifieth in plain words where he saith, *If God will be with me, and defend me in the way which I travel, and give me bread to eat and clothes to put on, and bring me home with peace to my father, then shall the Lord be my God: And this stone, which I have set up for a pillar, shall be God's house, and of all which thou givest unto me I will give the tenth to thee* (Gen. xxviii. 20-22); where he clearly under this figure signifieth the Levitical, and afterwards the evangelical, priesthood, as it would be hereafter.

---

[1] Or, his Passion.
[2] Agony, and a troubled heart, because of sin.

The Fifty-Seventh Chapter

How *Jacob* came to *Laban*, and kept his sheep for him fourteen years for his two Daughters; what the Spiritual Figure of Christ's Bride contained under it signifieth. How God sets *Jacob* in Christ's figure, and so sporteth with the Type of Christ[1]

1. WHEN Jacob must now in sorrow go away from his parents, and so avoid his brother Esau, and commit himself to God in the blessing of him, then God brought him to his beloved bride, with whom he spent a while in joy with patience, till he returned again with great riches to his father.

2. This is first a worldly history and example,[2] under which the spiritual figure of the kingdom of Christ is represented, for if the poor sinner turn to God, then he attaineth, first of all the blessing, viz. the Baptism of Christ, whereby the Holy Ghost baptiseth him in the inward ground; and then[3] it setteth him in the process of Christ under the banner of his cross, and biddeth him go forth from his father's Adamical house of sin, and make towards the path of Christ's pilgrimage.

3. And there he must lay the hard stone of reason under his head, and rest and sleep upon this stone of reason; that is, reason must stand still, and the mind must in itself turn in to the grace of God in the most inward ground in highest humility, and most willingly enter upon the pilgrimage of Christ, as Jacob here did; and then meets him his most amiable bride and beautiful Rachel, viz. the noble Virgin Sophia of the divine wedlock enjoyment[4] in the love and humanity of Christ.

4. First he comes to the (Gen. xxix. 2) well, where the noble Sophia gives her sheep drink; that is, the soul is led to Christ's fountain, out of which the water of eternal life doth spring; there he first seeth and demandeth of the shepherds, where the noble Sophia

---

[1] Gen. xxix.   [2] Or, precedent.   [3] Secondly.
[4] Or, amorousness.

feedeth her flock. The shepherds signify the children of Christ, viz. teachers of the word of Christ, in whom the spirit of Christ is, who also feed his sheep. There the penitent man asketh for his eternal kindred and friends, viz. for the Paradisical house,[1] wherein his grandfather Adam dwelt; then those shepherds shew him that house, and also the beautiful Rachel, which is born in this house, viz. the noble Sophia.

5. Who, when the poor soul discovereth these things, looketh amiably upon the soul; whence the soul is kindled in great love, and rolleth away the great stone from the well, and giveth the sheep of noble Sophia drink (Gen. xxix. 10); that is, the soul rolleth away all its earthly lusts, which were a cover upon the wellspring of eternal life, and giveth drink and food to the poor needy sheep of Christ, the sheep of this noble Sophia, and kisseth the noble Sophia with its burning desire to the love of Christ.

6. And when the noble Virgin Sophia seeth this, and that the poor soul discovereth all its perils that it hath undertaken for her, then she runneth to her Father, and telleth him that her beloved suitor and friend is abroad with the sheep of Christ, and helpeth to give them drink. That is, the love of Christ presseth with the poor soul's desire into God the Father, and saith, This soul is my friend, my bridegroom. Then God the Father commandeth that he be brought into his house; as here Rachel did to Jacob, and told it to her father who Jacob was, and what his purpose was (Gen. xxix. 12). And so also Christ sheweth his Father what the poor, troubled, perplexed soul's purpose is, when it cometh to him.

7. And as Jacob was promised this Rachel for a spouse, for which he consented to keep the sheep seven years, and loved her dearly[2] (Gen. xxix. 19, 20), and yet afterwards, at the wedding, the other sister, with her tender eyes, was laid by him, which he desired not. So it goes also with Christ's children, when they turn to God and apply themselves to be shepherds of Christ's sheep, to take care of them,[3] then is the most amiable and beautiful Sophia promised and presented to them, whereat they find joy within them.

8. But when it cometh to pass that the soul thinks it will embrace this bride in its arms, and have perfect joy with her, then the other sister, viz. Leah, that is, the cross of Christ, is laid by it, and the beautiful Sophia hideth herself, and it must first take the cross of Christ for a spouse, and keep the sheep of Christ seven years more for

---

[1] Or, family.   [2] At his heart.   [3] Or, provide for them.

MYSTERIUM MAGNUM

Rachel, viz. for the noble Sophia, before he obtains her for his spouse.

9. For the humanity of Christ doth not presently give itself to the fiery soul for its own; but stayeth indeed in the betrothing[1] in the inward ground, in the image of the heavenly world's substance, which disappeared in Adam. But God the Father giveth the soul instead thereof, the other sister, viz. tenderness of heart, that the soul in this time may not sport in the garden of roses, but be in trouble and calamity, that it may be tried and humble, and always keep the sheep of Christ, and not in this marriage solace themselves in pleasures and pride, as Lucifer did.

10. And though it be so that this noble Rachel or Sophia be given in marriage to the soul, as is done to the stable children of Christ, so that the soul keeps this great wedding of joy with this bride (which they alone understand who have been guests at this wedding), yet afterwards the noble Sophia is as it were barren, the wedding joy passeth away, and the soul is as if the love of this bride were taken from it.

11. In the meanwhile (Gen. xxix. 31 et seq.) Leah, under the cross of Christ, breaketh forth and beareth fruit; that is as much as to say, when the soul receiveth[2] the spirit of Christ, then beginneth the great joy of this marriage, concerning which Christ saith, *There is more joy in heaven for one sinner that repenteth, than for ninety-nine righteous that need not this repentance* (Luke xv. 7).

12. For that is the wedding of the Lamb, that God and man is married, and Christ is born; and then he standeth in our poor and simple form[3] in our most inward ground, and hideth his great sweetness, which the soul tasted in the marriage, and covereth it with his cross; and then must the poor soul in the meanwhile take the tender Leah, viz. patience, and labour with her for fruit in the vineyard of Christ.

13. And it is very well that the soul faultereth with this Leah, and then this Rachel in the inward ground of the soul is a stranger, and is as a stranger towards it. As Rachel towards Jacob, when she said to him, *Give me[4] children, or else I die* (Gen. xxx. 1). So also the noble Sophia saith indeed to the soul, Work [or bring forth] in my love-desire divine fruit, or else I will depart from thee; whereas yet the soul cannot do it in its own power.

14. But this is therefore done that the soul may the more earnestly

---

[1] Or, promise of marriage.   [2] As a conception.
[3] Condition or disposition. [4] Create.

apply itself to prayer, and pray to God for the divine working of the divine fruit. As Jacob prayed to God, so that *Rachel was fruitful, and did bear unto him Joseph* (Gen. xxx. 22-24), the prince of all the land of Egypt, who preserved, fed, and nourished them in the famine.

15. So also when the noble Sophia seems barren to the soul, as if it could not bring forth the power of God in the soul, and yet the soul mourneth to God in patience [praying] that he would work in it and bless it; whereupon the soul often converteth in very great repentance, and casteth itself upon God's mercy, till this noble Sophia become stirring, fruitful, and pregnant; and so it certainly generateth the true Joseph, viz. a lowly, humble, chaste, temperate and modest soul; which afterwards becometh a prince over the Egyptian house of flesh and blood. In which house the heathenish Pharaoh dwelleth, viz. the bestial spirit. Over that is this Joseph set for a ruler and governor, and is a ruler over reason, and governeth it with Joseph's, viz. with God's, spirit.

16. This is thus, as to one part, the spiritual figure of Jacob, wherewith the spirit alludeth to the future kingdom of Christ, where now at present in the fulfilling it alludeth thus also in the children of Christ, and doth yet so always lead them.

17. But we see especially in this figure the way of God, how God's mind is far other than man's. What man loveth, in that God hideth himself; for that pleaseth him well which in the eye of the world is simple and despised, which dependeth on him alone, and feareth him.

18. Jacob loveth the beautiful Rachel, and desireth her. But the line of the Covenant, in which Christ should be born, would not pass through Rachel, but Leah; also Rachel could not conceive till Leah had brought forth the root or line of the kingly priesthood and princedom,[1] viz. Levi and Judah.

19. For the priesthood came from Levi, and out of Judah came the sceptre of the kingdom, and the Prince Christ according to the humanity; to signify that Christ will be born and manifested in these men alone, and bringeth and worketh his priesthood of the Holy Ghost in them, who go forth from the love of themselves, and the pleasure of the flesh, and are in the eye of the world softly, bashful, simple and despised; who esteem themselves unworthy of such honour, and do not account such divine working to be their own, and pride themselves therewith, as the proud Pharisees did, and still do.

[1] Principality.

20. For this Leah desireth only to bear children for Jacob, that she might be acceptable to him, seeing otherwise, in respect of her bleareyedness,[1] she was disregarded. Thus also the true children of God desire therefore only to walk in the divine power, with teaching[2] and a simple life in the ways of God, that they may please God and serve him.

21. And again: we see here by Jacob's seed that the line of Christ would not manifest itself in his first seed with Leah, that Christ might not be manifested in human pleasure or lasciviousness of fleshly lust. For Leah first bare Reuben (who defiled the bed[3] of his father) (Gen. xxix. 32), to signify that this root sprang from human lust.

22. But when Leah was discouraged, because she was despised, and would fain go out of that contempt, then she bare Simeon, who was of an acute wit,[4] of whom Jacob said, when he was to die, when he prophesied concerning all his children, from what root each of them was: *The brethren, Simeon and Levi, their swords are murdering weapons. My soul, come not into their counsel, and let not my honour be in their churches or assemblies* (Gen. xlix. 5, 6); to signify that he was sprung from the line of zeal or jealousy, wherein Leah was jealous and discontented that she was thus disesteemed, as she then said, *The Lord hath heard that I was thus disesteemed, and hath given me this [son] also* (Gen. xxix. 33).

23. But when she cried unto the Lord in her zeal for deliverance from her disesteem, then she was pregnant, and bare Levi (Gen. xxix. 34), viz. the root of the Levitical priesthood, a type of the kingdom of Christ. For she cried to God that her husband might be again joined to her in love, as she speaketh after this manner: *Now will my husband be joined to me again*; to signify that God, with the Levitical priesthood, in a type, would be joined again to man, and would, in a type of the kingdom of Paradise, dwell among them again, as was done in the time of Moses.

24. But the spirit of God said by Jacob, when he was about to die: *Let not mine honour come in their churches or assemblies*; that is, they are of murderous, Cainical minds, and serve me only in a figure, pointing at the future kingdom of Christ; but the spirit of my love and grace is not with them in their sacrifices and worship of God; which love and grace he calleth his *honour*, which he would manifest through the line of Judah, in Christ.

25. Which honour was, that he should break death in pieces, and

---

[1] Or, tender eyedness.　　[2] Instructing.　　[3] Marriage bed. Gen. xlix. 4.
[4] A strict, severe man. Text, a sharp, piercing mind.

destroy hell, and take away the throne of the devil in man. This the Holy Ghost calleth his honour; and that was not in the Levitical priesthood, nor among the titulary priests in their churches. But when Leah gave up her will wholly into the will of God, and said, *Now will I give thanks unto the Lord* (Gen. xxix. 35), who hath delivered me from the disgrace of the devil, and of the world, then she bare Judah, viz. the line of Christ.

26. So here now the spirit saith, very secretly and covertly under a veil, *And she left off from bearing* (Gen. xxix. 35). To signify that Christ was the last, who was the end and fulfilling of the Levitical law; under which the spirit signifieth that men would not find Christ in the priests' churches, laws, and ordinances of preaching. He would not dwell in their churches with his honour of victory, nor suffer himself and his honour to be tied to the houses of stone, where they exercise a hypocritical show, and have within them only murdering proud hearts, and with the murdering swords of Levi, disgrace and slay one another with words.

27. But in the souls of men, when they give thanks, and praise the Lord in great humility, as Leah did, when she bare Judah, the line of Christ; there will he dwell, and not be at all in the counsel of these priests and Levites, the titulary priests, who contrive only specious glistering ways for their honour and voluptuousness, and forget the true thanksgiving in humility, and honour and love themselves alone; and so give that honour to their feigned or supposed office, which belongeth to God alone, and to the love of our neighbour in great humility.

28. We see clearly by this figure that God will not manifest himself in the fleshly love of ourselves. For *Jacob loved Rachel more than Leah* (Gen. xxix. 30), and would have only Rachel in the beginning. But his seed must continue shut up with her, till Rachel humbled herself before God, and that Jacob prayed for her; to shew also that God will not work in the love of ourselves, in that we love and honour one another according to fleshly lust, worldly honour and riches, where men flock together, associate and love one another according to their greatness, state, riches, glory, beauty, bravery and pleasure of this world.

29. But the spirit of God requireth humble, faithful and sincere love, where the soul is resigned up into God, and seeketh not its own pleasure or self-love; but looketh upon the way of God, and joineth itself to the humble children, who love God and constantly give him

thanks. There God manifesteth himself, and worketh in them, that they bear fruit to the Lord.

30. Jacob first served seven years for Rachel, which he himself had chosen in his own love, yet she was not given to him for the first seven years' service; but Leah was, unknown to him, laid by him. Jacob desired Rachel as wages for his service: yet seeing the Covenant of the Lord lay in the line of Christ in him, therefore he first received the spiritual wages of the grace of God.

31. For Christ is the wages of God's children: As they must serve their Lord for worldly wages, so God first payeth them with his Covenant of grace, and then afterwards they receive also temporal wages: As Jacob must first receive the gift of God, as God appointeth it for him, though it went very ill, as to reason. Afterwards he also received the wages according to his will, for which he must serve yet seven years more.

32. Which seven years, in the inward ground in this figure, signify the seven properties of the natural life, which must be given up to the service of God, into which God gives himself for wages in a co-working power, where the seven forms of life first help the Lord to bear a spiritual figure and image or type, and to manifest the line of Christ. Then afterwards that same spiritual form discovereth also the natural form, and beareth a prince in the natural life, in whom God worketh, and through whom he ruleth the world; as is to be seen by Jacob.

33. He served seven years for Rachel, but seeing he feared God, the divine wages, viz. the line of Christ, was first given him. Afterwards God blessed also the human self-love, according to the kingdom of nature in him; so that of Rachel, whom he had taken in natural self-love, he begat a prince and wise man, even Joseph, by whom the spirit of God ruled, and made him a lord and governor.

34. And this figure presents to us that first Christ should be born in us, and so then Christ in us beareth also the natural man, with understanding and wisdom, and appointeth him to his service in the kingdom of nature, and also in the kingdom of grace; as he did Joseph.

The Fifty-Eighth Chapter

How *Jacob* served his Father-in-law[1] Twenty Years, and begat Twelve Sons and One Daughter, and how God blessed him, that he gat great Riches, and how *Laban* often changed his wages, and yet could not hurt him: What is to be understood thereby[2]

1. WE see in this history especially, how it goeth with the children of God in this world, how they must live in mere crosses and adversity, as Jacob did with his wives. For *when Rachel saw that she was barren, she envied Leah, her sister* (Gen. xxx. 1); to signify that man's own love seeketh not the honour of God, but itself; as now Rachel envied Leah because she had a name that God had blessed her, and said to Jacob, *Give me children also, if not, I die.*

2. Where we see how the ways of God are quite hidden to reason, although reason standeth in the figure of the divine wonders, as here Rachel, which here signifieth the own Adamical nature, which desireth of Jacob the life's power from the blessing of God, and if it get not the same it must die. Which indeed the spirit of zeal in her desire doth very well signify, according to her inward ground in the Covenant of God; but her reason understood it not, but only desired children, that she might be delivered from disgrace; but her inward ground stood hidden, and panted through the human nature to manifest itself in the human essence. Therefore the inward ground in the Covenant of grace signifieth, through its own Adamical essence, that if the inward ground should not be manifested through the human essence it must then die eternally. Therefore saith reason, *Give me children, or else I die*; which seemeth outwardly to be an opposition and discouragement: But the spirit of God hath here its figure, under which it hath its signification.

3. And then we see in both these sisters, who yet were daughters of God's Covenant in the Promise, how the poison of the Serpent, in

---

[1] Stepfather. [2] Gen. xxx.

the wrath of God in flesh and blood, so vehemently sets against the line of Christ in the Covenant, and always despiseth the same; and, as a proud Lucifer, elevates and puffeth up the rational human ownhood of self-will, and would have the dominion.

4. As here Rachel despiseth her sister because she was outwardly fairer and more beautiful than Leah, in that Leah, in the sight of the world, was simple and blear-eyed, and Rachel had the spirit of the world in reason elegantly, as an ornament. And so the Adamical nature in Rachel ruled over the manifested blessing of the Covenant in Leah; to signify that the line of Christ in this world would be manifested in a mean, simple and despised form in men of such-like dispositions.

5. Which men would, by the reason, pomp and beauty of the world, be esteemed fools and blear-eyed; who in such scorn and disregard would go away and sow in tears, but in their inward ground in the line of Christ would bear, and at the end reap in joy: to signify that *Christ's kingdom is not of this world* (John xviii. 36); that in this world it must be thrown into God's anger and disdain, and into death. And by this throwing-in, satiate the anger of God with love and meekness, and with love spring forth through the anger and death, and bring the proud Lucifer, in the human own-will and fleshly lust, to scorn, and to naught, as an unstable life; which life cannot overpower the divine humility.

6. Which humility springeth under all scorn, and also breaketh through death and the anger of God, and maketh death to be life, and taketh from hell the victory, and changeth the sting of the false Serpent's essence with sweet love. As we see here by Leah, although she was envied by her sister, as by reason, yet the line of Christ in the Covenant springeth forth in her under all scorn, and maketh her fruitful, and Rachel barren, till she gave her maid to her husband for a wife. Which signifieth the Adamical, viz. the servile line, which in the kingdom of Christ attaineth the marriage of the line of Christ in the manner of a servant.

7. For Adam hath negligently forfeited the line. The right of nature in the kingdom of God was lost in Adam, and attaineth in the manner of a servant to the marriage, as the maids of Jacob's wives did. Whereby we then see that Rachel, viz. the right self-nature, could not work or bring forth fruit till the line of servitude (under the yoke of the Adamical nature of self-love) did first become fruitful. To signify that the human nature must give itself up to be a servant under the

HOW JACOB SERVED HIS FATHER-IN-LAW

line of Christ; if it will be married in the line of Christ, and be engrafted as an heir of God.

8. And then first springeth forth the kingdom of nature in the kingdom of God, and in the blessing becometh fruitful. As Rachel was first fruitful when her maid had brought forth; to signify that Rachel also must be a handmaid to the Covenant of God and the line of Christ. And that the line of Christ in her also [must] be her Lord; so that she also attaineth the marriage of Christ's line in the manner of a handmaid; and that she had not the line of Christ in her in self-power by the right of nature, but as a gift bestowed of grace, that standeth in another Principle.

9. And signifieth under it that the line of Christ was not propagated in human self-ability, but that itself doth press into their branches, and that the great or high name or stock[1] or tribe of men is not respected; but it presseth as soon upon the meanest and most miserable in the world (which are but servants and handmaids), as upon the most high and noble.

10. As we have a powerful example of this in Jacob, who must be in a servile condition twenty years as a servant, till the twelve stocks of the tribes of Israel were begotten by him. To signify that a Christian must be born under the servile yoke of the corrupt, domineering, self-willed Adamical nature; but if any should as a Christian be born of the line of Christ, then must the parent[2] be given up as a servant to God, and be in the kingdom of nature, only as a servant of God, who in his heart forsaketh all temporal things, and accounts nothing his own, and in his condition and employment esteemeth himself but as a servant, who serveth his Lord therein.

11. As Jacob, who under this service of his begat the stocks or tribes of Israel, signifieth that they should be strange guests in this world, and serve God their Lord in the kingdom of nature therein, who himself would vote[3] them their wages; that they should with great riches go out of this world and enter into the kingdom of Christ, viz. into their first Adamical Paradisical native country, as Jacob in his service got his stepfather's goods, with great blessing.

The inward spiritual figure standeth thus:

12. When Adam was fallen he must go forth out of Paradise, and yield up himself to be a servant under the spirit of the world in the

[1] Stock, family or genealogy.   [2] Mother.   [3] Promise or appoint.

kingdom of this world, and be subject to the stars and the four elements, and serve them in their dominion, and provide for and take care of their children, viz. the creatures of this world, as we see before our eyes.

13. But when he was to go out of Paradise, as Jacob out of his father's house, the Lord meets him, and sheweth him the entrance in again into Paradise, through the seed of the woman, and destroyer of the serpent; as he shewed the same also to Jacob, by the ladder which reached to heaven (Gen. xxviii. 12).

14. And when Adam was gone out of Paradise, then he must submit himself to be a servant under a strange yoke, and serve the kingdom of nature in its wonders, and provide for or take care of the children of nature, which kingdom of nature in the fall became strange to him, in that it now holds him by constraint, and vexeth him with heat and cold, sickness and misery, and holdeth him captive in itself, and useth him in its service, which before was his best friend and patron.[1]

15. And as Jacob in this figure must flee to his friend, his mother's brother, and serve him whom he kept as a servant, and yet also, in respect of his daughter, as a son-in-law; so also must Adam serve under the servile yoke of his great father,[2] viz. the kingdom of nature, which kingdom gave him its daughter to wife; of whom under this yoke he begat the children of God in the blessing of God, and also placeth his children as ministering servants in his father's house, viz. in the kingdom of this world.

16. And as Jacob obtained great riches in the blessing of God, and acquired the goods of his master with subtlety, in that he subtly used the half-peeled, streaked sticks before the drinking troughs, where the sheep drank, upon which they conceived, and brought forth ring-straked[3] sheep, particoloured (Gen. xxx. 37 et seq.); so also when Adam was come under the servile yoke of the kingdom of nature, wherein also the envy and subtlety of the devil domineered according to the kingdom of wrath, God shewed him that he should with subtlety acquire to himself the kingdom of nature, viz. the working of nature, with its wonders; and procure the power of nature for an eternal propriety, that his works, which he operates in the kingdom of nature, must follow him into his eternal native country, and be his own.

17. Which subtlety was that which God shewed him, viz. the Destroyer of the Serpent, which Adam put on in the Covenant, which

---

[1] Text, grandfather.   [2] Text, grandfather.   [3] Pied or spotted.

HOW JACOB SERVED HIS FATHER-IN-LAW

put on the kingdom of nature [assumed] from us men, and with divine subtlety took away the strength and power of our lord and master, viz. of the kingdom of God's wrath, which held us captive under its yoke, and put on all human power, and took away our lord and master's own power, viz. the kingdom of nature's own power, as Jacob took his lord and master's goods.

18. And as the spirit of *God shewed Jacob in the vision that the he-goats and rams that leaped upon the goats and sheep were ringstraked, speckled, and grisled* (Gen. xxxi. 10): so was Adam also shewn, in the spirit of the Covenant of promise, how the spirit of grace in the Covenant came upon the streaked, particoloured human nature, and blessed it, so that it became pregnant of the spirit of the Covenant.

19. Which human, streaked or particoloured nature is no other than the half-earthly, corrupt, and again in the Covenant, new-born heavenly nature. Upon this came the spirit of God as to the heavenly part, and made it fruitful, so that under the earthly yoke it drew the power of nature in the divine power into the heavenly; and so was his master's or lord's, viz. the kingdom of nature's, goods taken away, and the heavenly man in the Covenant gat them to himself with the divine wit and subtlety, and returned therewith from his lord and master, viz. the kingdom of the outward nature, again into his Father's house, viz. into Paradise, as Jacob into his father's house.

The figure is fundamentally thus:

20. In Adam the kingdom of nature lay in the temperature, that is, all properties were of equal weight. But when the will of the soul went with subtlety into the separation, then the properties were stirred up, and the temperature was broken. And then the separation was his lord and master, and held the will captive as a servant, who now must serve this master.

21. But when God spake or inspired again his grace with the Covenant of love thereinto, then the inward, inspoken or inspired ground of grace drew the kingdom of nature with its wonders to it; and came away with the riches and self-might, and brought them again, with the inward new man, into Paradise.

22. For the riches of the natural outward mortal man, in that it bringeth forth the wonders of God with its exercise, doth not belong to the kingdom of nature as its proper own, but to the inward spiritual new man, born of Christ; he shall draw these wonders to him, and take

them with him to be an eternal vision and contemplation of the wonders of God.

23. When the body of the outward nature falleth away, then shall the works follow the new man as a treasure, which he hath gotten to himself by divine wit and subtlety, and put off the evil Adamical nature's house of self-rule and dominion. As Jacob, who stood in the figure of the new spiritual man, with whom the spirit of God alludeth in the prefiguration to the future kingdom of Christ. Shewing how Christ would obtain all the goods of this world, and all the riches of the power and might of nature, in the formed, expressed[1] word of God, under his servitude, wherein he yielded himself up to be a servant of God in the kingdom of nature; and so make himself lord and master over it, and bring it with him into his eternal kingdom in our assumed humanity; and lastly manifest it at the end of the day of this world, and give it us again in our Father's first house.

24. Thus we should not at all look upon this figure in Jacob as if God had bidden Jacob to deceive his father-in-law with subtlety, and bereave him of that which was his, as if God had pleasure in the natural false subtlety of man. No, the spiritual subtlety is only represented in the figure, shewing how we shall obtain, in the kingdom of Christ, *the unrighteous mammon* (Luke xvi. 9–11), which we have not as by a natural right, but obtain it by the divine wit. And then *the kingdom of heaven suffereth violence, and they that use violence take it*[2] *by force* (Matt. xi. 12), with such wit of divine science, knowledge or skill, as Jacob did in the figure of Christ's kingdom.

25. And it is shewn to the Jews (who with this figure help themselves in their subtlety and earthly fraud and treachery), that this subtlety of Jacob prefigureth a spiritual type, and doth not at all cover their wickedness and falsehood.

26. For he that saith, *Thou shalt not covet* or lust after *that which is thy neighbour's* (Exod. xx. 17), hath forbidden all outward subtlety, fraud and deceit; but in the genealogies the spirit of God hath thus, with the kingdom of Christ, signified and alluded in the figure at the inward ground of the new man, with an outward figure.

27. As with Ishmael, Abraham's first son, from whom the goods also were taken away. To signify that they belonged not to Adam in the corruption and perdition, but to Christ, as the second Adam, which he took with divine wit and subtlety from the kingdom of God's wrath in man; where he must first be subject to the wrath of

---

[1] Or outspoken.   [2] Tear and snatch it.

HOW JACOB SERVED HIS FATHER-IN-LAW

God, and serve in the assumed human nature; yet so he obtained the goods, and took away all its goods: and that is it which this figure of Jacob signifieth.

28. The spirit presenteth here a most wonderful figure, in Jacob, shewing how Laban changed his wages ten times, and yet could not hurt him (Gen. xxxi. 7). To signify how it is with the children of God in this service, that under the yoke of nature they shall acquire the goods of the kingdom of nature in the divine wit in the inward new man. Thence happeneth such great alteration to man in his purposes, so that when he hath resolved upon the course that he will take, the devil comes with his envy, and hindereth him of his purpose by evil men, that it goeth not forward. As Jacob, when he thought the speckled sheep and goats shall be my wages, then his master disappointed him of his wages.

29. So it is also with the children of God in their labour and travail, when they think, now they shall reap the blessing of God, now they will apply themselves to the children of God, with whom they may work and bring forth fruit, and there they will effect their good purposes,[1] and comprehend this work in their faith's desire, that it *may follow after them* (Rev. xiv. 13). Then will everywhere all his work and purposes be broken, so that it goeth not according to his meaning and will: he must now trust and rely upon God alone, as Jacob did. And so no enemy can hurt him; and though it seems as if it would hurt him, and that his work should be vain, yet thus they work and bear fruit, incomprehensible to reason. And in the end that man departeth with much goods out of the kingdom of this world, and returneth again into his native country, as Jacob did.

30. For the Scripture saith, The works of the children of God follow after their faith; they take them with them; they are the wages of their faith (Rev. xiv. 13). The faith taketh Christ into itself, and Christ taketh the works of faith with him; and thus a true Christian returneth home again into his native country, with much goods, which he hath introduced and laid up in hope with his faith's desire.

31. Which hope God filleth for him in Christ with the heavenly ens, and taketh also herewith his works of nature, and draweth them to itself for an eternal wages, which is Christ, with the expressed[2] word, viz. the kingdom of nature, wherein lieth the wonders and being of man, kept to God's Great Day of Separation, wherein *every one shall reap what he hath here sown* (Gal. vi. 7).

[1] Text, do good.   [2] Or outspoken.

32. When we rightly view and consider this history, how God did begin the kingdom of Israel with a servile shepherd, and exalted him before all the potent rich men on earth, even to eternity; and consider that the twelve stocks or tribes of Israel were begotten under a servile yoke, as servants (out of which stock Christ, according to the humanity, was to be born); so we see that all highness of the world, also all art and wit of nature, is foolish in the sight of God, wherewith yet men so boast and esteem their worldly matters, doings or pomp, and their high state, for great things; and yet in the sight of God, are not by far so acceptable as an honest shepherd.[1]

33. A shepherd, in whom the spirit of God worketh, is more highly esteemed before God than the wisest and most potent in self-wit, without the divine dominion. And we see very well how God erecteth his kingdom in simple, lowly and mean men, who are not esteemed by the world, but are accounted in the eye of the world no better than herdsmen. As Christ also chose such for his Apostles who were but poor, mean, contemptible people, by whom he manifested the kingdom of Israel in divine power.

34. Where are the learned and worldly-wise men? Again, where are the potent lords, who contemn the simple? where is their might, strength, art, and wit? They must all come, in dust and ashes, and fall down to the simplicity of such shepherds, and bow their hearts in servitude under Christ's yoke, if they will be partakers of the line of these shepherds. Yea, they must be as the maids of Jacob's wives, if they will come to this marriage.

35. For the line of Christ in the beginning was manifested in Abel, a shepherd. So also afterwards, in Abraham, Isaac, and Jacob, Moses and David, they were all but shepherds when the line of Christ was manifested. There is no potentate, noble, rich, learned, or high worldly-wise, hath attained it; but mean people of no account, who have put their trust in God.

36. Where are now the high priests, schools, and universities, who ascribe to themselves and assume the authority and power of these Mysteries, and often tread underfoot the gifts of the Holy Ghost in such shepherds, and laugh at them, and count them fools? Are they not, all of them, Cain, Ishmael, and Esau, of the left line from the kingdom of this world's nature, in the hypocrisy of self-reason? which in the sight of God is not so acceptable as a shepherd.

37. O ye poor blind men in Adam! cast your eyes down from

---

[1] Like unto an honest shepherd.

above, and lay yourselves low under the simplicity of Christ, in the line[1] of these shepherds, and look not upon the pomp of art and loftiness, or you will be miserably deceived. If you will be capable of this line, you must not attain it from loftiness, which boasteth itself in hypocrisy in this office of a [pastor or] shepherd; but in humility and mean simplicity, where the soul submitteth itself under Christ's yoke: there will the poor soul, blind as to God, get root in this marriage, and be capable of this line.

38. The twelve children of Jacob are even the lines, which the spirit of God, from Adam to Noah and his children, signified, which sprang from the line of the Covenant in Paradise, and pressed from Adam to Abel, and so on to the children of Noah; and there also twelve lines or stocks [or tribes] were manifested. Here the same tree openeth itself again out of one stock, which was Jacob; and signifieth how those lines should all be sanctified in one stock; which stock is Christ, who also chose him twelve Apostles to manifest this tree, which was grown out of the line of the Covenant.

39. And as Jacob begat these twelve sons, *he begat also a daughter, Dinah by name* (Gen. xxx. 21), *who went out to see the daughters of the land* (Gen. xxxiv. 1), and thereby lost her honour and virginity; and he begat her of Leah, in whom the line was manifested out of the stock [or tribe] of Judah, to signify that the line of Christ at this time as yet stood hidden in the woman's tincture, and yet was manifest through the masculine, viz. the fiery tincture, till Mary, the mother of Christ. As we see in the Covenant of Abraham, Isaac, and Jacob, that the Covenant pressed forward in their seed; we see it also in the circumcision, which was given only to the man [or male].

40. And much more do we see in the Law on Mount Sinai, which was also given in a way of fire; to signify that men, before Christ, were led in the Father's property, which held us captive in the wrath, till his love, viz. his Son, through the wrath, manifested himself in the woman's tincture, and changed the man's and the woman's tincture into one again: therefore the line of Christ, with the Father's, sprang forth in the woman's tincture through the man's.

41. In the man's tincture it was stirring in the Covenant of faith in Abraham, and was manifest out of the man's tincture in the woman. But in the fullness[2] of time it was manifest in Mary, in the woman's tincture, viz. in the highest love; in which love Adam loved himself before his Eve [was], for God was manifest therein.

[1] Or, true succession. [2] Fulfilling.

42. There we see here in Dinah a figure of Eve, for after Leah had borne six sons, she bare a daughter, which signifieth the female tincture, which in her vain curiosity squandered[1] away her honour; as Eve would see and know the daughters of the world, viz. the bestial creaturely lust, and in this lust lost the Paradisical virginity.

43. Thus the spirit of God here in Dinah sets a figure of Eve near the line of the Covenant, seeing he who should seek and save the poor children of Eve should come out of the line of the Covenant.

44. For Leah did bear six sons, which signify the six properties of the natural life, and the seventh is the substance or corporeity of the six; in which spiritual substance Adam died or was extinguished as to the kingdom of God, when his will brake itself off from God. And that same seventh property of nature is now even the woman, viz. the mother wherein the other six are continually borne, which rightly signifieth the Adamical Eve, when Eve was yet in an image or type in Adam.

45. The figure whereof the spirit of God represents in Dinah with Jacob, signifying how that seventh property of nature in Adam is become a whore, perfidious to God; and sets this figure near the line of Christ, [signifying] that Christ should come and change this whore, viz. the seventh property of the human life, into the virginity again.

46. Therefore was Christ born of a virgin, that he might sanctify the woman's tincture again, and change it into the man's tincture, that the man and the woman might again be one image of God, and no more man and woman, but masculine virgins, as Christ was.

47. In Rachel we see now the self-love of the kingdom of nature, where both tinctures, the masculine and the feminine, according to the kingdom of nature in self-love, bind themselves in conjunction; as Jacob loved Rachel according to the kingdom of nature, according to the tincture of self-love, and on the other side so did Rachel love Jacob. Therefore must these tinctures of natural self-love be so long shut up and bring forth no life, till *the Lord remembered Rachel, and heard her* (Gen. xxx. 22), as the text in Moses saith. That is, till the Lord stirred up the tinctures of the kingdom of nature with his blessing, then she bare a prince in the kingdom of nature, viz. JOSEPH, in whom we see, by his great chastity and fear of God, that the blessing of God stirred up the tinctures of the kingdom of nature, which

---

[1] Or, trifled.

HOW JACOB SERVED HIS FATHER-IN-LAW

lay shut up in the seeds, and manifested the Covenant of grace therein.

48. For Christ should deliver from wrath the kingdom of nature in man; therefore also the spirit in this figure presenteth an image or type in Joseph, which it sets down also in the figure of Christ's humanity, how it would go in the future with Christ's humanity, which he took from us men.

49. In Leah Christ was represented according to his heavenly hidden humanity, shewing how the heavenly world's substance would be hidden in our humanity under the yoke of God's anger, and how Christ must appear in a servile and contemptible form.

50. In Rachel with Joseph now the figure is represented, which sheweth how he would overcome, and in our human nature should be a Lord and Prince over all his enemies, who have held us poor men in flesh and blood captive; and how he would bring us forth out of the misery and famine of Adam, into a good land, and not remember how we in this world have cast him into the pit, as Joseph's brethren cast Joseph.

51. The spirit of God presents this figure in the twelve patriarchs, as a glass, to see by whom God was atoned in his anger, pointing at the future fulfilling, for the text in Moses speaketh very hiddenly in this figure, and saith, *Now when Rachel had borne Joseph, Jacob said to Laban, Let me depart and travel to my own place, and into my country. Give me my wives and my children, for whom I have served thee, that I may go* (Gen. xxx. 25, 26).

The inward spiritual figure is thus:

52. When the blessing of Jacob, viz. Christ, in the kingdom of the human nature was manifest, so that man stood in Christ's image, then he desireth to return from the servitude of this house wherein he must serve, and go again to his Father's first house, and desireth to take with him his fruits, viz. his children, brethren and sisters, and all the children of this birth; he hath a great longing after that, as Jacob had after his father's house. But the Lord saith to him, Stay and serve here a while, and feed my sheep, *appoint the wages that I shall give thee* (Gen. xxx. 28); that is, ask of me, so will I give it thee, as Christ saith, *Whatsoever ye ask the Father in my name, he will give it you* (John xvi. 23).

53. Thus then this Jacob demerseth himself in humility, and keepeth the sheep of Christ, in hope of the eternal wages, which

followeth after him; for in Joseph, that is, in Christ, the wages will be first given him; as Joseph was the wages of Jacob in the outward kingdom, and preserved and nourished him and his house in the famine. Which signifieth Christ, who will eternally nourish us in himself, and bring us home with him into his Father's house, as Joseph brought his father and children into his lord's country.

The Fifty-Ninth Chapter

How *Jacob* departed from *Laban*: What this Figure signifieth, and what is to be understood thereby[1]

1. IN this chapter for the most part is the outward history set forth, under which yet the spirit hath its secret figure wherewith it playeth, for the text saith, *And the words of the children of Laban came before Jacob, saying, Jacob hath gotten all our father's goods to himself, and of our father's goods hath he procured this riches. And Jacob looked upon Laban's countenance, and saw that it was not towards him as formerly* (Gen. xxxi. 1, 2).

2. This is a figure represented in the spirit of Christ. When the spirit of Christ in man hath gotten the kingdom of the human nature to himself, then the envy of the Serpent in the wrath of nature in flesh and blood awaketh, understanding and feeling that the power of nature in man is taken away from him, and opposeth the spirit of Christ in the power of nature.

3. Then proceedeth the opposite will in man, so that the poor soul is everywhere faint and in an agony, perceiving that it dwelleth among strange goods, and that the devil is its neighbour, and hath a continual access to its own nature, and opposeth the soul, because it hath, in Christ's spirit, taken away from him the kingdom of nature, viz. the land and country which he had for his possession. And therefore the mortal nature in the wrath of God sets its desire and endeavour against the poor soul, as a stranger, unfriendly, when it seeth that it looseth its voluptuous earthly inheritance (which right is intimated in the children of Laban, where reason looketh to get temporal honour and pleasure), that all its natural right is taken away, as Jacob by subtlety took away Laban's goods.

4. Then thus saith God to the soul, as here he did to Jacob, *Return again into thy father's country, to thy kindred: I will be with thee* (Gen. xxxi. 3). That is, the poor soul should enter again into its first country of its father, viz. into the eternal Word, out of which it proceeded; and therein God blesseth it, and therein it can also call its

---

[1] Gen. xxxi.

children and members, and bring them along out of the servile house of God's anger in the kingdom of nature, as Jacob called his wives and his children, and brought them out of the servitude of his father. Thus also the enlightened soul bringeth the power of its life in the kingdom of nature, together with its fellow-members, out of the servile house of flesh and blood, again into the first house, viz. into God's Word.

5. And as *Jacob did flee* from the servile house of his stepfather, and *Laban pursued after and would hurt him* (Gen. xxxi. 21–23), so also in like manner is done to the children of Christ, when they begin to flee out of the servile house of Satan, viz. out from fleshly pleasure and voluptuousness, and would again enter into its first land of its father, viz. into righteousness and the fear of God. Then instantly the fleshly crew of the wicked world, with rage and folly pursue after it and would slay it, and take away with evil and false tongues all its riches and goods in God's righteousness.

6. But the Lord aweth them, that they cannot do it (as was done to Laban), though they stand up and reprove the children of God as unrighteous, because they turn away from their idols and abominations, and follow their hypocrisy no more, neither will they bear their evil yoke any more, and serve them in their unrighteousness, and call their falsehood, good. As the present world playeth the hypocrite under this yoke, and serveth their wickedness only that their god Mäusim may live and be fat.

7. The spirit of God here also presenteth a figure, shewing how Christ would for a while put himself under this servile yoke in the kingdom of nature, and would betroth to him Adam's daughter, that is, our flesh and blood, and acquire to himself Adam's possessions, goods and riches, viz. the kingdom or dominion of the human nature; that is, draw many men to him, and in the end go therewith out of this servile house of this world, again into his Father's eternal house, in which departure to his Father would the devil and the wicked world scorn him and quite slay him, and would take away and rob him of his goods, as also of his children which he hath here begotten. Even as the devil, by the Pharisees and wicked Jews, did, who would take away and rob Christ of all his faithful children, as Laban pursued and hunted after Jacob, and would take away his purchased goods from him again.

8. But as *God would not suffer Laban to hurt Jacob*, (Gen. xxxi. 7), so God would not suffer the devil and the wicked high priests to rob Christ of his purchased goods. Although they slew his outward

HOW JACOB DEPARTED FROM LABAN

humanity, yet he rose again from the dead, and brought his purchased goods into his Father's country.

9. The spirit of Moses representeth in this chapter a wonderful figure, which ought well to be observed, because he intimates a secret mystery under it: For he saith, *When Jacob did flee away from Laban, Rachel had stolen away her father's idol gods*: and further saith, *Thus Jacob stole away the heart of Laban the Syrian, in that he told him not that he fled*: and we see further, *how Laban, when he came to Jacob, was eager after his idol gods, and searched all Jacob's household stuff for his idol gods*. Also we see in this text, *how Rachel was she that loved those idol gods*, and sat upon them, and so hid them that her father could not get them again (Gen. xxxi. 19, 20, 30, 33, 34).

10. In these words there is represented to us an outward and an inward figure, shewing how it would go with Israel in the future. For these idol gods were not heathenish idols, according to the constellation or star (Acts vii. 43) Moloch, as the heathen had. But as we read, they made images, monuments, statues or pictures of their friends that were dead, as a pattern for instruction, which images among the heathen afterwards were turned to idols; and these might well be such images of his kindred that were dead, which Laban was loath to lose, because they were patterns of instruction, and memorials to him of his ancestors and deceased kindred whom he loved.

11. But the true figure under which the spirit pointeth at the future, is this: First, That Israel would not continually cleave to God with their whole heart, but would always take these idol gods of fleshly self-love along with them, and love themselves and their images, viz. genealogies of human greatness, state, high birth and noble pedigrees of gentility, more than God, even as it came to pass.

12. Especially this departure of Jacob intimates the departure of Israel out of Egypt into the promised land, when they took with them also their fleshly idol gods, and presently after *served their own idol gods* (1 Sam. viii. 8), viz. human greatness; and forsook their God, and regarded their Mammon, and would have *kings among them according to the custom of the heathen* (1 Sam. viii. 19), and forsook their right King, who had brought them out of Egypt.

13. Secondly, It intimates how Christ, in whose figure Jacob stood, would take to him this Rachel in our flesh and blood, viz. these, in Adam, idol-wills of the soul turned away from God, which hath acquired to itself images and idols, and possessed them as Rachel; and would bring the averted wills of the soul, with their acquired idols

and images, out of the idol's house or temple, which idols, viz. idol-wills and desires, must afterwards be all broken to pieces in the death of Christ.

14. As presently the figure is represented to us, when God said to Jacob, *Arise, and go to Bethel, and dwell there: and make there an altar to God, who appeared to thee when thou fleddest from thy brother Esau. Then said Jacob to his household, and to all that were with him, Put away from you the strange gods that are among you, and cleanse you and change your garments: And let us arise, and go to Bethel; that I may there make an altar to God, that heard me in the time of my trouble, and hath been with me in the way which I have gone* (Gen. xxxv. 1-3).

15. Which history of Jacob signifieth nothing else but this, viz. when Christ would with this Rachel's idol gods, viz. our flesh and blood, depart from this servile house, and go to his Father, then he would by his going forth, when he should build the high altar before God (which altar is himself), lay off these our idols in human self-will, viz. every imagination of self-love, before the altar of God in his death, and cleanse our hearts, viz. our soul's will, and change our garments, viz. our flesh and blood; as this text in the thirty-fifth chapter clearly signifies, and wholly intendeth it, that Christ would offer us up upon that same Altar of his New Testament, to the God who appeared to us again in our trouble and misery after the fall, in his Covenant of grace.

16. But that the text of Moses saith, *Jacob stole away the heart of Laban the Syrian, in that he secretly fled away with his daughters* (Gen. xxxi. 20, 21): it hath the very same inward spiritual figure contained in it. For *the Word became man*, and took Laban's, viz. the earthly Adam's daughters, and brought them by divine subtlety away out of Adam's house into God's house, which in that place is called *stealing*, in that the children of Adam are thus stolen from the kingdom of God's wrath, that is, brought away in the divine wit and subtlety.

17. For the anger of God had possessed men in the right of nature, but Christ came and married with them, and stole them, together with the idol gods, away from the anger, and offered them up to God upon his Altar, which is himself, and laid off the images of man's self-love, and cleansed our garments before God, that we might serve him at this Altar.

18. This is properly understood concerning Rachel's idol gods: the figure indeed sets down only the outward history, but the spirit of God hath its figure under it. For the whole history of Abraham,

HOW JACOB DEPARTED FROM LABAN

Isaac and Jacob stands inwardly in the figure of Christ; for the covenant between Laban and Jacob, and all that happened therein, is a figure of Christ; for Laban here standeth in the figure of the kingdom of nature, and Jacob in the figure of Christ.

19. *Laban upbraids Jacob, that he fled from him, and did not suffer him first to kiss his children, and that he might conduct them on their way with mirth and with tabrets* (Gen. xxxi. 27, 28). Thus also doth nature with the children of Christ, when they secretly flee from it, and forsake the idol's house [or temple]; then the children of nature's kingdom upbraid these children of Christ, for fickle forsworn people, for heretics, novellists, new lights, enthusiasts, or whatsoever sect can be named. And say unto them, When you will depart from your wicked way and enter into another life, why do you not tell it to our high priests, that they may lead you onwards with their ceremonies, viz. confession, sacraments, intercessions? Why do you not observe the usage of the Churches, where the kingdom of Christ is in mirth, with roaring, organs, and pipes? Why do you steal away from us secretly, and go another way than our ordinances and decrees prescribe? and therefore are enemies unto them, persecute them, and hunt them with censurings and disgraces, as evil children and forsworn, which had robbed them of their idol gods, and will not honour their hypocrisies for gods; as Laban pursued after Jacob and upbraideth him, because he had not first kept that pageantry and solemnity, and told him beforehand that he would travel and be gone.

20. Thus Babel also would fain have it, that the children of Christ should only enter in to God through their pageantries and solemnities, and belly-ordinances; and whosoever will enter in to God otherwise than through their ordinances, and flee from this servile house [of bondage], he is damned and cannot come to God.

21. But Jacob can well go to his father without Laban's pageantry and solemnity; and though he upbraid Jacob and calleth his way wrong, yet his way was right in the sight of God. For God had commanded him so, and Laban could not withhold him at all. So also Christ's children, when the spirit of Christ in them commandeth them to flee out from Babel, cannot be withheld; also it doth not hurt them, though the world blameth them never so for it, and scorn, deride, disgrace, and upbraideth them for fools, heretics, and enthusiasts.

22. Yet the Most High reproveth and chargeth Laban that he speak not otherwise to Jacob than friendly;[1] that is, the disdain[2] of

---

[1] Courteously and kindly.   [2] Blasphemies, reproach, misusage.

Babel towards the children of Christ must, in the end, turn to their mere joy and kindness, and now Laban must let them depart with their goods and riches. For God commandeth his children to flee from Babel (Rev. xviii. 4), and to go into the first country of their father (out of which they are departed with Adam), not through the solemnity and pageantry of Babel, but through the conversion of the mind and will: viz. a new obedience.

23. For God hath as much pleasure in the solemnity and pageantry of Babel, as in Laban's tabret and piping. He requires a penitent, converting heart, which in highest simplicity and humility, without any solemnity or pageantry, draweth near unto him, and departeth from Babel: with such a one he goeth along and blesseth him.

24. For *when Jacob was gone forth*, without solemnity and pageantry, *then the angels of God met him, whom he called God's host* (Gen. xxxii. 1, 2); which signifieth that when the children of God go forth from human inventions[1] and imaginations, and account all earthly things as nothing, and slip away from the hypocrisy of all their titulary brethren, then they get the angels of God for a guard, who go along with them, and lead them on their way in their going out from Babel, as here was done to Jacob.

25. For as soon as Christ is born in a man, so that the mind goeth forth out of the Adamical servile house of images,[2] then the angels of God are appointed his guardians.

---

[1] Trifles, fables, chimeras, fantasies. [2] Or imaginary conceits.

The Sixtieth Chapter

How *Esau* went to Meet *Jacob*, with four hundred Men, Soldiers: what this signifieth. And how *Jacob* sent a Present to his Brother *Esau*; and how a Man wrestled with him the whole Night. What all this meaneth[1]

FOR THE READER HIGHLY TO CONSIDER OF

1. MOSES saith, *And Jacob sent messengers before him to his brother Esau into the land of Seir, in the borders of Edom. And commanded them, saying, Tell my lord Esau thus, Thy servant Jacob saith thus, I have been long abroad with Laban until this time: and I have oxen, and asses, sheep, menservants, and womenservants: and I have sent forth to thee my lord to tell thee, that I might find grace in thine eyes. The messengers returned again to Jacob, and said, We came to thy brother Esau, and he also cometh to meet thee, with four hundred men. Then Jacob feared very much, and was in distress: and divided the people that were with him, and the sheep and oxen, and the camels, into two companies; and said, If Esau come upon one company, and smiteth it, the rest will escape* (vv. 3–8).

2. This whole chapter stands eminently in the figure of Christ. For when the Word was become Man, and would now go forth from this world and with our humanity possess his eternal mansion, then meets him this host of soldiers in the kingdom of nature in the anger of God.

3. For the kingdom of nature, viz. the natural Adam, was the firstborn Esau, which was angry with Jacob, that is, with Christ, for the blessing and heavenly inheritance, viz. for the eternal life; because it must die, and lose its right; in which kingdom the anger of God had gotten the dominion. That same anger of God came to meet Christ, when he was about to bring his acquired goods into the eternal country of his Father, viz. into the love of God; as Esau did Jacob, in the type or image of the figure. And Christ was astonished at this warrior, viz. the anger of God, as may be seen on the mount of Olives: as Jacob was astonished at the anger of Esau.

4. And as Jacob divided the herds into two parts, because of the

---
[1] Gen. xxxii.

wrath of Esau, that if Esau should smite one company the other might escape: so also was the humanity of Christ divided into two substances, viz. into a heavenly, whereof he speaketh, saying, *He was come from Heaven, and was then in Heaven* (John iii. 13); and also into an earthly, from our flesh and blood; that if the anger of God did smite the one part, viz. our humanity, with death, yet the heavenly part should escape the wrath, and penetrate through death, and therein make our humanity living. For the messengers which Jacob sent to Esau are nothing else but the prayers of Christ, which he sent through the anger of God into his love, viz. into the mercy, that our humanity might find grace and favour with God.

5. For as Jacob sent to Esau, saying he had been long abroad with Laban, even till this time, and had with him menservants and womenservants, and camels, with other cattle; that he might with all this find grace and favour with his lord Esau: so also Christ saith to his Father, in our humanity (viz. in Adam) which he hath assumed, he hath been long abroad absent from the kingdom of God, and hath brought forth,[1] in the kingdom of this world in God's works of wonder, many images out of the divine wisdom through the formation of nature, that he might with these formations of wonders find grace and favour with God, seeing these wonders were brought forth through the nature of his manifested wrath; that so they might come to the eternal divine vision and contemplation.

6. But the anger went to meet him in the four elements, and would devour the earthliness and evil of them. For Esau's four hundred men signify nothing else but the wrath of nature in the four elements of the body: and they went to meet the humanity of Christ. When Christ was bringing the created image of Adam in our humanity into God, viz. into Paradise, then would the wrath of God first kill the Adamical image, that it might no more live in the kingdom of anger, seeing it was to live in God.

7. And as Jacob humbled himself before God, and said, *O God of my father Abraham, and God of my father Isaac, Lord, thou who hast said unto me, Return again into thy country, and to thy kindred, and I will deal well with thee: I am unworthy of the least of all thy mercy, and all thy faithfulness and truth, which thou hast afforded unto thy servant; for I had no more but this staff with which I went over this Jordan; and now I am become two bands. Deliver me from the hand of my brother, from the hand of Esau: for I am afraid of him, lest he come and smite me, with the mother and the children* (Gen.

---

[1] Born, generated, or begotten.

HOW ESAU WENT TO MEET JACOB

xxxii. 9–11). So also Christ humbleth himself in our assumed humanity before God; and though God in the prophet David, in our assumed humanity, *hath bidden him sit at his right hand until he hath laid all his enemies under his footstool* (Ps. cx. 1), yet he humbleth himself, even as Jacob did before the anger of Esau: so also did Christ before the anger of his Father.

8. And as Jacob said, When I went over this Jordan I had only this staff, but now am become two bands; so also when Christ, viz. the eternal Word of divine love, came to us in our humanity, then it was only the staff of divine grace. But in our humanity, in the servile house of Adam, he was enriched with two bands, viz. a twofold humanity, the heavenly, extinguished in Adam, and the earthly from the limus of the earth. Therefore he saith, in this twofold humanity, as Jacob said to God: *O God of my father Abraham, and God of my father Isaac, O Lord, thou hast said unto me, Return again into thy country, and to thy first kindred; I am less than the least of all these mercies which thou hast bestowed on thy servant*; to signify that it was only in divine mercy that these two bands, viz. the twofold humanity, returned home again into its first country of Paradise to the angelical kindred.

9. And when Jacob had humbled himself before God, and his brother Esau, *He stayed there all night, and took of that which came to his hand, for a present to his brother Esau, two hundred she goats, and twenty he goats, two hundred ewes, and twenty rams, and thirty milch camels with their foals, forty cows and ten bulls, twenty she asses with ten foals. And put them under the hand of his servants, every herd by itself; and said to them, Go on before me, and leave room for one herd after another. And he commanded the foremost, and said, When my brother Esau meeteth thee, and asketh thee to whom dost thou belong? whither goest thou? and whose these are that thou drivest? thou shalt then say, They are thy servant Jacob's, who sendeth them for a present to his lord Esau; and he followeth behind after us* (Gen. xxxii. 13–18).

10. This type is now the great earnestness, whereby the spirit of God in the figure pointeth at the future. For this present of Jacob to his angry brother Esau, pointeth at the place and condition of Christ. When he should appease the anger of his Father, then he must first send these beasts in our implanted humanity for an atonement, which should be presented to the anger of God.

11. But these beasts, which Christ sent to the anger of God before his passion and death, were our implanted beasts, viz. pride, covetousness, envy, wickedness, lying; whereby one man slandereth, disparageth, disgraceth, shamefully censureth with words, discourageth,

suppresseth and exclaimeth against, as wicked and ungodly; and, summarily, all abominations of the devil and the wicked world.

12. These evil beasts are in Adam in sin all awakened and become living. These very forms or conditions of life, wherein Adam generated his evil beasts, wherein the temperature of nature was rent asunder, Christ took all upon him in our humanity: as they are well intimated in the figure of Jacob by five hundred and eighty; and sent them to the anger of God for an atonement, when he was redeeming the humanity from these beasts.

13. And these beasts were, as to Christ, his being despised, scorned, spat upon; whatsoever the Jewish priests did to him, were all our beasts, which Christ, in his body, gave up to the anger of God, as if he himself were the transgressor: and yet he had generated none of these beasts in his will. But Adam had generated them: and Christ took them on him as a lamb, and presented them to the anger of God on his body and life, and did it as if he himself were the transgressor; so that the anger of God devoured them on his body and life, viz. his inheritance which he had in man, as a natural right; whereby the anger of God laid hold of its own; and his wrath and hunger after this vanity to devour these beasts was appeased.

14. And the spirit of Moses speaketh further in the figure of Christ, and saith, thus, *The present of Jacob went before him, but he stayed that night with the company. And arose in the night, and took his two wives and handmaids, and his eleven children, and went over the ford. And he took them and sent them over the water, and sent over that which he had, and stayed alone* (Gen. xxxii. 21-24).

The figure of Christ standeth thus:

15. When Christ had sent this present, before, to the anger of God, he stayed with his company, viz. with his disciples, and arose in the night of the great darkness in our prison of misery, and took his two wives, viz. the twofold spirit of man, viz. the soul and the *spiritus mundi* (the spirit of this world), the outward soul, and the inward eternal soul, together with the two handmaids, viz. the twofold humanity of the body, and the eleven children, which are the eleven apostles;[1] and passed over the ford Jabbok; that is, he went over the brook Kidron, in the dark of the night, over the water (as here Jacob), with all whatsoever he was, or had assumed from us men.

[1] 11 Apostles.

HOW ESAU WENT TO MEET JACOB

16. For the right twelfth Apostle[1] of Christ was not yet chosen in Judas his stead (as here with Jacob), the twelfth son lay yet in the mother's womb unborn. And as Jacob with his eleven sons went over the water in the great night or darkness: so went Christ with his eleven disciples, in this night of Jacob, over the brook Kidron into the garden, and wrestled with the anger of God, so that he sweat a bloody sweat, till he overcame.

17. And as in this night a man wrestled with Jacob till the daybreak (v. 24), so also the spirit of God, viz. the love of God in our assumed humanity, wrestled with God's anger in our humanity till the love of grace brake through the anger, and the daystar of divine love arose in the soul, and overcame the anger (2 Pet. i. 19). As the text in Moses hath here very secretly, and yet very clearly, signified in this figure, saying:

18. *When Jacob in this night was passed over with his eleven children, and both his wives, and the handmaids, and all his company, and afterwards was alone, there wrestled a man with him till the break of day appeared. And when he saw that he prevailed not against him, he touched the ham[2] of his thigh; and the ham of his thigh was displaced with the wrestling with him. And he said, Let me go, for the day breaketh. But he answered, I will not let thee go, except thou bless me. And he said, What is thy name? And he answered, Jacob. And he said, Thou shalt no more be called Jacob, but Israel: for thou hast striven with God and man, and hast prevailed* (Gen. xxxii. 22–28).

19. This text stands wholly in the figure of Christ: for this man, who wrestled with Jacob this whole night, is nothing else but God's righteousness and truth, in which righteousness, in Adam and in all men, the severe judgment of God was awakened. And it signifieth the same Man who, on Mount Sinai, gave the Law to the people of Israel, in fire and terror; where he appeared in his righteousness, in the type of the Judgment, and commanded man to keep the law of righteousness under pain of the eternal curse; where he required the possibility and ability from man, viz. from the image of God that he had created in Adam.

20. But man having not stood in the trial,[3] therefore God inspake or inspired into him the ground, viz. the fountain of his most inward hidden love, in the promise of the Serpent-Destroyer, viz. the holy name JESUS. This name JESUS stood now as a Covenant of grace in God's severe righteousness, hidden in the most inward ground of the

---
[1] 12th Apostle. [2] Or, hollow.
[3] Proba or Temptation.

human soul; and opened itself in the holy fathers,[1] Abraham, Isaac, and Jacob, in their faith's ens.

21. But Jacob at present standing in the figure with his brother Esau, viz. Jacob in the type or image of Christ, and Esau in the type or image of God's righteousness in the anger, according to the kingdom of nature, so at present in this night, when Jacob was in great anxiety, this figure was manifested to him, that he perceived how God's love, in the Covenant of grace in the incorporated name JESUS, wrestled with God the Father's righteousness in the anger of the judgment, viz. in the great night of the darkness of God's anger, wherein the poor soul lay captive, and was so hard tied and bound[2] and put thereinto; and that the anger in the righteousness will not give over, unless it give itself into the love of grace, that the love may break through the anger, as the shining of light doth out of the fire, or as the morning breaketh out of the dark night, and changeth the dark night into day.

22. For the Covenant of grace in the love, and the soul, stood at present in one person. Therefore at present the soul of Jacob must, in Christ's figure and type, wrestle with God's righteousness about the heavenly ens, viz. about the substantial wisdom, which the name Jesus brought along with the poor soul in its heavenly substantiality, which faded in Adam; whereby Adam's faded [substantiality] sprang forth again in this living [substantiality], as a new birth.

23. Therefore the spirit of God saith to Jacob, Thou hast wrestled with God and man (viz. with God's love in the Covenant, and with the future heavenly substantiality, which substantiality became man in the seed of Mary), and hast prevailed. For Christ, in whose figure Jacob stood, should thus, in our assumed humanity, wrestle with God's righteousness, and conquer.

24. And the spirit in Moses saith here, *And when he saw that he prevailed not against him* (understand, God's righteousness in the anger of the judgment prevailed not against the grace) *then he touched the ham of his thigh, and the ham of his thigh was displaced by the wrestling with him.*

25. This signifieth the destruction and displacing of the Adamical humanity: that when Christ would stand out this victory, then would the human self-might and own-will be displaced, and broken and killed. But as Jacob died not by this wrestling (though the ham of his thigh was indeed displaced), so also our humanity should not die eternally, but be only displaced, that is, be changed.

26. This signifieth especially how the repentant man must enter

---

[1] Patriarchs. [2] Coarcted.

HOW ESAU WENT TO MEET JACOB

upon this combat of Jacob, and so wrestle with God and man, in the spirit of Christ in God's righteousness, in the anger. And when he overcometh, then will the ham of his fleshly self-will be broken, that he must go up and down in this world as one half lame, that cannot well walk in the way of the world, but goeth halting, as if his limbs were half broken, with which the wantonness and vanity of this world is driven on. For the spirit in the victory of Christ toucheth his thigh, that he is half lame in the pride and malice of this world, and never regardeth it more; but goeth up and down as a despised lame man, who in the pride of the world in their hale or frolic jollity [the world] little regard, but hold him for a lame halting man, who cannot follow the garb of the antic tricks, conceited jests and lasciviousness of this world. But he hath wrestled with God and man, and is with this victory touched and marked.

27. This, the pride and wantonness of this world understandeth not, for it goes up and down still in God's severe righteousness, in the kingdom of nature, in the might of the fire, in self-will, and thinks itself very well, till the judgment possesseth its place; then must the poor soul stand in the eternal judgment, and live in pain and torment.

28. And as Jacob stood in the wrestling, and had his thigh touched that he halted, then the man said to him, *Let me go; for the daybreak dawneth. But he answered, I will not let thee go, except thou bless me.*

29. This is first the figure of Christ, when he yielded himself up in the righteousness of God in the Father's anger, so that the anger according to our humanity slew him. Then said the righteousness, Now let me go, for at present the eternal morning breaketh forth in me. But Christ had taken hold of the righteousness, and said, I will not let thee go, except thou bless the humanity again; that the judgment may cease; except thou bring the morning of thy inward power forth through the humanity, that the curse may cease, and that man may wholly stand in the divine working again, in the blessing.

30. Secondly, it is the fair type or image, shewing how it goeth with the repentant man, when he giveth himself up through earnest repentance into this combat of Christ, in Christ's suffering and death, in his victory, and in the spirit of Christ wrestleth with God's severe righteousness, which continually assaileth him in his conscience.

31. For God's righteousness in the conscience saith, Let me go; thou art dead in sins, and hast no part in the divine grace; thou hast purposely and wilfully sinned, and set the grace behind thy back. Now thou art mine, praying will not avail thee, I will not let thee in

thy conscience attain the grace; thou wilt obtain no comfort more from God, the morning will no more rise to thee in thy conscience, for thou art a child of death. Now leave off and let me alone, that I may shut thee up below in the dungeon or chamber of death.

32. When this comes to pass then the poor soul wholly immerseth itself into the death of Christ, and giveth itself up to the severe righteousness of God, into the judgment, for the judgment layeth hold on it. But the soul catcheth hold of the incorporated grace in the death of Christ, and diveth therewith into the most inward ground of the judgment of God; in which ground God's Love is broken forth through the righteousness, and through the judgment, viz. through the eternal night, and hath made that same night in man to be day.

33. Into this day, viz. into the abyss without all human possibility or ability, it diveth as a child, that neither can nor will do any more, [as a child] that is too unworthy of all grace, and must indeed give itself up to the judgment. But with this diving the soul yieldeth all its utmost will and ability, and is in itself as it were void of nature and creature, and falls again into the Word wherein it stood in the eternal speaking before its creaturely nature.

34. For God's righteousness and judgment hath no deeper ground than merely the creaturely life; but when the will of the soul yieldeth itself up in going forth from the creature, and sinketh into the abyss, then is it again as a new child; for the abyss in the eternal speaking Word, out of which the highest love and grace of God hath manifested itself, layeth hold on it, and penetrateth into it, as the sun doth into the ens of a herb, whence the herb becometh half solar [or of the nature of the sun]. Thus in this diving the soul in its will is half divine; and then it wrestleth with God's severe righteousness in flesh and blood, and will overpower the anger of God.

35. Then saith God's righteousness in the conscience, Let me alone. That is, Leave off, and slay me not, for thou seest very well that the divine morning ariseth in me: cease from striving against the judgment of God. But in the right combat the soul saith to God's righteousness, I will not leave thee except thou bless me. That is, except thou givest me the promised grace out of the death of Christ in his conquest, that I may put on my Saviour Christ, that he may be mine and I his. And then thus saith God's righteousness (as [was said] to Jacob), What is thy name? And then the poor soul nameth itself according to its own creaturely name; as Jacob did here, when he called himself Jacob. But as the Lord said to Jacob, *Thou shalt no more*

HOW ESAU WENT TO MEET JACOB

be called Jacob, but Israel, that is, a tree of life, thus also saith God to the soul: Thou shalt no more have self-names in me, but thou shalt be called a Christian in Christ, viz. a branch in the Tree of Israel, *a sprout on the vine Christ* (John xv. 5). For thou hast fought with God and man, and hast prevailed. Thou hast overcome God's righteousness in the wrath of the anger, in thy combat in the spirit of Christ, and art now an essential Christian, and no more a titulary and verbal or mouth Christian, from whom grace is yet far off.

36. And Moses saith further, *And Jacob asked him, and said, Tell me, I pray thee, what is thy name? But he said, Wherefore askest thou what is my name? And he blessed him there. And Jacob called the place Peniel: for I have seen God face to face, and my soul is preserved*[1] (Gen. xxxii. 29, 30).

The inward holy figure standeth thus:

37. When Jacob with the desire of faith in his wrestling apprehended the morning or daybreak of God in the spirit of Christ, and saw Christ afar off, without the creaturely humanity, then he said, What is thy name? But Christ said, Wherefore askest thou what is my name? That is, I am no stranger, but am even the Israel in thyself, I have no other name, but thy name and my name shall be one.

38. For God, without nature and creature, hath no name, but is called only the eternal GOOD, viz. the eternal ONE, the abyss and profundity of all beings. There is no place found for him, therefore can no creature rightly name him; for all names stand in the formed Word of power. But God is himself the root of all power, without beginning and names. Therefore saith he to Jacob, Wherefore askest thou what is my name? And blessed him.

39. As the creatures and also all vegetables of the earth cannot know how the sun's power is named, but they stand still for the sun, and the sun giveth them power and warmth and blesseth them, that they grow and bear fruit: so also here is to be understood concerning Jacob and all men. When Jacob saw and felt the morning or daybreak of God in his soul, then the Divine Sun, in the name JESUS, blessed him through an essential working.

40. And this must thereby signify, as it went with Jacob and all the children of God, and yet still goeth with them in this sunshine. When the sun of grace, with its working power, ariseth in the soul, then the soul rejoiceth, and would always fain behold the countenance

[1] Healed.

of God after a creaturely manner; as also Moses desired; and always thinketh God is of some form. They look not yet rightly upon God, but will know God in imagery: thus hard lieth the creaturely imagery upon us, in the departed apostate self-will in the mind, that we cannot at all understand what God is, viz. that he himself is the abyss of all nature and creature, viz. the eternal ONE, that dwelleth in nothing, but only in himself, and hath no form, nor any thing.

41. And it were very well and good that we were not so led by the masters of the letter in an imaginary form, when they teach and speak of the only God, as hath been done hitherto, where men have led us on in vain images of[1] the essential will, as if the only God did will this or that; whereas [he] himself is the sole will to the [being of] nature and creature, and the whole creation lieth only and alone in the formation of his expressed Word and will, and the severation of the only will in the expression; and is understood in the impression to[2] nature.

42. If the pride of Lucifer might be torn out of the hearts and eyes of these masters, then men would soon see the countenance of God. But the Babylonish tower, upon which men will climb, and in opinions climb up to God into a severed heaven, where God sits cooped up, this withholdeth the true knowledge and understanding; and makes us always ask, What is the name of God? Where is God? What is the will of God? Also, they say God willeth good and evil, from which they make a multitude of decrees[3] in the divine purpose; as a prince in his land makes laws; and they have as much understanding of God and his will as the pot understands of the potter.

43. It is to be lamented that we are so blindly led, and the truth withheld in images;[4] for, if the divine power in the inward ground of the soul were manifest and working with its lustre, and that men did desire to go forth from their ungodly ways, and give up themselves to God, then is the whole Tri-une God present in the life and will of the soul; and the heaven, wherein God dwelleth, is opened in the soul; and there, in the soul, is the place of God, where the Father begetteth his Son, and where the Holy Ghost proceedeth from the Father and the Son.

44. For God maketh use of no circumscribed place, he dwelleth even in the abyss of the wicked soul, but incomprehensible to it, as to his love; but as to his anger he is manifest and comprehensible in the wicked soul.

---

[1] Or, in. [2] Of. [3] Or, determinations and conclusions.
[4] Imaginary conceits.

45. For the eternal speaking[1] of the Word, incomprehensible to nature and creature, becomes imaged[2] in the will of the soul; of which the Scripture saith, *With the holy thou art holy, and with the perverse thou art perverse* (Ps. xviii. 25, 26). Also, such as the people is, such a God they have.

46. For in the thrones of the holy angels God is manifest in his love; and in the thrones of the devils he is manifest with his wrath, viz. according to the darkness and torment; and yet there is but one only God, and not two. According to the tormentive nature he willeth torment, and according to the love he willeth love: as a burning fire desireth hard brimstone like itself, and the light of the fire desireth only an open place where it may shine: It taketh away nothing, but giveth itself for the joy of life; it suffereth itself to be taken; it hath no other will in itself but to give forth itself, and work that which is good. So God, as to his holiness, hath no other will in himself but to manifest the power of his love and shining lustre, in a creaturely form.[3] As the sun manifesteth itself in a herb, and tinctureth it and maketh it wholesome and good: so also is to be understood concerning God.

47. Therefore all is but vain jangling, babbling, and a creaturely imagination,[4] for men to ask what is God called, or what is God's name. Or for men to talk much and say, God willeth this or that evil and good, and know not how to say upon good ground how he willeth evil and good, and how a man shall understand the texts[5] of Scripture to that purpose.

48. This contention and strife about the letter is, indeed, the very confused divided tongue or language on the high tower of the children of Nimrod in Babel; for that high tower is a figure of the exercises in the Universities,[6] where the one divine language is divided or confounded and wrested into many speeches;[7] that one people doth not understand another, and that men contend about the only God, in whom we live and subsist, and whereby even the kingdom of nature in its wonders is manifested, and brought into figured wonders.[8]

49. But the true ground, what God is, and how he is, what the Being of all Beings is, remains as blind to them, as the visibility of this

---

[1] Or, expression.
[2] Conceivable, or perceptible, or gets an idea.
[3] Or, manner.
[4] Or, imagery.
[5] Or, sayings.
[6] Disputations in the High Schools.
[7] Perverted in phrases and expressions.
[8] Fashioned wonderfully. Ps. cxxxix. 14.

world is to one that is born blind. And though they are called Masters of the Letters, yet they have lost the five vowels, which are the power of all words; which is much to be lamented, that men understand nothing at all more of the Holy Ghost's language, what the spirit of God hath spoken in Moses and the Prophets, and how he hath in his speech declared and pointed at that which is future, eternal. Men cleave merely to an historical action,[1] and see not what is signified by this or that action.

50. For God's spirit hath not done such wonders for the history's sake of a plain simple shepherd, as it standeth in the outward form of it; and hath so exactly expressed those things in writing, as if he were so much concerned in a history, that he hath preserved it among all people, and suffered it to be proclaimed for his word. No, sure: but for this cause; that under such plain, simple, historical relations is signified (and wherewith God's spirit in the figure alludeth at), that which is future, eternal. Therefore should men look upon the Scripture of the *Old Testament* with clearer eyes, for the whole *New Testament* is couched under it in the figure of the plain simple acts or actions.

51. *When God had blessed Jacob, then Jacob called the place Peniel* (Gen. xxxii. 29, 30). That is, God's inspection into the soul, where God is manifest in the soul. Then saith the soul, I have seen God face to face in me, and my soul is preserved in this inspection. *And when he passed over Peniel the sun arose to him.* That is, when God's sun, viz. his power, is manifest in the soul, then the essence of the soul carrieth the power in itself; and then the divine sun ariseth in the soul's essence, and then the Father hath there begotten his Son in the soul, which is the sun of righteousness, as also the divine love and joy. And then self-nature halteth, for the sinew of its natural will is displaced, so that the self-will is lame in its ability; as here Jacob. And the text of Moses saith, *Hereupon the children of Israel eat not of the sinew upon the ham of the thigh, to this day: because the sinew of the ham of Jacob's thigh was touched.*

52. This sheweth clearly that Jacob and his children understood this mystery, and have instituted a memorial in this sinew. For what doth that which was done to Jacob concern a beast? The sinew of a beast is not therefore displaced or venomed: only, the children of the saints looked upon the ground of the divine mystery.

53. Concerning which the present Jews are very blind, and hang only on the Law. If they did so eagerly seek after Jacob's sun as they cleave fast to the Law, then would that sinew in them also be dis-

---

[1] Act or thing done.

placed, and they would not so hunt after covetousness and gain: But *they wash the outside of their cups and dishes, and inwardly remain foul* (Matt. xxiii. 25; Luke xi. 39).

54. Even as Christendom cleaveth to the history, viz. to the purple mantle of Christ, and hunt away Christ in his power from them, and will not, with Jacob, have the sinew of the wild bestial properties of the voluptuous will of flesh displaced and lamed, but walk nimbly with the beast, under the mantle of Christ.

55. This displaced sinew signifieth that Adam in his innocency, before his Eve, was not such a gross beast as afterwards. Therefore when the spirit of Christ in the Covenant was manifested in Jacob, then it touched the bestial ham of his thigh. To signify that in Christ it should be broken and cease, so that a spiritual man should arise from death, and not such a gross bestial man.

The Sixty-First Chapter

The Excellent and Wonderful Figure, shewing how *Jacob* and *Esau* met, and how all Heart-burning and Evil Will was changed into great Joy, Kindness, and Compassion: What is to be understood thereby[1]

1. AT this text blind reason should better open its eyes than hitherto it hath done, and better consider the figure of Jacob and Esau, and learn rightly to understand the decree concerning Jacob and Esau; where the Scripture saith, *Jacob have I loved, and Esau have I hated, when the children lay yet in the mother's womb, and had done neither good nor evil, that the purpose of God might stand* (Mal. i. 2, 3; Rom. ix. 13).

2. Here men should rightly look upon the purpose of God, what the spirit of God meaneth thereby, for Esau stood in the type or image of the corrupted Adam, and Jacob in the type of Christ, which came to help poor Adam. Therefore must these two brothers come of one seed, to signify that God would become man, and that God's seed, viz. his Word, and Adam's seed in its own nature, should be manifested in one person, and become man; and that God's seed should overcome the corrupted Adam's seed with great divine love, and quench the Father's anger with love, and the love should wholly give itself into the anger of the soul, that God's grace, compassion and mercy in the love may pass through the anger, and also change the anger into compassion; as here Jacob, with his present, and in great submission and humility, yielded himself to his brother Esau, and changed his anger, which he bare towards Jacob, in respect of the natural right of the first-born, and of the blessing, into such great compassion that Esau fell about his neck and wept in great compassion, and his anger in him was turned into love; even as Christ, with his great love and humility in our assumed humanity in our fiery burning angry soul,[2] changed his Father's anger into such great mercy and compassion, that the divine righteousness in the anger ceased and departed from our souls.

3. For as Jacob appeased his brother Esau with the present and

[1] Gen. xxxiii.   [2] Anger-soul.

SHEWING HOW JACOB AND ESAU MET

[with] humility, when he gave up himself into the anger of Esau, so also Christ appeased the anger of God, when he gave up his heavenly blood with the great tincture of love into the anger of God to be devoured; then was the anger, viz. the nature of the dark world which was manifested in Adam, turned again into the divine light of love, viz. into a love-fire.

4. Moses saith, *Jacob lifted up his eyes, and saw his brother Esau coming with four hundred men. And he divided his children to Leah and to Rachel, and to both the handmaids. And set the handmaids with their children foremost, and Leah with her children next, and Rachel with Joseph last. And he passed over before them, and bowed himself to the ground seven times, till he came to his brother* (Gen. xxxiii. 1-3).

The inward precious figure standeth thus:

When Christ, in our assumed humanity, entered into his suffering, then the anger of God in the four elements of the body came to meet him; and then Christ divided his Deity and his humanity, viz. the heavenly world's substance, which he brought from God in our humanity, and the kingdom of the natural humanity from Adam, into two several Principles: for the Deity, as to the omnipotency, stood yet still. Therefore saith the humanity on the cross, *My God, why hast thou forsaken me* (Matt. xxvii. 46; Mark xv. 34; Ps. xxii. 1)?

5. The two wives of Jacob, with their children, signify here, in Christ's state and condition, the twofold soul, viz. that from time and that from eternity. And the two handmaids, with their children, signify here, in this state and condition of his, the heavenly and the earthly corporeity, viz. Leah, in her blear-eyedness signifieth the *spiritus mundi in limo terræ*,[1] wherein the corruption in Adam was effected, wherein God promised the Destroyer of the Serpent; and wherein Christ should be manifested. And therefore in Leah the line of Christ, viz. the Destroyer of the Serpent in the type and prefiguration, was born, viz. Judah; and Rachel signifieth the extinguished ens of the heavenly world's substance, wherein the true soul dwelleth, which faded in Adam's fall and became unfruitful; as Rachel; till God in the spirit of Christ made her fruitful; as was done to Rachel.

6. And as Jacob set the handmaids with their children foremost, so was the earthly image in the human nature set foremost in the suffering of Christ, which should pass through the sharpness of death;

[1] The spirit of the world in the dust of the earth.

next after would follow Leah, that is, the body out of the limus of the earth, wherein the Destroyer of the Serpent lay, in the suffering of Christ; and after that, Rachel, viz. the heavenly limus with the prince Joseph, that is, with the true Adamical image of the divine world's substance; and the name *Jesus* passed before into the suffering of Christ; as Jacob before his wives and children.

7. And as the name and power *Jesu*, viz. God's sweetness and love, saw and felt the wrath of God in the human flesh and soul, then the name *Jesus* bowed itself through all the seven forms of nature's life, wherein the anger of God was become manifest; that is, he then pressed essentially through the centre of nature, through all the seven forms of nature, quite through the wrathful fire-source.

8. As Jacob bowed himself seven times to the earth before the anger of Esau, and appeased Esau in this humility, so also here the love in the name *Jesu* appeaseth the anger of the Father's property in the fire, in soul and body. For the natural life from the spirit of the world, viz. the soul from time, which was breathed into Adam's nostrils, must yield up its natural right and die. As Jacob yielded up his riches and also his outward life to his brother, to do what he would with him, thus also Christ yielded up our life to the anger of God, and left it willingly. But the name *Jesus* went before, and brought our natural life quite through death, and took it to himself again, and triumphed with our natural life over and through death.

9. And as Esau his brother, in this humility and submission, ran to meet him, and fell about his neck and kissed him, and in great compassion wept upon his neck: so also in like manner, when the essence of the anger of God [kissed and] tasted the sweet love in the name *Jesu* in the blood of Christ, then it was transmuted and converted into such great compassion towards mankind. As Jeremiah in the spirit declareth, where he speaketh in this figure, *Ephraim my dear child, my heart is troubled, I must have compassion on him* (Jer. xxxi. 20). Where he speaks concerning this compassion.

10. And when Esau wept upon Jacob's neck, *He lifted up his eyes, and beheld the women with the children; and said, Whose are these with thee? Jacob answered, They are the children which God hath bestowed upon thy servant. And the handmaids drew near with their children, and bowed themselves before him. Leah also drew near with her children, and bowed themselves before him: afterwards Joseph and Rachel drew near and bowed themselves before him* (Gen. xxxiii. 5–7).

SHEWING HOW JACOB AND ESAU MET

The inward figure stands thus:

When the anger of God held man captive in the darkness, then was he not, in the anger, known to God's holy image. But when the love in the suffering of Christ in the humanity brake through the anger, so that the anger was changed, then the only God looked on it again in his image, and spake to the name *Jesu*, saying, Who are these that are with thee? And *Jesus* answered God and said, They are the children which God hath vouchsafed and bestowed upon his servant.

11. For here Christ presents himself as a servant of God, with his children that are born in him in the faith, viz. with us poor children of Eve. And there passed through the death of Christ, and were presented before the countenance of God: first, the handmaids with their children; that is, man that had been sinful he sets him first in God's countenance; which Jacob's handmaids do signify.

12. Afterwards there pressed forward the line of the Covenant, with the spiritual Leah, viz. the first created image out of the limus of the earth, wherein the five prints of the nails, the wounds of Christ, stood; they should be shewn to the only God, that therein he should receive the handmaids' children, who all bowed themselves before God.

13. Then afterwards came Joseph with his mother, viz. the image of the heavenly world's substance, and bowed before the only God, which had been angry with him.

14. Men should not understand this in divided figures, types or images, but as the properties of the humanity are manifested before God through the suffering of Christ in one only image, viz. in Christ's humanity in the kingdom of the restoration or redemption, viz. in the kingdom of heaven. The reader should understand our sense properly: for we write here in the vision of all the three Principles, how it went, and still to this day goeth, with the new birth. Our exposition will not bear any dividing of the figure or creature: we understand it in one creature.

15. Our earnest and hearty consideration is this: That we may see and understand how we poor children of Eve were brought through Christ's suffering and death, and set before God's countenance, and how first the soul, with the body of sin, must pass through death, and in the resurrection come again with the body before God, where the body from the limus of the earth is esteemed strange in the presence of God. Therefore it is prefigured in the type in the condition

of a handmaid, and then presently, in that body, the prints of the nails and the suffering of Christ is set before God. Out of which death of Christ the fair image created in Adam appeareth again; as the whole figure together of Jacob thus fairly typifieth, and as the spirit hath signified thereby.

16. *And Esau said further to Jacob, What meanest thou by all this herd which I met? He answered, That I might find grace in the sight of my Lord. Esau said, I have enough, my brother; keep what thou hast. Jacob answered, O no, if I have found grace in thy sight, then receive my present at my hand: for I have seen thy face, as if I had seen the face of God; and let it please thee from me. Take, I pray thee, the blessing from me which I have brought thee; for God hath bestowed it upon me, and I have enough. Thus he constrained him that he took it* (Gen. xxxiii. 8–11). This now is the fair figure wherewith the spirit alludeth, how Christ appeareth before God, with his Christendom, viz. with his purchased goods. Then saith the Father to the Son, Whither wilt thou go with these thy children, who meet me daily, in that they come to me? And Christ saith, O Lord, that I might find grace from thee with them. And the Father saith, They are thy purchased goods, keep what thou hast, I have without them enough, even all things.

17. But Christ saith, O no, my Lord, receive, I pray thee, the blessing which God hath bestowed upon me in my children, which I have brought to thee; for God hath bestowed them on me, and I have enough: and he constrained God his Father that he received the kingdom again from him. And it is a true figure [shewing], how Christ, after he sits at the right hand of God and ruleth over his enemies, would deliver up the kingdom again to his Father. And then also will the Son be subject to the Father, together with his Christendom, as the Scripture saith (1 Cor. xv. 24–28). Which the spirit in this figure powerfully prefigureth, and representeth in a type or image.

18. This is an excellent figure, where Jacob cometh to his brother Esau that had been angry, and perceiveth how Esau falleth about his neck and weepeth, that Jacob saith, I saw thy face, as if I saw the face of God. Which signifieth to us that the wrath of God in the kingdom of nature was become an enemy in Adam's soul and body, viz. the fiery soul itself, which standeth in the Father's property in the eternal nature.

19. But when this great love and humility pressed through in the blood of Christ, then was this wrath, viz. the fiery soul, converted

SHEWING HOW JACOB AND ESAU MET

again into God's most clear countenance, and attained again the eye of God's love. Thus also we are to understand concerning Esau. When the Covenant of grace in the figure of Christ, in Jacob's humility, was discovered to him, then was his curse and malice, through the spirit of Christ, turned into love, that he was no more he of whom the Scripture saith, *Esau have I hated* (Rom. ix. 13). For in the kingdom of the Adamical nature was God's hatred manifested in him, and he was himself that hatred; and of that saith the Scripture, *Esau have I hated*. Now so long as the hatred in him had the dominion, so long he was in God's hatred, and was himself the hatred; but when the Covenant of grace in Jacob discovered itself to him, and that Jacob's humility pressed into his hatred, then began he to lament and weep, and God's clear countenance was manifested in his hatred, so that in great compassion he fell upon Jacob's neck and wept.

20. Which denoteth the repentance of poor sinners. When the malicious wicked soul which lieth captive in the hatred of God turneth to God, then beginneth first this compassion and repentance and sorrow for its former sin. When the spirit of Christ afflicteth the soul, then it weepeth and sorroweth that it hath been so wicked; and then instantly the sun riseth upon it, and the hatred of God is turned into the countenance of love; where, of a hateful spirit, he is made an angel.

21. And though clearly the Scripture saith in a certain place, *Esau sought repentance with tears, and yet found it not* (Heb. xii. 17). But this text giveth us to understand much otherwise, namely, that indeed Esau, and all the children of corrupt Adam, do not find repentance in their own willing, going, and running; else would it stand in the ability of man to attain grace; but the grace and divine mercy and compassion worketh repentance: Yet man must give up his will to the divine working.

22. The soul's will must incline itself towards the promised grace; and then will the divine sun shine into its will, and dissipate the hatred of wickedness.[1] And then the soul graspeth after the sun of grace, and so beginneth the working of repentance in the power of grace; and then the anger of God in the soul giveth its severe righteousness to the spirit of Christ. And so Christ then saith to his Father, *I have lost none of them that thou hast given to me* (John vi. 39).

23. The Scripture saith, *God willeth that all men should be saved* (1 Tim. ii. 4). And *Christ is come to seek and save that which is lost* (Matt.

---

[1] Or, the hatred in wickedness.

xviii. 11). And *He hath no pleasure in the death of a sinner* (Ezek. xxxiii. 11). Then, saith reason, If God will that all men should be saved, and willeth not the evil, can he not then save all? Why do they remain hardened, if he willeth not their hardening?

24. Answer. The soul standeth in the unsearchable[1] will of God, in the eternal speaking Word. It is a spark from the divine speaking, whereby the abyss, viz. the eternal One, expresseth or speaketh forth itself in the science, understanding, and knowledge of the severation.[2] In the speaking it is come into nature and creature, and hath now the ability to express again, viz. an image of itself.

25. Also in its knowledge it speaketh forth the wonders of the divine possibility in good and evil. It speaketh itself in its essential speaking, out of the eternal science itself, in evil: where it should speak God, it speaks in itself, want: where it should speak in its science, into the eternal One, viz. into God's love and wisdom, there it speaks into severation, viz. into multiplicity; and bringeth the science of its ability, which standeth in the eternal speaking Word, out of the temperament into a self-will, which breaketh off from the only will of God and entereth into self.

26. Therefore then it changeth the eternal will of the Unity in it, into the centre of severation, wherein the only God introduceth his only will, in the speaking forth of the Word, into nature and painfulness, to the divine perception and feeling, viz. into an essential spiritual fire; and out of the fire into a light, whereby the abyss becomes majestic and working. Thus the false or wicked soul speaks itself only into a source of fire.

27. For its will to the speaking, which in God stands in the abyss, which brings itself through the desire into the fire-speaking, viz. into properties, that goes not easily back again into the abyss, viz. into the eternal One: But if it go back again, viz. into the eternal One, viz. into God, then the fiery science becomes majestic and light, and then is the soul an angel of God, viz. an image of the eternal divine science.

28. But if the will continue in the fire as a magical fire-source, then is the soul that very fire-source. Who shall now advise and persuade this fire-source, seeing it hath its ground in the abyss, and is itself its ground? The power of the majesty shineth through it; but the desire shuts it up, and maketh it dark, so that the light cannot be manifest therein. As it stands in John i. 5, *The light shineth in the darkness,*

[1] Unfathomable. [2] Separability.

and the darkness comprehendeth it not. They dwell one in another, as day and night: the soul, in its imprinted desire, maketh itself darkness.

29. The eternal One, viz. God, is in it, and it comprehendeth him not; it maketh an angry God to itself. Where God's word in the anger speaketh, and formeth itself into nature and creature, there it worketh in itself, evil. But if it stood still from its working [for] the twinkling of an eye, then it would dive again into the eternal One, viz. into God; and so the divine science in the light would begin to work in it, and so it would come to repentance, even as it cometh to pass with the penitent. Concerning which Christ saith, *Except ye be converted, and become as a child, you will not see God* (Matt. xviii. 3).

30. The soul's will, which hath its ground and rise in the divine revelation (whence it is become a working life), should and must turn again into its mother out of which it proceeded; and then it is as a child in the mother's womb. And so in its mother it beholdeth God, viz. the Abyss of all beings; and is new-born in its mother; that is, the mother giveth it the light's power, and in that power it attaineth the ability to work repentance. And then the eternal unsearchable will of God, which is called the Father of all beings, begetteth his only Son, viz. his power of love, in and through the science[1] of the soul, as in the particular or parcel of the whole will of God; for the ground of the soul, and God's eternal speaking Word, is one only ground, undivided.

31. And as we know that the same only eternal-begetting and speaking Word expresseth itself in heaven, viz. in the power of the light, in holiness, viz. the holy wisdom: so also the same only Word expresseth itself in the hell of darkness, in flames of torment, viz. in hellish essences; according to which God calleth himself, *An angry God, and a consuming fire* (Deut. iv. 24; Heb. xii. 29). For without and beyond the only Word, or speaking, of God, there is nothing. So also it is to be understood concerning souls, as also angels, and devils.

32. In the resigned soul God the Father expresseth the holy name *Jesu,* viz. the grace, mercy, and compassion; that is, he begetteth Christ in it, and bringeth the Adamical, evil, innate will, through the suffering and death of Christ, again into the eternal *One,* where *the Son delivereth up the kingdom* of the soul's nature *again to the Father* (1 Cor. xv. 24).

33. But if the soul will not stand still from its working of wickedness, then the Father, through the Word, speaketh hell torment in

---

[1] Or root.

the soul; and the desire of the soul imprinteth and fixeth itself therein, and its impression maketh the eternal gross darkness, viz. a gulf between God [and it]. And yet no strange foreign speaker must be here understood, which from without shall speak into the soul; but the word, that is, the soul itself, speaketh itself thus into wickedness.

34. But it hath lost in Adam the good speaking [or expression of good], viz. the divine ability. But of God's mercy it is inspoken or inspired again of grace, in Paradise, as a self-centre of the soul; and it stands now at present in the soul as a self-centre or principle, and speaketh continually into the soul [saying], It should stand still from its false [and wicked] imagination, and then will that good[1] manifest itself again in the soul. But if the soul will not stand still from its ungodly speaking, then cannot the good inspeaking or inspiration manifest itself in the soul; and so it cannot be converted.

35. Therefore this is the conclusion: that God, in the false [and wicked] soul's speaking, cannot be good; and in the resigned soul's will, he cannot be evil. In himself he is indeed good, but not in that soul.

36. God is only called God where his love is expressed, and known and manifest operatively and feelingly. Of which the Scripture also saith, *The Word* (John i. 1) *which is God, is nigh thee, namely, in thy mouth and heart* (Deut. xxx. 14; Rom. x. 8). Also, *The kingdom of God is within you* (Luke xvii. 21): *with the holy thou art holy, and with the perverse thou art perverse* (Ps. xviii. 26).

37. In heaven he is called God, and in hell he is called anger; and yet he is in the Abyss, both in heaven and in hell, the eternal One, viz. the only Good.

38. And man can speak no further or deeper concerning God's will, but merely and only as in his manifestation through the Word; where the Word bringeth itself into nature and creature: there God willeth through the expressed Word of evil and good. As the science of every thing is in the formed Word, so also is God's will therein: That same expressed Word is in the angels, angelical; in the devils, diabolical; in man, human; in beasts, bestial. And yet in itself, in its eternal speaking, in the One, is only God, viz. one only holy Word, a ground and root of all beings.

39. Therefore salvation lieth in the will of the soul,[2] whether it will suffer itself to be saved, or whether it will stand still in its will. Not that it can take salvation to itself: no, it is given of grace, only the

---

[1] Good speaking, motion, or inclination of the spirit in the mind.
[2] Note the Grace of God.

SHEWING HOW JACOB AND ESAU MET

divine sun shineth into it in the abyss; and it lieth in it,[1] whether, with its will, which it hath from God, it will again for the twinkling of an eye dive down in its mother, viz. in God's unsearchable will, and so it will attain the ability.

40. For the ability hath opened its mouth to the soul, and saith, *Come ye to me* (Matt. xi. 28). As the sun shineth the whole day into all plants, and giveth them power, and the sun is not in fault that the thistle is a thistle, but the first ens is the cause whence it is a thistle.

41. So also a false and wicked soul from the ens of God's anger in the curse, and from the inherited wickedness, as also from the actual wickedness, becometh a thistle, in that the will, viz. the science of the soul, speaketh in [the quality] a thistle; and from such a false and wicked ground there grow more thistles. As God in Moses saith, *He will visit or reprove the sins of the father upon the children unto the third and fourth generation* (Exod. xx. 5); and Christ saith, *A corrupt tree cannot bring forth good fruit* (Matt. vii. 18).

42. Thus we see that perdition cometh from the soul. And we see that God's holy will cannot be manifest in false and wicked working. So long as the soul's will worketh evil, so long God's speaking formeth itself therein in anger; but when it beginneth to stand still from such working, then is God's power of love manifest therein: for if it worketh no more, then worketh in it the Abyss, viz. the One.

43. For God worketh from eternity to eternity, but no other than his Word; and *that Word is God* (John i. 1), viz. a manifestation of the Abyss. Now if the soul speaketh no more its own will, then is the unsearchable will speaking in it: where the creature standeth still, there God worketh.

44. Now if the creature will work with God, then must its will enter into God; and then God worketh with and through the creature; for the whole creation, both heavenly, hellish, and earthly, is no other than the working Word, the Word itself is All.

45. The creature is a compacted, coagulated vapour and exhalation from the Word. And as the Word is exhaled out of the free will, where the free will bringeth itself out of the Abyss into the profundity, so also the free will of the angels and souls bringeth the Word into a profundity. And that profundity is the creature, viz. a fire-source to its re-speaking-forth; and out of that re-speaking-forth proceedeth evil and good; and according to that re-spoken-forth substance and power the soul hath its judgment and sentence.

---

[1] The soul.

46. For that is the judgment: that the evil be separated from the good, and that every thing possess its own principle. Whatsoever soul now speaketh forth hellish source, viz. the curse, it must [speak it] into death, that it no more bring God's Word into evil and good, but [into] the evil alone, that every thing may remain with its own.

47. And therefore because in the place of this world, through the Word, evil and good are spoken forth, therefore in that place is a final day of separation appointed, when good and evil shall cease to be spoken in any place. And the wicked shall have their place prepared, where evil shall be spoken in its eternity, that the good may be known, and in the good the joy be manifest. Also that it may be known what evil and what good are; also what life and death are; and that the children of God may rejoice.

48. For if evil were not known, joy would not be manifest; but if joy be manifest, then is the eternal Word spoken in joy: to which end the Word, with nature, hath brought itself into a creation.

49. And this is the true ground wherein all conceits and opinions are known, and all sophistry thrown to the ground; also all strife and contention hath an end. Whosoever rightly seeth and understandeth this, hath no further question about anything; for he seeth that he liveth and subsisteth in God, and he giveth himself up to God, that God may further know and will through him, and speak what and how he will. This party seeketh only the estate of lowliness, that God in him may alone be high.

50. But so long as Lucifer hath his dominion in man, so long the creature presseth forward to advance itself, and will be its own God. And this is also a wonder: as God's wisdom standeth in the wonders in the love, so it is also in self, and in the appropriation of the creature.

51. Every thing is good in its own principle wherein it liveth, but to another it is opposite: Yet it must be so that one may be manifest in the other, and the hidden wisdom may be known; and be a sport in the severation, wherewith the profundity, viz. the eternal One, may sport with itself, before itself.

52. We should therefore learn to understand the Scriptures aright, how God willeth good and evil, namely, the determination is not in his very self, but in his expressed word, viz. in nature and creature. God hateth Esau in the corrupt nature, in Esau's self-nature: Esau was the type of hatred itself; but in God's self, viz. in the impressed or inspired Covenant of grace, he loveth him.

53. Therefore he presents the type of Christ, viz. his brother

SHEWING HOW JACOB AND ESAU MET

Jacob, together with him, and lets them both come out of one seed; to signify that, in the corrupted Adamical nature in the hatred of God, Christ should call Esau to repentance, and beget him anew; as Jacob brought Esau to repentance, so that he let his malice fall, and wept bitterly, and departed from his evil will towards Jacob.

54. This therefore is the understanding of the Scripture: that the earthly Adam in the kingdom of corrupt nature, in his own will, findeth not, nor can find, repentance, for there is no ability therein to good; but the incorporated grace in him awakeneth or stirreth up the ability, when the will turneth to it: For if self-will could work repentance and become good, honest and virtuous, it needed not grace.

55. The decrees in Scripture point only at two kingdoms, viz. the hardening respects the false and wicked will; the false will hardeneth itself: God's anger in the will's own substance hardens it; this hardening doth not enter in from without, but is manifested in the will's own substance. The will is from God, and the same God in the will introduceth himself into the hardening, in that manner as he introduceth himself into hell in darkness and torment. The same is also to be understood concerning the kingdom of grace.

56. God willeth in man only that which is good, in the kingdom of his grace; where the free will yieldeth itself up into the grace, there God willeth that which is good in the will, through the grace.

57. But when a man will say, Man cannot turn his will towards that which is good, viz. towards grace, that [saying] is groundless: in all wicked men grace indeed standeth in the abyss of the creature, and the will need only stand still from wicked working, and then it beginneth, as to its self-will, to dive down into the abyss.

58. For that which standeth still, standeth still together with the eternal One, and becometh one substance therewith, for it goeth into its nothing. Must not the false will or desire for a worldly law's sake, for fear of punishment, forbear or stand still from unrighteous works? Wherefore then not also for the sake of the commandment of God? Can it be obedient to a worldly lord and master, and for that end stand still for [that] which he would have him? Wherefore not also to God? especially when the ability is as soon given, as a man doth but incline his will to stand still.

59. But the cause why the total false, wicked will doth not stand still, and incline itself to grace, is this: that it is clearly a thistle born, wherein grace lieth too deeply hidden; and the wrath of God is too

strong in nature. Grace draweth it, and sheweth to it its own falsehood and wickedness; but it contemneth grace, and worketh as a thistle doth in the power of the sun. Such a one is to God *a good savour of death to* the *damnation* in hell, that grace may be severed from the false and wicked will (2 Cor. ii. 15, 16).

60. But the conclusions of reason which pronounceth that God in himself, so far as he is called God, hath determined that one part of men, and indeed the greatest number, shall and must be damned, and that of his own purposed will he hardeneth them, is false; and hath no ground, either in the Scripture or in the light of nature: if a man but rightly consider the Scripture, and doth not blindly look upon it.

61. For in God, so far as he is called God, there is no purpose nor beginning to will: he is himself the will of the profundity, viz. One, alone. And he himself willeth nothing but good, and therefore he is himself also that same good will, or willing of good: For the good that he willeth is the birth of his power, viz. his Son.

62. God willeth in himself nothing but to manifest his own good, that he himself is; and that could not be done if the only good power did not introduce itself, with the exhalation, into the desire to nature, and into a severation, viz. into the science; for if the good did remain alone, there would be no knowledge or skill.

63. But now the good, viz. God in himself, maketh not evil or separation, but the science, viz. the Fiat, or the desire to severation, bringeth itself into nature and creature; and from the science springeth evil and good, and not from God, or in God, in his Trinity.

64. For there is no decree: but there is a consultation therein. And then there must also be a cause of that consultation therein. And then again, there must be a cause of that also; and so there must be something before God, or after God, wherefore he so consults and determines.

65. But he is himself the profundity, and the One; and is one only will, that is, himself, and that is only good; for one only thing cannot be opposite to itself, for it is but one, and hath no quarrel with any thing.

66. Therefore it is the folly of reason, that they speak of compulsion and inevitable necessity, and understand not the Mysterium Magnum.[1] Or that they say, God of his purpose willeth the evil desire or will, which he hath hardened that it should not attain the grace.

[1] The Great Mystery.

SHEWING HOW JACOB AND ESAU MET

67. I shew to this blind reason a thistle to consider of, which the sun for a whole day toucheth, and giveth it light and power: yet it remains a thistle. So also the wicked will: the divine sun shineth to it the day of its whole life: but its ground is an ens of a thistle.

68. Otherwise, if God did of purpose harden it, the righteousness could have no judgment therein: for that which doeth what it must do liveth according to the will of its Lord. But if *God willeth not that which is wicked*, as in Ps. v. 4, then the evil cometh out of the root; and in the root of knowledge out of nature's ground to the creature, and by accident. And for that cause hath God manifested his will, and given his Law and Gospel; that is, hath manifested his threatenings and his grace, that a day of separation might be kept with righteousness, and that no creature might have excuse.

69. And the history saith further, after Esau had received the present of Jacob, he spake unto his brother Jacob, saying, *Let us take our journey, and go forward, I will go with thee. But Jacob said to him, My lord, thou knowest that I have with me tender children, and, moreover, cattle that are great with young, and sucking calves: if they be overdriven for one day the whole flock would die. Let my lord pass over before his servant, and I will follow on softly, as the cattle and the children are able to go, until I come to my lord into Seir* (Gen. xxxiii. 12–14). This text appeareth to be only an outward history, but the spirit hath also its inward figure under it, for Jacob stands in that figure of Christ.

And the figure is thus:

70. When Christ through his suffering and death appeased his Father's anger in the kingdom of nature, thus said the appeased anger: Now will we arise, and take our journey together (understand, in the life of man). But the love said, Man is too tender, feeble and impotent, and can scarce go in God's ways, *I will remain with them even to the end of the world* (Matt. xxviii. 20). And lead them slowly,[1] as they are able to go, lest they fall into temptation and error, and be blind as to grace. Go thou before, my lord, I will lead them on softly under my yoke of the cross, that they die not; for if they should now presently be led in the Father's severe righteousness, they would not be able to go: though they are indeed redeemed, yet they live still in flesh and blood, I will come after with them to thee into Seir; that is, into God's righteousness.

[1] Gently and moderately.

71. *And Esau said, Let me now leave with thee some of the folk that are with me. He answered, What needeth it? let me but find grace in the sight of my lord* (Gen. xxxiii. 15). That is, God the Father said, Let me leave some of my severe righteousness, commandments and laws with thee. But Christ said, What needeth it? let me, with these redeemed children, only find grace with thee, for they cannot fulfil the Law.

72. *Thus Esau went his way again that day towards Seir* (Gen. xxxiii. 16). That is, thus God's righteousness pressed into its own principle. *And Jacob went to Succoth, and built him an house, from whence the place is called Succoth* (Gen. xxxiii. 17). This, in the figure, is as much as to say, Christ led his Christendom, viz. his children, not to *Seir*, that is, into the proof or trial of God's righteousness (though indeed grace was manifested in them), but he erected a house, viz. the Christian Church upon earth, and made his children tents,[1] that is, Christian ordinances, wherein they might dwell. And hence it is called Christendom, as Jacob's city is called *Succoth*. So also the place or city of Christendom is called *Suchet* (seek), *so shall you find* (Matt. vii. 7; Luke xi. 9) Christ, who is always in these tents with his children, to the end of the world (Matt. xxviii. 20).

73. And the text in Moses saith further: *Afterwards Jacob went to Shalem, the city of Shechem, which lieth in the land of Canaan, when he came from Mesopotamia;*[2] *and set up his station before the city. And bought a piece of ground of the children of Hamor, the father of Shechem, for an hundred pieces of money, and there he set his tent up, and erected an altar, and called on the name of the strong God of Israel* (Gen. xxxiii. 18–20). In this text the spirit alludeth rightly to the future Christendom; for after his resurrection Christ led his children to Shalem, that is, into salvation, or the anointing or unction of the Holy Ghost, as Jacob led his children to Shalem; but it was to the city of Shechem, that is, among the heathen.

74. *And set his station before the city.* That is, Christ should have his habitation by the heathen, and set his temple and doctrine near the idols' temples of the heathen, and purchase the city of his holy Christian Church from the heathen; that is, with his blood purchase it from God's righteousness, even as it is come to pass; and there erect his altar among the heathen, and preach the name of the God of Israel, that is, Christ.

75. For the name *Shechem* signifies that the Christian Church must be in misery and trouble: As Jacob buildeth his habitation before the

---

[1] Tabernacles, booths. [2] Padan-aram.

city Shechem, so must also the children of Christ be but strange guests in this world, and be but as household servants to the heathen, potentates, and children of this world. Though indeed they have their habitation, viz. the temple of Christ in them, which Christ hath purchased for them with his blood, yet they are outwardly but strange guests and pilgrims, and dwell without, before the city of this world, viz. in an earthly tabernacle and tent, in flesh and blood.

The Sixty-Second Chapter

Of *Dinah*, *Jacob's* Daughter, which he begat of *Leah*, how she was deflowered by *Hamor's* Son, and how *Jacob's* Sons slew *Shechem* for it, and all the males that were in that City, and took *Dinah* again: And what is to be understood by this figure[1]

THE GATES OF CHRISTIANS WAR, FOR THE BABYLONISH WHOREDOM, NOW HIGHLY TO BE CONSIDERED

1. MOSES saith, *But Dinah the daughter of Leah, which she had borne to Jacob, went out to see the daughters of the land. And when Shechem the son of Hamor the Hivite, the lord of the country, saw her, he took her, and lay with her, and deflowered her. And his heart clave to her, and he loved the damsel, and spake kindly to her. And Shechem said to his father Hamor, Get me this damsel to wife* (Gen. xxxiv. 1-4). The Reader should very seriously consider this figure, and rightly meditate on the text in Moses, and look thoroughly into it;[2] then he will well understand our sense and meaning and most precious apprehension, opened to us by the divine grace; and learn to look upon the Scriptures of the first Book of Moses with clear eyes.

2. Leah the wife of Jacob bare to him six sons, viz. the half stock of Israel, and of her came Judah, viz. the root of David, of whom Christ was manifested according to our humanity. Afterwards she bare this Dinah, a daughter, by which figure the spirit powerfully prefigureth Christendom, that after Christ's ascension into heaven, after the work of human redemption, the true Christendom should be born; as Jacob first begat the twelve patriarchs, but afterwards of Leah, that is, of the mother of Christendom, a daughter of fleshly self-love would be born, which daughter would go agadding to see the daughters of the land, among whom she should be a stranger.

[1] Gen. xxxiv. [2] Into the face of it.

OF DINAH, JACOB'S DAUGHTER

That is thus much in the figure:

3. When Christendom would be born, that its number might be great, it would go forth in self-love and seek the pleasure of the flesh; and would set its heart upon the customs and behaviours of the people, and depart from lowliness and humility, and would look after the wantonness and pride of the daughters of the land, that is, of the people. And then they would beget this daughter, Dinah, and appear before God in fleshly voluptuousness of spiritual whoredom, and would play the whore with the heathenish customs, but yet would present itself beautiful, and trimly dressed, as an amorous virgin which runneth abroad to be seen, that she might take lovers, as Dinah did, which went thus forth agadding.

4. Thus also would Christendom trim itself, and dress itself with great ostentation and solemnity, with churches and schools, and put on glittering, sumptuous, appearing-holy garments, that they might have respect with the daughters of the land, as with strange people; and yet would be full of flames of self-love and fleshly menstruous pollution under such habits, and have a whorish heart, as a whore outwardly flatters, beautifies and trims herself, and will throughout be called a chaste virgin. Thus also would this trim Christendom be called holy: but her heart would only play the whore with fleshly voluptuousness.

5. She would fain see the dress of the daughters of the land, which dress is no other than the heathenish wisdom and philosophy; and would draw the same into Christ's kingdom, and would live under Christ's purple mantle, in those rites and customs, and trim herself therewith, and thereby quite forget that her tents and habitations are without the city of these peoples' customs, as *Jacob dwelt without, before the city of Hamor* (Gen. xxxiii. 18); and also Christ said, *His kingdom was not of this world* (John xviii. 36).

6. But this Christendom would set her heart upon the kingdom of this world, and so, in the dress of a virgin, trim herself with many churches, priests and ceremonies, under the habit of a virgin; but in this departure from the simplicity and humility of Christ, she would but gad abroad in the world, and look after fleshly whoredom; as Dinah did, which is a type of fleshly Christendom, which is always born after the true children of Christ: as Dinah was born after the twelve patriarchs. That is:

7. When Christendom is born and manifested among a people, it

begetteth in that place, first, the twelve patriarchs, viz. the ground of the Apostolic doctrine. But when she mixeth again with the heathenish wise men, and with the lust of the flesh, then that place begetteth a Dinah, viz. a whoredom with Christ; that is, a seeming Christian, yet the heart is but a whore; and then this whore goeth abroad gadding to find the habitations of that people. That is:

8. She seeketh again the heathenish ground, and mixeth herself with the heathen, and is with child by the heathenish philosophy, and bringeth forth a bastard, half Christian and half heathenish, viz. a new sect or doctrine, which doth not fully agree in form with the first customs of that people among whom it did spring forth; and yet in her heart is no whit better than they.

9. And then this people raise themselves up against that strange opinion, and cry out in anger, These have deflowered our sister Dinah, and have made her a whore, and are enraged against the new-found opinion, as the sons of Jacob against Shechem; and with fighting and the sword, with storming and cursing, run on against the deflowerer of their sister Dinah, and murder him; and not only him, but all the males that are with him, as Jacob's sons did the Hamorites. And then the innocent must thus suffer with the guilty; to signify that they all of them, both the one and the other, live in such religious whoredom. For the whore, for whose sake they take vengeance, is their sister, and born of their stock, as Dinah their sister was, and they came of one mother.

10. We see here eminently the type of contentious Christendom, how Christendom would be headstrong and furious in opinions, and that, in great blindness; and not know wherefore, and would not see themselves, that they thus rage in their own whoredom, and strive not about the power of true Christianity, as about the true Christian life; but about their contrived opinions, as about their sister Dinah, which goes abroad gadding from them, and gazeth upon the strange opinions; and cry out upon the opinion for a whore, and yet see not how they should help their sister's heart, wherein sticketh the lust of whoredom. As Jacob's sons did not see how to help the evil, that their sister might save her credit; and though Hamor and Shechem sent to them to give her a dowry, and would marry their sister, and love her, and be circumcised, and become one people with them, and would perform all love, faithfulness and friendship towards them, yet all this did not help.

11. And although they told them, that if they would be circum-

OF DINAH, JACOB'S DAUGHTER

cised, and be one people with them, they would give them their sister, yet they were furious in killing and slaying; to signify that this is a figure of future Christendom, which would arise out of this stock. As we see that it so comes to pass before our eyes, that men strive about the gadding separated opinions, and kill and murder one another for them; and yet this is but for the opinion's sake of false whoredom, which the titulary Christendom hath taken up, wherein they trim themselves in hypocrisy and whoredom, and look not how their sister might be helped, who is gone astray in a strange opinion. But they take their swords, and would slay the new opinion, and snatch their sister, who is with child with another opinion, forcibly again with her bastard out of Hamor's house, and slay Hamor and Shechem and all their males.

12. And though they would unite themselves with them, as with the true Christian ground, viz. with the chief Articles of Christian doctrine, yet it avails not; they will, against all faith and promise, slay and kill, and keep their opinions, which they have contrived in their ease and pampered jollity, with their fat bellies and heathenish festivals. As it is seen at this day in the contentions and opinions.

13. Men of self-love have introduced their Christianity into a fleshly kingdom, and finely trimmed it with laws, ceremonies and opinions, and have covered it with Christ's purple mantle, and yet live in mere spiritual whoredom under it, with a hypocritical show. But their hearts constantly beget this lustful Dinah, which runs abroad from the simplicity and humility of Christ, and plays the whore with the idols of fleshly lust, viz. with pride and covetousness, merely with their own honour and reputation, and a voluptuous life; quite contrary to the true Christian ground.

14. But seeing the spirit of Christ dwelleth yet always in his Christendom, he often stirreth up men which do thus acknowledge and see the sleep and whoredom of the titulary Christendom in their Sodomitical life, and turn away from them, and search in the Scriptures, and also in the light of nature, whether this their fleshly ground can subsist in the presence of God; and when they see that it is false, then they fall upon some other ground, and reprove the whoredom of the titulary Christendom.

15. And when the hypocrites in their voluptuous glory hear and see these things, that thereby they are blemished and defiled, and that their God Mäusim is made manifest; then they cry, O, there's a heretic, he deflowereth our sister Dinah, viz. our opinion, and maketh

the Church a whore. And though some should offer to give a good account of his ground and opinion, and reconcile and marry himself with the true Christian ground, and marry with their sister Dinah, viz. to espouse the first true virgin Christian ground, and to be of one and the same heart and will with them in the Christian ground, all this avails not; they snatch their sister, viz. the name of a Christian from them, and had rather keep the deflowered damsel with her bastard by them, whose shame the truth hath discovered; than they may see how to help their sister's shame, that she may attain the wedlock with Christ.

16. They suppose, when they can with power rescue and keep their opinions, and though indeed the whoredom in their opinion is laid naked, that it is weakened and blemished; yet they will have their Dinah to be taken for a virgin, and though her shame of whoredom be open to the daylight, yet they will defend the same with the sword, and with slaughter. As we see before our eyes, and the present strife intimates no less, but that it is manifest that Dinah is become a whore, viz. titulary Christendom that playeth the whore in the presence of God, and hath lost her virgin chastity, and the purity of her conscience. And so at present the brethren of this Dinah fight for her, and will preserve her honour and reputation with the sword and with killing; and will murder all those who do deflower and defame their Dinah.

17. This Dinah is at present nothing else but the stone churches and great colleges of their ministers, wherein men use the name of Christ, but seek thereby only their own honour, voluptuousness, and good days,[1] how a man may be honoured in the world.

18. For the true Apostolic temple is the temple of Jesus Christ, viz. the new man, who liveth in righteousness and purity before God, who walketh in humility and in the simplicity of Christ. And his ministers are such as do declare the peace in the love of Jesus Christ, who labour that the deflowered Dinah might be married with Shechem, and that Hamor and Shechem with their males might also become Christians; who leave the sword in its sheath, and teach with the meek and gentle spirit of Jesus Christ; and shew instead of the murdering sword the spirit of cleansing, how this deflowered Dinah might get Christian honour again, and be married to her Bridegroom.

19. Behold, O Christendom! the spirit hath set this before thee in

---

[1] Fat days.

OF DINAH, JACOB'S DAUGHTER

the figure of the twelve patriarchs, and signifieth that thou wouldest do thus: not that thou shouldest do it. Though this strife must come, that the true children of Christ might be exercised and made manifest; otherwise if no strife did arise among the Christians, all wicked men could appear as Christians. But the strife maketh it manifest that the false ground of verbal Christians is brought to light, and they are distinguished from the true children of Christ; which will be also a witness against them at the Last Day of Judgment.

20. Man's true Christianity standeth in the inward ground of the soul in the ground of man, not in the ostentation and fashions of this world, but in the power of well-doing in the spirit and conscience.

21. The strife wherewith a true Christian striveth is only the spirit of righteousness, which casteth away from it the falsehood and wickedness in flesh and blood, and suffereth and endureth all things willingly for Christ's sake, who dwelleth in it; that it may not live to itself, and please itself, and have satisfaction in itself, and triumph with the earthly Lucifer; but that he please God his Creator in Christ Jesus.

22. He hath nothing in this world to strive for, for nothing is his own. For in Christ he is not of this world, but as the Scripture saith, *Our conversation is in heaven* (Phil. iii. 20). All things for which and wherewith he striveth is about the earthly, voluptuous, fleshly Lucifer, in the mortal flesh and blood. For Christ saith, *His kingdom is not of this world* (John xviii. 36). So also a Christian's kingdom, so far as he is a Christian, is not of this world, but in Christ in God.

23. Therefore now all the strife of Christians is only about their Dinah, viz. about their fleshly whoredom. A Christian ought not to strive otherwise than in spirit and power against the ways of unrighteousness and falsehood.

24. Outward war that Christians make is heathenish, and is done for the bestial mortal man's sake. For immortality cannot be attained or kept with the sword and forces, but with prayer, and with entering into the fear of God. But the earthly Lucifer striveth about the belly, and about worldly honour and pleasure, wherein Christ is not; but it is the deflowered Dinah, where men make war about the houses of stone, and temporal goods, and thereby declare that the spiritual virginity in the spirit of Christ is made a whore, who plays the harlot for the kingdom of this world.

25. Hearken, all ye who call yourselves Apostles of Christ, Hath Christ sent you to fight, and to make war, that you should strive

about temporary goods and outward power and glory? Is that your authority (John xx. 23)? When he gave you the sword of the spirit did he command you that? Hath he not sent you to make known the peace which he hath brought us? What will he say to you, when he shall see that your Apostolic heart hath put on armour, and that you have instigated your worldly kings and princes to the sword and wars, and have allowed them that, as of Christian liberty? Will he find you thus, in his ministry? Do you that, as the disciples of Christ?

26. Are you not the apostles of the anger of God? Whither will you go with your reproach? Do you not see, that, as to Christ who hath taught you peace, you are become forsworn or perjured harlots? Where is your Christian virginity? have you not with Dinah squandered it away in worldly pleasure? What will Christ say to you, when he shall come again, who on earth had not whereon to lay his head (Matt. viii. 20; Luke ix. 58), when he shall see your pomp, state, and glory, in such palaces [and colleges], which you have built in his name, for which upon earth you have made wars?

27. When have you striven about the temple of Jesus Christ? Have you not always striven about your colleges or palaces, and about your own laws, wherein you have lived in opinions, and disputed about those opinions? What need hath Christ thereof? Christ bestows himself upon his children substantially, in a living manner, to dwell in them, and will give them his flesh for food, and his blood for drink. What needeth he opinions, that men should strive about him, who and what he is?

28. When I consider a true Christian, then I understand that Christ is and dwelleth in him. What means then your outward worship of God? Wherefore do you not serve him in your hearts and consciences? He is present within you, and not in the solemnity and ostentation of outward things. Ye have the sword of the Holy Ghost by right, with that you should strive: Use you the power of the true Apostolic Churches, and not the sword of man's hand.

29. The excommunication is your sword; but yet it must be used in the power of the Holy Ghost, in divine zeal against the wicked and ungodly, and not for that purpose to maintain human inventions and fictions, that a man must call your spiritual whoredom in opinions a chaste virgin: as for a long time the Babylonish Church hath used it to such a power.

30. All outward ceremonies, without the inward ground, that is, without Christ's spirit and co-operation, is whoredom in the sight of

OF DINAH, JACOB'S DAUGHTER

God, that a man will approach to God without Christ the Mediator. For none can serve Christ but a Christian, where the spirit of Christ itself co-operateth in the service. But how will he serve Christ, who holdeth in one hand the cup of Christ, and in the other hand the sword of self-revenge? Christ must, in a Christian, overthrow sin by his spirit, and not [by] the Father's fiery sword in the law of severe righteousness.

31. O ye children of Simeon and Levi, the spirit at Jacob's end hath signified concerning you, that your swords were murderous, that Christ is not in your councils. As Jacob saith, My soul, that is, the Covenant and grace of Christ, be thou not in their Churches and congregations, nor in their council. Read *Genesis* xlix. 5, 6, where the council of the Pharisees and Scribes, who institute themselves pastors without the divine calling, is thereby signified.

32. All spiritual whoredom proceeds from hence: that Christ's ministers possess worldly power and authority; and so one playeth the hypocrite with another; the inferior that is without power and authority playeth the hypocrite with the potent, that he may advance him also, and bring him to honour and [plenty, to deliciousness and] fat days; whereby the spirit of zeal declines and falls to the ground, and the truth is turned into a lie, and the spirit of zeal of the mouth is stopped with power, and man is honoured in God's stead.

33. This history, relating how *Simeon and Levi went into the city to Hamor and his children and people, and slew all the males in this city* (Gen. xxxiv. 25), may well be understood to be a figure, whereby the spirit signifieth that he declareth in the figure concerning the future time, and is so written as a figure.

34. Also the history is clear, that *Hamor and his son Shechem, and all the males of the* whole *city, were circumcised* and became Jews,[1] *and* then presently *were slain by these two brethren, Simeon and Levi* (Gen. xxxiv. 24–26), which indeed is a hard figure to be understood, seeing reason questioneth whether it were so done or no, that two men should slay a whole city. But seeing it is a figure, and was done even by Simeon and Levi, viz. by the stock and root of the Levitical priesthood, and signifieth the future Christendom: This therefore is to be understood under it:

35. These two brethren required first, and proposed, that if they would be circumcised, and receive their Law, they would give them their sister; and afterwards, as it came to pass, they slew them all,

---

[1] Or, Israelites.

both the innocent and the guilty. This is that which Christ said to the Pharisees: *Woe unto you, Pharisees! ye compass sea and land to make a proselyte, and when he is one, you make him twofold more a child of hell than yourselves* (Matt. xxiii. 15).

36. This also may be said of the Christian Levites, they persuade people to be baptised, and called Christians; and when that is done they stick their murdering sword into their hearts, that they learn to slay other people with words, which are not called after their name, and are not of their opinion. They curse and damn them, and they give occasion that one brother persecutes another, slanders, condemns, hates, and becomes his malicious enemy, and yet understands not wherefore. Here it is rightly said, These Levites have promised me their sister to wife, so that I am become a Christian, and now they slay me with false doctrine, and not only me but all my generation, who hear them and receive their blasphemy for divine truth; and believe them that it is right, that one man should thus judge and condemn another, which yet Christ hath earnestly forbidden. And thereby now that man judgeth himself, since he doth that himself which he judgeth in another.

37. Thus is the murdering sword stuck into many innocent hearts, so that they are guiltlessly slain by the Levites. But seeing Simeon and Levi are placed together, and Jacob also, when he was at his end, prophesied concerning them, and putteth them together, calling them murdering swords, it hath this signification: that they will not only slay them with the sword of the mouth, but they would also set themselves up in worldly power and authority, and for the truth's sake kill their bodies, and would do it even to them which are under the circumcision, or under the Gospel, whom first they had persuaded to be circumcised, or to be baptised.

38. As it is also come to pass among the Christians, when men have first persuaded them unto baptism; afterwards, when they have for a while seen their abominations, that they live worse than the heathen, and will not in all things give their consent and approbation, then they begin persecution with fire and sword, and slay them, with their innocent children, both in soul and body, which is powerfully prefigured in this type of Simeon and Levi; else that were a grievous gross murder of the children of the saints, for them to persuade people to their faith, and give them their promise, and then afterwards, under such hypocrisy, to slay all, both innocent and guilty, when they had so deeply humbled themselves before them.

OF DINAH, JACOB'S DAUGHTER

39. Therefore men should carefully and accurately look upon the Old Testament, especially the first book of Moses: for the veil of Moses hangeth before it; there is always somewhat more signified under the text. Although we will have the text left also standing as a history, and doubt not at all thereof; which is known to God, who hath thus suffered it to be described.

40. For the text saith, *They fell upon the city, and slew all the males, and took all their children and wives captive, and plundered and spoiled all that was in their houses* (Gen. xxxiv. 25-29). Which though it doth indeed seem that these two men were not able to do it, yet even Jacob himself witnesseth that there were no more than these two, when he said to Simeon and Levi, *Ye have raised mischief unto me, that I stink before the inhabitants of this land* (Gen. xxxiv. 30). Which stands very right in the figure, that the murdering sword of the Levites hath raised such disturbance in the world that Christendom, for their base murdering practices, stinketh before the strange nations; so that they say, If they were God's people they would not be such tyrants and outrageous scorners. And they hate them for that very cause; and slay and kill them as a turbulent evil people, that contend only about religion, and kill one another for it; therefore there can be no certainty among them, and their divine service and worship of God must needs be false, say they. For which cause the potent countries of the east are departed from them, and have subjected themselves to a doctrine of reason. As is to be seen by the Turks, which ought further to be considered of.

The Sixty-Third Chapter

How God called *Jacob* to depart from *Shechem*, and what happened upon it. And how afterwards *Rachel* bare *Benjamin*, and died in the birth; also how *Isaac* died: And what is to be understood thereby[1]

1. WHEN Simeon and Levi had committed that murder, *God said to Jacob, Get thee up, and go to Bethel, and dwell there: and make there an altar to God, who appeared unto thee when thou diddest flee from thy brother Esau. Then said Jacob unto his household, and to all that were with him, Put away from you the strange gods which are among you, and cleanse yourselves, and change your garments: And let us arise, and go to Bethel; that I may there make an altar to God, who hath heard me in the time of my trouble, and hath been with me in the way which I have gone. Then they gave unto him all the strange gods which were in their hands, and their earrings; and he buried them under an oak which was by Shechem. And they went forth: and the fear of the Lord came upon the cities which lay round about them, that they did not pursue after the sons of Jacob. Thus Jacob came to Luz, in the land of Canaan, which is called Bethel, with all the people that were with him. And he built there an altar, and called the place El-Bethel: because God there appeared to him, when he fled from his brother* (Gen. xxxv. 1–7). This history once again prefigureth powerfully the future times, how it would go both with Israel and also with Christendom. For when Levi and Simeon had committed that murder, and slain all the males of Shechem, and taken captive all their wives and children, having plundered and spoiled all, then Jacob was afraid of the people of the land. And then God called him from thence to go to Bethel, and make an altar there.

The inward figure standeth thus:

2. When men, both the Jews and afterwards the Christians, were grown up in fleshly whoredom and unchaste life, and became wicked, then would God's spirit depart from them, and then they began a spiritual whoredom and idolatry, and were erroneous in their

[1] Gen. xxxv.

JACOB TO DEPART FROM SHECHEM

opinions, and would fall together by the ears, and say one to another, He deflowereth his sister Dinah, that is, his worship and service of God. And would fall one upon another, and murder, kill, plunder, spoil and rob one another with wars, and bring their country to desolation and misery. And then when they should stick in such misery and trouble, they would attain the fear and trembling, as here Jacob, upon the murder which his children committed. For the Lord would touch their evil consciences, and call them again to repentance, as he did Jacob and his children, when he commanded them to come away from the place of this murder, and commanded Jacob to make an altar to him, viz. to the Lord, at Bethel, that is, in the lowliness of the fear of God.

3. So the spirit here signifieth, that God would then again send them prophets and teachers, who would dissuade them from their idolatry and wicked life; as here Jacob exhorted his family that they should put away the strange gods, and the pride of their earrings from them. And then, when they had thus seen the anger of the Lord, which destroyed their land, and exceedingly devoured them for their whoredom, pride, and idolatrous life, then would they follow and obey the prophets who reproved them for it; and bring their idols and strange gods, viz. their idolatry, before God, and put it away from them; and would again seek the temple of God within them. And then would God again build up his altar in them, and they would again rightly offer sacrifice to him, viz. offer up their souls; and would cleanse their garments, that is, their hearts, as Jacob here commanded his people. This also would the prophets, and among the Christians the true apostles and teachers, command and direct.

4. And we see further here a powerful figure, how Jacob took their idols and earrings, and buried them under an oak by Shechem, where the murder was done. O thou great and wonderful God! what does this signify? Nothing else but that these their errors and idolatry, together with their wars and contentions, should thus for a long time lie buried in the anger of God.

5. And seeing the spirit mentioneth an oak, under which these idols and pride are buried, the figure is clear to us. For an oak is of a magnetic attractive kind, and maketh a tenacious[1] hardness in its property; moreover blackness, duskiness and darkness. This signifies that the former idolatry, sins and blasphemies, which they have committed, shall there, in the hungry wrath of the anger of God in turba

[1] Tough.

magna, viz. under the great oak in *spiritu mundi*, viz. in the hidden mystery, stand still a long while.

6. And what sin they shall commit anew, all that will this magnetic oak draw to it, and bring it to the treasure of the former idolatry and pride, till they become so great that the earth under the oak can cover them no more. Then shall these their old and new whoredoms and idolatries, together, be naked before the anger and judgment of God, and their measure be full.

7. And they would stink before God for these abominations, for the sake of which the spirit of God would hide its countenance from them, and take away from them the light of his countenance; so that they would run on in vain errors, and enter again upon the way of such whoredom, and with their evil zeal for Dinah their sister, which yet is but a deflowered whore, trample all under with murder and robbery.

8. As is come to pass among the Jews and Christians, that afterwards, in the zeal of their idolatry and whoredom, they have slain and murdered the prophets and ministers of Jesus Christ, which are sent from God (Rom. xi. 3); that they might live in their pride and Sodomitical whoredom, till *God hath given them up to a perverse mind* in their hearts (Rom. i. 28), that they are become wholly evil before him. Then is their measure full, and the horrible punishment followeth. As may be seen by the castaway Jews, which for such abominations' sake were driven out of their country and kingdom; as also by the Christians, who in the fair country of the east were the best Christians, and now must have the *Alcoran* instead of Christ, and their country horribly wasted in the anger of God.

9. Thus it goes now also with thee, thou warring Babylon and titulary Christendom, full of idolatry and earrings of pride, which have lain for a long time under the oak, and the magnet of that oak hath drawn to it all thy abominations, idolatry, and proud evil life, that the earth can cover them no longer; but they now stand naked before the face of God, therefore also thy judgment is near at hand.

10. The prophets call thee and reprove thee, but thou ravest for thy sister Dinah, viz. for thy fleshly kingdom, full of pride, which thou hast built with thy idolatry and fleshly love, and murderest thy brethren for thy sister's whoredom's sake, viz. for the Pharisaical whoredom's sake; and dost not discern how thou shouldst remedy thy sister's whoredom, that she may be married; and thou takest thy sister with her bastard, which in the presence of God and all the

JACOB TO DEPART FROM SHECHEM

world stand in shame, to thee again, and wilt have her called a virgin. If thou didst give her to Shechem for a wife, and let him be circumcised, and wouldst live with him in peace, then would thy sister's whoredom be covered.

11. But thy wrath, O Lord, maketh it to be thus: for the misdeed is too much, and the earth can no more cover it under the oak, in *spiritu mundi*, it standeth naked before thy face. Therefore, ye wise children, flee out of Babel (Jerusalem); the overthrow thereof, and the earnest judgment, draweth near, the measure is full, the anger burneth, sin hath killed the understanding, that they no more perceive or feel the understanding,[1] and these children are blind concerning it, and always say, This is a golden time, it will be good for us, and not so come to pass. Thy prophets among thee are esteemed fools and madmen, till that be done unto thee, and till thou thyself doest what they have said unto thee.

12. Beware now, and leave off to war about the whore, that the Lord may call thee with Jacob, and bring thee again to his holy altar in Christ Jesus. Put away the idols, viz. the opinions, and build thine heart to be an altar in the temple of Jesus Christ; then wilt thou be brought away from the murders, and the fear of God will come upon those men who would pursue thee, as is to be seen by Jacob. But if thou wilt not leave off to make war about the whore, then wilt thou, together with the whore, come to shame and desolation.

13. But learn to know her: she giveth Shechem occasion to uncleanness, for she runs out of her house, and seeketh lovers. Behold her pride, tear her earrings from her neck, wherewith she boasteth, and then she will no more thus shew her folly. Bereave her of her idols, bury them, with Jacob: build thyself an altar in thee, and bring thy children to the offering. Bid them not strive for Dinah, but leave Dinah to the man with whom she hath bedded; else it is in vain to make war for her virginity, for it is manifest to all people that she hath played the whore.

14. Mark what is told thee, it is high time, her shame can no more be covered, for she hath brought forth the bastard. Dost thou not see it? and dost thou not know the whore with her child? Then thou art blind.

15. She sitteth in high honour among men, and cries all hail to herself. This is she to whom thou prostitutest thyself, and forsakest thy God and his altar, Jesus Christ in thee. Take pity on thyself, and

---

[1] Have no more sense or understanding.

behold the misery, how this whore hath sat instead of the altar of God in thy soul, and hath taken thy body and soul in possession, and rideth upon thee as upon her beast; she leadeth thee with her reins, and thou seest it not, thou sayest likewise, It is right. O thou evil beast, full of thy whore's pride! how will the Lord throw thee, together with the whore, to the ground, as is to be seen in the *Revelations*![1]

16. The spirit here further setteth down an excellent fair figure, shewing how God manifested himself to Jacob, after *he made the altar in Bethel, and called the place El-Bethel* (Gen. xxxv. 7), viz. an angelical dwelling, where God conversed with Jacob in the form of an angel; as the high tongue renders it, that God spake with him in vision in an angel's form, viz. in the angel's form of the future humanity of Christ, and signified to him, that *he should no more be called Jacob, but Israel* (Gen. xxxv. 10-12), that is, a great tree, or company of nations. Him hath God thus blessed, that he should possess all this country; and he shall be so great that even kings should proceed out of his loins, whereby he signifieth concerning the future kingdom, of Israel, and of Christ, how it would come to pass.

17. *And when the Lord had spoken with Jacob, in that very place Jacob set up a pillar of stone* (Gen. xxxv. 14); which signifieth the temple of Christ, as also the temple at Jerusalem in a type prefiguring Christ, also the true Christian Church among the Christians, that from the word of the Lord men would build a place and pillar, where they would assemble and declare the wonders of the great God, and call upon him there, and offer up the drink-offering of prayer there.

18. And the spirit saith further, So God went up from him, when he had spoken with him (Gen. xxxv. 13). That is, when he had appeared in a visible form, in the image and type of Christ, he withdrew and hid himself again in that royal place; from whence afterwards he would manifest and make himself visible in his seed in this figure in the humanity.

19. *And Jacob called the place Bethel* (Gen. xxxv. 15), viz. a humiliation[2] of the Deity in the humanity, so that the divine altar becomes manifest, where a man offers praise and thanksgiving to God. And the spirit by Jacob concerning this Bethel pointeth at the future Bethlehem, where Christ should be born man; as this place, Bethel, was exceeding highly esteeemed by the patriarchs, which all pointeth at the future Bethlehem, where the true altar, Christ, should be erected

---

[1] *Apocalypse.*   [2] Or, condescension.

and built; upon which Jacob and his fathers and children had offered in the faith and prefiguring type, and under it God led them in the visible type from thenceforth, till the appointed time that this altar was erected at Bethlehem by the birth of Christ.

20. And the spirit in Moses speaketh instantly very darkly thereof in this figure, and saith, *And they went from Bethel* (Gen. xxxv. 16); whereby he pointeth at the going forth from the figure of Christ, that men should go forth from this figure to the birth of Christ; and saith, *And it was a field-breadth from Ephrath, where Rachel brought forth; and she was in hard labour at the birth* (Gen. xxxv. 16).

21. This field-breadth signifieth the time that is between that and the altar of Christ, as Adam was gone a field-breadth from the altar of God, that is, out of the spiritual world into the earthly, where it goeth very hard with Rachel, viz. with the human nature, as to the patriarch Benjamin. That is, to bring forth a Christian even the old Adam must die and perish in this birth, as Rachel died when she bare Benjamin.

22. Which Benjamin signifieth, that when we erect God's altar in us, so that Christ dwelleth in us, then is Benjamin, that is our last man [or second Adam], born. Then dieth the old mother who hath generated the kingdom of nature in man, and the new spiritual man is manifested.

23. This Benjamin is born after Jacob is first gone out of Mesopotamia, as the spirit hath prefigured the type of Christ's passion and victory by Esau and Jacob in their meeting. And it was a figure of the Apostle Matthias, who was elected to be an Apostle in the stead of Judas, after Christ had first consummated his passion and ascension into heaven.

24. And it is a figure shewing how man must first enter into Christ's passion and death, and that the altar of Christ must first be erected in him, before the human nature from Christ can be born. For Judas must first, in his falsehood and treachery in the old Adam, with sorrow for his committed sin, hang himself (Matt. xxvii. 5), and, as to his own ability, despair and die. And then will Benjamin, viz. the new creature in Christ, first be born, and Matthias, viz. the first created Adam, be elected an Apostle (Acts i. 26).

25. For Matthias was indeed born before the passion of Christ, and was with Christ; but he was then first an Apostle when Christ in him was dead from sin, and Judas had hanged himself. Thus also the Adamical man, which shall be an Apostle or Christian, is indeed born aforehand, before Christ suffereth in him; but Christ must first

arise from the dead in him, and Judas, viz. the Serpent's will, must hang himself and die to his own evil will in the death of Christ: and then first is the Adamical man a Christian.[1] It is not the historical man by an imputed grace, wherein Judas still liveth under the purple mantle of Christ, that is a Christian, as Babel playeth finely under the veil concerning the virginity of her daughter Dinah, that the fair dainty damsel may play the whore, and finely sleep with her pandour Judas, and lie with her lovers in the bed of fornication.

26. Great things are prefigured in this text, for the text saith: *When she was in sore labour in the birth of Benjamin, the midwife said to her, Fear not, for thou shalt have this son also. But her soul being ready to depart that she must die, she called him Benoni* (Gen. xxxv. 17, 18). That is, she looked upon the inward ground, upon the new birth, what he would be in Christ, and regarded not the name of the outward creature.

27. For *Benoni* is altogether a spiritual name after an angelical kind and manner; for she said, in spirit (when the midwife comforted her concerning it, that she should have this son also), I have him no more in the world, the outward passeth away; and it pointeth at the angelical new name. *But his father called him Benjamin* (Gen. xxxv. 18), as with the name of this world, that he should represent how a Christian must be born under the cross of Christ in smart pain, at which also his mother looked, as if she should say, Through smart pain and sorrow we come to life, as this son of my smart and sorrow.

28. Then saith the spirit, Thus Rachel died, and was buried in the way towards Ephrath, which is now called Bethlehem. And Jacob set up a pillar upon her grave: and that is the pillar of Rachel's grave unto this day (Gen. xxxv. 19, 20). This is a secret mystical figure, that Rachel died and is buried at the city Bethlehem; and it signifieth that she shall there rise again through the birth of Christ, for Christ should there be born.

29. And it is signified that when we shall flee to Bethlehem to the birth of Christ, then shall Benjamin, viz. the new spiritual man be born of Rachel, viz. of the mother of the old Adamical man, in the spirit of Christ. And then presently will the mother yield up her birthright to the spirit of Christ, and die to her right of nature; and then will the spiritual eternal birth begin, and Eve pass away; for there Jacob setteth up the gravestone or pillar. And the spirit saith it is her gravestone unto this day, to signify that it pointeth at the future, and

---

[1] Adam's man a Christ.

JACOB TO DEPART FROM SHECHEM

that this gravestone should continue, and Christ be born there where Rachel died.

30. In this history of the acts of Jacob we see clearly that the spirit hath in this description a figure, under which it signifieth. For Rachel was big with Benjamin when Jacob departed from Laban, when *she sat upon the idol-gods, when her father sought for them, and she said, It is with me after the manner of women, so that I cannot rise up before thee* (Gen. xxxi. 34, 35). But now the text relateth how Jacob first pitched his tents before Shechem, and dwelt there, and afterwards went first to Bethel, and then Rachel brought forth. So that it appeareth that the spirit speaketh wholly in the figure, for the acts do all follow very orderly one after another in the figure of Christ, as it hath come to pass with Christ, which ought well to be observed.

31. The spirit of Moses saith further, *And Israel went forth and spread his tents on the other side of the tower of Edar. And it came to pass, when Israel dwelt in that land, that Reuben went and slept with Bilhah his father's concubine: and it came before Israel* (Gen. xxxv. 21, 22): What manner of figure is this, which is very deeply hidden? but the circumstances make it as clear as the sun.

32. Israel went on the other side of the great Babylonical tower, and dwelt there with the children of that people, which may well be a pretty way from Ephrath (Bethlehem); but the spirit hath here its figure under which it signifieth: that is, when Jacob had taken away the strange gods from his people, and also their earrings, and buried them, and built the altar of the Lord, converting to God, and they were sitting in rest and ease, then the natural fleshly man turned again to the lust of the children of Babel, even as the text saith:

33. Jacob went and dwelt there, and then Reuben lay with his father's concubine, viz. with Bilhah, Rachel's handmaid, the mother of Dan and Naphthali, and committed incest,[1] which was worse than that of Shechem with Dinah. But the spirit hath thus with this action presented a figure, pointing at the future, how it would come to pass, how Israel would turn away from the divine ordinance from the altar of their God, and mix their father's worship and service of God with natural whoredom, viz. with heathenish sacrificing to idols, as is to be seen by Jeroboam. And the spirit signifieth thereby, that the first Adamical man would have only fleshly desires and lusts.

34. For Reuben was the first son of Jacob by Leah, viz. by her of whom also sprang the line of Christ; to signify that every one that

[1] Blutschande.

would be called Jews or Christians, and are generated out of those stocks, would forsake God, and lie with their father's concubines, viz. commit fornication with the idolatry, human inventions, and babblings of the Pharisees and Scribes, and with their laws and canons, and forget the truth of God, and of his commandments, in their hearts, and imprint those whoredoms[1] in their hearts' lusts.

35. For Reuben was indeed Jacob's first son, as Adam also was the first man, but the line of Christ was not manifested in Reuben, as also not in Adam, but it was manifested in Abel and in Judah. And as Adam, in *spiritu mundi*, in the spirit of the world, committed adultery with God's concubine, through whom he[2] bringeth forth his fruit, and gave up himself to the woman, viz. to the mother of the outward nature, and lay with her, and committed whoredom with her, and defiled the holy heavenly marriage-bed of chastity; thus also stood this figure of Reuben with his father's concubine portrayed before the figure of Christ; for Christ should bring this Adamical whoredom into the heavenly marriage-bed again, and cover the incest of man. And therefore it is here prefigured together with the figure of Rachel, viz. with the new regeneration.

The figure of Christendom stands thus:[3]

36. This concubine in Christendom signifieth nothing else but the stone churches,[4] which are indeed God's concubine, wherein his Word and Testaments are handled, in which God generateth his children, in which a man should work [together] with God, and turn his heart to God. But Reuben, viz. the Adamical man, forsaketh God, and committeth fornication and whoredom with the stone churches, and hath embraced her in his arms of love, and goeth in unto her, and playeth the hypocrite with her; and thinketh it is enough if he do but go thither and hear sermons preached, and make use of Absolution and the Sacraments, and believe that all is true which is there taught, and comforts himself with this: that he goes cheerfully, willingly, and constantly thither, and esteems that for right and good, and approveth and assenteth to all that is there performed, thus covering himself with the purple mantle of Christ; and goeth out of the Church just as he entered in, and goes twenty or thirty years together, and so to his

---

[1] Einbilden, make to themselves images of these.
[2] God.
[3] Or, is thus to be understood.
[4] Or, temples built with materials.

very end; and committeth whoredom with the churches, and thinketh he doth God good service when he appears there among others, sitting and hearing the preachers' sermons, and when he cometh forth knoweth nothing of what hath been done there.

37. Also in that auditory he had his heart at home, or about his trade and business, or casteth his eyes upon the beauty of fair women and men, and upon their brave clothes and fine fashions of pride; and filleth his heart with imaginations of lascivious lust, and broadly commits whoredom with these, or in these, concubines, the churches.

38. And that which is yet more: when the preacher often reproveth sins and abominations, and often indeed out of passion soweth thorns, that are caught up presently, he tickleth himself the whole week therewith, and contriveth how to find fault with and censure others, and to backbite and blemish them, how they may scoff at people, and gall them with cutting and stinging words, pricking like thistles and thorns, and holds that for the best of what he hath heard; and so setteth this Lucifer in the place of God, and constantly committeth fornication in the whoredom, viz. in the burning lust of these concubines.

39. And the greatest whoredom of all in this concubine is this: that men so quite take their hearts off from God, and set them upon the ministers of these concubines, and commit whoredom with them, and honour them with presents and gifts, so that they many times in their encomiums praise evil, malicious, proud, wicked, covetous people, who do but squeeze the miserable, and oppress them with power and authority. They make great epitaphs and eulogies, and give them high and stately titles, with high respect and reverence, ascribing to them great devotion, with the fear and love of God, and do highly advance their genealogy[1] and stock, and so set up the trade of juggling for money, as a common juggler, and so reproach the concubine of God, viz. the Church, with hypocrisy and lies. Of this it is rightly said, Reuben is climbed up to his father's concubine, and hath committed whoredom with her. For they are they that dwell by this concubine, and are her curates and bishops or overseers. But they fill this concubine full of their false fleshly seed, and generate bastards in God's concubine, that so the false lust of the flesh may wholly bring their heart into her, and [they] think it availeth before God and is very right. Their sins are thus covered by the venom and poison of money, and this hypocrisy filleth their imagination, so that they think they

---

[1] Or, pedigree.

are better than others, and live thus in such proud lofty thoughts continually, in such Church whoredom.

40. And thus Reuben begets, of his father's concubine the churches, a company of bastards, proud, stately, boasting, covetous people, which defile the poor mother of the humility and simplicity of JESUS CHRIST, viz. the line of Christ which lieth hid in this concubine, and shall be generated and manifested, and cast the whoredom upon her. And thus God's concubine, viz. the Church, is made to be a whore; and so very much deflowered that her reproach is come before Israel, viz. before the eyes of all the children of God; who cry fie upon her, and account her for an unclean deflowered whore, wherein such whoredom, as also pomp, pride and pageantry is exercised, that the devil, with the imagination and false lust, doth more teach and govern in such lust, than the spirit of Christ; and it is more a proud whore and a dark valley [and dungeon] than a temple of JESUS CHRIST.

41. And that which is yet more abominable: many very vain affectations, scornings and derisions are therein managed and taught, where, for an opinion's sake, which every one frames to himself, they disgrace and persecute one another, and cry out against one another for heretics, and sow abroad such poison and venom in this concubine the Church; whereby simplicity is seduced, and such poison of defamation riseth up and groweth in their hearts, that in the churches nothing but contention, disputation, scorn and blasphemy is exercised and taught, that one brother despiseth the other, calleth him heretic, and damneth him to hell fire for an opinion's sake, whereby all love, truth, unity and concord is vanished.

42. The grossest impudence, at which the heavens and the elements at present stand amazed, which is practised in this concubine, is this: That men take the writings of the holy children of God, viz. of the Prophets and Apostles, and their successors, and make use of them falsely, putting them on for a cloak to cover such whoredom, corrupting and embittering them, and making mere sects and swarms of schisms of them; and thereby reproach, slander and persecute one another, giving thereby cause of wars and bloodshed; and so they make a mere impudent whore of the Bible, wherewith every one exerciseth and manageth their whoredom, and sucketh opinions out of it, and therewith despise the opinion of another, and scorneth and condemneth it, and yet take all their matters out of the Bible. Thus they make their father's concubine, viz. the holy Prophets and Apostles all whores, and falsely commit whoredom with them,

JACOB TO DEPART FROM SHECHEM

practise impudence, unchastity and pride with their writings, and teach the lay people their unchastity and scorn; so that one Christian learneth to scorn another out of the Holy Scripture, and trim their scorn with the writings of the saints.[1] Of this it is rightly said, Reuben, thou art my first strength, but thou hast climbed up upon my bed, and defiled it with unchastity; thou hast used my concubine, viz. my formed Word, to thy whoredom, and hast made of the churches of my children a whore-house, and hast defiled my marriage-bed, which I have in the churches, where I beget my children.

43. This the spirit of God signifieth clearly, by the declaration of the patriarch Jacob, where he saith thus concerning these churches and their sacrifices: *Reuben, thou art my first son, thou art my first power, and my first might, the chief in the offering, and the chief in the kingdom: unstable therein as water, thou shalt not be the chief; for thou hast climbed up upon thy father's bed, and there hast thou defiled my bed by thy climbing up* (Gen. xlix. 3, 4).

44. The spirit speaketh clearly in this text: for Reuben signifieth the ordinance of the first Church, viz. the power out of which it was built, that is, the first power of the Christian Church or congregation, and is God's concubine, by which he dwelleth. But their ministers are climbed up into God's marriage-bed, and have gotten the concubine to themselves, and taken her into their power, and have gotten her with child, with human fictions, fleshly honour and voluptuousness. And it saith clearly, *Thou art the chief in the offering, and in the kingdom*: for so it must needs be, when the whoredom is not committed. But seeing Reuben exerciseth whoredom with the churches, it saith thus, *Thou shalt not be the chief; for he was unstable therein as water*; and signifieth thereby that he would give himself to fleshly lust and self-love, and that in unstability: and in that regard is rejected of God.

45. Thus the spirit signifieth under this figure, how this concubine, viz. the Church, would be reproached with its first power, viz. of its own children; so that it will be said by the churches, It is a spiritual whore-house, which a man must distinguish from the temple of JESUS CHRIST. For the spirit saith, Thou shalt not be the chief, neither in the offering, nor in the kingdom: and thus she hath lost the true divine power[2] by the whoredom of her ministers, and standeth at present rightly as a deflowered one that is made a whore, which is despised of Israel for her unchastity, which is practised by her; which is cried out upon by almost every one, each party crying out against

---

[1] Holy men.   [2] Jus Divinum.

the church of the other, for a whore-house, as is enough manifest; and all libraries are full of such a cry, and men at present are ready to storm and fall in upon the whore-house.

46. But let this be said to the children of God: that the churches hurt no man, and they were instituted out of a good meaning by the first Christian power; and were very good and profitable, and they need not be thrown down and demolished, if Reuben would but leave his whoredom, whereby he reproacheth them; that her ministers might be renewed, and not, without the unction of the Holy Ghost, give forth that they are the ministers of this concubine of God, as is now done only for temporary honour and pleasure's sake, which are as profitable to the Church as a fifth wheel is to a wagon: unless they go with five wheels to their wagon, where the fifth moveth in the air, and entereth with their contention into the abyss of hell.

47. The stone houses of the churches have no greater holiness in them than other houses, for they are built of stone and such materials as other houses are, and God is no more powerful in them than in other houses. But the Church or congregation that entereth thereinto, and there meeteth together, and there bind themselves with their prayer into one body in Christ, whose type and resemblance the Church is, that [Church] hath the holy temple of JESUS CHRIST in it.

48. Their songs of praise and thanksgiving are the cradle of the child JESUS CHRIST, in which the child Jesus is rocked with unanimous consent in the hearts of men, and not within the bounds of the church which is a dumb and dead thing.

49. Its ministers are no more than all other men; but the power and virtue that is poured forth in the unction of the Holy Ghost hath the power in the offering, and is the key.

50. Whosoever will worthily enter into the church, must bring with him the temple of Jesus Christ within him, or at least he must fully take such a resolution and purpose that he will bring it out with him in his heart; otherwise his going in and coming out is but a committing of spiritual seeming holy, but indeed hypocritical, whoredom; and [he] is no whit the holier when he cometh out, and had as good have been standing in the market, shewing his pride in his fine clothes, for the people to see him: and then perhaps he had not caused many honest hearts to err.

51. This we had a purpose to signify by the knowing of this figure: That a Christian should not look upon the show of churches, but consider that the Church is but a type and resemblance of Christ;

JACOB TO DEPART FROM SHECHEM

and that he is not a Christian that entereth into the resemblance, and approveth of that; but he is a Christian that wholly giveth himself up into Christ's incarnation, suffering, and death, and dieth to his hypocrisy in the death of Christ, and riseth from the death of Christ in a new will and obedience, and who, according to his inward ground, is and liveth in Christ, who himself becometh the temple of Christ, wherein Christ worketh with his power and virtue, and thereby killeth sin in the flesh. Such a one is a Christian in Christ, and may rightly enter into the resemblance of Christ, and exercise his Christianity therein. Such a one will hear God's word, and keep and ponder it in his heart.

52. And though a cow's lowing, in its sound, should declare the name of God, yet Christ preacheth in himself: but none that is dead can awaken another that is dead, nor *one that is blind shew the way to another, but both will fall into the pit*, saith Christ (Matt. xv. 14).

53. Further, the spirit of Moses sets down in its figure the death of the patriarch Isaac, and saith: *And Jacob came to his father Isaac to the head city in Mamre, called Hebron, where Abraham and Isaac were strangers. And Isaac was an hundred and eighty years old, and gave up the ghost and died, and was gathered unto his people* (Gen. xxxv. 27-29). This is a figure, shewing that the children of Christ in this pilgrimage are but strange children, and have nothing for their own in the world, and come all again in the end to their Father who hath created them; as Jacob came again to his father before his end. Thus also are we, in this pilgrimage in these earthly churches, but household servants and strange children, for we must in the end go into our Father's right country, viz. into the angelical Church of Christ.

The Sixty-Fourth Chapter

Of *Esau's* Genealogy: And of the very excellent and emphatical Figure, which is signified by *Joseph* the Son of *Jacob*. And what is thereby to be understood[1]

1. THE thirty-sixth chapter of *Genesis* is the genealogy of the potent and princely family of Esau, shewing how God gave him much wealth and many children, and children's children; and the spirit setteth down a great register in describing his children, and children's children, relating what great princes [and dukes] were descended of him, and possessed the glory of the world: whereas on the other side, when he speaketh of Jacob, he doth not mention any present worldly glory; but only speaketh in the figure of Christ concerning the kingdom to come.

2. Whereby we see very clearly that Esau doth stand in the figure of the kingdom of nature, and that the glory of nature fell to be his lot; and that he became a great prince, and begat many princely families. Also we see how God blessed him, and made him great, and how the Holy Spirit, with especial observation,[2] hath recorded and specified his posterity; to signify that we should learn rightly to understand the figure of Jacob and Esau, and not go on so blindly as to condemn Esau into the bottomless pit of hell, as too frequently is done. For we see how his father Isaac did appoint and assign unto him a very rich and wealthy habitation upon the earth, and that to him God would give many temporal blessings. But his figure in Adam's nature must perish; and Christ must arise in him, so that from ESAU the SAU[3] might be done away, and he remain steadfast in the E,[4] as (*ein Engel*) an angel, whereunto Christ in Jacob's figure would help him.

3. The spirit of Moses giveth also to Esau a name, and calleth him *Edom* (Gen. xxxvi. 8), who dwelt upon mount Seir, under which a very secret understanding is couched. For *Edom* doth signify, in the High

---

[1] Gen. xxxvi.
[2] Care and diligence.
[3] The swinish, bestial, earthy property.
[4] The angelical eternal property.

OF ESAU'S GENEALOGY

Tongue,[1] one red coloured, who, in his hard, strong and rough[2] nature, should be tinctured red by the red blood of JESUS CHRIST.

4. And the spirit saith further, that *the two brothers did separate themselves one from another* (Gen. xxxvi. 6), which signifieth the natural Adamical Esau, who must be separated with his [evil] will from Jacob, that is, from Christ; for the natural self-will shall not see God. Moreover, it signifieth how evil and good should separate themselves in the kingdom of this world, and each possess its own Principle.

5. These names of the children of Esau do, in the Language of Nature, contain their worldly kingdom and dominions, intimating how they have divided themselves, even unto the ends of the world: whereof, in another place,[3] seeing it would take up too much room, and *the time also of the clear signifying of it* is not yet fully at hand. Enough to those that are our schoolfellows.

NOTE

The Third Part of the Mysterium Magnum *was published in Germany as a Complete Treatise of itself, under the Name of* Josephus Redivivus.

But when the whole Book came to be printed together, there was only the First Part, and the Second Part, which comprehended the Third Part also as one with the Second.

Yet because the History of Joseph, *being an Exposition of the last* 14 *Chapters of* Genesis, *is so excellent and entire a piece, it may well go as a Third Part of the* Mysterium Magnum, *as it is here distinctly divided and printed by itself, with a several Title Page, as followeth.*

[1] In the Hebrew.
[2] Text, mountainous.
[3] *Note.*—Another place in other writings of his.

THE THIRD PART
OF THE
Myſterium Magnum:
BEING
THE MOST EXCELLENT HISTORY OF
JOSEPH,
WHICH IS

The Cleerest Figure of the New-Man
Regenerated out of the Earthly Old
A D A M.

AND IS

A Looking Glasse, wherein Every one may
try, examine, and discerne what Spirits
Childe himselfe is.

Written by JACOB BEHM, *Teutonicus.*

Beginning at the XXXVII Chapter of *Genesis,* and the 64
of this *Mysterium Magnum,* and at the 6 Verse, and ending at the
L and last Chapter of *Genesis,* and the 78 and last Chapter of
the *Mysterium Magnum.*

LONDON,
Printed by *Matthew Simmons.* 1 6 5 4.

OF ESAU'S GENEALOGY

6. THE thirty-seventh chapter,[1] concerning Joseph, is indeed the most pleasant and excellent figure of the new man regenerate out of the old Adam. Which [new regenerate man] is become a prince over the kingdom of nature, and also a lord over all his Adamical members, being the brethren of the little child Jesus in him; as *Joseph became a prince in the whole land of Egypt, and a lord over all his brothers, and whole kindred and family* (Gen. xlii. 6). And it shews us very emphatically and pregnantly in its figure in the history, how a man must become such a Joseph; also how it then goes with him, and how the world dealeth with him, before he be made a prince over the Adamical kingdom of his nature, and that the new man may obtain the government and power over his earthly members: How the devil in the wrath of God doth assault the precious lily-twig in the power of God, out of which the chaste Joseph springeth, groweth, and is brought forth; and first casteth him down into the pit of darkness in flesh and blood, and there hides him, that so he might be destitute of all help, comfort and assistance, and be even forced to perish.

7. As Joseph's brethren did to Joseph, even so the earthly members of the old Adam do likewise to this lily-twig of the new birth in the chastity of Christ's spirit; whereat the devil is also busy, and continually stirreth up the evil beasts, full of carnal, greedy, and burning lust in flesh and blood, so that they strive to domineer and have the upperhand.

8. Externally, or from without, the devil also bringeth Potiphar's wife, viz. unchaste lewd people to him, who would fain defile the chaste countenance of the inward ground, and egg on the earthly flesh to feed upon the whoredom of the world, and all lascivious lewdness, wantonness and vanity, and draw the same unto it with the imagination; and bring the new Joseph to commit adultery with Potiphar's wife. But he must so violently and resolvedly break through, and force his way from thence, that he must be fain to leave his garment, that is, his substance,[2] and fly from thence nakedly, and resignedly in spirit and power, that his chaste virginity may abide steadfast before God.

9. And if Joseph doth thus wrestle, and suffers not flesh and blood nor the base world to hinder or over-master him; then it will become his utter enemy, and betray him to death, because he will not commit lewdness and whoredom with her. And then Joseph, viz. the wrestling

---
[1] Gen. xxxvii.
[2] All whatsoever he hath, or is.

man,[1] is cast into prison, viz. into reproach and contempt for the sake of his chastity and fear of God; and he must hide himself under Christ's cross, under his yoke, in his suffering and death, and live as a prisoner in misery; the world rejecting him as one not at all worthy to tread upon the earth; accounting him as a prisoner, that is imprisoned and despised for whoredom's sake; desiring to have no converse nor intercourse with him, seeing that the chief masters and great ones (viz. Potiphar's wife) do revile him, and accuse him of unchastity.

10. Which wife doth also signify the false [Babylonish] hypocritical whore, with all her dissemblers and flatterers in the fine adorned house of Christendom; who, when they cannot catch and hold Joseph with their whoredom, but that he doth strongly get away from them, then they exclaim out against him falsely, and keep his garment for a sign, accusing him of unchastity, viz. of idolatry [and heresy],[2] and call him a dreamer, a phantastical fellow,[3] and a schismatic: as happened to Joseph.

11. And when the master heareth it, then he believeth this Potiphar's wife, viz. the painted, and fine, accomplished hypocrite, in the house of hypocrisy. And so Joseph cometh to be suspected of the master, and is rejected of him, and cast into the prison of affliction, and there he must live in misery and scorn, as a guilty person: and yet not guilty.

12. But this contempt, banishment and affliction is good for him; for thereby he is drawn from the pride and whoredom of the world and all its falsehoods, which might assault his flesh and blood, and hinder the new birth. And thus the precious pearl-plant grows under Christ's cross, in the disrespect and tribulation of the world, and becomes great and strong.

13. But in the meantime God doth send honest people to such a Joseph, who take pity and care of him, and maintain him, and acknowledge his innocency, and shew themselves friendly and kind towards him, and consider his chastity and fear of God, and do also respect him, and provide for him, till the inward prince in God's power be fit for the government. And then God bringeth him out of prison, and giveth him the sceptre of government, to be a prince in his wonders, and to rule and govern in divine knowledge over God's wonderful works: as Joseph over the land of Egypt. In which type and

---

[1] The real, earnest, conflicting Christian.
[2] One, of dangerous principles or opinions.
[3] A whimsical fellow.

figure[1] this pen is likewise born, and indeed no otherwise; which yet is hidden unto reason.

14. This is now the sum of the exposition of the history of Joseph: But seeing it is so very rich and full, we will make a fundamental explanation upon the text, for a direction and manuduction to the loving Reader, who also intendeth to become a Joseph. If he shall be in earnest, and learn to observe and know himself in this figure, he will see what spirit's child hath made these writings; for he will find this pen [engraving or writing][2] in his heart.

15. The text saith, *Jacob dwelt in the land wherein his father was a stranger, namely, in the land of Canaan. These are the generations of Jacob: Joseph, being seventeen years old, was feeding the flock with his brethren; and the lad was with the sons of Bilhah, and with the sons of Zilpah, his father's wives: and Joseph brought unto his father their evil report. Now Israel loved Joseph more than all his children, because he had begotten him in his old age: and he made him a coat of many colours. And when his brethren saw that their father loved him more than all his brethren, they hated him, and could not speak friendly to him* (Gen. xxxvii. 1-4).

The inward figure is this:

16. Jacob had cast his fleshly natural love upon Rachel, seeing she was fair; and seeing that the line of Christ in the Covenant did lie in Jacob, Rachel was shut up. So that his seed was not manifested in her in the natural manner of the flesh, until Jacob and Rachel were grown old, and neither of them loved each other so any more according to fleshly love, but only desired a fruit of their seed; wherefore also Jacob and Rachel prayed unto God, that he would open her, and make her fruitful. And when this was brought to pass, out of this seed of Jacob sprang forth a line, which did set forth and represent a figure of the pure natural and right Adamical humanity. Which birth, in the figure, typifieth how Christ would again beget the Adamical humanity in[3] its primitive chastity, purity, and fear of God.

17. For in Leah, viz. in the simplicity and lowliness, the line of Christ arose and sprang forth, and in Rachel the line of the first Adamical man in his innocency, viz. a figure of the same; which figure did represent how a Christian should stand at once both in Christ's

---
[1] In such a condition.
[2] That pen of iron or point of a diamond it is that engraveth in the heart (Jer. xvii. 1).
[3] Unto.

image and in Adam's image; and what a Christian in this world should be inwardly and outwardly, and how he must become a Christian. Therefore saith the text, *Jacob loved Joseph more than all his children.* The cause was this: Joseph was sprung forth out of Jacob's own natural line, of his peculiar natural love to Rachel, wherein the line in Christ's love in the Covenant had also imprinted and manifested itself; and it was a punctual representation in the figure of a new regeneration, how a true Christian should stand, after that Christ should be revealed in the flesh of the human nature.

18. And therefore Joseph was so inclined in his mind that he could not conceal any falsehood, but when he heard any evil of his brethren he told the same to his father. This his brethren could not brook, and therefore they called him a betrayer, and envied him: for the spirit which reproveth wickedness and falsehood was revealed in him. For Christ should reprove the world for sin (John xvi. 8). But seeing he now did represent a Christian, he told it his father, out of whom HE should come who should reprove the world. And we see very clearly how flesh and blood [viz. Joseph's natural brethren] in the type of Christendom became an utter enemy to the type [viz. to the true Christian Joseph], and they could not speak a friendly peaceable word unto him; for it doth sorely vex and offend the Serpent in flesh and blood, when Christ comes and will bruise its head.

19. Moreover, we see very evidently how the spirit of God did manifest itself in Joseph, and signified to him the figure of his constellation; so that he could understand dreams and visions, after the same manner as the prophets in the spirit of Christ saw visions, and could expound them: so also Joseph.

20. As it was shewn unto him in a vision how he would be a prince over his father, and all his brethren; which doth directly point out the inward man in the spirit of Christ, who becomes prince over his Father's Adamical house. In the type and figure whereof Joseph stood outwardly, and therefore the external figure was set forth and personated in him by the hatred of his brethren towards him; signifying how the multitude of the world would be hateful, scornful, and opposite enemies to the new child in Christ's spirit; and also how it would be done by those who were Christians, and did boast of Christ, and were also such in the inward ground; and how the Adamical man would not know and acknowledge Christ in a true outward and manifest manner, but ignorantly despise and contemn him in his brethren and members.

OF ESAU'S GENEALOGY

21. To signify that in this world Christ hath taken on himself the reproach, in the righteousness of God; and that he would not only in his own human person suffer scorn, and bear Adam's reproach (seeing Adam departed from the image of God), but that he would also suffer himself to be reproached in all his members and children; so that he would also bear Adam's reproach in them, and *make them like to his image* (Rom. viii. 29).

22. Therefore must Jacob's children, who also were in Christ's line according to their natural Adamical man, reproach, revile and hate the image of a true Christian man in Joseph. To shew how one Christian would exercise, provoke [and persecute] another in zeal, and despise his fellow-Christian for a natural opinion's sake; as it now is and ever hath been practised in Christendom [namely], that the one party hath despised, contemned and hated the other, because of natural laws [rights or privileges] and the opinions of a supposed service of God.

23. As Joseph was hated of his brethren because he had visions,[1] so nowadays is the divine wisdom (which revealeth itself in God's children) vilified and hated of the natural Adam. Which scorn and enmity doth wholly proceed and arise from the Pharisaical laws and canons, from the concubine of Christ, the stone-churches, and their ministers, which do disgrace and vilify the concubine of Christ themselves, as it appears very evidently; and thereby they contemn and despise the children of Christ.

24. For by the concubine of Christ, the churches, the Babylonish tower of the high schools and universities is built; and from thence come the confused languages,[2] so that Christ is not understood in his children. When they, in the simplicity of Christ, declare and expound the visions of Joseph [the Mysteries of Christ's kingdom], then these strange languages despise it, for they have gotten upon the tower other languages, from the compaction of the sensual tongues, where every sense of the literal spirits hath brought itself into a form of a several peculiar tongue or speech.

25. And the height of the tower giveth the difference or distinction of speech to this sensual tongue, so that they do not understand one another in their understanding [or ground of their meaning]. Which height signifieth the pride of self-love, from which the five vowels do hide themselves, so that they understand not the power of God (Matt. xxii. 29) in God's children, in the simplicity of Joseph, but call

---

[1] Or, for the knowledge of his visions.
[2] The confusion of several opinions and conceits in men's minds.

him a dreamer, an expounder of signs, a schismatic, a phantastical fellow, an enthusiast and a fool.

26. Thus, in the room and place of our Adamical guilt and crime, Christ is despised in his children; and thus Christ fulfilleth the righteousness of God (Matt. iii. 15) in his children; and hereby the old man is also mortified. And it is well for the Christian Joseph that it goes thus with him, for otherwise he would not be thrown into the world's pit, and be sold to the Midianites, that he might come to Pharaoh, and there become a prince.

27. Therefore a Christian must not be grieved and perplexed at the hatred of his brethren (in that they hate Joseph), but rather think with himself: O! that thou also were cast into Joseph's pit, that thou mightest thereby be brought away from the house of sin, and come likewise into Joseph's prison, that so thou mightest have cause to fly from the world; and that this prince (that giveth Joseph to understand the divine visions in his word of power) might be also manifest and born under the banner of Christ's cross; that in thee also the divine chastity of Joseph (the pure Christian virginity) might be manifested, that thou likewise mightest obtain such a godly, chaste heart. This ought to be the wish and will of a Christian, and not that he may become great by means of the tower of Babel in the strange languages; of whose difference and several variety the height [of the tower], viz. pride, is the author and cause; so that men will not understand one another in love, meekness, humility, and in the simplicity of Christ, in whom notwithstanding we live and have our being (Acts xvii. 28).

28. Therefore, O thou poor, confused and distracted Christendom, thou art bidden and entreated, by the affliction of Joseph, to see from whence thy affliction and misery cometh: from no whither else, save only from the hatred of thy brethren, which also are in Christ's line, as Joseph's brethren. Observe it aright, thy wound and hurt, thy misery and affliction, doth come only from the tower of Babel, from the titles, dignities and preferments of thy brethren, who, in their pride of the confused tongues, are entered into self-love. Observe it, I beseech thee: all strife, division and contention in the world ariseth from thence.

29. But thou sayest, This tower [doth advance me to honour and esteem, and] makes me high [and rich]; so that I, by means of the strange languages [of my literal endowments and scholastic learning], can ride over Joseph, and am able to bind him, so that he must lie in the pit; and thus I am lord in Christ's kingdom upon the earth.

OF ESAU'S GENEALOGY

30. Hearken, and mark it. We have heard a watchman say, The Midianites come and take Joseph with them, and bring him unto Pharaoh. And there thine unfaithfulness and unrighteousness shall be discovered. How wilt thou then stand before the face of Joseph? The time is nigh at hand.

31. Or dost thou think that the affliction of Joseph shall not be avenged? Behold! in thy miserable famine and distress, when thou shalt hunger and thirst, even then thou must make thy address and supplication to him. The high tower will give thee neither comfort nor deliverance: the time is come about that Joseph's affliction is to be avenged, and Reuben's whoredom with Jacob's concubine is come before Israel.

32. Why makest thou such long delay, and flatterest thyself, playing the hypocrite, and sayest: Not yet, a good while? Behold! it is come before the eyes of Israel, that thou hast committed whoredom a long time with the concubine, and defiled the line of Christ. Israel will no longer endure it; thou shalt with Reuben be cast out of the high office of sacrificing and governing: This is the voice which the watchmen have pronounced.

33. When Joseph had had the two dreams: the one, of his sheaf standing upright, before which the sheaves of his brethren bowed; the other of the sun, moon, and eleven stars, which had done obeisance to Joseph: envy forthwith arose amongst them, and they supposed he would be their lord (Gen. xxxvii. 5-10); and seeing that they were the elder they desired to rule over him.

34. Whereby we see how the outward man hath only sought and aimed at the kingdom of this world; which was even the bane and undoing of Adam, in that he forsook the inward and sought after the outward.

35. Joseph's parti-coloured coat which his father made (Gen. xxxvii. 3) signifieth how the inward power of God would again be revealed through the outward man, whereby the human nature would be variously coloured (that is, mixed with God), as the inward spiritual kingdom with the outward.

The spiritual figure standeth thus:

36. Joseph, with his coat of many colours, was as yet a lad, both tender and young, and had not yet the wit, craft and subtlety of the world, but spake the truth in simplicity; for his soul was not yet

defiled from without with the craft of lying; and the spirit of God began to drive him forward:[1] for his coat of many colours was a figure of the inward.

37. This figure prefigureth and representeth to us the image of a true young scholar and beginner in Christianity, how he must be when the spirit of God shall drive and act in him; namely, he must turn his heart to God his Father, and learn to love him heartily. As Joseph loved to be with his father, and told him the evil that was committed among his children, so must a beginner in Christianity daily bring before God all his own miseries, and the miseries and sins of all that belong to him; yea, of all Christendom. As Daniel confessed the sins of the people of Israel before God; and Joseph the evils of his brethren before his father; so also a true Christian doth daily confess the misery and sin of his people and nation, in hearty compassion, that God would be merciful to them and preserve them from great evils and sins.

38. And when this is brought to pass his heart becometh very simple, honest and upright, for he desireth no craft, but would fain have all things proceed righteously and justly; and he cannot abide any unrighteousness or subtle dealings; for he always confesseth the people's unrighteousness before God. And thus his mind becometh altogether simple, and seeketh no kind of craft or subtlety; but putteth his hope and confidence in God, and liveth in the simplicity and lowliness of heart before God and the world. And he is as the tender young lad Joseph; for he hopeth for good continually from God his Father.

39. Now when a man is come so far, then Joseph [viz. the chaste virgin child of Sophia] is even born; then God his Father clothes his soul with the parti-coloured coat, viz. with the divine power; and forthwith the spirit of God in him beginneth to play with the soul: as he did with Joseph. For the spirit of God seeth through the soul, and with the soul (as Joseph, in the type, saw things which were to come, represented to him in the vision of dreams, whereby the spirit did also play with the soul), even so the spirit of God doth forthwith take delightful communion with the soul of a new Joseph, viz. with the inward spiritual world. So that the soul understandeth divine mysteries, and seeth into the eternal life, and knoweth the hidden world, which yet is to be revealed in man: as this pen hath found by experience, from whence it hath received its spirit of knowledge.

[1] Work, act, or move in him.

OF ESAU'S GENEALOGY

40. Now when this man beginneth to speak of divine things and visions, of the hidden world's divine mysteries, and speaketh forth the wonders of God, and that his brethren (viz. the children of the outward world in whom the hidden spiritual world is not yet manifest) do hear it, they count it a mere fable and a melancholy chimera and whimsey, and esteem him foolish, in that he speaketh of those things which they cannot understand and comprehend; they make a mere fancy and fiction of it. Also they account it some astral instigation or false enthusiasm, or the like; especially if he revealeth and reproveth their evil works and ways, as Joseph did; then they turn his open enemies, and grudge him his very life, as happened to Joseph.

41. Now when it is thus, reason beholdeth itself at a stand as if it were confounded, and knoweth not the ways of God, viz. that it must be thus with the children of God. It thinketh, Thou seekest God, and he bringeth thee into distress and misery: thus this man doth now wander up and down; as Joseph wandered in the wilderness when his father sent him to his brethren to see how it was with them.

42. So it goeth likewise with God's new children, when God's spirit sendeth them to be zealous about the affliction of Joseph; and the world doth every way hate and persecute them for it. Then they think, in the reason of this world, Dost thou not go in the ways of God? wherefore then doth it go so with thee, that thou art but the fool of the world? And then the mind beginneth to be troubled, and knows not how it is with it; for he heareth that he is everywhere accused for a frantic wicked person, and hated; for the young mind in flesh and blood understandeth not the divine process; viz. how reason must become a fool, and how Christ doth very willingly take upon himself, in man, the reproach and scorn of the devil, and of the world; and how God's righteousness, and Adam's propagated guilt, must be always fulfilled with suffering, [and] how a Christian must stand in Christ's figure.

43. And now when it comes to be thus, then reason goes truly a-wandering in great sorrow and desertion with Joseph in the wilderness; and is every way in distress: and yet he must perform his father's commandment and will. But God forsaketh not his Joseph; but sendeth him a man to comfort him, and shew him the way to his brethren; as happened to Joseph, when he was a-wandering in the wilderness.

44. That is, he sendeth to him also a truly zealous Christian, who knoweth his ways, and comforteth him, exhorting him to persevere

constantly in the ways of God. Whereby this new Joseph doth again receive courage and strength, and cometh into the right way, and goeth readily and boldly to his brethren, and seeth what they do, and what they intend.

45. That is, he setteth the command and will of God before them (as Joseph did the command of his father). And when they see that he will reprove them with God's word, then they cry out, Lo! there is a dreamer (Gen. xxxvii. 19), and a frantic fellow; he will come and make us believe strange things; he inveigheth against our good customs, wherein we have honour and good days. What, shall this fellow reprove us? He is not come from the high schools [and universities]; and yet will take upon him to teach and reprove us; let us consult how we may take him out of the way, and slay him. What, shall we endure this poor silly fellow to teach and reprove us? What is he? He is but a layman; and shall he control us? Moreover, he is not called; and it is none of his vocation; he puts himself forth only that he might be taken notice of, and get himself some name and fame among the people. But we will so silence him that he shall be the fool of all the world; we will lay his honour in prison, and make him be scorned, hated and persecuted, for an example to others that shall offer to assault or trouble us; that so he may learn to tarry at home, and attend his worldly vocation, and leave it to us to judge of divine matters, who are appointed and authorised by the magistrate, and have studied in the universities, and there have learned such things.

46. Thus they take the poor Joseph, which cometh to them by his father's command, and bind him with reproach and shame, and exclaim against him falsely; and rob him of his coat of many colours in the sight of all his brethren, which coat God his Father hath made him; as Jacob's sons did to Joseph, and continually consult how to kill him, and take him wholly out of the way, as Joseph's brethren did (Gen. xxxvii. 18–20).

47. But as Reuben the eldest brother did hinder it, and would not suffer them to kill Joseph, and yet, that he might not be wholly against their council, he said, *Behold, here is a pit in the wilderness, into that we will cast him. And send his coat of many colours to his father, that he may think some evil beast hath devoured him* (Gen. xxxvii. 22). So God raiseth in their council, Reuben the eldest brother, who hath power to hinder the counsels and decrees of the false Pharisees; viz. some honest, pious man in authority, who resisteth the murdering council of the Pharisees.

48. And although he doth not wholly oppose their counsels, yet he resisteth and stoppeth the actual execution of their wills, and saith, Kill him not; cast him only into the pit, and strip him of his coat of many colours, that he may have no more dreams. And this he doth that he may deliver him from the murdering sword.

49. But they take him (as Joseph's brethren did Joseph) and strip him of his coat of many colours, and cast him into the pit in the wilderness, and take his coat of many colours and dip it in goat's blood, and send it so to his father (Gen. xxxvii. 23, 24, 31, 32). That is to say, they deprive and bereave him of his honour and good name by their slanderings, and take his words and doctrine, and make false constructions and conclusions thereof, and bedaub them in goat's blood, that is, with false understanding and sense; and send forth such reproaching pamphlets and libels among the people, and before his father, viz. before the whole Church and Commonwealth, and cry out, Lo! this defiled coat is this man's. And thus they murder the spirit of his father, in the coat; that is, in his name they scandalise, slander and reproach him falsely, and say of him that he doth vilify the blood of Christ with his coat of many colours. And thus they deceive his father, viz. the whole congregation, with the false goat's blood, wherein they have dipped his coat; so that the people think, A wild beast hath torn Joseph in pieces (Gen. xxxvii. 33); that is, they think the devil hath possessed this man, and that he is a false [wicked] man.

50. Thus the father, viz. the people and the magistrates are, by this defiled coat, deceived by [the sleight of] Joseph's brethren; that is, by those who themselves are to teach the way of God, so that they think that the devil hath devoured this man, and hath possessed his heart. And thus the poor Joseph is thrown down into the desolate pit in the wilderness, and lieth in misery, as *in a pit wherein there is no water* (Zech. ix. 11), and wherein he can neither be drowned, nor receive any refreshment; but sitteth as wholly forsaken of all the world; and waiteth now what God will do with him, since he thus rejecteth him by men.

51. Here now he hath no help or succour from any man; his best friends also account him mad and foolish; his name is as an owl among the birds; for thus he must pass through the judgment of God, and be even the scorn of all men. If he shall attain to the contemplation of the Divine Mysteries, then he must first be judged, and come under the censure and judgment of the world; that they may judge his inbred

sins, and sacrifice them before God, that he, in the figure of Christ,[1] may force through the judgment of God, and come to the divine vision within himself.

52. Thus a right true Christian [before he attains the science of the Divine Mysteries] must be wholly severed from the pleasure and honour of the world, and become altogether foolish, and a child to his own reason in himself; and also outwardly be accounted a fool, as the world likewise esteems him a foolish silly fellow, when he forsaketh temporal honour and goods for the hope of the eternal good which he seeth not.

53. And when it goeth thus with poor Joseph, that he must lie in the miserable pit, his brethren are not yet content that they have cast him into the pit, but *they draw him out from thence, and sell him to the Midianites, that he may be carried from them into a strange and foreign country* (Gen. xxxvii. 28). That is, they take his name and doctrine, and send them into foreign countries, whereby Joseph's coat of many colours doth by divine appointment and providence come to be known.

54. But they intend treacherously and falsely towards him, and so sell Joseph to reproach, derision and servitude, to serve the world, and to be their footstool and scorn; as happened to Joseph from his brethren, and hath also happened to this pen.

55. Thus *Joseph is brought into Egypt, and sold for a slave* (Gen. xxxvii. 36). *But God is with him, and giveth him understanding and wisdom, that he is made his master's steward, so that his master doth[2] nothing without him, but entrusteth him with all things* (Gen. xxxix. 1-4). So also when the spirit of Joseph (though in a spiteful manner) is sold into strange countries, where his person is not known; yet the wise do take especial notice of the spirit [of his sense and meaning] and know him, and see that God hath given him his wisdom and spirit, and receive his writings and doctrine, and order their whole life according to it. And thus Joseph cometh to sit in the chief office of Pharaoh's steward, and governeth his whole house.

56. But for all this Joseph is not yet passed through the judgment, for even in this government he first meeteth with the greatest danger of his life: for there the steward's wife burneth in lust towards him (Gen. xxxix. 7). That is, the false sects, who would fain woo and wed themselves into his spirit, and therewith adorn their doctrine and doings, for temporal honour, art and science. And if this Joseph's

---

[1] Or, as a follower of Christ.   [2] Or, undertakes.

spirit will not mix itself with their human fiction and fables, then they exclaim against him, and say all manner of evil of him, and accuse him of unchastity, viz. of false doctrine; and appeal him before the steward, that is, the magistrate.

57. And then *Joseph must be cast into prison, and lie there captive* (Gen. xxxix. 20), and be tried to purpose, till God shall bring him out again from thence, and set him before Pharaoh. And then his wisdom and fear of God is revealed, that it is plainly discerned and known that his understanding is given him of God; and so his understanding is made ruler over the land of Egypt, so that he ruleth not only strange nations, but his own brethren must at length also come unto him in their famine, when the right understanding of the divine manifestation [and mystery] is scarce and rare with them; and he nourisheth them also by his wisdom. Thus God hath sent him aforehand to be their father, that they afterwards must be fain to come and seek and enjoy their brother Joseph's wisdom among other[1] nations.

58. For so also did *Israel persecute the prophets* (Matt. v. 12), till they [Israel] were brought into darkness and idolatry in the lust of their flesh; and all those things came upon them of which the prophets told them; and then, when they sat in hunger and misery, and their land was full of abomination, they sought out the writings of the prophets; and even then they acknowledged that what they [the prophets] had spoken was true, and that they had done them [the prophets] wrong, and *adorned their graves, and said, Had we lived in our forefathers' time, we would not have killed them* (Matt. xxiii. 29, 30). But the Most High doth so order his judgment that it beginneth at the house of Israel; and he extinguisheth his anger and indignation in the children of grace: for the blood of the saints, in the power of Christ, hath at all times resisted the anger, so that *Israel hath not been consumed* (Mal. iii. 6).

59. *Joseph was sold for twenty pieces of silver* (Gen. xxxvii. 28), and *Christ for thirty* (Matt. xxvi. 15); to signify that the humanity of Christ is higher and more perfect than the humanity of others which are his children, seeing he was not conceived of the seed of man, but sprang forth in the natural tincture in the light's property. But the Adamical soul is from the fire's property, from whence the light receiveth its original and manifestation; so that the light's property in Christ assumed the fire's property, viz. the Adamical soul; and the inward hidden [divine and heavenly being] which was sealed up and quite

---

[1] Or, strange.

faded as to the light's life, in Adam, did again open and put forth itself afresh.

60. Therefore, seeing a Christian is under Christ, and in Christ becometh again manifest in God, the figure of Christ is represented here in this figure in the number of 30, and that of a Christian in the number of 20: for a Christian is sold into the hands of men to suffer; but Christ must not only suffer in the hands of men, but give himself up also to the wrath of God, whereupon he sweat blood.

61. And this whole history of Joseph doth excellently decipher to us how a Christian standeth in his figure before God and the world: for the whole acts[1] of Joseph do point out how Adam cometh to be a Christian; how he must in the process of Christ be put into Christ's figure, and become an image of Christ; and how God doth in Christ's process exalt him again in the kingdom of Christ, and setteth him at the right hand of God: as Joseph was set at the right hand of King Pharaoh after that he had continued in the process of Christ, and was brought through it.

[1] Or, history.

The Sixty-Fifth Chapter

Of *Judah* and *Tamar*: being a Mystical Figure of *Adam* and *Christ*, in which the New Birth is excellently prefigured[1]

1. WHEN we consider the history of Joseph according to outward reason, then reason demandeth, wherefore Joseph's history is not set down together in the Bible without any interruption, whereas one act followed so upon another. Why doth Moses put this typical figure of Judah and Tamar between? But if we look upon, examine and consider this history of Judah and Tamar, and likewise the figure of Joseph, with a right understanding, we find and see that the Holy Ghost hath of set purpose so ordered and disposed them in their right and true order.

2. For Joseph representeth a true Christian, shewing how he must behave himself before God, and the world, and how he is put in the process and figure of Christ. But this history of Judah and Tamar is a figure of a Christian's growth out of Adam's image, according to the humanity in the kingdom of nature; shewing how he must spring forth out of the first Adamical image, and how this same Adamical image is evil and must die, which the anger of God killeth; and yet that the first right must stand; that a Christian, according to the human nature and property, is only the Adamical image, and no new or strange thing; and how Christ manifesteth himself in this Adamical evil image, and killeth the evil; and yet during the time of this life outwardly it hangs to a Christian: this the spirit here powerfully prefigureth.

3. Here we see a powerful figure in Judah, in whom stood the line of Christ in the order of the genealogy, out of which Christ was to be manifested: *This Judah went away from his brethren, and applied himself to a man of Odollam* [Adullam], *called Hirah. And there Judah saw a Canaanitish man's daughter, called Shuah; and he took her and went in unto her, so she conceived and bare a son, and he called his name Er. And she conceived again and bare a son, whose name she called Onan. And she conceived once more and bare another son, whose name she called Shelah; and she was at Chezib when she bare him. And Judah gave his son Er a wife, whose name was Tamar: but Er*

[1] Gen. xxxviii.

was evil in the sight of the Lord, and therefore the Lord slew him. Then said Judah to Onan, Lie thou with thy brother's wife, and take her in marriage, that thou mayest raise up seed to thy brother. But Onan, knowing that the seed should not be his own, when he should lie with his brother's wife, he let it fall to the ground and destroyed it, lest he should give seed to his brother. And it was displeasing in the sight of the Lord, which he did, and the Lord slew him also (Gen. xxxviii. 1–10).

This figure stands thus:[1]

4. Judah stands here in the figure of Adam, in that condition as when the Covenant of grace concerning the seed of the woman was again inspired or inspoken into Adam: just so he standeth in that same figure. Shewing that the Covenant of grace stood in the evil Adam, as Adam then was; for as in Judah the time of Christ, viz. the Covenant of grace, was in motion, as a boundary reaching to Mary: so also it was in Adam, and so along to and in Judah.

5. And Tamar standeth in the figure of Eve, into whom God had inspired or inspoken his Promise, the Word of Regeneration, that the seed of the woman, in the power of the Word, should break the Serpent's head. So she standeth as an earthly Eve, in whom inwardly the Covenant of grace stood; and outwardly there was the corrupt Eve, which in this figure standeth outwardly as a whore, out of whom yet the line of Christ sprang in Pharez her son: as Abel out of Eve, though Eve were indeed become earthly. And we see here the type very plainly, how the spirit playeth and taketh delight in this figure with the old and new Adam, as also with the old and new Eve.

6. For Adam was, in his lust, gone forth from his Father's house, as Judah to the Canaanites, and had taken to him in his lustful desire the Canaanitish woman, the four elements, of whom he begat three sons. The first called [Er or] Ger, viz. self [will or] desire, wherein the kingdom of the nature of man stood in self-desire or own will. And this son was the first world before the deluge or flood; to this the father gave him his name, to signify that he lived in the father's nature.

7. The second son she called Onan, whom the mother called so, which pointed at the second world after the flood, for the nature of the Father, in man, said to God, *O nein* [*O no*], my Lord, drown me no more. And the mother, viz. the woman of this world, *in spiritu mundi* [in the spirit of the world], in the expressed or out-spoken word and life, gave her son this name. For God had inspired his grace again into her,

---

[1] Or, is thus to be understood.

OF JUDAH AND TAMAR

that this her second son, viz. the other world, should not be drowned with water: therefore this name standeth thus in the high figure, and is called *Onan*, for the spirit hideth it in the High Tongue, and calleth him *Onan*, or *O nein* [O no].

8. The third son she called Shelah, and she was at Chezib when she bare him. *Chezib* signifieth in the High Tongue[1] an exhaling in and recomprehension. That is, this Shelah signifieth the time of the manifestation of the Law, wherein the divine will in the Word hath manifested itself through the expressed Word, and comprised it in a law or commandment.

9. These three sons signify the three times, from Adam to Christ: Er is the time before the flood, in self will, lust and desire; Onan is the second time after the flood. This son, viz. the world after the flood, hath known God's judgment and punishment, which began to weep and lament before God, saying, O nein [O no], Lord, punish us no more thus.

10. The third time, is the time of the Law, viz. a manifesting and laying open of sin, and is justly called Shelah: for this son saith, I have found my soul again in the Lord. But it was not he yet which Tamar (that is, the hidden Eve, in whom the Covenant of grace lay) could marry: he could not raise up the seed of the woman. For Christ was as yet hidden in the law, therefore Tamar must wait till Shelah be grown up; that is, the Law must wait till the fullness of time. Yet nevertheless Tamar (that is, the new Eve, which lay hid under the veil of sin) must conceive through the spirit in the Covenant, and bear the line of Christ, hidden to the outward Tamar or Eve: as this figure of Judah and Tamar sheweth it.

The inward figure standeth thus:

11. Judah gave his first son a wife, called Tamar; but he was evil in the sight of the Lord, therefore the Lord slew him. That is, in the inward understanding, as much as to say, God gave to the first world, viz. to the first son Er, this Tamar, viz. the promised incorporated Covenant in the seed of the woman. But they looked only upon the outward Eve, and committed whoredom with her; so Tamar remained unfruitful by this son, and bare only the outward Eve in her whoredom. And thus Er, viz. the fleshly desire, was evil in the sight of the Lord, therefore the Lord slew him with the deluge.

[1] Either the Hebrew is here meant, or, rather, the Language of Nature.

12. When this son was slain, the spirit of God said to the second son after the deluge: Take thou thy brother's wife, and raise up in Tamar a seed out of the line of the Covenant. That is, enter thou into the first Covenant of the woman's seed; and bring thy will into the obedience of God, and work in the promised grace. But the second son, viz. the second world, would not marry with the divine will either, nor work in the grace, but spilt their seed upon the earth. That is, they set their desires upon earthly things, and would raise up no seed in the inward Eve in the Covenant of grace; but introduced their seed into earthly vessels, and bare children of fleshly voluptuousness: as is to be seen in the children of Nimrod, and presently after in Sodom and Gomorrah.

13. But God having signified his Covenant of grace to them by Noah, that he would no more slay them with water, when they said, O nein [O no], Lord, slay us thus no more, and they had promised to walk before him, and bring forth fruit to him; but they brought their seed into vanity, and spilt it before the Lord, and would not marry Tamar, viz. the inward Covenant of grace, but committed adultery with the earthly Eve, and spilt the seed of their soul before the inward Eve in the Covenant: then the Lord slew this Onan also, viz. Sodom and Gomorrah, and the heathen, when Israel drove them out of their land, and slew them. For those heathen would not marry the woman in the Covenant, but they married[1] their own reason, and made them idols, and spilt the seed of their faith before them upon the earth, and therefore the Lord slew them also, as he did Onan.

14. And the spirit speaketh further in the figure under an outward act done, and saith, *Then spake Judah to Tamar his daughter in law, saying, Remain a widow in thy father's house, till my son Shelah be grown up: for he thought, Perhaps he may die also, as his brethren. So Tamar went home and remained in her father's house* (Gen. xxxviii. 11). In the first world before the flood, as also in the second world after the flood, the world lived free, without the divine law: for they were married with the Covenant of grace, and should have lived under the Covenant of grace, viz. under the promise of the woman's seed. This woman's seed married herself with them, as Judah's son with Tamar; but they only committed adultery with the earthly Eve, and so the true woman in the Covenant remained unfruitful in them.

15. But when God gave the Law, then he promised this woman, in the Covenant of grace under the Law, the true Shelah. But she, viz.

---
[1] Wedded themselves to.

the woman's seed in the Covenant, should remain a widow, under the Law, till Shelah grew up; that is, till the Law had attained its time and limit: in that, should the woman in the Covenant remain in her father's house, hidden under the Law, as a widow in her state and condition: for the Law should govern under it. But she, viz. the holy woman of grace, should be still and quiet, that the wrath of God (for the sake of this high grace which he gave to men, when they regarded it not, nor did not receive it and live therein) should not slay Israel also, as Judah thought the Lord would slay Shelah also.

16. And we rightly see in this figure, that this woman in the Covenant was not given to Shelah, viz. to the Law, though the Law waited long for it. Yet Shelah might not marry this woman in the Covenant of grace; but Judah, that is, God's word and power, must again lie with this woman's seed in the Covenant, and raise it up, that this woman conceived and bare the woman's seed. Which was fulfilled in Mary, as we see by the figure of Judah and Tamar, how Judah (when Tamar sat before the door, and waited for his promise that he would give her Shelah) did get her with child himself: for the Law could not get the right Tamar in the Covenant with child, but the word in the Covenant must move itself and get Tamar with child.

17. For we see here the most powerful figure of the whole Old Testament: where Judah standeth in the figure in the line of the Covenant, as his father Jacob declares concerning him; and Tamar his daughter in law, of whom the children of the Covenant should raise up seed in the time of Judah, standeth in the figure of the inward and outward Eve. Inwardly she signifieth the mother of the Covenant of grace, in which stood the incorporated Word of grace; and outwardly she stood in the figure of corrupted Eve, in whom the Covenant lay inwardly.

18. And now the line, that was sprung up out of this Covenant, should sow divine seed, and bring forth fruit in God's kingdom: and that they could not do, for their own self-power and might was lost. Therefore the first eternal speaking Word, that had inspired or inspoken the woman's seed into Eve, must again move itself, in this incorporated Covenant of grace in the woman's seed, and itself get this woman with child, that she may bring forth Christ: as Judah gat his daughter in law with child in this type.

19. The text of Moses saith clearly, thus: *When many days were overpassed, Shuah's daughter, Judah's wife, died; and after Judah's time of mourning was out, he went up to shear his sheep at Timnath, with his shepherd,*

Hirah of Odollam [Adullam]. *Then it was told Tamar, Behold, thy father in law goeth up to Timnath to shear his sheep. Then she put off her widow's apparel that she wore, and cast a mantle over her for a veil, and sat without, far from the door, in the way to Timnath: for she saw that Shelah was grown up, and she was not given unto him to wife* (Gen. xxxviii. 12-14).

The inward figure stands thus:[1]

20. In Judah lay the root of the Covenant, which pressed on to the limit, where it should be manifested in Christ: and so stood Judah here in this figure in the place or stead of the divine Word: which Word, God inspired or inspake into Adam for an understanding life (*John* i). Therefore the text saith here: *Judah's wife, the daughter of Shuah, died.* This woman died to Adam: for it was the mother of the heavenly birth, in the heavenly world's substance, for which Adam mourned. And when God had ordered him for this world, then his mourning ceased; for he thought he was now at home, and went forth out of Paradise, to eat earthly fruit, like the beasts or living creatures: therefore saith the spirit here: *He sheared his sheep*; which might well be done so by Judah. But the spirit hath here the most secret figure, under which Adam is comprised: for the spirit saith, *Judah took his Shepherd Hirah of Odollam* [Adullam] *along with him.*

21. In the figure, this Hirah is the [Cherub] Cherubim, which sticketh in the earthly desire and bestial clothing of man; which Adam took with him, when he went out of Paradise, to shear the sheep of this world; for the same, viz. the earthly desire was his shepherd: for that now keepeth the beasts and sheep, and did shear them also, so that Adam had clothes and things necessary.

22. And the spirit calleth the place *Timnath*, where Judah had his sheep. In the High Tongue this understanding lieth very clear in the sense; for *Timnath* is nothing else but the expressed word in its powerful re-expression; and it signifieth the spirit of this world in the elements, wherein the outward mortal life consists; wherein Adam had his sheep, and now also therein hath them in his children.

23. For in this place Shelah is born, viz. the law of nature, which offereth righteousness to man; for which law, Tamar, viz. the Covenant of grace, waited a long time during Shelah's youth, to see whether the law could be married with the Covenant of grace. But it could not be, that God's righteousness could be fully performed by

---

[1] Is thus to be understood.

OF JUDAH AND TAMAR

the law, and that Tamar, viz. the Grace in the covenant, and the law, might enter into marriage.

24. Now the spirit here signifieth clearly, that when God's word had manifested itself in the world by the law; that Tamar, that is, the Covenant of grace, laid aside her widow's apparel, and had set herself in the way of the word in the law, where, under the law, the spirit of the prophets out of the line of Judah went onward concerning the kingdom of Christ. This spirit would have the Covenant of grace for a spouse, for it was the right [spirit] from which the prophets under the law pointed at Christ.

25. But Tamar, that is, the Covenant of grace, veiled her beautiful countenance from the earthly Adam, and was ashamed of the deformity of the earthly man, in that the children of the law, as also the prophets, were outwardly so earthly: even as Tamar veiled her countenance from Judah. But when the time was come that the Covenant should be manifested, then the spirit of the Covenant sets itself before Shelah, viz. before the law, for the grace should receive Adam into itself again: as Tamar received seed from Judah her father in law, and suffered herself to be gotten with child.

26. But the holy countenance of the Covenant of grace in its power remained yet hidden to Adam in the law, as also to the prophets, till Christ: as Tamar veiled her countenance from Judah her father in law, that he knew her not, so also the Covenant of grace stood in the law, but with a veiled countenance. And the spirit speaketh further in Moses, and saith:

27. Now when Judah saw her he supposed she was a whore, for she had covered her countenance; that is, when the children in the law heard the prophetical spirit speak of Christ, they supposed it was in their law, and of the law: but it had veiled its countenance, like Tamar. And Judah went towards her on the way, and said, Prithee let me lie with thee: for he knew not that she was his daughter in law. That is, Adam's nature in the law said, to the prophetical spirit of grace, Pray let me come in unto thee; lie with me, I will give thee seed of my nature. And it knew not that God was in this spirit, and desired to mix with him after a creaturely manner; neither knew it that this prophetical spirit was the incorporated spirit in the Covenant, in man himself: so very blind was the Adamical nature concerning the Covenant.

28. The Adamical nature thought it was a whore, that setteth itself forth so in the prophetical spirit before it: therefore have the

Jews so often slain the prophets; for they supposed they heard a false whore's spirit speak. But here the figure of Judah sheweth that the first Adamical nature should mix with the Covenant of grace, that the heavenly ens would receive the Adamical human ens again into itself; and man himself would not understand what God would do with him.

29. The Adamical nature would indeed in its lust long after the heavenly ens, but would not know it. Although it should see the same, yet it would think, That is like unto me, I will commit whoredom therewith: so strange a thing is paradise become to Adam.

30. And *when Tamar, with her face covered, presented herself before Judah in the way, and that he said to her, Lie with me; then said Tamar to Judah, What wilt thou give me to lie with me? He said, I will send thee a kid from the flock. She answered, and said, Then give me a pledge till thou send it. And he said, What wilt thou have me give thee for a pledge? She answered, and said, Thy ring, and thy bracelet, and thy staff which thou hast in thy hand. And he gave them to her, and lay with her, and she was with child by him. And she arose and went away, and laid off her mantle, and put her widow's apparel on again* (Gen. xxxviii. 14-19).

31. Here the spirit alludeth very finely in the figure, how Adam's nature lieth with the presented new Eve in the Covenant, and yet knoweth her not; also how the Covenant lieth with Adam's first right nature, and how they meet together in strange apparel, when Adam's nature saith, Lie with me, and would have this Eve in the Covenant only for a little pleasure's sake, as the Adamical nature doth in its selfhood, that it might only, in its false seeming holiness, lie with the new Eve. And its heart is far from the true wedlock marriage, and only draweth near her in a hypocritical whoredom, as is done in the office of the Pharisees: Then saith this Eve to the Adamical nature, What wilt thou give me? Then this Adamical nature promised her a kid, that is, a bestial [desire and] will, full of the burning lust of flattery and hypocrisy.

32. But this Eve, viz. Tamar, saith, Give me for a pledge thereof thy ring,[1] staff and bracelet. The ring is the soul, which came from the Word of God: the bracelet is the *spiritus mundi* [the spirit of the world], viz. the outward spirit; and the staff is the body. These will the new Eve, viz. the line of Christ in the Covenant, have for a pledge: these ornaments[2] must Adam give for a pledge to the Covenant of grace, viz. of the woman's inward seed in the incorporated grace of the heavenly world's substance.

[1] Seal, ring, or signet.   [2] Habiliments, or precious jewels.

OF JUDAH AND TAMAR

33. When this dear Eve in the seed of Mary should lie with Adam, and receive Adam's seed into her holy birth; as Judah, in whom lay the line of the Covenant, must give Tamar, who stood in the image and type of the new Eve, viz. of the heavenly world's substance; these ornaments and jewels, viz. his ring, bracelet and staff: Both which stood in the figure, shewing how Christ should be manifested out of Adam's nature in Mary, wherein lay and was manifested the right Tamar or new Eve.

34. And when Tamar had gotten the ring, bracelet and staff for a pledge, she took them and laid them up, and asked not after the kid, but kept these jewels and went from thence with them, and changed herself again into her former widow's estate, and hid herself from Judah, that he knew not who she was, nor whence she came.

35. This now is the most excellent figure, shewing how the spirit in the Covenant mingleth and uniteth itself again with the heavenly world's substance, viz. with the new wedlock or Eve, viz. with Adam's faded substance, which is from the heavenly world's substance, which substance faded or vanished in the fall; viz. how God becometh man, and man becometh God, and how this image or type (conceived in the new divine seed) even then again hideth itself from the earthly Adam,[1] that Eve must put on and wear her widow's apparel again, that the noble seed might not be known in this world. As is to be seen by the children of Christ, who are conceived of Christ according to the inward ground, how they must, after the wedding of the Lamb, viz. this divine wedlock or coition, which is indeed done in the soul with great joy; enter again into the state of mourning, and be forsaken in this world, as a poor widow.

36. And as Tamar inquired not after the kid, but would have an eminent pledge; so the spirit of Christ in the Covenant inquireth not after the outward solemnity and pageantry, wherein men will offer gifts to it: It will have the body, soul and spirit for a pledge.

37. In this figure it representeth the Jewish offerings as a whoredom in the sight of God. For as Judah committed whoredom with Tamar, and intended only the whoredom, and would give a kid for it, so also stood the priests of the Law, and in seeming holiness and hypocrisy play the harlots with God, with the blood and flesh of beasts. Which indeed was a figure of the inward, and God was pleased to bear with it; but he would not accept their offerings, neither did he mix himself with the offering, but with the faith in the body, soul

---

[1] One copy saith Eve.

and spirit of man: whereof we have here an excellent example.

38. Judah had begotten three sons of the Canaanitish woman. But the line of the Covenant which lay in him would not pass on in the Canaanitish woman and her children, but opened itself in this whoredom of Judah with Tamar, in Pharez; whom Tamar conceived of Judah by this coition or lying together. With which figure God represents the misery of man, and presents his Covenant of grace with the opening of this precious line of the Covenant, which pressed on to the limit, Christ; in this whoredom of Judah and Tamar, viz. in the earthly Adam, and in the earthly Eve; but, in the inward ground of its essence. To signify that even the children of God, in their corrupt nature, do but commit whoredom in the presence of God, and that their state of wedlock is but whoredom and a defiled bestial thing in the presence of God; and hath nothing at all therein chaste or pure in the sight of God. Therefore the line of the Covenant manifested itself in this whoredom of Judah and Tamar, to signify that Christ should come out of this line of the Covenant, and enter into the middle of this whoredom [as a Mediator], and break the head of the false whorish desire and earthly Serpent, and purify our fleshly impure bestial conception with its heavenly virgin seed, and in himself change it into the Paradisical image again.

39. Also God doth therefore manifest the line of his Covenant in this whoredom of Judah and Tamar, that his wrath in our human impurity might not burn up and devour body and soul, but that the Covenant of grace might withstand the anger in our impurity, lest God should devour Israel in their abominations and impurity in his wrath.

40. Now seeing the line of the Covenant as to its manifestation and propagation lay in Judah, and that Israel also was impure according to the Adamical nature, therefore God did represent his Covenant of grace at the first propagation from the stock of Israel in such a figure; that the faith of Abraham, of Isaac and of Jacob, in the first branch from them, viz. in Judah and his children, might withstand his wrath, and that continually the faith of Abraham, viz. the spirit of Christ in Abraham's faith, might be a mediator between God and the impurity of man.

41. We see also such a figure in the royal prophet David with Bathsheba, upon whom also the line of the Covenant pressed on in Solomon, and though clearly David caused her husband Uriah to be slain, and used deceit that he might get Bathsheba to wife, which in

OF JUDAH AND TAMAR

the human nature was an abomination and great sin before the face of God; yet the spirit hath its figure in David thus, seeing God had renewed his Covenant of grace with him concerning Christ. Therefore God set the line of his Covenant in David's unrighteousness in the woman that he had gotten to himself with unrighteousness in whoredom by murdering her husband. To signify that all human matters and doings are vain and evil in the sight of God, and that he will come himself with his grace to help our sins and impurity, and introduce his grace into our sin and slay it with the grace. Therefore God represents this image and type in David, for an atonement, pointing at the coming of Christ, who, when he rendered himself into this figure, took on him the sins of all men, and cleansed again the whoredom of Judah and Tamar, as also of David and Bathsheba, and of Adam and Eve; and laid himself in the marriage bed with them, as he did with Judah and Tamar, and with David and Bathsheba, in whom the line of the Covenant was manifested in their evil purposes and doings.

42. For here the old proverb was fulfilled: Where God erects a church, there also the devil builds a chapel. God had built a church of his covenant in Judah and David; close by also the devil in God's anger buildeth his chapel in man's lust: but the church of God always resisted the devil's chapel.

43. For here in this figure the seed of the woman presents itself, shewing how it would break the head of the Serpent in man's impurity. And so the type of God's anger, and the type of grace, were represented in one figure, viz. Adam's fleshly whoredom with his Eve, and all her daughters; and then the woman's holy seed of the heavenly world's substance, which, with the Word of grace, mediated, interceded, and set itself in the middle.

44. A much more excellent figure we see in the most wise king Solomon, who stood just in the figure of Judah; as Judah was the son of Jacob, who received and embraced the promise, and Jacob stood wholly in the figure of Christ; so David also received and embraced the renewing of the Covenant of the first promise; and David begat this Solomon also of an unrighteous marriage; though he took her to wife, yet the unrighteousness and murder stood behind the door.[1]

45. This Solomon was endued with high divine wisdom, and the line of the Covenant pressed and passed through him. But at length he became such an insatiable luxurious person,[2] that the Scripture

---
[1] Lay under the green leaf.
[2] Uxorious luster after women, lecherous person.

saith of him, he had three hundred concubines, and seven hundred wives, and mixed himself with the daughters of heathenish kings, and took them to wife, and allowed his heathenish women to set up their idols' images for idolatry in the high places at Jerusalem (*1 Kings xi. 1-8*).

46. In this eminent figure the spirit signifieth that man is fallen away from God, and [is] merely idolatrous; that Adam and all his children, in their own nature, are such a bestial adulterous and idolatrous generation: and, in this, King Solomon represents the line of the Covenant subjoined with these heathenish idolatrous adulterous concubines, who in their own nature were but an abomination in the presence of God, to signify that Christ, out of this line of the Covenant, should set himself in the midst amongst the heathen, and tear idolatry out of their hearts, and convert them all to Christ.

47. Also to signify that God did bear with the wise heathen under the patience of the figure of Christ, and that he did represent by the Jews only a prefiguration or type of the temple of Christ; and that the Jews in their nature were but idolatrous adulterers, as well as the heathen, only that in their law they had the type and prefiguration of Christ in their sacrifices and offerings, at which the Covenant had respect, shewing how God would redeem and purify both Jews and heathen from Adam's abominations and idolatry, and that the one people in his sight were as the other, and no whit better, but every one of them was the evil Adam. Therefore the spirit represents them perspicuously in the figure of Solomon in the line of the Covenant, *that he may have mercy* and compassion *upon all* (Rom. xi. 32), for Christ's sake who should fulfil and accomplish this line.

48. And hereby is signified to the teachers in Babel, part of whom account Solomon damned in regard of those heathenish idols, that they themselves lie under the veil, as the Jews did under the type of Christ, and do really understand the Scripture as little as the Jews, and stand in contentious idolatrous whoredom in the presence of God, as Solomon with his concubines did, and the Jews.

49. For Solomon had the Law: but at length with his heart he committed whoredom with the heathenish women's idols: And so doth Babel, who calleth herself a pure child, pretending the name of Christ, and striveth zealously and vehemently about it in opinions; and all the opinions about which she contendeth are Solomon's heathenish women and idols, and no polemic or contentious opinion is any whit better.

50. For Christ sticketh in no contentious opinion, but in the line of

OF JUDAH AND TAMAR

his grace he is entered into the midst amongst us; and if we receive him, then he taketh us also in it to himself. And there needs no strife or opinion about it, but this one thing he requireth of us: that we continue in him, and then he will continue in us; and that we love ourselves in him, as he loveth us in himself; that all of us may be cleansed from the wrath of God in his love, and that his grace and love may wash all of us that come to him from our sins and idolatrous abominations, and make of Judah, Tamar, David, Solomon, and all the children of the Jews, heathen, and Christians, a pure virgin, prepared for himself by his love in his blood, which he hath bestowed upon us in his grace, that we may acknowledge and put on him in that love, and be one spirit and body with him: and then Adam is helped and restored again.

51. The spirit of Moses in the text saith further, thus: *After three months it was told Judah, saying, Tamar thy daughter in law hath played the harlot; moreover, behold she is with child by whoredom. And Judah said, Bring her hither, that she may be burned. And when they brought her forth she sent to her father in law, and said, From the man, whose these are, I am with child, and said, Dost thou know whose this ring, these bracelets and this staff is? Judah acknowledged it, and said, She is more righteous than I; for I gave her not my son Shelah. Yet he lay with her no more* (Gen. xxxviii. 24–26). This is a powerful figure, shewing that whoredom is an abomination in God's sight, and how God sets man's sins before his eyes; and here it signifieth this to us: that the Adamical whoredom and abomination are manifest before this Covenant of grace, and that Man in such abominations is guilty of hell fire, as Judah judged his daughter in law Tamar to be condemned to the fire, and knew not that he himself was the whoremonger, who stood in the like condemnation.

52. And here in this figure the spirit presenteth men's false judgment, that they even do the same thing which they condemn; as here Judah condemned the whoredom of Tamar to the fire, and saw not his fall, that he himself was guilty; to signify that Christ also had set himself in the judgment of the world in this line of the Covenant, as a righteous judge, who would separate right from wrong, and condemn the whoredom and idolatry of the world. But on the other side, we see in this figure how Tamar presented the pledge, viz. the ring, bracelet and staff before the judgment, and before the severe sentence of Judah, and therewith did overthrow Judah's determinate sentence, and still his wrath, that he must take compassion on her and justify her.

53. Thus also stood this figure before God in the inward ground in

Judah and Tamar, with Adam and Eve. For Adam had brought himself into fleshly earthly lust, and committed whoredom with his feminine property through his imagination in a bestial manner, and had forsaken the heavenly magic way of the divine wedlock: therefore also the heavenly woman died as to him, and in the stead thereof the earthly bestial one awaked, with whom he now useth the bestial manner in whoredom. This God presents in him, viz. in Adam himself, in his judgment, and would condemn Adam to death, as indeed God's righteousness then condemned him.

54. But the re-incorporated Eve in the Covenant of grace, which hath incorporated itself in Eve, viz. in the faded seed of the woman from the heavenly world's substance, presented itself before the severe judgment of God, and said to God's righteousness, Behold, I am with child from the man whose these are. That is, Behold, I have taken Adam's soul, spirit and body, for a pledge, when I joined myself with him, and am betrothed to him, and have received the Father's nature in the awakened anger into my love, and am now with child of the human nature, and shall bring forth a God-Man.

55. And when the Father's property in the soul's nature in the anger knew that the Father had sown himself again into the grace, viz. into the new Eve in the Covenant, then said the anger of the Father in the soul (when this grace went to meet it), to this new Eve, Thou art more righteous than I, for I have caused Adam's impurity, that he is become earthly, and hath committed whoredom before me. And I have not given Shelah for a husband to the new Eve; that is, I have not given the Word of the new regeneration by and in the Law. Therefore hath Tamar, that is, the new Eve, under the time of the Law, lain and copulated with Judah and his children for and about the soulish or animal and human nature; and left Shelah, viz. the Law, standing in the figure; and the grace of the new Eve in the Covenant hath always [joined and] mixed itself with God's children, as is to be seen in the saints, especially in the prophets, who outwardly lived under the Law and exercised themselves therein, and yet always [joined and] mixed themselves with the new Eve in the grace, and yet lived not to the Law, but to grace.

56. And this is the powerful figure in this place, shewing how the Covenant of Promise in Judah, and the awakening of the Covenant in the woman's seed, stand always set one opposite to the other, and lie and copulate one with the other in the love, pointing at the future manifestation in the flesh in Christ.

OF JUDAH AND TAMAR

57. For this figure of Judah and Tamar, in the inward ground, is nothing else but this: that outwardly the adulterous evil Adam, with his fleshly Eve, is represented in the figure, viz. outwardly the man of sin with a sinful figure, and inwardly the betrothing of the new Eve in regeneration.

58. And the spirit speaketh further in Moses, and saith: And when Tamar was about to bring forth, behold, twins were found in her womb. And as she was upon the birth one of them put forth a hand: then the midwife took a red thread and tied about it, and said, This is the first that cometh forth. But when he pulled back his hand his brother came forth, and she said, Wherefore hast thou for thy will made this breach? and his name was called Pharez. Afterwards his brother came forth, who had the red thread about his hand, and his name was called Zarah (Gen. xxxviii. 27-30).

59. O thou wonderful great God, who art so high and deep: how simply, and to the capacity of a child, dost thou modelise thy wisdom to us! What is all art and wit of human greatness before thee, who dost so very much condescend, bow down, and humble thyself; and presentest thy deepest wisdom and highest profundity in a childish simplicity, which may justly shame all human state and self-wit, when they see so great Mysteries of God stand in such childishness!

60. O world, how foolish art thou! that thou elevatest thyself in a blind life, and still cleavest to the husk, and seest not what thou art, and understandest not the divine simplicity. And then, how wilt thou apprehend the divine depth? O leave off thy wit, and cleave to simplicity, that thou mayest yet obtain a child's understanding, and be not accounted in the sight of God more unwise than the beasts, which remain in their clothing and condition as God hath created them. O thou world! why sleepest thou in the devil's arms, who suckles and dandles thee in himself, and bringeth thee to his will and life by his might? O do but see it!

61. This potent figure in these twins, one of which put forth the hand, which the midwife bound a red thread about, and thought it would be the first, but it drew the hand back again, and his brother came forth, prefigureth this to us: How Christ in this line of the Covenant assumed the human nature, and so the human nature according to Adam's right and self will, in this world, first puts forth and manifests itself, about which Adamical nature in the humanity of Christ must this red thread, with the shedding of his blood, be bound.

62. When this is done, then must the human nature with its right draw back again; that is, Adam's will that was gone forth must again return into the mother's womb, viz. be turned into the Word; and then cometh the inward new Adam forth, after which followeth the Adamical nature with the red thread. Then saith the mother to the new Adam in Christ, Why hast thou for thy will made this breach? For thy will, saith the mother, not for thy will's sake, but for the sake of that which driveth thy will forth; and Adam's will goes back. Thus hath the will in the Covenant of grace powerfully broken through the strong bar and enclosure of the first Principle, viz. of the kingdom of God's anger; for the good will in Adam was shut up in death and in hell, and in Christ he rent that powerful rent, and brake through death and hell back again into the kingdom of the eternal nature, and turned itself forth again into the natural life, so that the kingdom of God was again manifested in the human life.

63. This the spirit represents by Tamar in the line of the Covenant, and modeliseth Christ's breach through death and hell, how that should be; and by this premodelling was the whorish will of Tamar and Judah healed, and their children of whoredom in the line of Christ were espoused into the Covenant of grace.

64. In Esau and Jacob stood the figure, how according to nature Adam had the right of the kingdom, and how he squandered it, and is therefore in his natural will thrust out from the kingdom of God, and how Christ came to help him. Here now stands the figure, shewing how Christ hath gotten the kingdom, and turned Adam back again, and in Adam turned himself forth, so that now Adam is called Christ, and presents himself very excellently in the figure of Joseph: and this standeth fitly and rightly between, in the interval of Joseph's history.

65. For Joseph is the figure of a Christian; and this of Judah and Tamar is a figure shewing how a Christian springeth out of Adam's nature, and how Adam's nature is turned in again, and Christ turned forth; and how this image of a Christian man in this world is covered outwardly with the earthly Adam, so that men cannot know it; also how thus Christ in Adam took his guilt upon him, and how Adam must be marked with this red thread, which mark is rightly the pledge that Judah gave to Tamar. And I would have the Reader of this admonished in love, not to reject our exposition of this text, but to consider it and look narrowly and perspicuously into it: and then he will well perceive who was the Expositor, if he be worthy of it.

The Sixty-Sixth Chapter

The Most Excellent History of *Joseph*: How he was sold to *Potiphar*; what befell *Joseph*; and of *Joseph's* Chastity, and fear of God[1]

1. *Joseph was brought down into Egypt, and Potiphar, an Egyptian Pharaoh's officer, captain of his guard, bought him of the Ishmaelites, who brought him thither. And the Lord was with Joseph, and he was a prosperous man; and was in his master's, the Egyptian's, house. And his master saw that the Lord was with him, and that the Lord made all that he did to prosper in his hand. So that he found grace and favour in the sight of his master, and was his servant which he set over his house. And all that he had he put under his hand; and from the time that he set him over his house, and over all his goods, the Lord blessed the Egyptian's house for Joseph's sake; and the blessing of the Lord was every way upon all that he had in the house and in the field. Therefore he left all that he had under the hand of Joseph, and he meddled with nothing while he had him, but what he did eat and drink. And Joseph was a goodly person and fair of feature* (Gen. xxxix. 1-6).

2. The history prefigureth to us a true Christian man, what he is, and how he is, in this world, and what his office is; that is, when Christ is manifested in him he is no more his own, to do what he will; also in this world he hath nothing for his own of which he can in truth say, This is mine, or I, I am he that hath it, I possess it, it is mine own, I may do therewith what my flesh and my own will listeth, I may use it for my honour and pleasure, that I may thereby be aloft[2] in the world: No, a true Christian hath none of that in his power.

3. He indeed ruleth of right over that which he hath and possesseth with truth and righteousness, but yet as a servant of his Lord Christ. For a Christian is a Christian in Christ, and is bought to a Christian life, and to the obedience of faith, by the blood of Christ, with Christ's thirty pieces of silver: whereof his Lord Christ hath committed to him Joseph's twenty pieces of silver, and set him as a steward over it, that he may trade therewith and employ it, till he make it come to thirty pieces of silver, which he should wear in him and about him as a mark or badge of his Lord Christ, as a treasure of his Christianity.

4. But seeing his Lord Christ was sold and betrayed to death for

---

[1] Gen. xxxix.   [2] Or, high.

MYSTERIUM MAGNUM

thirty pieces of silver, and Joseph was sold by his brethren to be a bondslave[1] for twenty pieces of silver; in both these numbers standeth the figure of a Christian, viz. Christ, when he is manifested in a man, sheweth man the thirty pieces of silver for which he was sold to suffering and death, and this his suffering and death he putteth upon him, in which is founded the figure of the thirty pieces of silver, viz. that he was sold and betrayed: and therein man becomes such a Christian as is founded, implanted, ingraven,[2] upon and into Christ's sufferings and death; and therein a man becometh a Christian in Christ's sufferings and death, and standeth in the figure of Christ, and looseth the right of his natural self will, as also the kingdom of this world.

5. For in Christ's death, as to his inward spiritual man, he dieth from this world, and, according to that inward man, is no more in this world, but in Christ in God, viz. in the kingdom of God, as it is written: *The kingdom of God is inwardly within you* (Luke xvii. 21): Also, *Examine yourselves, whether Christ hath gotten a form in you* (Gal. iv. 19): Also, *Ye are the temple of the Holy Ghost who dwelleth in you* (1 Cor. iii. 16): Also, *Ye are the servants of Christ* (Col. iv. 12), *and should eat the flesh of the Son of Man* (John vi. 53), and so *he abideth in you and you in him* (John xv. 7): and *without him ye have no life* (John vi. 53). As a herb and grass, and all earthly things, without the power and virtue of the sun, have no life, growth or vegetation and operation in them, so man, without the Divine Sun, which through Christ hath manifested itself in his Christians, hath no life or happiness or salvation without Christ in him.

6. And as Christ was sold for thirty pieces of silver to suffering and death, which thirty pieces of silver signify the thirty years of Christ before his baptism (Luke iii. 23), ere he entered into his office and divine government according to the humanity, when he gave up his human will to God, and the creaturely self will ceased in him: so also must a Christian, when he is in truth in his own natural will, sold for twenty pieces of the thirty pieces of silver, to be a servant of God in Christ, to be a minister or officer, and obedient to his Lord who liveth in him; then his bypast years of the Adamical natural time of this world are sold, in and with Christ, for twenty pieces of silver; and so the Adamical time of his natural will, in this being sold, ceaseth in Christ's suffering and death; and he is by his Lord (who is

---

[1] Over whom the master hath power of life, and all he hath.
[2] Etching of plates with aqua fortis.

THE MOST EXCELLENT HISTORY OF JOSEPH

arisen from Death in him, and ruleth and reigneth over Death), set to be an officer over Christ's goods, to dispose of them through the spirit of Christ, viz. in the power and virtue of his Lord who is in him, in this world, according to the kingdom of Christ.[1]

7. As Joseph was taken away from his father's house, and was first cast into the pit, wherein he should have perished, and was afterwards sold by his brethren for twenty pieces of silver to serve as a bondslave; so also a Christian is first taken away from his father's house, viz. from the Adamical nature, and is cast into the pit, viz. into Christ's suffering and death, and then loseth the Adamical inheritance of the kingdom of this world, and is with his will and mind brought away from it. Then he must yield up his father's house, viz. all his selfhood, together with his natural life, to his brethren in his father's house, that is, to the power of God in the government of this world; and suffer himself to be cast into the pit of the death of his natural will, and therein give up himself to the death of Christ, and willingly die to the will of this world, viz. to his own Adamical house, and willingly suffer all whatsoever his brethren of this world do to him.

8. And then if he thus lie in the pit or grave of Christ, and hath given himself up to the death of Christ, that he willingly would forsake all for Christ's sake, and die the death of his own will, then Christ his Lord putteth on him his resurrection from the dead, and maketh him living with his power, and draweth him with Joseph out of the pit and grave of death, and bringeth him into his service: as Joseph into the service of Pharaoh's captain of the guard. And then all goeth prosperously in and with him, for the divine power ruleth him; and now he attaineth divine understanding and wisdom, and knows how to manage his master's goods. That, in the Christian figure, is as much as to say:

9. When a man is thus a Christian in such a process and way, then he hath given up all whatsoever he hath of temporal goods, or is able to do, as also his own will, to God, who bringeth him first into Christ's image, and maketh him conformable to Christ, and taketh nothing away from him of that which he had before of natural right, viz. the disposal of temporary goods; but he taketh away the authority and power of his own nature, viz. his evil self will which Adam had brought away from God and introduced into a creaturely selfness of his own willing and working in earthly things, whereby Adam bereaved God his Lord of the government in him, and made the

[1] As to the dominion of Christ.

essence and things of this world his own; as if he had made it, and would not be God's servant therein, and be his fellow-branches' guardian and nourisher, and give them his virtue, will, essence and substance, but saith, [It is] *Mine*; that is, it is mine own, I will keep it only for myself, and it shall remain with me. And would not work therewith in the life of his brethren, and give them also of his life and power; and bereave them also (through that appropriation of it to be mine) of the power in the kingdom of nature, viz. of the growth [and fruits] of the earth which God gave in common, and would only fill his own body, and thereby be accounted great, and a lord of his miserable despised fellow-branches, whom he wickedly bereaveth of the sap wherewith they should strengthen their life, and bringeth it into a propriety [calling it mine]. This authority God taketh away from a Christian, and maketh him a guardian and nourisher of his brethren again, viz. a steward of his Lord: He lets him possess the temporary goods which he had, so far as he possessed them in a natural right with righteousness and truth, and maketh him a Joseph therein.

10. This Joseph now saith not, This is mine, that village, city, country, principality, kingdom, empire; also that house, land, field, money; those goods, those cattle, that woman, that child, is mine. But he saith with his whole heart and conscience from a new good Christian will, It is all my God's and his children's. He hath set me as a ruler, disposer, and steward of it, that I should manage it to that purpose which he will have me. I should sustain myself and his children, the needy, with it; and I should be their curator or guardian, and give them also my power, virtue and understanding of the divine gift; and instruct, tutor or take care of them for their good. And as God governeth me with his spirit, so also should I that am his officer in this world, with my understanding and office, govern my fellow-members in such power and virtue, and take care of them. For all that I rule over is not mine, but God's and theirs; but I should do to them as God doth to me.

11. To such a one God giveth Joseph's understanding and wisdom, and governeth the house of this world by him; be he in what state and condition soever, therein he sits in the office of God, and is only a servant or minister of the office, and a guardian over divine creatures. For the right Christian government of his will is in heaven, his conversation is alike in heaven and on earth; as the Scripture saith, *Our conversation is in heaven* (Phil. iii. 20). For according to the inward

THE MOST EXCELLENT HISTORY OF JOSEPH

ground of his soul and spirit he is in Christ in God, viz. in the eternal speaking Word, from which Adam's will had turned itself away, and turned itself out into this world, which will Christ hath turned in again into the eternal Word. And so now he governeth with that re-inturned will through and in the outward substance and matters of this world, viz. in the formed outspoken or expressed Word, as a servant, minister and instrument of the eternal speaking Word in its secret mystery of wisdom, viz. in the visible creaturely word.

12. Therefore to thee, O thou governor in the office of the Joseph of this world, in every state, condition and degree, this is told thee, and set before thy eyes: that though thou callest thyself a Joseph, thou dost not yet govern as a Joseph; that is, not as a Christian, but as a child of the stars and elements; thou governest no otherwise than the brethren of Joseph, who will not that God should choose Joseph for a governor. They will be governors themselves, and will rather kill Joseph than wait to try what God would do with Joseph's dream or vision; they would not suffer that Joseph should tell their injury to his father; but would do what they thought fit. For they said among themselves, We are the elder, and should govern; what will the least and youngest persuade us to? we possess the government in a just way by the right of nature; the power and authority is ours, we will dispatch Joseph out of the way, and cast him into the pit, and then we shall do what we will.

13. Thus doest thou also, thou governest Christendom in all states and degrees. The stars, and the evil averted Adam in his own will, governeth through thee in God's office in the kingdom of this world; thou hast only cast the mantle of Christ over it, that men should not know thee, that thou art the evil Adam, and governest with the starry wit and ingenuity, and through the subtlety and policy of the devil, in mere self-willed ways of thine own, to advance thy own ostentation, pomp, might, authority and stately proud glory.

14. O hearken! art thou a Christian? then art thou dead with Christ to the wicked false will of Adam, and of the devil's pride. But if thy will and life be heathenish, why dost thou then boast thyself to be a Christian? Why dost thou make wars for lands, countries, cities and villages, if thou be not with Joseph called and instituted of God to be a governor? Why dost thou in Christ's kingdom enslave the country, if thou art a prince and minister in God's office, and servest him?

15. Art thou thy own lord upon earth, and doest what thy own will listeth? Then thou doest not what God will, also thou governest not from heaven, but from the world, and with the world's might. But whence hast thou that in Christ's kingdom, and from what power and authority, that thou, in God's office, drawest to thyself the sweat of the poor and miserable, and takest away his strength and virtue, and lettest him starve in want? Also, that thou squeezest or crushest him down with thy burden, that thou mayest but possess much riches, and heap up much for thyself, with which thou makest thyself potent, and liftest up thy mind into pride. Whence hast thou that in Christ's kingdom, that thou wilt be better than the members of thy own body? Whereas in Christ we are one, viz. one tree with many twigs and branches, and Christ alone is our sap and virtue, and taketh care for us all in common: for the officer as well as the branch; no otherwise than the twig upon which the fruit groweth.

16. Thou potentate in God's office! dost thou not know that in thy office thou art a branch in the tree of Christ, and that fruit should grow upon thy twigs? Now if thou withdrawest thy sap from the twigs, and with thy rubbing breakest them off, what fruit can they bear to thee? They must needs wither in thee, and bring forth no fruit: of which thou art guilty, that the branch, thou being in God's office, standeth without fruit. What dost thou profit thy Lord who hath planted thee? Shalt thou not be hewn down, and cast into the fire (Matt. iii. 10; Luke iii. 9) of God's anger, as a dry piece of wood? Are ye not the Great Tree in the field of the world, standing in your twigs without fruit? What fruit do you bear? Nothing but leaves, which fall off by the wind, and rot and go to the earth again without fruit. And now what profit to life is a tree without fruit? No other but for the fire, or for the building of a habitation.

17. Thus also thou art only in thy office a building and habitation, wherein God's children are to dwell; but they grow not out of thy stock, thou art only an officer of or belonging unto a constellation and asterism, and servest the kingdom of separation in evil and good: as that pulleth down and buildeth up, so dost thou also. What one officer buildeth up, another teareth down to the ground. But he that serveth in Christ's spirit in this office, he worketh with Joseph: the blessing is everywhere in his office, so that his twigs bring forth much fruit in Christ's kingdom.

18. Ye nobles and potentates under the name of Christ; whence cometh it to you in Christ's kingdom that ye are such, under a

Christian name? Your office is God's; if ye govern therein as a Joseph, as a minister of Christ, then it is right and pleasing to God. But whence comes it in the kingdom of Christ that there is nobility and slavery? Is not that heathenish? Wherein stands the ground thereof? It proceeds from nothing else but from the pride of the devil, and self will.

19. Who planted you in the beginning? Your princes and kings, whom ye have served: to what end are they? That pride might be arrayed in brave apparel, and that men might not say of the high offices of God, They are clothed with common apparel; but that they might be distinguished from the lowly and simple: and that was even Lucifer's fall.

20. *But Christ on earth had not whereon to lay his head* (Matt. viii. 20), neither house, nor anything else. So also a Christian hath nothing for his own, but what he hath, he hath it for his office sake, and serveth his Lord therein; but he that serveth otherwise, he serveth the Adamical self, and not Christ; and is no Christian, but a mere titulary Christian. But he is a child of nature, of the kingdom of this world, in whose inward ground hell standeth, and serveth the kingdom of darkness: outwardly he serveth indeed the type of God according to love and anger, where all things together stand in strife, till the day of separation, and the restoration of that which was before such doings.

21. For in this world all goes on in free will, that which hath no law hath also no judgment; but that which hath a law, that hath its judgment in itself: therefore seeing man, especially a Christian, hath a law, viz. that he is no more his own, in that he is given up to another, viz. to Christ, and yet will not be subject to him, then is the judgment in the law, and condemneth the own will and self.

22. We do not disallow of the offices, which are God's, as also the officers are God's servants: we distinguish only what a minister of Christ is, and what a minister of nature in human selfhood is. If any one be in a noble office in the kingdom of Christ, then is his office noble; but he is a minister or servant under this noble office, and is justly honoured in respect of the office; we detract not from his honour, which his office deserveth; but all selfhood in the kingdom of Christ is the evil Adamical nature, which is departed from God; for in Christ there is no nobility, but we are all only children and ministers or servants.

23. Our Adamical nobility is lost in Adam; but whoever in this world in the kingdom of Christ is noble, he is noble in respect of his

office (as a king and prince is noble in respect of his office in which he serveth); but if he serveth not Christ therein but only the nobility of his office and his selfhood, and saith, The power and the kingdom is mine, he bereaveth God of his power, and maketh it appropriate to himself, and becometh a Lucifer under the office of God.

24. Even as Lucifer, who also was a prince of a throne, and a king in God's office, but when he appropriated the office to self, then he was thrust out (Isa. xiv. 19), and another got the office which he had in the kingdom of God: but he remained indeed a prince in his own office, but not in God's love, but in his wrath, wherein he must now also serve him: as also is to be understood concerning the offices in this world.

25. For a wicked prince and nobleman remaineth indeed in the office, but he serveth not God's love but his anger; as is done at present, where the princes serve the anger of God with murdering and wasting countries and people, as in vengeance, and in the power of selfhood, wherein God's anger also becometh creaturely: but they do not that to Christ in Christ's office, but to the anger of God, who thereby punisheth the false and wicked titulary Christendom with his office of anger.

26. For in Christ's office there is only love and righteousness, as also humility and fear of God in self. But the office hath the power to separate the evil from the good as a minister[1] of God, yet with righteousness, and not with self will. He who saith, Thou shalt not kill, saith also to the officer, that without the authority of his office he should kill none, neither should he do injury to any [though by virtue of his office].

27. For the office requireth a just judgment, and then the office killeth the wickedness,[2] and severs it from the good, and the officer is free from the commandment of death; but if he hath any evil intent in his will, there the judgment passeth upon the officer himself.

28. In Potiphar, Pharaoh's officer, we have a powerful figure; who set Joseph over his whole house, and gave him full power to rule in his government; shewing how God hath set his officers in his house of this world, that they should do and direct, judge and manage things in a creaturely manner, as God doth in them after a spiritual manner.

29. For Potiphar took upon him no disposal of anything, but let Joseph manage the government: Thus also are all officers instituted

---

[1] Diaconissa ministresse.   [2] Wicked thing or substance.

in the kingdom of this world, that they should outwardly manage God's government; as Christ giveth a similitude or parable of stewards whom a lord appointed over all his goods, and went into a far country, and after a long time returned again to require an account of his stewards, where he distributed to the officers, and gave one of them five talents, and the other four talents, to the third three talents, to the fourth two, to the fifth one talent, wherewith every one should trade and get gain. And then when he that had but one talent had gained nothing, he commanded him to be bound hand and foot, and to be cast out into darkness; and commanded also to destroy those murderers, and to burn their cities, who after their lord was gone away, and had committed his goods to them, and they presently in his house began to fight, and beat their fellow-servants, and to be drunken, and play, and kill his messengers which he sent to them (Matt. xxv. 14–31; Luke xix. 12–28). All which are similitudes and parables concerning his officers in the house of this world, shewing how he will punish the evil householders with hell fire, and burn their cities, viz. their kingdom which they have built in their own voluptuousness to their own glory and honour, and shut them out from his face for ever. But the others, who were faithful in his ministry and service, he gave full power over his house, and gave them also the government (Luke xix. 17) and talent of him that had buried it in the earth (Luke xix. 24), and would not execute his office that was appointed him.

30. Thus all potentates and magistrates in offices ought well to consider this, that they ought to work in God's office, and have a care of his house, and not think only to look after nobility and high estate, and think how to fill their belly, and satisfy their pleasures with gourmandising and guzzling, gluttony and drunkenness, and to wrest the sweat of the miserable with unrighteousness, and lay it out upon their pride and bravery, and constrain and press upon the miserable and inferior with power. All these, one with another, are the evil and wicked officers, and the murderers, which the Lord commandeth to be destroyed, and their cities to be burned with the fire of God's anger.

31. But at present the world is full of such officers, to whom the Lord clearly for a long time sent many messengers, but they have vilified and contemned them. Therefore now is the time of the Lord's coming; for they have even now also killed his son (Matt. xxi. 39), viz. the plain truth of his word, and turned it into mere self lust [and

wantonness]; therefore these householders must give an account of their offices (Luke xvi. 2).

32. Moses speaketh further concerning Joseph, and saith, *And it came to pass after this was done, that his Master's wife cast her eyes upon Joseph, and said, Lie with me. But he refused, and said to her, Behold, my master taketh no notice what is with me in the house; and whatsoever he hath, he hath committed it under my hand and charge; and there is nothing so great in the house which he hath withholden from me, but thee, because thou art his wife: how should I then do so great an evil, and sin against God. And she pressed such words upon Joseph daily, but he obeyed her not, to lie with her, or to be near about her* (Gen. xxxix. 7–10). This is now the mighty type,[1] shewing how it goeth with the children of God, when they have attained the divine government in the new regeneration, in that they must now converse in this house of flesh and Adamical prison with their holy blessed governments. Also how the soul hath taken in marriage this unchaste whorish woman in the spirit of this world in the bestial desire in flesh and blood; which whorish woman now sets upon the chaste Joseph, and continually would urge and draw him to her amorous lust, that the new virgin child might lie with the bestial whore again, as Adam did, from which lustful bed the earthly Eve proceeded, with whom afterwards he copulated in his lust, as all beasts do.

33. This lecherous Eve sticketh yet to the children of God in flesh and blood, and it is the animal soul, viz. the mortal spirit, full of evil lust and impurity, whereinto the devil hath yet stuck his Serpent's sting; for which cause the body must die, and rot; also this bestial spirit must be destroyed,[2] and go quite into its mother again, out of which it proceeded in the beginning.

34. In this whore the devil assaulteth the noble virgin child daily, viz. the chaste Joseph in Christ's spirit, encompassed with heavenly spiritual corporeity, viz. with Christ's flesh and blood. This virgin child is the woman in the *Apocalypse*, that standeth upon the moon (Rev. xii. 1), viz. upon this earthly whore, and hath twelve stars in the crown upon her head, which woman the dragon in the earthly whore would continually devour, when she bringeth forth the holy child, viz. the noble Joseph, viz. the chaste and divine purity, which causeth woe to the dragon in flesh and blood, that it must resign its kingdom, and in that respect poureth forth the great

---

[1] Or, image.
[2] Or, corrupt.

THE MOST EXCELLENT HISTORY OF JOSEPH

deluge[1] of earthliness upon her, to slay the child together with its mother.

35. But the earth cometh to help this woman (Rev. xii. 16), that is, the earthly desire in flesh and blood openeth its throat wide and swalloweth this dragon's flood into itself, seeing it is its like, that it may not hurt the virgin child; as Potiphar's wife's unchaste dragon's whorish floods and streams did not hurt Joseph, in that he fled from her and did not yield his will to her.

36. And this is first the most powerful proba or trial of the children of God; that as soon as they attain the new birth, then the devil comes and stirreth up the fleshly whore in flesh and blood, and all false and wicked desires and imaginations, and then injecteth and frameth in this whore the honour and glory of the world; also riches and the pleasure of this life; also he modelleth and represents the great misery and desolation, wherein the poor soul, in this world, must stand in shame and scorn; also the great unworthiness of the soul; also he represents covetousness, to think all temporal good things and necessaries will fail, and so it should come into great misery.

37. To the potent and rich the devil modelleth and represents, in this their fleshly serpentine whore, their nobility and highness, their great honour, might and power; also voluptuous eating and drinking [of dainty fare], and how they may acquire it with power and subtle policy; also he represents unchastity and wantonness; and to think, that if they should walk in humility and lowliness they should lose the respect and reputation of the world: for who would fear and honour them, if they did not put themselves forward with ostentation?

38. All these are the words of Potiphar's whore in flesh and blood, which the devil stirreth up in the Serpent's insinuated poison, with his imagination, wherewith he plagueth the poor imprisoned soul in flesh and blood, and provoketh it to such and the like unchastity and sins. And this whore in the flesh saith continually to the soul, Lie with me, copulate with me, thou wilt be blessed, happy, and saved well enough, use thy lust with me. And this she doth daily, that she might bring Joseph into lust, viz. the new child, that the soul might bite at that bait, and defile the new child, and its fair crown.

39. For this whore is ashamed before this new child: she resembleth a dirty swine compared with the sun. When she heareth mention made of the wantonness of the world, she rejoiceth at it; but when

---
[1] Flood or water-stream.

men speak of such chastity and purity she is ashamed of it, and then bespattereth or sullieth the speech of the holy child with the above-said abominations, and despiseth it: for she knoweth that if Joseph holdeth the government she must die.

40. But honest, virtuous and chaste Joseph, viz. the inward new man, saith to this whore, Behold, my Lord and Master hath trusted me with all his eternal goods, and the whole kingdom of Christ, how shall I then do so evilly before him? I will not lie with thee, thou art thy Lord's wife, viz. the wife of the spirit of this world, I will not lie with thee, nor be near thee.

41. And Moses saith further, *It came to pass on a day, that Joseph went into the house to do his employment; and there was none of the people in the house. And she caught him by his garment, and said, Lie with me: but he left the garment in her hand, and fled, and ran forth out of the house. But when she perceived that he left his garment in her hand, and was fled forth, she called the people of the house, and said, Behold, he hath brought in an Hebrew man to us to defame us; he came in unto me and would have lain with me, but I cried with a loud voice: and when he heard that I cried out, and called, he left his garment with me, and fled, and ran forth* (Gen. xxxix. 11-15). This now is the figure, shewing how the devil, through this whorish woman, strongly sets upon the soul, especially when the devil observeth that the soul is alone, that the spirit of God stirreth not in it. Then he falls a-storming of it, and layeth hold of it in its life's essence, and will force it in such whoredom, that the precious virgin child might be defiled, and that she might with the Serpent's power copulate with the soul.

42. This also is a powerful figure of the whorish and unchaste world, shewing how the fair daughters of Eve, in the instigation of the devil, run after the tender youths and allure them with flattering hypocritical behaviour, with wicked burning lust, which trim and adorn themselves, as if an angel sat under their dress; and have drawn to themselves many an honest virtuous child, that never desired it, and bound them with the devil's chains, and have bereaved them of their honour and chastity.

43. And if there were an honest and chaste Joseph, who would not go into these hogstys and jakes of the devil, they cry out against such a one, and accuse him of unchastity, as willing to betray him and rob him of his honour, and yet are even the lustful panders, which strow sugar, and give gall to eat; which strange people strow sugar so long as he hath money in his purse, till they bereave him of his livelihood, honour and goods, that he have no more to give them; and then they

scorn him and leave him without a garment, as Potiphar's wife did Joseph, as he was going out of the house; so the devil hath the soul, and the whore the garment for a pledge; in which whore nothing else governeth but the Serpent with its brood of young ones, and he that joins himself unto them is poisoned by the Serpent. For the Serpent sheds its spawn into body and soul, and poisoneth him so exceedingly that his heart cleaveth to the whore, and runneth after her, as if he were fast tied to her.

44. At present the world is full of these vermin, among high and low, and therefore also at present the Serpent itself is pregnant and will shed forth its spawn, which the zeal of God will consume. For Joseph with his governing office lieth as yet in prison, and Potiphar's wife governeth in her burning lust which she bare to Joseph. But since she could not betray Joseph, she set herself in Joseph's government, and governeth the house of this world, and accordingly hath generated many bastards, which now govern in her stead; and therefore the judgment cometh upon her whoredom, and breaketh her to pieces; that men will say, *She is fallen, she is fallen, Babel, the mother of the great whoredom, and is become a habitation of all devils and unclean spirits* (Rev. xviii. 2), she is for ever sealed up in the abyss.

45. On the contrary, we here see in this image and type also the great chastity and purity of Joseph, who, when he was drawn and held with power, yet fled from this whore, and had rather leave his garment and good name at stake that he might but keep a good conscience.

The holy figure standeth thus:

46. When this chaste new virgin child in the spirit of Christ seeth this whore in flesh and blood draw near it, that her desire layeth hold on this chastity, then it fleeth out of the house; that is, this virgin child hideth itself in its own Principle, and may not come near the soul, seeing the soul is defiled by this whore's poison, so that it is brought into lust. Thus strongly the divine purity shields itself from the devil's vanity.

47. For in this new child there standeth the fair carbuncle stone of the highest love of God in the name JESUS, which suffers itself to be sullied no more, for it once passed through death and hell in man. It will be pure, and possess the throne of God, whereupon the Scripture speaketh strongly, that, *Whosoever hath once tasted the sweetness of the world to come, and departeth from it again, that this soul hath no*

forgiveness more for ever (Heb. vi. 4-6); that is no other than where the noble virgin child is born anew again out of the soul in its substance that faded in Adam, and the soul departeth quite from it again, and severeth itself from it with its will, so that it fadeth again once more; there is no remedy for it more eternally. For in the birth of this virgin child the foretaste of the eternal joy is given to the soul, and that is done in the wedding of the Lamb, known to our schoolfellows.

48. Therefore this noble virgin with her fair stone[1] hideth itself frequently from the soul, but she breaketh not off from the marriage, except the soul breaketh itself off from her; and there is great weeping and lamentation towards the soul, if it defile itself again, as in the little book of *Repentance* is set forth, and cannot easily befall Joseph; for the soul is hugged, embraced and kept in Christ's arms, as it is John x. 28, *My sheep are in my hand.*

49. Thus we understand in this figure, how very chaste, modest and pure hearts are given to the children of God in their inward ground, and how they must be strongly proved and tried, before the government of Divine Vision will be given them, to be able to see the Mysterium Magnum [the Great Mystery].

50. And Moses saith further, *And Potiphar's wife laid up his garment by her until his master came home, and told him those very words* (Gen. xxxix. 16, 17). We see in this figure the perfidious treacherous dealings of the world, how wickedly they recompense and reward their Christian faithful servants and ministers. Joseph carried himself faithfully in the sight of their whole house, and all succeeded happily that went through his hand: but when he would not lie with this whore, to pollute himself with her, then she persecuteth him in his body and life, and studieth how to steal away his honour from him by falsehood and wickedness; when she cannot take it away with subtlety and devilish plots.

51. This now is a figure, shewing what grievous enemies a true Christian hath, and that he is everywhere encompassed with enemies; and though perhaps he standeth in temporal felicity, and have the favour and good will of many men, yet he ought not to be secure. For the devil continually hunteth after him to find how to make him fall; for what the devil cannot do by himself to God's children in flesh and blood, that he attempts by his instruments, falsely to betray the children of God, and that, even for their fear of God, their honesty and virtue.

[1] Or, star.

52. For if the new heavenly Eve be born in God's children, then the devil in the earthly Eve will not endure it: for a whore and a modest virgin will very ill stand together.

53. And thus the children of God have no greater danger than when they are exalted to worldly honour. For the devil is a spirit of pride, and sets himself with his lust in worldly highness and magnificence, in high offices;[1] for he will always still be a prince of this world (John xiv. 30), as Christ also calleth him; and he is so indeed according to the property of vanity, falsehood and wickedness, and always sets his [throne and] stool readily there, where great offices and honour are, where might, power and authority is administered and put in execution: there he involves himself,[2] so that he might be sure to sit [for one] in the government of the world.

54. Therefore he will not readily endure that a Joseph should sit near him, but those that are rich, noble, lofty and stately, honouring themselves, which hunt only after worldly honour, pleasure and voluptuousness; who fill their bellies daily, and are bold, stout, furious, and full with plenty, and hunt only after subtlety and policy, seeking how they may wrest from the miserable his sweat, and convert it into pride; who trim and set themselves forward in every place, taking pleasure in themselves in such dresses and ornaments, giving one another great compliments and courtship, and ascribe great titles of honour to them. Where the house is stuck full of such trimmed dressed whores under a modest and chaste show and appearance, there is the devil a frolick guest: for it goeth according to his own heart's desire and will.[3]

55. But if God send a Joseph thither, who would fain live and do according to the will of God, then it happeneth to him as to Joseph; and to Daniel, whom they wickedly and with falsehood brought to the lion's den; and Joseph they brought into prison: but in the end the devil's kingdom is put to shame, as in Joseph and Daniel.

56. Therefore if any will be a Joseph, and also sit in worldly offices and honour, he must do it with great earnest sincerity and humility of his heart, and continually pray, and resist the devil, that he may not be able with his stool of pride to dwell with him; if not, let him stay without it, or else he will fall to the ground in such offices. If Joseph be not armed with Christ, who hath overcome the devil, let him let the high offices alone; for the devil will not endure him in it, while he

---

[1] Or, high places (Eph. vi. 12). [2] Insinuates or wraps up himself.
[3] Property and condition.

is against him: He must either be a right Joseph and Daniel, or must have the mind of the world, if he will govern the world.

57. For this world hath a twofold office, viz. God's office, and Satan's office; the one in God's love, the other in God's wrath, viz. according to the property of light, and according to the property of darkness, which, in the nature of this world, rule near and in one another, and are two kingdoms: as the one is Christ's kingdom, the other is Satan's.

58. Therefore, if thou art not armed and wholly resigned to God, that thou canst upon occasion, with Joseph, leave thy garment, also thy honour and welfare, for the sake of God, and for righteousness, and overcome the devil with divine power and strength, press into no office, except thou art rightly, duly and orderly called thereunto: and then also thou standest either in the throne of Joseph or in the throne of the world.

59. Thou must in an office either serve God or the devil, for thou canst not serve two masters alike; for self and resignation are two [distinct]. He that serves God is resigned up into him, and in all things hath respect to truth and righteousness, and will promote that. But he that serves self hath respect to favour, and the highness and magnificence of the world, that he may have it all at his disposing: This officer is in the ministry and service of the evil Adam, in whom the devil hath his throne, and helpeth him to pronounce the sentence of justice.

60. O thou worldly judge! rely not thou upon the tower of Babel, upon worldly determinations, ordinances and conclusions, upon human institutions, statutes, laws and decrees: the top thereof reacheth not into heaven; that is only the height of the confusion of strife and a misunderstanding.[1] God seeth thee in thy very heart, he proveth and trieth thy will [and desire]; the law pleads not for thee before God, though thou orderest thyself according to that, when thy heart knoweth it ought to be quite otherwise; and then think no otherwise with thyself but that thou pronouncest the sentence of justice for the devil, and servest him under a hypocritical mantle or cloak. The justice and right is God's, and *it is God himself*; but wrong[2] is the devil's, and *it is the devil himself*: that master which thou servest is he that will reward thee and pay thee thy wages, *he himself will be thy wages*: and this thou art to expect in thy office.

61. And Moses saith further, *Then his master took him and put him into*

---

[1] Or, mistake.   [2] Or, unrighteousness.

prison, where the king's prisoners lay: and he lay there in prison. But the Lord was with him, and vouchsafed protection towards him, and caused him to find favour in the eyes of the officer of the prison, that he committed all the prisoners in the prison under his hand, that whatsoever was done there must be done by him. For the officer of the prison took not any thing upon him; for the Lord was with Joseph, and what he did the Lord made it successful (Gen. xxxix. 20–23). In this figure we see the final and last proof and trial of God's children, how they must leave their honour and welfare, and also put their life in hazard, and resign themselves wholly to God, to do whatsoever he will with them; for they must forsake all for God's sake, and leave the world, and be as a prisoner who expecteth death, and relyeth no more upon any man; and knoweth not how to get any comfort from any creature, but relyeth barely and merely upon God and his grace: and then is a man passed through all proofs and trials, and now stands waiting the commands of his Lord, what he will have him to be.

62. For he saith very inwardly to God, Lord, wilt thou have me in prison and in misery, that I shall sit in darkness, then I will willingly dwell there; if thou bringest me into hell, I will go along; for thou art my heaven. If I have but thee, I inquire not after heaven and earth, and if body and soul should fail,[1] yet thou art my comfort; let me be where I will, yet I am in thee and thou in me, I have fully enough when I have thee, use me for what thou wilt.

63. In this last proof and trial man becomes the image of God again, for all things become one and the same, and are alike to him. He is all one with prosperity and adversity, with poverty and riches, with joy and sorrow, with light and darkness, with life and death. He is as nothing to himself, for in his will he is dead to all things. And he standeth in a figure, representing how God is in and through all, and yet is as a nothing to all things, for they comprehend not him, and yet all is manifested by him; and he himself is all, and yet hath nothing, for any thing is to him in the apprehension of it even as nothing, for it comprehends him not. He is as it were dead to all things, and yet himself is the life of all things. He is ONE, and yet NOTHING and ALL. Thus also a man becomes according to his resigned will, when he yields himself wholly to God, and then his will falls again into the unsearchable will of God, out of which he came in the beginning, and then standeth in the form as an image of the unsearchable will of God, wherein God dwelleth and willeth.

64. For if the creature willeth no more than what God willeth

---

[1] Or, be famished.

through it, then it is dead to itself, and standeth again in the first image, viz. in that wherein God formed it in a life; for what is the life of the creature? nothing else but a spark of the will of God, which creature now standeth still to the will of God, whose life and will is God's, who driveth and governeth it.

65. But that which willeth and runneth (Rom. ix. 16) of itself, that rendeth itself from the entire will of God, and bringeth itself into selfhood, wherein yet there is no rest, for it must live and run on in self-will, and is a mere unquietness. For unquietness is the life of self-will; for when the will willeth itself no more, then nothing can torment it more, its willing is its own life; and whatsoever willeth in and with God,[1] that is one life with God.

66. It is better to know nothing, than to will according to self; for that which knoweth nothing, the will of that passeth away with the creaturely life, and its strife hath an end, and hath no more source [or torment]: as we may understand in irrational creatures.[2]

67. For it is the source [and torment] of all the damned that they are wishing and woulding,[3] viz. they would that which is self, and in their woulding they generate ideas, species, and formations,[4] viz. contrary wills and desires, the will being at strife; so that one [only] thing is manifested in multiplicity, wherein it is at enmity with itself; but when it is one with the Eternal One, then can no enmity be therein, and there is also no possibility of enmity therein.

68. Therefore it is man's last proof or trial when he standeth still to God in all things; then in him light proceeds out of darkness, life out of death, and joy out of sorrow; for God is in and with him in all things, and blesseth him. As was done to Joseph in the prison: his prison became joy to him, for he became also a governor over the prison in the prison; he was as a prisoner, and yet as a master of the prisoners; he governed the prison, and the prisoners, and was a patron, fosterer and guardian to the distressed; his master took nothing upon himself, and was well pleased with what Joseph did, for all was very pleasing and right in his sight.

69. Thus understand us here according to its precious worth: When man is entirely resigned to God, then is God his will, and God takes nothing upon himself about what man doth; nothing is against him, for God's will doth it in himself, and all sin ceaseth; and though

---

[1] Willeth or desireth that which God willeth or desireth.
[2] Or, sensitive creatures.
[3] Have a longing desire, and yet cannot attain the least satisfaction.
[4] Representations in their thoughts.

God's will of anger stirreth in him, and bringeth fire from heaven from the Lord (as was done by Elias), yet all is right in the sight of God, for the party doth it not, but God through him: he is the instrument through which God speaketh and acteth.

70. Now as God, in so much as he is God, can will nothing but that which is good; or else he were not God, if he himself would any thing that were evil: so also there can be nothing in such a man's will but blessing only, and the will of God. As was said of Joseph, God was with him in all his doings, and blessed all things through his hand. Thus to the honest and virtuous, a light ariseth in the darkness (*Ps.* cxii. 4), and the night is turned into day to him; and adversity is turned into prosperity, and the curse, wickedness and malice of the world is turned into Paradise. And it is with him as St Paul saith, *All things must serve to the best to them that love God* (Rom. viii. 28).

71. For Joseph's prison brought him before king Pharaoh, and set him upon the throne over that land and people; and made him lord over his father and brethren, and to be a guardian[1] and officer of the king, and to be God's regent and governor, through whom God ruled great countries and kingdoms: as the like may be seen also in Daniel.

72. Therefore a Christian should learn to bear the temptation,[2] when God casteth him into Joseph's pit and prison, and rely upon God in all his doings, and entirely resign himself into God; and then God would be more potent in him than the world and hell is; for all those would at length, after he hath stood out all the trials, be put to scorn in him.

[1] Steward.   [2] Affliction.

The Sixty-Seventh Chapter

How *Joseph* in Prison Expounded King *Pharaoh's* Chief Butler's and Baker's Dream to each of them; and what is to be understood thereby[1]

1. IN this chapter the spirit representeth a figure, shewing how the spirit of God seeth through man's spirit, and bringeth man's spirit into his seeing or vision, so that it can understand hidden secret things. For, to expound dreams is nothing else but to see and understand the figure, how the *spiritus mundi* [the spirit of the world] in the constellation of man frameth itself into a figure with those things which, in the human life, are clearly in working, or indeed are framed in a figure in the constellation by a great conjunction, the working not being yet begun, and yet is modellised naturally, where the spirit of man by divine power knoweth in the prefiguration what working and effect it hath. Also it may be understood by the diligent consideration of astronomy[2] according[3] to astrology (wherein the natural effect and working is prefigured), what naturally is wrought and represented by this power.

2. But [the interpretation of these dreams was given] while Joseph was a child, and did not outwardly busy himself in this art; therefore it is to be understood that the spirit of God, with his seeing or vision, brought him into the image or idea of the dream, and that the spirit of God explained the dream through the spirit of Joseph; as was done also by Daniel. For, to expound dreams is nothing else but to understand a magic image or representation of the astrum, aspect or constellation in the human property.

3. For every man beareth the image of his constellation, viz. a magic asterism,[4] in himself, and when the time cometh that such

[1] Genesis xl.

[2] By an astronomical figure of the outward heavens, in a scheme, thus, and a judgment of the effects by astrology: predicting, before the stars be in that posture in the heavens, or before the effect be wrought by the stars.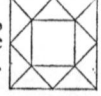

[3] Or, in.

[4] As Orion, the Pleiades, *Amos* v. 8. Mazzaroth, the 12 signs. Or, Arcturus, *Job* xxxviii. 31, 32. Ursa Minor or Ursa Major, or any other constellation that consisteth of many stars together. Or a figure of the whole heavens erected upon a point of time.

HOW JOSEPH EXPOUNDED DREAMS

magic image of the superior constellation is kindled, then it entereth upon its working; and then the astral spirit beholds itself in the elements, and seeth what figure it hath.

4. But the elements are void of understanding,[1] and afford only a bestial body[2] in their figure, therefore the astral spirit can discern nothing else but the form of some such earthly creature: except the soulish spirit[3] be concomitant in the working of the astral spirit, then is it premodelled in a human form, and in a true, natural way and manner of figure. For the soul alone hath true, human eyes, but the astral spirit hath only a bestial appearance, and seeth after the manner of a beast.

5. Yet seeing there is a great difference between a false and wicked soul (which daily imagineth in a bestial manner of figure, and willeth and desireth bestial things) and a pious divine soul, wherein the spirit of God is manifest; so also are the magical imaginations and representations in the astral spirit different. For a beast dreameth according to phansie,[4] and so doth a bestial or animal man: though indeed the image or idea[5] of the constellation doth certainly co-modellise itself, whether in evil or in good, according as the astral spirit eagerly longeth or lusteth in itself when it so vieweth what stands naturally as a working in it. But seeing it is a beast, therefore it introduceth in its image with its desire, commonly, the model of[6] a phantastic image; and turneth it from joy to sorrow, from sorrow to joy; but the soul is faint and sick in such a spectacle or glass and prefiguration, whence oftentimes there ariseth great unquietness to the body.

6. But where a true vision is seen in man, that is done by the soul's modellising, when it co-imageth or co-modelleth itself in the figure through its imagination; then the image or representation standeth in the right human understanding, though indeed the astral spirit continually imageth or frameth itself in earthly forms, so that very seldom an entire perfect vision appeareth as the work or effect in itself shall be; also man's own imagination itself doth often alter it: what a man thinks or imagineth in the day, viz. that magic form, makes it so, that the figure is according to his imagination.

7. Yet the right visions are when man's will resteth in God, and then is God's will manifest in man's will, and then the soul seeth with God's eyes from its most inward ground, where it stands in the Word

---

[1] Inanimate.   [2] Animal body.   [3] Or, spirit of the soul.
[4] Or, from phansie.   [5] Or, figure, the schema cœli.
[6] Or, in.

of God. And then the speaking Word goeth with the soul's [word] into the magic image of the constellation, and then the astral spirit cannot image or fashion itself in the phansie, but must stand in the image in the figure as the constellation is; and then the soul seeth what the Most High hath prefigured, and what shall come to pass. And then the Word of God, viz. the ground of the soul, expresseth the figure in the soul, so that the soul understandeth it; as here Joseph and also Daniel expressed and expounded. As soon, now, as the figure of the vision was told before Joseph, the spirit of God was together in the voice of the relator, and in Joseph expounded the vision: for so also are the magic visions of all the prophets.

8. For after God hath once appeared to a prophet in an audible voice, and called them to be prophets (as to Samuel) (1 Sam. iii. 4, 6, 8, 10), then afterwards he appeared to them in magic visions, and answered them upon their questions.

9. The right prophetic ground of the magical seeing and understanding is thus: Every prophet is a limit, wherein a time is included or an age comprehended; and he is the mouth of that kingdom or dominion; that is, when that kingdom hath awakened and generated the turba in it, then is he the mouth of the inward ground, which declareth and expresseth the vanity in the turba, and also the grace of God which hath taken compassion on the human misery, and opposed the wrath of the turba, and [he] reproveth that kingdom for their vanity and idolatry, and comforteth them with the introverted grace again.

10. For his spirit standeth in the figure, in the eternal speaking Word of God (from which the life was expressed or spoken forth, and became a creature), introverted again as an instrument of the spirit of God, whereby the spirit of God speaketh and intimateth. For the prophetic spirit could not, in its own might and power, declare future hidden things, if the spirit of God did not see through it, and that the Word of God did also go together through his Word into the magic figure which the prophet seeth.

11. For the prophet knoweth not anything beforehand in his own power and authority, which he declareth, but when the word modelleth itself together in the figure, then the prophetic spirit seeth through God's seeing, how the word of God goeth also together upon the figure. And then the Word expresseth, declareth and expoundeth the figure through the prophetic spirit: as here was done by Joseph. When the king's officers told their dreams, then the Word set the

HOW JOSEPH EXPOUNDED DREAMS

figure in Joseph's understanding how it should come to pass, so that Joseph knew what their visions meant.

12. But he knew it not beforehand; but in the telling of the dream, the word of understanding modelled itself in Joseph's understanding, that he knew it. For Joseph's spirit stood in a magic figure, introverted again into the Word, after the manner as the new birth in the spirit of Christ standeth introverted again. So also the other prophets, through whose mouth God's Word expounded and expressed from the inward ground, through their mouth, the wonders of God in nature, viz. in the formed creaturely word.

13. By this figure of Joseph, in that he obtained divine knowledge and skill, and could expound hidden things, we see how the introverted spirit of man resigned up into God, when he forsaketh all that is his own, doth attain the divine eye to see and understand; so that he gets much more again than he forsook, and that he is much richer than when he enjoyed his own. For in his own will he had and possessed only a particular; but in the resignation he gets into the total, viz. [into the universal] into all; for ALL is from the Word of God.

14. Therefore if he cometh into that he cometh into the ground wherein all lieth in the eternity, and from being poor becomes rich. As Joseph's figure declareth, that a poor prisoner became a prince, and that only by the divine Word that had manifested itself in him, when the Word, in his submissive dereliction and forsaking all, expressed or spake forth itself again, and so spake or pronounced Joseph into a regal government and dominion, through whom the Word of God would rule in Egypt, and give the understanding for such a kingly government.

15. We see further in this figure of Joseph, How at length all must serve for the best to God's children (Rom. viii. 28): all the wrong they must suffer that will turn to mere joy in the issue. For in trouble and affliction they learn to know what they are, how very weak and miserable they are in their own selves, and how near death and misery attend them; and how all the trust, confidence and expectation they have of men, in that they will rely upon man and trust to the favour of man, is a very fickle uncertain thing; also how man should turn his hope towards God, when he expecteth to be delivered out of trouble by the favour of man: yet [even] so at length the favour and counsel of man must stand him in stead.

16. But if a man will expect the favour and counsel of man, he

must set his hope upon God, and look whether God will give him comfort by human means, and release him from misery; and [he must] not set his hope upon the favour of man, but look upon God, to see what he will work by means. And though it seem as if God had forgotten, as here with Joseph, who must remain two years in prison, then he must consider with himself that God will have him here; but if he will through means have him in another place, then he will afford means for it, and send it in due time, as is to be seen here.

17. The mishap of the king's officers, in that they were put into prison to Joseph, was a means whereby God would bring Joseph before the king. But it was not done suddenly: because Joseph hoped the king's butler would speak a good word for him to the king, and tell his innocency. But the butler forgot him, and left Joseph lying in the dungeon: that Joseph might wholly despair of human means, and flee to God; and when he doth that, and despairs of all human means, and barely relyeth on God, then must even that means, in which Joseph had hoped and yet also had long despaired of any help from it, break forth again and stand him in stead.

18. By this a child of God should learn, that all which he prayeth to God for, that it should stand him in stead by man, that he should not set his hope upon man, but upon God; then at length everything is done which he hath prayed to God for, that should stand him in stead by human means: when the mind despairs of human means, and diveth down into God again, then God's help breaks forth through human means. Thus the mind is instructed to learn to trust in God.

The Sixty-Eighth Chapter

Of the Dreams of King *Pharaoh*: How *Joseph* is fetched out of Prison, and presented before the King, and Cometh to Great Honour[1]

1. MOSES saith, *After two years Pharaoh had a dream, that he stood by the water, and saw seven fair fat kine arise out of the water, and went to feed in the meadow. After this he saw other seven kine arise out of the water, which were ill-favoured, lean and meagre, and drew near the kine that were by the water side; and the lean, meagre and ill-favoured devoured the seven fair fat kine. Then Pharaoh awoke. And he slept again, and dreamed once more, and saw seven ears grow out of one stalk, full and thick. But afterwards he saw seven thin blasted ears spring up, and the seven thin and black ears devoured the seven full and thick ears. Then Pharaoh awoke, and observed that it was a dream. And when it was morning his spirit was troubled, and he sent forth to call all the magicians*[2] *of Egypt, and all the wise men, and related to them his dreams: but there was none that could interpret them to Pharaoh* (Gen. xli. 1-8).

2. These dreams of Pharaoh were represented to him from God, therefore no magus and naturalist[3] could interpret them. For the natural magus hath power only in nature, only in that which nature frameth in its working; he cannot apprehend that, nor advise in that, which the word of God modelleth and frameth. But a prophet hath power to interpet that; for he is a divine magus; as here Joseph.

3. With the Egyptians the magic art and skill was common. But when it was misused to witchcraft, it was extirpated; although it remained among the heathen till the kingdom of Christ, till the divine magia sprang up. Then the natural magia was suppressed among the Christians, which in the beginning was well that it was suppressed, for the heathenish faith[4] was thereby allayed and quenched; and the magic images of nature, which they honoured for gods, were rooted out of men's hearts.

4. But when the Christian faith was common, then came other magi up, viz. the sects in Christendom, which they set up for gods, instead of the images of heathen idols, and drove on greater delusions than the heathen with their magic idols.

[1] Gen. xli.   [2] Truth-sellers, soothsayers.   [3] Skilful in nature.
[4] Or, religion.

5. For the heathen looked upon the ground of the possibility and working of nature. But these set themselves above the ground of nature, merely in a historical faith, and say that men ought to believe that which they contrive.

6. As at this very day titulary Christendom is full of such magi as have no natural understanding, either of God or of nature more among them, but only an empty babbling of a supernatural magic ground, wherein they have set up themselves for idol-gods, and understand neither the divine nor natural magia, so that the world is made stock blind by them. Whence the contention and strife in faith [and religion] is arisen, that men talk much of faith, one drawing this way, another that way, and make a multitude of opinions, which are altogether worse than the heathenish images, which indeed had their ground and foundation in nature. But these images have no ground, either in nature or in the supernatural divine faith, but are dumb idols, and their ministers are Baal's ministers.

7. And as it was highly necessary and good that the natural magia was discontinued amongst the Christians, where the faith of Christ was manifest: so now at present it is much more necessary that the natural magia were again manifest; that indeed titulary Christendom's idols which it maketh to itself might, through nature, be made manifest and known, that man might know in nature the outspoken or expressed formed Word of God, as also the new regeneration, and also the fall and perdition. That thereby the contrived supernatural idols might be suppressed, that men might at length in nature learn to understand the Scriptures, seeing men will not confide in the spirit of God in the divine magia of true faith, but lay their foundation upon the tower of Babel, in the contention and contrived idol-opinions, viz. in the edicts and traditions of men.

8. I do not say that men should seek and preach the heathenish magia again, and take up heathen idols again, but that it is needful to learn to search the ground of nature, viz. the formed Word of God in love and anger, with its re-expression; that men might not be so blind concerning the essence of all essences.

9. For the Fathers of the first faith were not so blind concerning the kingdom and dominion of nature, but did know in and by nature that there was a hidden God, who had made himself visible by the Word of his exhalation and information of the created world, and have known God's Word by the creation; which is now at present much the more necessary, that the opinion-idols might

OF THE DREAMS OF KING PHARAOH

come to light and be known, that man might at length see what faith is, that it is not an opinion and conceit, but a divine substance or essence (Heb. xi. 1), which substance or essence in the visible man is hidden to outward eyes, as the invisible God is hidden in the visible substance of this world.

10. But that the magi naturales [the natural magicians], could not expound Pharaoh's dreams, this was the cause: Pharaoh's dreams sprang from the centre of nature, which the heathenish magicians understood not; for their magic ground in their understanding was only in the working and figure[1] of the constellation or asterism, and in the elements. They understood not the ground of the eternal nature, out of which the nature of this world had its original, and wherein it standeth: but the dreams of Pharaoh had their original out of the eternal nature, and were represented in a visible image in the outward nature of time, and in the outward figure of man.[2]

11. For the seven fat kine in the pasture signify, in the inward ground, the seven properties of the eternal nature in the holy, good substance or essence, viz. in the kingdom of heaven, where the divine power is substantial. And the seven lean, ill-favoured, meagre kine signify, in the inward ground, the seven properties of the eternal nature in the wrath of God, viz. in the kingdom of hunger and thirst, where nature is without the divine substance of the good power of God: and the seven thick, fat and full ears, and also the seven dry, blasted ears signify the same also.

12. But that this dream appeared twofold to Pharaoh, it signifieth in this figure, First, the ground of the eternal nature in its seven properties, what God would shew thereby. Secondly, as to the second appearance, it signifieth the human ground, which in its substance hath its creaturely original out of the seven properties. Moreover, it denotes the twofold man, according to the outward body and the outward spirit, and then according to the inward soulish [or animal] spirit and according to the inward holy substance of the divine substantial power; and standeth in the figure[3] of a holy divine man, who is fair, and full of divine power and virtue, who walketh and feedeth

[1] Or, scheme,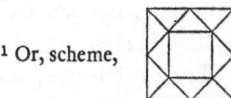

[2] Or, representation to the outward man.
[3] Condition, quality or property.

in the true heavenly pasture of the substance of the substantial wisdom of God.

13. And it denoteth secondly a wicked and ungodly man, who is withered, meagre, lean and ill-favoured as to that divine substance, and yet is even the same nature's property as the divine is: But he is withered and corrupted as to its good substance; the wrath of the eternal nature in the seven properties hath consumed its substance, so that it is now as a hungry fire-spirit.

14. Thus the great God representeth before Pharaoh what at this time stood in the figure of the Egyptians, for he would visit them: First, he sheweth them his great grace, in giving them Joseph, a prophet and wise prince to govern them: also he sheweth them in this vision, that in his grace in the kingdom of the inward and the outward nature in the seven properties, there is mere blessing and good things. If they would walk therein, they would be as the seven fat kine and ears:

15. But if not, then his wrath would come upon them, and consume their good things in body and soul, and make them lean, dry and withered. As was done to the devils, when of angels they became devils; then their good things, viz. the substantial divine wisdom in them, faded, and their seven properties of the eternal nature became so ill-favoured, lean and dry, as the seven withered kine, and the seven blasted ears, wherein was no more power and virtue.

16. And so the seven withered kine, and the seven dry ears, devoured the good fat kine and ears, and were yet more lean and ill-favoured than before, that a man could not discern that they had devoured them. Thereby the great God also signifieth that the wicked man, with his seven properties of Nature enkindled in the anger of God, devoureth the good and fair image of God in him, by introducing himself into self-desire; in which self and wicked desire nature becomes painful, and falls into unquietness and disturbance of its peace; and yet afterwards is still ill-favoured, abominable, loathsome and dry: as a covetous, churlish, hungry dog, though he devour much his covetous nature in his envy consumeth him; even his flesh, so that he hath not that which he will not afford to other dogs.

17. Thus the great God represents by this, before the Egyptians, seven good fat years, and seven dry barren years which devoured the other seven, so that a man could not know the good any more: under which yet very powerful things are prefigured, as shall be mentioned hereafter.

OF THE DREAMS OF KING PHARAOH

18. But that Pharaoh was troubled at this vision, and yet understood it not, neither could his wise men interpret it, this signifieth that God himself would interpret it by his power and virtue in Joseph, and that the time of this visitation was at hand: therefore was Pharaoh so moved in himself that he would fain know it.

19. But that the wise men in the light of nature could not interpret it, signifieth that the works of God are hidden to the natural man, without grace, and that he knoweth or understandeth nothing of the ways of God, unless God reveal or manifest them thereby in and through him: for this was a motion of the eternal nature through the outward nature, therefore the natural wise men could not understand it.

20. And when none could interpret it to the king, the king's butler thought on Joseph, that Joseph had interpreted his dreams for him, and [he] told this to Pharaoh. And here in this vision of Pharaoh, God called Joseph, and that which he had desired two years ago through man's help was fulfilled and granted unto him.

21. *Then Pharaoh sent and commanded Joseph to be called, and they brought him speedily out of the dungeon: and he was shaved and put on other garments, and came in to Pharaoh. Then said Pharaoh to him, I have dreamed a dream, and there is none that can interpret it: but I have heard of thee, that when thou hearest a dream thou canst interpret it. And Joseph answered Pharaoh and said, That is not of me:*[1] *yet God will prophesy good to Pharaoh, and Pharaoh related his dream to him* (Gen. xli. 14–16).

22. This figure, that Joseph put on other garments and was shaved, when he was to enter in before Pharaoh, signifieth this to us: that God at present had put off the garment of his misery, and had now put on him the garment of wisdom, and would have him now in another place than he was in before; and set him before Pharaoh with the garment of wisdom, and would give him for a guardian to Pharaoh. For the spirit of Moses setteth down the figure excellently, accurately and properly, as if he had a great desire to play and delight himself therein.

23. And we see further, that Joseph said to the king, that it stood not in his natural power and might to know such hidden things, but that God alone gave him to know it; so that he needed neither art nor magic images about it; but God would interpret good to Pharaoh through him.

24. Therefore should a magus give up his will to God, and fix

---

[1] In my power.

his magic faith (wherewith he will search the figure of nature in its forms and conditions)[1] in God, that he may apprehend the word of God, and introduce it into the figure of nature, and then he is a right true divine magus, and may master the inward ground with divine power and virtue, and bring nature into a figure.[2] He that practiseth otherwise herein, he is a false and wicked magus, as the devil and his witches are.

25. And it is no way to be thought, as if a Christian ought not to dare to meddle with the ground of nature, but that he must be a clod and dumb image in the knowledge and skill of the secret mysteries of nature; as Babel saith, Man ought not to dare to search and know it, it were sin; which all of them, one and other, understand as much of the ground of sin as the pot doth of the potter.

26. When they should tell how sin is sin, and how man doth cause God to be angry and in wrath, then they have no other way to turn themselves to evade it, but images or conceits of opinions, which shut up the conscience in such images [and conceits], so that the conscience is afraid of their images; and the ground of sin, according to the seven properties of nature (how their fat kine are made lean and dry) they know not.

27. O ye makers of images, how doth the anger of God, in the inward ground of your own nature, threaten you with the seven barren kine and ears! Joseph is out of prison, and declareth the counsel of God to Pharaoh.

28. The time is even at hand wherein the figure of Pharaoh shall be brought to effect: your images of false and wicked magic shall be manifested to the whole world, by Joseph's exposition of the vision. Break off from the images, and pray to God, that he would give you the understanding of Pharaoh's visions; and then you may be partakers of the seven good kine and ears within you.

29. If not, then must all your images of false and wicked magic be turned into such barren kine and ears, as they are indeed for the most part already in the inward ground, and outwardly at present are devouring, and always devour, the good times and years; for they have almost quite devoured and swallowed up into the abyss all love, faith, truth, righteousness, humility and fear of God; and at present also they devour all outward food and sustenance. They have devoured the silver, and there is nothing left but meagre and base copper: and yet they are so hungry and greedy that they lie gnawing

---

[1] Or, qualities.   [2] Type or representation.

at the copper, as a dog at a hard bone, and would fain have more to devour, and yet there is no more for them.

30. Therefore they are so hungry, that they themselves worry and devour one another for hunger, and bring their land and country into death and famine. But hereby they are made bondslaves to the anger of God in the seven properties of nature, as the whole land of Egypt was made King Pharaoh's own in the dear time of Joseph.

31. This anger of God will hereafter give you seed, that you must sow images and idols, and devour them again yourselves, as you have clearly done for a long time, and must be its bondslave servants, as Egypt was to Pharaoh.

32. Let this be told thee, O Egypt of Christendom, by Joseph's interpretation in the spirit of wonder of the sixth number of the seals: It concerns thee, awake and behold, the great famine of body and soul is at hand, or else thou must be famished.

33. Thou standest at present in no other figure[1] in the sight of God, but that of the seven ill-favoured, hungry, withered, lean kine and ears: the blessing of God in body and soul is departed from thee, that now thou huntest after good things and temporal sustenance, and yet are not satisfied with it. And the more that thou dost hunger and suck upon bones, thou wilt be still the more hungry, till thou hast devoured all thy good kine in conscience, both in body and soul, as also land and people. And thy form and feature is so ill-favoured, that the princes of the inward and the outward heaven cannot endure to behold thee, but help to judge thee to the damnation of death, saith the spirit of wonders in Joseph's interpretation.

34. Behold thyself now aright, art thou not thus ill-favoured and hungry? Consider all thy faculties:[2] thou art raving blind with great hunger, for thou hast swallowed that up into the abyss which should bless thee and make thee happy, and hast set up the hypocrisy of thy idol ministers instead thereof. Righteousness, truth, love, faith, humility, chastity and the fear of God were thy blessing by which thou wouldest become fat again, but thou hast swallowed up all these properties, and set thine idols in their stead, and covered them with Christ's purple mantle; and now the evil hungry form, feature and properties of a devourer are awakened in thee.

35. The first devouring property covered with Christ's mantle is *pride*, viz. a desire of self-might, under the lowly humble mantle of Christ resolving to be potent and splendid, as Lucifer under his black

---

[1] Or, resemblance.   [2] Powers, virtues and abilities.

hood, who yet always supposeth he is the most potent, when yet in the presence of God he is but a lord in phantasy.

36. The second property of thy hunger covered with Christ's mantle is *covetousness*, viz. the devourer, who devoureth himself, and getteth from others their sweat, and flesh from their bones, and devoureth it: and yet hath nothing, but always lieth like poison, sucking out itself. This hath devoured all truth, righteousness, patience, love, hope, faith, and the fear of God, and yet is but a mere hunger: at present it hath eaten all silver from the copper, and yet looketh as if it had devoured nothing, for nothing is to be seen in it. But that it is more hungry than before it hath devoured all good times into itself, and still always devoureth all provisions, which God of his grace bestoweth, and yet is every day more hungry with devouring: and though he could devour heaven, he would devour hell also, and yet remaineth a mere hunger still.

37. The third property of this hunger covered with Christ's mantle is *envy*, viz. the son of covetousness, and pride is his grandfather. This stingeth and pricketh and rageth in the hunger, as poison in the flesh; it stingeth in words and works, and poisoneth all; it lieth and cheateth, and is never quiet. The more greedy covetousness is to devour the greater is this its son, *envy*; it will possess all alone to itself, and yet hath no place of rest, either in heaven, this world, or hell: It can remain neither in heaven, nor in hell, it standeth only in the hunger of covetousness, and is the life of covetousness.

38. The fourth property of hunger covered under Christ's mantle is *anger*, which is the son of envy, and covetousness is its grandfather: what envy cannot sting to death, that will anger strike and fell to death. It is so evil and wicked that it breaks and shatters the bones to pieces. It always thirsteth after murder, only that its father and grandfather, viz. covetousness, envy and pride, may have room enough. It destroyeth body and soul in their kind of fatness, and wasteth country and city, and is further so wicked that it would destroy heaven and hell, and yet hath nowhere any rest.

39. These are the four elements of hunger, which devour and swallow up the seven fat kine and ears of Pharaoh, and yet are as they were before. At present Joseph hath seen and manifested them in Pharaoh's dream, so that they are become manifest in the world, and are set before the eyes of the watchmen who sit in council for judgment, what is to be done more with these dry ill-favoured kine, for God hath given them the seven fat kine of the manifestation of his

OF THE DREAMS OF KING PHARAOH

grace; but they devour all, and yet are so very hungry that hell dwelleth in their four elements, and the kingdom of the devil standeth in their figure.[1]

40. O Egypt of Christendom! thou hopest for good, and yet desireth only to work wickedness. No good shall come to thee; except thou diest from this hunger, thou wilt burst thyself asunder in it. Whence shall good be interpreted to thee by Joseph, when thou thus hungerest the more? Nature generateth in thee such a thing as thy hunger and desire is. Thou oughtest to hope for nothing, except thou convertest and puttest on Joseph's new garment. And then the Lord will give thee his spirit, so that thou wilt see and understand thy images, and put them away, and stand with Joseph before the face of God, as Joseph before the face of Pharaoh, and wilt be able to see and interpret the wonders of God.

41. And then the Lord will set thee with Joseph over the kingdom of his mysteries, that thou wilt rightly understand the magic ground of faith, and wilt search no more in the images of the outward natural magic, as thou hast done for a long time. But thou wilt see the inward ground, and with Joseph rule over Egypt, that is, over the mysteries, and wilt therein praise the Lord, and draw in his fountain, and drink water of life.

42. For *the word*, which thou shalt now learn and understand, *is nigh thee, namely in thy mouth and heart* (Rom. x. 8; Deut. xxx. 14); thou art God's formed word, thou must learn to read thy own book, which is thyself, and then thou wilt be free from all images, and wilt see the place of which it is said, *The Lord is here* (Gen. xxviii. 16). And then thou wilt attain the life of power and virtue again, and become fat, and put away the mantle of Christ, and say, Here is the man that will walk in the footsteps of Christ, and will follow and imitate him, and be like and *conformable to him* (Phil. iii. 10) in his life and image.

43. This whole history of the dreams of Pharaoh is an image, whereby the spirit under an outward action portrayeth and typifieth the human ground, how good, God created him, and set him in his fatness, and how he is thus destroyed by Satan's envy and poison, and changed into so ill-favoured an image.

44. But in Joseph the spirit representeth a figure, shewing how a man must again spring up through the new birth out of this poison; and how he should be set before God again, and how God giveth him

---

[1] Consisteth in that which their posture, condition or quality doth represent and express.

his spirit, and maketh him ruler in his house; how he shall gather in heavenly fruits in faith and a good conscience, against the time of temptation, when the dearth or famine, viz. God's anger, sifteth the soul.

45. In which sifting then, that fruit which is for food, which stands by the soul in repentance, and in which its little pearl-plant with its branches groweth, it takes along, and beareth good fruit.

46. Those fruits are then Joseph's interpretation, as he declared God's counsel, and taught it to Pharaoh. So the new birth bringeth forth such good fruit and doctrine, which makes known the way of God to mankind, and standeth before him with wisdom, as Joseph before Pharaoh. And this we see in Joseph's counsel, after he had interpreted his dream. He said to Pharaoh, *Let the king look out for a wise and prudent man, who may build granaries for Pharaoh, where provision may be laid up, that men may have necessary sustenance in the famine* (Gen. xli. 33–36). Which the spirit secretly represents in the figure of man,[1] that a man should look out for wise men, fearing God (Exod. xviii. 21), which should help to gather in the divine treasury and provision, with wisdom and understanding, with doctrine, life and prayer; that thereby the divine treasure and provision might be gathered in.

47. And then when the time of trial, sifting and hunger cometh, that God's anger might be thereby kept back and prevented, and not so suddenly make both body and soul, land and people, lean, and devour them, but that there may be something for provision. Concerning which God saith he will do well to them that fear God, unto a thousand generations (Exod. xx. 6); and this provision shall continue to a thousand generations.

48. And Moses saith further, *This saying of Joseph pleased Pharaoh, and all his servants, well. And Pharaoh said to his servants, How can we find such a man, in whom the spirit of God is; and said to Joseph, Seeing God hath made all this known to thee, there is none so understanding and wise as thou: thou shalt be over my house, and all my people shall be obedient to thy word, only in the regal throne will I be higher than thou. And further, Pharaoh said to Joseph, Behold, I have set thee over the whole land of Egypt, and took his ring off his own hand, and gave it to Joseph into his hand, and clothed him with white silk garments, and hung a golden chain upon his neck; and caused him to go in his second chariot, and caused it to be proclaimed before him, This is the father of the land; and set him over the whole land of Egypt. And Pharaoh said*

---

[1] Or, condition of such a man: the Man Christ, or a Christian man.

OF THE DREAMS OF KING PHARAOH

to Joseph, I am Pharaoh, and without thy will shall no man stir his hand or his foot in the whole land of Egypt. And he called him his secret council, and gave him a wife named Asenath, the daughter of Poti-pherah, priest of ON (Gen. xli. 37-45).

49. This now is the most excellent figure in the whole Bible, that there is nowhere the like to it of any man. And he standeth in the figure of an approved tried Christian, who hath out-stood all trials: whom the spirit of Christ hath lead with himself quite through his sufferings, death, hell, prison, and misery; as the only God, viz. the Great King, set him before him, and tried his wisdom, which he had received in the process [or imitation] of Christ, when he received him with joy, and giveth this testimony of him: There is none so wise as thou, who would so hiddenly introduce his life in patience, through death and hell, to God, as thou.

50. And as God giveth him full power over his kingdom, and in his love maketh him his helper and assistant, as a council of a king helpeth and assisteth a king to govern his kingdom; so also God sets him in his kingdom, and ruleth by him, and giveth him his seal-ring, viz. the humanity and Deity, in the love of Jesus Christ, to his soul; and causeth him to ride in the second chariot after him, that is, where God's spirit goeth, there always goeth such a man after it; and the devil, death and hell dare not touch him any more, for thus he getteth power over the devil, death and hell, and also over his mortal flesh and blood, as Joseph over the land of Egypt.

51. And as Joseph quickly withdrew and built the king granaries to lay up provisions; so also such a man, who according to his inward ground sitteth in the kingdom of God, buildeth for God his Lord many such human houses, viz. men's souls, in which he lays up in store the divine overplus which God giveth him in Christ Jesus, viz. the divine knowledge and wisdom, with good instruction, doctrine and life, so that his doctrine spreadeth abroad and multiplieth as sands in the sea; so innumerable spreading branches his pearl-plant putteth forth, that many hundred thousand souls eat thereof, as of Joseph's provision in the famine.

52. And then Poti-pherah's daughter, that is, the daughter of the priest of On, viz. the true Christianity, is given him for a spouse, which he is to cherish and love, and begetteth of her these two sons (Gen. xli. 50), as always travelling in this way, and then they walk with washed hearts. As Joseph before the time of the famine in Egypt begat of his wife, Manasseh and Ephraim; and so it was represented to

him with these names, how God had in the house of his misery caused him to grow great and gave him much.

53. And then also a child of God sets open his chests of treasure when the famine cometh, that the anger of God sifteth the world, as Joseph did his granaries, and imparted to his fellow twigs therewith out of his chests of treasure, that they perish not in that famine.

The Sixty-Ninth Chapter

How this Famine went through all Lands, and how *Jacob* sent his sons into the Land of *Egypt* for Corn, and how they came before *Joseph*, and how he shewed himself to them. What is thereby to be understood[1]

1. THIS forty-second chapter of *Genesis*, concerning Joseph and his brethren, is a figure, shewing how such a converted Christian, which hath already entered with Christ into his process, and hath now overcome, in the end also forgiveth and rewardeth his enemies with bounty, who have brought him into Christ's process with their persecution and wicked devices and counsel. And how also their sins are set before them, and how they are brought into anxiety and necessity, and how in the end, of mere grace they are released from pain and punishment; and how God is so gracious to them upon their conversion, that he not only releaseth the punishment, but blesseth them with his gifts and benefits: as here Joseph did to his brethren.

2. But then next is also represented in this figure, how earnestly and severely God sheweth himself against sin: as here Joseph against his brethren. And yet God is not earnest to punish the repenting sinner according to the sharpest severity, but he sets himself strictly against the soul in its conscience; that sin may awake and be acknowledged, and that repentance may be the greater, that man in such terror may be humbled for sin, and quite depart from sin, and be angry with it, and utterly hate it; when he knoweth that sin hath so terrible a judgment in it.

The history saith thus:

3. *But when Jacob saw that there was plenty of corn in Egypt, he said to his sons, Why do you look so long about you? behold, I hear there is plenty of corn in Egypt: go down thither, and buy us corn, that we may live, and not die. Then the ten brethren of Joseph went down, that they might buy corn in Egypt.*

[1] Gen. xlii.

But Jacob would not suffer Joseph's brother Benjamin to go; for he said, Some mishap may befall him. (Gen. xlii. 1-4).

4. Now this is a figure, first, shewing that when man findeth himself in the divine anger in this famine, that as to righteousness he is in want, as Jacob and his children in the famine; then the Father saith in the conscience to the soul, Why lingerest thou so long looking about thee? Go down into repentance, where there is plenty of righteousness in the death of Christ, where Christ giveth righteousness for and instead of thy sins, if thou heartily turnest to him: And thus the Father bestoweth his will, and introduceth it into the sinner's repentance and conversation.

5. But Benjamin, Joseph's brother, that is, the humanity of Christ, he giveth not to it presently therewith: he first bestoweth upon it its sinful brethren, that is, he giveth it first his terrors into its conscience, and hideth his comfort in his grace, viz. the true Benjamin, Joseph's brother, from the properties of sins,[1] and sendeth the properties of sins, viz. those wherein sins have been wrought and committed after grace, to buy this corn of Joseph, viz. of Christ.

6. The sinner must himself enter upon it, and with earnestness enter into the suffering and death of Christ, and die from his sins in the presence of grace, in the prison of God's anger, and cast himself upon Joseph's, viz. Christ's, mercy and grace, and not stay without and say, *With Christ there is plenty of grace,* and so tickle and comfort himself with grace. No, that quickeneth not the poor soul. Thou must go down into Egypt to thy injured brother, whom thou hast cast into the pit, by thy sins within thee, and must in great humility come into his presence. Though thou wilt not suddenly know it, till he in his mercy shall give thee to know it; and then thou must in Christ's power, might and glory, which he gat in his resurrection, buy corn for the poor soul, that it may live, and not die; as Jacob said to his children.

7. And Moses saith further, *Thus the children of Israel and others with them came to buy corn: for the famine was also in Canaan. But Joseph was the ruler of the land, and sold corn to all the people in the land. Now when his brethren came to him, they fell down with their faces to the earth before him. And he saw them and knew them, and carried himself strangely towards them, and spake roughly with them, and said to them, Whence come ye? They said out of the land of Canaan to buy food. But though he knew them, they knew not him yet* (Gen. xlii. 5-8).

8. This now is the first state and condition of the poor soul when

---

[1] Sinful affections.

it turneth to Christ, to fetch food from him. Then he looketh upon the soul in its will, totally in its essence, to see whether the free will had set itself towards him. And now if the soul be converted, then he knoweth it; but first he terrifieth the conscience, and setteth himself roughly, and seemeth strange towards the soul, as he did towards the Canaanitish woman (Matt. xv. 26), and hideth his grace from the soul, till it shed forth its repentance, and boweth its face in the presence of Christ, and acknowledge its transgressions, and totally bow down itself to the pit of judgment, and yield itself into God's anger and punishment, and to the dying of itself.

9. And then Christ looketh into it, and layeth fast hold upon it with the strict hand of God's anger; but his love and grace hideth itself therein, and that is it which stirreth up the sins of the poor soul, and disturbeth them, so that it is terrified and afraid in the presence of God. When the soul standeth and crieth to God, then saith Christ in the conscience, Who art thou? behold thyself now, whether thou art worthy of me: as Joseph did here, when he said, Who are ye? and set himself roughly and strangely towards them.

10. *And Joseph thought on the dreams which he had dreamed concerning them, and said to them, Ye are spies, and are come to see where the land is open* (Gen. xlii. 9). That is, Christ thinketh on his mercy, and on his bitter passion and death, and saith to the soul, Thou art a spy, and cometh to me only to see where the gate of my grace is open: but that shall not help thee, thou must do otherwise, thou must first enter into the gate of my suffering and death, or else thou art but a spy, and wilt see the gate of my grace stand open that thou mayest cover thyself with it as with a mantle; thou must be in earnest, or else thou wilt be but treacherous to me, and take my grace into thy mouth.

11. *And Joseph's brethren answered him and said, No, my lord, thy servants are come to buy food. We are all one man's sons; we are honest and true men, we thy servants were never spies* (Gen. xlii. 10-11). That is thus much in the figure: before the properties of the soul in their vanity rightly know themselves, when the anger of God is presented before their eyes, viz. passeth into their essence, then the soul thinketh it is wrong that is done to it; for it thinketh if it comfort itself with the merits of Jesus Christ, and believeth on Christ, that he is the son of God, and hath satisfied for the soul, then it ought not to be blamed for a divine spy and unrighteous hypocrite; it is righteous through the justification of Christ, seeing it believeth the same, that it is applied to it for its benefit.

12. But as Joseph said to his brethren, No, but ye are come to see where the land is open, thus also the spirit of Christ blameth the essences of the soul; for it proveth them that they are not yet broken, and have still self desires in them, and will instantly lay hold on grace, viz. the open gate, which availeth not the soul; it must first enter into Christ's suffering and death, and put them on first through earnest repentance and conversion of its will, and then it may enter through the open gate, through Christ's wounds and death, into his resurrection.

13. Further, Joseph's brethren say, *We thy servants are twelve brethren, sons of one man in the land of Canaan; and the youngest is still with our father, but one is not in being. Joseph said to them, That is it which I told you; ye are spies. In this will I prove you: By the life of Pharaoh ye shall not go from hence except your youngest brother come hither. Send one of you hence, that may fetch your brother, but ye shall be prisoners: so will I prove your saying, whether your ways be in truth or not; for if not then are ye spies, by the life of Pharaoh. And they put them together in ward for the space of three days* (Gen. xlii. 13-17).

The inward precious figure standeth thus:

14. When the soul doth thus draw near to Christ, and will instantly put on his resurrection, then saith the spirit of Christ in the soul's essence, This is that which I told thee, Thy essences are spies, by the life of God: in this will I prove them whether they come to me in a faithful and right path: whether they bring with them to me their youngest brother, viz. the true Joseph's brother; that is, the incorporated line of the Covenant of grace, in their (in Adam) faded heavenly substantiality, viz. the incorporated ground of grace which was effected in Paradise; so that the soul's essences, with their most inward ground, turn in to me and in me, else they come but as hypocrites and spies of the gate of grace.

15. This is rightly called fetching the youngest brother: for that same incorporated grace in the Promise, effected in Paradise, is the soul's youngest brother, which it hides and covereth with sin; and in the beginning of its repentance it leaves him at home by[1] the life of God.

16. Therefore saith the text of Moses very secretly: He will prove them by the Life of Pharaoh: which is as much as to say in the figure,

---

[1] Or, with.

by the life of God, with whom this youngest son stayed behind. Him must the repenting man bring along with him to the port of grace, or else he must lie three days shut up in prison, till he bring him, as Joseph's brethren did. That is, else must the three Principles in man lie so long in prison in the anger of God, and cannot buy divine food unless they have this their youngest brother with them; that is, the gate, wherein Christ in man, in that same image of the heavenly world's substance which faded in Adam, ariseth from death, wherein he may have his dwelling place.

17. Thus a man is proved by the life of God when he turneth to God, to try whether he turn wholly and altogether to him, and bring this incorporated ground of grace with him, wherein Christ will and shall manifest himself. If not, then saith Joseph, that is, Christ, to the soul's essences, Ye are but spies to the life of God, and search only for the justification of man from the sufferings and merits of Christ. That is, ye learn only the history, and take the precious Covenant of God in your mouths, and flatter yourselves with Christ's satisfaction, and remain still only as spies of grace. But that shall nothing avail you or help you. Though likely you may spy out the kingdom of Christ, my anger and righteousness in my zeal and jealousy shall yet hold you in prison with all the three Principles, as long as you bring not the most inward ground of your substance along with you (this is called, setting all the twelve sons of Jacob before Joseph, that is, before Jesus), and fall at his feet with body and soul, inwardly and outwardly, with all your faculties and powers, and yield them up into his grace.

18. For it is not said that they can *take* the grace, but that they should *sink down into* grace, that Grace may *give itself* to them; for man's ability to take it is lost: self-will is rent off from God, it must wholly sink down into God, and *leave off willing*, that God may receive it again into his grace.

19. O Babel! how [home] doth this hit thee? Thou art by or before the life of God, with thy hypocrisy, but a spy of the grace of God: thou dost but seek for the gate of grace, and how thou mightest with thy own will, without thy inward Benjamin, enter into the kingdom of Christ. Yes, thou wilt be outwardly an adopted child of Grace, whose sins are forgiven through the merits of Christ, and yet continuest to be Babel and a fable, and wilt not be a Christian in Christ. Thou wilt needs pass into heaven, but that will not avail thee: Joseph, that is, Christ, holdeth thee imprisoned in the anger of God, both in body and soul, unless thou givest him Benjamin, viz. the inward

MYSTERIUM MAGNUM

ground. And then heaven goeth into thee, and Christ standeth up in thee, out of the grave, so that thyself art risen from death: and then thy spying and prying hath an end.

20. O ye high schools [and universities], and all ye that will be accounted the ministers of God, and to teach the way of God, and contend and dispute about it; what are ye? Look upon yourselves in this figure: you appear to be no other than spies, you always search, and yet you lie still in prison. God will have it so no more; for he himself trieth the thoughts of man, and is himself present in all things; his is the understanding, his is the knowledge of the kingdom of God, without him ye know nothing.

21. Your spying and knowing helps you not into the kingdom of God: you cannot enter therein, except that go forth in your life, that is, except it be manifested in your life, that ye are God's children in Christ, in his sufferings, death and resurrection, in himself; not through an acquired historical seeming faith, but essentially, as a branch on the vine. Ye must be a twig on the tree; you must have Christ's life, flesh and blood operatively and substantially in the inward ground in you; and you must become Christ; else ye are all, one and other, but spies, searchers, and historical Christians, and no better than Jews, Turks and heathen.

22. O ye simple men, let it be made known to you: Go but forth from the tower of the confounded languages, then may you soon come to the right. Seek Christ at the right hand of God within you: he sitteth there. Unlock your wills: that is, give them up to him, and he will unlock them well enough. Your repentance must be earnest: or else you are all, one and other, but spies (Matt. xxvi. 64; Acts vii. 55, 56; Col. iii. 1).

23. Gaze about no more, it is high time. The time is truly born [or at hand] (Rev. i. 3; xxii. 10), your redemption draweth near (Luke xxi. 28). The Bridegroom calleth his Bride (Rev. xxi. 2): you must indeed into the prison of Joseph in his famine: if you will not [bring your inward ground of your hearts into repentance with you], Amen [so be it].

24. And Moses saith further, *But on the third day he said to them, If you will live, then do thus, for I fear God: If you be honest and true men, let one of your brethren lie captive in your prison. But as for you, go your ways, and carry home what ye have bought for your hunger; and bring your youngest brother to me, and so I shall believe your words, that you may not die. And they did so* (Gen. xlii. 18–20).

HOW THIS FAMINE WENT THROUGH ALL LANDS

The figure standeth thus:

25. When the soul draweth near to God, and will work repentance, and that its inward ground is yet wholly shut up in vanity, so that the mind is still hanging to self, yet if it will not give over repentance, and for all that cannot be free from the earthly desires, but continueth in prayer, then indeed God the Father letteth the soul's essences out of the prison of his anger, that the mind is well eased again, like one that is released out of prison. Then saith the mind thus: I am very well eased in my prayer in this repentance.

26. For God's anger hath released nature out of its prison, that it should with greater labour and industry press into God; for in its prison it cannot do so, for it is in anguish, and beholdeth only its committed sins which continually drive it back, that it is afraid, ashamed[1] and daunted in the presence of God. But when the anger lets it loose, then it gets power and virtue of prayer, and the work of repentance.

27. But the anger of God holdeth it continually with one band: as Joseph held one brother in prison, till they brought the last brother also. And thus must the poor soul remain tied with one band of the prison of death, till it shed forth the last brother, viz. the inward ground, and come before God, and say: Lord, I will forsake all for Christ's and my salvation's sake, and give up my will wholly to thee; cast me into death or into life, into derision or scorn, into poverty or misery, as thou wilt; I will cleave to thee, I will not play the hypocrite before thee, and give thee but half my will any more, as I have done.

28. And then if the earnestness proceed to practice, that God perceiveth that it is in earnest, then will also the last brother be let loose; that is, then will also the last band of the anger of God be loosed: but in the meantime, ere it thus come to pass, the soul must lie captive in one band.

29. But nevertheless God saith to the other released forms[2] of life: Now go your way with that which you have at present in this repentance bought or gotten of me; and carry it home, that is, defile it not again, live of it, and partake of this present grace bestowed, and carry it in, to the honour of God, that it may come before God with the operation of it.

30. Moses saith further, *But they said one among another, We trespassed against our brother, that we saw the anguish of his soul, when he wept to us, and we would not hear him; therefore now this trouble cometh upon us. Reuben*

---

[1] Abashed.   [2] Or, faculties.

answered them, and said, Did I not tell you as much, when I said, Sin not against the lad; and ye would not hear? and now is his blood required. But they knew not that Joseph understood it; for he spake to them by an interpreter. And he turned himself from them, and wept; and when he turned himself to them again, and spake with them, he took Simeon from among them, and bound him before their eyes (Gen. xlii. 21-24).

31. This figure now is the earnestness of repentance, when man in his repentance standeth before God, when he seeketh to God [and weepeth to him], when his conscience and sins awake: as here the brethren of Joseph did. Then he saith in himself, This have I merited and deserved by my sins, that I have helped to deride, scorn and crucify Christ within me, and without me in my fellow-members, and have not regarded the entreaties and beseechings in my fellow-Christians, but have scorned, derided, and judged them to damnation. At present it toucheth me home, when I will turn to God by repentance, now his sobs and tears withhold me, in that I have driven him away for my voluptuousness, jesting, sport and wantonness, now I stand here, and the heaven in me in my conscience is become as iron.

32. Then saith God in the conscience, hast thou not known well enough; moreover, have I not caused my word to be told unto thee; thou knewest well that thou diddest wrong, but thy evil stubborn self-will must reign; and now thou wouldst have grace. And the devil saith, It is to no purpose, grace is gone, heaven is shut up, hell is open, leave off, thou wilt not attain it.

33. But the great mercifulness in the grace of Christ in the inward ground presseth in with his pity and great compassion; although at present he still hideth his countenance of love from it, that the soul doth not know it, and maketh the troubled soul full of misery, that in self it beseecheth and weepeth before God, and accounteth itself guilty of all evil and wickedness; and beginneth in such kindled lamentation bitterly to complain of its sins, and to be sorry, and is also so full of shame in the presence of Christ that it hideth its countenance before God, and knoweth not what to do for lamentation. For it seeth in itself with its own eyes that the severe righteousness of God holdeth and bindeth it in its life: as the brethren of Joseph must see that their brother was bound for their sins before their eyes.

34. For though Christ be stirring in the soul's essence in the inward ground of the incorporated grace, and shattereth it, that it seeth and bewaileth its sins, yet he setteth himself very strangely against the soul, and will not touch it with any beam of love: as Joseph set himself

strangely, as if he understood not their speech, and spake to them by an interpreter.

35. This same interpreter is even that which bringeth the soul into such repentance, which otherwise could not be; for it hath nothing more in its own power but this: that it may turn its abyssal unfathomable supernatural will towards God, viz. that out of which it is proceeded, and there stand still, which yet is very hard for it, and yet possible.[1] Unless its will have quite broken off itself from the incorporated gate of grace, and given itself up to the poison and infection of the devil, so that the will of the abyss of the soul is entered into a figure[2] of a false or wicked thistle, and be wholly poisonous. Then it is hard, for then it asketh not after repentance at all, but is careless and negligent, and obdurate, and desireth at no time to convert, neither is it sorry for any evil or wickedness, but taketh delight therein and rejoiceth at it, so long as it carrieth the body about it; and then it is quite lost: but where there is yet a little spark of divine desire left, there is remedy.

36 And Moses saith further, *And Joseph commanded to fill their sacks with corn, and to put everyone's money into his sack again, also provision for their journey: and they did so to them. And they laded their burdens upon their asses, and went their way. But when one of them opened his sack to give his ass provender in the inn, he perceived his money that lay uppermost in the sack, and said to his brethren, My money is restored to me, see, it is in my sack: then their hearts failed them, and they were afraid, one with another, and said, Wherefore hath God done this unto us?* (Gen. xlii. 25-28).

37. This now is the most lovely rich figure, shewing how God taketh nothing away from the repentant sinner, when he in his will giveth up all, and resolveth to cleave steadfastly to God, he taketh no reward or bounty from him, or anything else; neither doth he take away his temporal good things, when he doth yield up all to God, and forsaketh selfishness. And then God filleth his sack and restoreth him all that money, which he giveth to the poor and miserable, in his blessing again, and layeth it aloft in his provision, that the man seeth that God hath afforded it to him again in his wonderful blessing.

38. At which a man often wondereth how it cometh to pass that temporal maintenance befalleth him in such a wonderful manner, when he hath not sought it or known anything of it, and likely stands amazed at it, questioning whether he should receive it or no, and

---

[1] Note the ability of the soul to attain grace.
[2] The condition, posture, and quality.

thinketh verily it is done for a temptation to him: as here Joseph's brethren thought that Joseph tempted them thus, that he might have an occasion against them.

39. And this signifieth the inward bounty of Christ, that when the poor sinner poureth forth his heart before God, for payment to the grace, and returneth what he hath to God, then God filleth the sack of his heart full with the grace of Christ, and giveth him still good provision, viz. understanding and wisdom, in the way of his pilgrimage, wherein he is to journey through this valley of misery, home again into his Father's country.

40. But by this journey and pilgrimage, wherein the Adamical man's sack is filled with heavenly good things, the kingdom of God's anger, as also the earthliness, is robbed of that which they have in man: as is to be seen in this figure.

41. For *when Jacob's sons came home to their father, and told him how it happened to them, and poured out their sacks and found the money again, and would have Benjamin also into Egypt. Then said Jacob, Ye have robbed me of my children: Joseph is no more in being, and Simeon is not, and you would take away Benjamin: all this goeth against me* (Gen. xlii. 35, 36).

42. Here Jacob their father standeth in the figure of the outward nature's self, shewing how nature complaineth, when it is bereaved and robbed of its right, and of that which it hath begotten and brought to light; and standeth very excellently in the figure; for the outward nature saith, when it seeth the divine gifts in itself, whereby it looseth the right of its selfhood, I am bereaved of my might and strength; Joseph, viz. the inward ground of the kingdom of heaven, which I had in Paradise, that is no more; and so will also these gifts of my power and authority, viz. my children, that is, the properties of my nature, be taken away: it all goeth against me: I must suffer myself to be bereaved.

43. But *Reuben said to his father, If I bring not Benjamin to thee again, then slay my two sons: give him into my hand, I will bring him to thee again* (Gen. xlii. 37). That is, God comforteth nature, and saith, Give me thy forms, quality and condition, viz. thy children, into my hand, I will but bring them into Egypt to Joseph, that is, to Jesus, and will give them to thee again, thou shalt lose nothing: if I do not, then slay my two sons with thee, that is, slay the first and second Principle:

44. Which is even done, if nature be bereaved of its forms and condition. Then must cease in the nature of man the kingdom of God in love, and also the kingdom of God in the might of the fire. So very

secretly doth the spirit of God delight to play in the figure of regeneration; which exposition will seem strange to reason: but we know what we write here, which is understood by those of our society.

45. *And Jacob said, My son Benjamin shall not go down with you; for his brother is dead, and he is left alone: if any mishap befall him in the way that you travel, ye will bring my grey hairs with sorrow of heart into the grave* (Gen. xlii. 38). That is, nature is faint, when it must enter into the death of Christ, and is afraid of dying, and will by no means come to it; it excuseth itself concerning its heavenly Joseph which it had, viz. the heavenly image, which while it cannot comprehend it, it saith, It is dead; now when these my forms and qualities of life in this way shall get mishap again, then must I perish with sorrow of heart, and my life hath an end.

The Seventieth Chapter

How *Jacob's* sons went into *Egypt* again because of the Famine, to *Joseph* to buy Corn, and take *Benjamin* with them. How *Joseph* caused them to be brought into his House, and to Eat at his Table. What is thereby to be understood[1]

1. Now this whole chapter prefigureth to us the most excellent image, representing how first the outward nature, in this process, when it shall give up its will thereinto, that its life's essences shall go into Egypt, that is, into the death of Christ, is very fearful, timorous, abashed and daunted, and yet in the end is willing and ready that all its forms and conditions of life might enter into the dying of self, viz. into the true Egypt, upon divine confidence, that it bringeth the will of God with it thereinto.

2. And then [secondly], how the forms and conditions[2] of life are afraid before Joseph, that is, before the face of God, seeing they feel in them an evil conscience: as Jacob's sons were afraid before Joseph, for they thought continually God would punish them for Joseph's sake, at which they trembled.

3. And thirdly, how God, with the forms of the soulish nature, carrieth himself first so friendly, and first giveth them heavenly bread of his own substance, and yet but in a strange form: as Joseph invited his brethren for guests, and fed them at his table, that they ate and drank plentifully, and were merry; and afterwards let them go in peace. But presently after came with a terrible trial, in that he caused his cup to be laid into Benjamin's sack, and pursued after them and fetched them back again. All which standeth powerfully in the figure of a repenting sinner, shewing how it goeth with him, till God in his love giveth him to know him.

4. Moses' words follow thus: *This famine was sore in the land. And when the corn was spent which they had brought out of Egypt, their father said to them, Go again, and buy us a little food. Then Judah answered and said, The*

---

[1] Gen. xliii.   [2] Powers or faculties.

HOW JACOB'S SONS WENT INTO EGYPT

man obliged and charged us strictly, and said, Ye shall not see my face, except your brother be with you. Now if thou wilt send our brother with us, then we will go down and buy for thee to eat: but if thou sendest him not, we will not go down: for the man hath said to us, Ye shall not see my face, unless your brother be with you (Gen. xliii. 1–5).

This figure standeth thus:

5. The soul of man standeth in three Principles, viz. in the eternal fire's nature, and in the eternal light's nature, viz. in the love-fire, which extinguished in Adam, for which cause at present the strife is. And thirdly it standeth in *spiritu mundi* [in the spirit of the world], in the kingdom of this world, viz. in mortality and restoration.

6. Therefore now understand us aright, thus: When the inward soulish ground, viz. the eternal soul from the Father's property of the Word of God, turneth back again, and looks about after its little pearl, viz. after the second Principle of the angelical world's property, then it will perceive that it was lost in Adam; *from whence ariseth its misery, and* [also its] *return again*. And as soon as it returneth again, God giveth his grace into it again, but unknown and not understood by it. And he[1] desireth that the inward fire-soul, viz. the centre of the eternal nature, should, with the voice of grace inspoken or inspired in Paradise (which was wholly incorporated), turn to God again.

7. In which divine desire this great unquietness ariseth in the soul, that it thus goeth into repentance. When it seeth that it hath lost its ability, neither may nor shall nor can it, in any other way, again attain its first pearl which it had, and come to divine salvation, unless it turn with its fire's might wholly again into the ground of the incorporated grace, and give itself up thereto.

8. And now when the outward mortal soul (viz. the nature of the third Principle) of the kingdom of this world seeth this, then it is afraid, as Jacob was of his children; and always thinketh they will lose body and life, goods and honour, and their forms or faculties of life will be bereaved of their outward might and authority, which they have in this world.

9. And then also the inward fiery soul cannot stir up its inward ground, viz. the true Benjamin, and bring it along with it into Egypt, into the presence of Joseph, into earnest repentance, into the presence of Jesus: unless the outward soul, from the spirit of the world, be

---
[1] God.

brought down and quite tamed and overwhelmed, that it also may in the end willingly submit to it, that the fiery inward great soul might thus move itself in all the three Principles, and stir up the most inward ground, viz. Joseph's brother, viz. the incorporated gate of grace, together with all outward essences or faculties of the outward soul, and bring them along into the work of repentance, into the presence of the right Joseph or Jesus.

10. For the fiery soul is threatened by Joseph, that is, by Jesus, that if, in its drawing near, it bring not along with it the most inward ground, viz. the brother of Joseph, or Christ, which in its manifestation becometh the temple of Christ, then shall its band of God's anger not be loosed: its brother Simeon shall remain in prison, till it also stir up and bring with it Joseph's brother, viz. the most inward ground.

11. Neither shall its sack be filled with heavenly manna for its food (Rev. ii. 17), that is, its faith's desire shall remain hungry and empty, and not be filled with divine power and virtue, unless it bring the temple of Christ, viz. the right sack, with it, whereinto the heavenly Joseph filleth his food.

12. This now in the text stands in a figure: shewing how the old Adamical man, viz. the old Jacob, thinketh it to be very hard that he should let all the powers of his life be carried along into Egypt, that is, into repentance, into the presence of Joseph, or Jesus; especially when he seeth that he must break his will, and part with all temporal things for it: as old Jacob must part with all his children for this food.

13. It went hard with him; and yet the famine and hunger did so press upon him that in the end he must yield and be willing that all his sons should go into Egypt; and his youngest son went along, and he was alone as one who had no children: So wholly must the outward nature leave whatsoever it hath or is in itself; as having no more power and ability as to earthly things, and give up the selfhood of its inward soul, which standeth in the drawing of God, that the inward soul may take the outward soul's will along with it into conversion. And then the old Jacob, that is, the old earthly Adamical body, remaineth alone in its house of sorrow, and knoweth not now what will become of it, when its spirit must go along into conversion. Then thinketh the earthly Lucifer in it, viz. the fleshly desire, Hereby thou wilt lose temporal honour and good things, and be the fool of the world; this will not serve thy turn and lust.

14. But the great famine, viz. sin, presseth the poor life in all the three Principles, that it must make ready and go into Egypt, that is,

HOW JACOB'S SONS WENT INTO EGYPT

into repentance, and seek divine food, and pray for it, and desire it, from the true householder Joseph, or Jesus, and in such prayer and desire fall on his face of great humility before Joseph, or Jesus, and desire food of him.

15. But that Jacob's sons must go twice into Egypt for corn, and at the first time receive corn enough, and yet they came into danger thereby, and were kept as a pledge,[1] hath inwardly this figure: when man at first turneth into repentance, then first the terrible figure or aspect of his sins standeth before him, for they rouse him up, and the conscience standeth in the anger of God.

16. As the brethren of Joseph stood the first time before Joseph, when he held them for spies, so also man standeth before God as a spy of divine grace; for he thinketh he will this once enter into repentance, that his old sins may be forgiven him; but he hath not yet so strongly tamed his will, that the will should think all days of its life while the body lasteth to remain in such begun repentance, but it thinketh only for once thus to destroy sin in the conscience, and to drown the old sins in repentance and sorrow.

17. And it cometh also to that pass, that his conscience, though perhaps at first it be terrified, is in the end appeased, and divine food is given to him from the heavenly Joseph, into the sack of his desire, so that the anger of God letteth him go. But the anger of God in his righteousness taketh a pledge[2] from the conscience, and keepeth it, to see whether man would continue to rest satisfied with this burden of food; if not, then the anger of God hath [in the pledge] its first right in soul and body.

18. As it happeneth to us poor men, that we very slightly and lavishly spend the first food which the heavenly Joseph giveth us in repentance, and come again with great hunger, want and misery of conscience, and must come to be poor again; and even therefore, because we did not the first time bring along with us our Benjamin, viz. the most inward ground, in that our will was not quite broken, and that we suppose we shall continue till our end in repentance and divine resignation. But if it were done in the first repentance, then could not God's righteousness in the anger take any pledge, but must leave us quite free.

19. This figure now, that Jacob's children must go down into Egypt for food twice, and at the second time Joseph was first manifested unto them, and the third time they took along with them their

---

[1] Were kept in pawn, or custody.   [2] Or, pawn.

wives and children, and all that they had, together with their father, prefigureth that when man through sin hath spent and consumed the first divine food, that he must hunger again and be in want in his conscience, so that his conscience presseth him and complaineth (as a hungry belly complaineth for food), then he thinketh on the first repentance again, how grace happened to him before.

20. But his most inward ground, viz. the band of God's anger, complaineth against him and condemneth him, that he did not preserve grace. It blameth him for an unfaithful perjured man, who hath tasted God's grace, and how it was bestowed on him of mere mercy, and that he hath for the lust's sake of the flesh spoiled and lost all again. And then he standeth as one that is not worthy of anything, so much as to look up to heaven, or that the earth should bear him, that he hath for such base lust's sake of the flesh squandered so precious a thing again, and thinketh yet with the poor publican and sinner, and with the lost son, the keeper of swine, He will turn again, and come to the salvation of God. And then first it is in right true earnest, and then goeth Jacob's sons all one and other the second time into Egypt into repentance, to buy heavenly corn, and then must the old Adamical Jacob, viz. the body, stay at home in calamity.

21. In this earnest it is that Benjamin, viz. the inward ground, is first taken along. And now the first will is broken, and goeth no more in and with such a purpose as at the first time. And they come now no more as spies before Joseph, but as earnest hungry men, viz. with an earnest hungry life, which from all its powers and virtues hungereth after God's mercy, after the food of Jesus Christ.

22. Here now beginneth the earnestness, in fear and trembling. And this is the true going forth after heavenly food, wherein the conscience stands in anxiety, and reason despairs of its own ability, and thinketh, Alas, God is angry with me: where shall I seek for grace? I am not worthy of it; I have trampled it underfoot, I must stand ashamed before God. Into what deep shall I go, where I may dare to lift up my face to God, and bewail my wants to him?

23. Then comes the poor conscience, in need, and with trembling, before God, and hath not many confessions or words, for it accounteth itself too unworthy to speak one word before God, but setteth itself before his face, and boweth down to the ground; and thus in itself *demerseth* itself into the most mere and deepest mercy of God, into Christ's wounds, suffering, and death, and beginneth from its most inward ground to sigh, and to fly into grace, and wholly give up itself

HOW JACOB'S SONS WENT INTO EGYPT

thereto: as Joseph's brethren came thus the second time before Joseph, and fell down before him.

24. And when Joseph saw them thus, that they were all there and stood so humbly before him, he had so great compassion upon them that he could not speak a word either: but turned him and wept. And this is the state and condition wherein the inward ground of the heavenly world's substance which faded in Adam (into which God again inspoke or inspired his Word of grace in Paradise, for an ensign, banner, mark and limit), became living again in this compassion, wherein Christ is assuredly born in man in this ground, and now instantly ariseth, through his sufferings, from death in man, and there sitteth at the right hand of his Father; which right hand is the fiery soul from the Father's property in the Word of the eternal nature, and presenteth the soul in this ground before the anger of God, and satisfieth and filleth it with love.

25. And here a Christian beginneth to be a Christian, for he is one, in Christ, and is no more a spy and verbal or mouth-Christian: but that is in the most inward ground. And here Simeon is loosed, and *there is no more condemnation to those that are* thus *in Christ Jesus* (Rom. viii. 1). Although perhaps the outward body is in this world, and subjected to vanity, yet it hurteth it now no more: but every failing which it now committeth in the flesh must turn to serve for the best to it. For now it beginneth to kill the works and contrivance of the flesh, and continually to crucify the old Adam; for its whole life is now a mere repentance, and Christ in it doth help it to work repentance, and bringeth it now to his glorious feast or banquet: as Joseph did his brethren when they came again to him, when he commanded to make ready and gave them of his table.

26. Thus now Christ feedeth the converted soul with his flesh and blood, and in this feast or banquet is the true *Wedding of the Lamb* (Rev. xix. 7, 9). Whosoever hath been a guest here, he understandeth our sense and mind. And no other doth, they are all of them but spies; though perhaps they suppose they understand it, yet there is no right understanding of this feast or banquet in any man, unless he hath been at it and tasted of it himself; for it is a very impossible thing for reason to apprehend it without Christ's spirit in himself, who is himself the food at this feast or banquet of Joseph.

27. And it is told thee, Babel, in thy spying by Joseph's feast or banquet, that thou deludest Christendom: in that by this feast thou pointest them to the resurrection of the dead thou errest. A Christian

must here *eat the flesh of the Son of man,* or *he hath no life in him* (John vi. 53): *In the resurrection God will be All in All* (1 Cor. xv. 28). Here *Christ sitteth at the right hand of God* (Col. iii. 1) in man, and presenteth him with his body, and with his innocent blood that was shed; and that, he covereth the soul withal, and floweth into it with the same, when God's anger will stir, being instigated by the desire of the flesh.

28. O thou poor old Jacob of spying[1] Christendom! let thy hungry sons, who are very lean for great hunger in the conscience, go to Joseph: keep them no longer back in thy fear. What, I pray thee, is thy fear? Thou supposest, that if this ground should come to light in the world, thou wouldst lose thy sons whom thou lovest. But who are thy sons? There is thy own honour, in that thou thinkest to sit in the stead of Christ upon earth. Also there is thy Lucifer of fleshly honour, which thou takest care for, and thy countenance is dejected about it, if a man should require an Apostolic life from thee, and seek thee in the process and imitation of Christ. It pleaseth thee better that thou livest in honour and voluptuousness of flesh, in spying, and honourest thy belly, and so bringest thy poor Christianity under a veil.

29. O thou poor old Jacob! trouble not thyself so about temporal momentary things. See how it went with old Jacob, when he let all his sons go from him to Joseph, how Joseph caused him to be fetched to him, and did so much good to him and his children, and nourished them in the famine, and placed them in a better land. And so it will go also with thee, if thou wilt let thy sons go to Joseph; but if thou wilt henceforth keep them back longer, then thou must starve, thou and thy children, and be famished in misery: saith the Spirit of wonders, by Joseph's feast or banquet.

30. O Israel, mark this text very well, it concerneth thee, and hath clearly concerned thee, but that thou art yet blind in thy hungry misery, and waitest for the sword of the turba: that shall awaken thee, since thou wilt needs have it.

31. Every one thinketh, If three parts of men were destroyed then I should have good days with those that remain, and then we would be honest and virtuous, and lead an upright honest life. Also men gaze about to see whence that salvation will come, which is so much written of; and say and think, salvation will enter into the lust of the flesh from without: men always gape for an earthly kingdom of Christ.

32. O Israel, if thou knewest these present times wherein thou

---

[1] Or, inspecting.

HOW JACOB'S SONS WENT INTO EGYPT

livest in blindness, thou wouldest repent in sackcloth and ashes. Thou lookest for the signal-star,[1] and it hath appeared: it shineth, whosoever hath eyes may see it; it is indeed as big as the world is, and yet men will be blind. Enough, to those that are ours.

33. And as Jacob's children spake much with their father concerning Benjamin, and promised to bring him again, he said at last: *If it must be so, let it be so; and take of the best fruit of the country in your sacks, and carry down a present to the man, a little balsam and honey, and spices and myrrh, dates, and almonds. Take also other money with you; and the money that was put above in your sacks again carry with you: it may be it was done by mistake: Moreover, take your brother, arise, go again to the man. And the Almighty God give you mercy before the man, that he may let your other brother and Benjamin go. But I must be as one quite bereft of his children* (Gen. xliii. 11–14).

34. This now is the figure that is above explained. And we see a very excellent clear type and image therein, shewing that Jacob commanded his sons to take with them of the most precious rich and costly fruit of the land, and carry it with them to Joseph. In which the spirit portrayeth in the figure how the Christian Church, when it seeth itself in such trouble and spiritual famine, hunger and want, and now is on the way of repentance, should carry these good fruits with it before God, viz. hope, faith, and divine affiance, and not wild fruit, as covetousness, self-willed lust, and hypocrisy, but a purpose and resolution towards truth, righteousness, chastity, love and meekness.

35. Thus must the old man take a resolution, to go in such a purpose to Joseph, that is, to Christ; and then he yieldeth up all his sons for the journey of this pilgrimage, and saith, Now I am bereaved of all my sons, I have nothing more in the desire of fleshly voluptuousness, I have yielded them altogether into the will of God.

36. Also, we see in this figure how Jacob commanded them to take with them again the unrighteous money that they had brought back in their sacks, and restore it again: thus also must a man who will be or is a Christian put away from him all unrighteous things; all that he hath gotten to himself by subtlety, craft, and wrong, that, he should repay again, or else indeed give it to the poor.

37. For that which he giveth to the needy and miserable that suffer want, he giveth to the hungry brethren of Joseph, and the heavenly Joseph receiveth it in his hungry brethren and fellow members, and returneth it to him again manifold: as Joseph's steward gave

---

[1] Such a star as leads the wise men to Christ.

them again the money, which they carried home in their sacks the first time and brought it again, and said, Peace be to you, your father's God hath bestowed treasure on you.

38. A man must put away all unrighteousness from him, if he will enter into the wedding of Jesus Christ. Hypocrisy and flattery in comforting oneself availeth nothing; it must be earnestness: and this is that which keepeth men back from the ways of God, even their walking upon the ways of hypocrisy, and flattering themselves. Whereas they should leave off and forsake unrighteousness and extortion, and restore that which is gotten by falsehood. Thus they have cast the purple mantle of Christ over the crafty wretch, and covered him with the satisfaction and merits, only that the thief may live under that cloak.

39. O thou poor Christendom, how hath Antichrist deluded thee with this cloak and covering! O flee away from him, it is time! The covering will not avail any wicked and unrighteous person: so long as any is such a one he is the devil's servant.

40. A Christian is a new creature in the ground of his heart, his mind is bent only to well-doing: not to steal, else were Christ, [by consequence, accounted] a thief in man. Let but the mantle of Christ fall off, and restore what thou hast stolen, and gained and extorted with unrighteousness and injury; and cast away the old quarrels, strivings and litigations[1] from thy soul, and go naked and empty under the cross to which Christ hangeth, and look upon his fresh bleeding wounds, and take his blood into thy hungry soul; and then thou wilt be healed, and redeemed and released from all want: else no comfort of satisfaction and merit will help thee. All true comfort is but this, That a Christian comforteth himself that he shall in this repentance in Christ Jesus obtain a gracious God: and that shall even be his comfort, that he may not despair.

41. The satisfaction wherewith the unrighteous comforteth himself, and saith, My works avail nothing, Christ hath done all, I can do nothing; and continueth under such comfort in sins, that is the devil's fishhook, whereby he catcheth his fish with Christ's mantle.

42. Christ had his purple mantle on him when he was in his suffering; but when he hung on the cross he had it no more, much less in his resurrection: So also should a man take this mantle about him only when he goeth into Christ's suffering and death in repentance. In repentance it is alone available, and no way else, that a soul should

---

[1] Lawsuits.

HOW JACOB'S SONS WENT INTO EGYPT

wrap itself up in it, when it is ashamed in its sins, before the face of God.

43. All that is taught and believed otherwise is deceit, a fable, and Babel. All teachers that teach otherwise are but servants and slaves of the belly, the devil's fishermen, and a deceit of the world: of these let men beware. For he that will be a teacher must also be a true Christian, that so he may also thus live in Christ: else *he is a thief and a murderer, that climbeth up some other way into the sheepfold* (John x. 1), of whom Christ speaketh.

44. And Moses saith further, *Then they took their present, and the double money with them, and Benjamin; and arose and went into Egypt, and presented themselves before Joseph. And when Joseph saw them with Benjamin, he said to his steward, Bring these men to my house, and slay and make ready; for they shall eat with me at noon. And the man did as Joseph said unto him; and brought the men into Joseph's house* (Gen. xliii. 15-17).

45. This now signifieth thus: That he that hides himself under the mantle must come forth, and bring his unrighteous wrong gotten goods again, and come before the face of the heavenly Joseph, and come naked and empty of his I-hood or own ability, and bring the right Benjamin that is in him along with him. Then Joseph draweth near him, and seeth him, and commandeth his steward, viz. the spirit of power, to bring these men into his house, viz. into his humanity. And then the Lamb of God shall be made ready, and these men, or the life's essences of the right soul, shall eat at Joseph's table with him at noon (then it is noon when the high light of grace shineth as at noon or midday in the soul); and here Joseph's brethren are reconciled, when they eat with Joseph, that is, with Christ, of his food.

46. This now is the supper (Apocalypse iii. 20). Here a man casts away the mantle, and becometh a brother of Joseph, and needs no more flattery or comforting of himself, but becometh a Christian in Christ, who is dead with Christ to his sins, and is become living in him, and is risen again in him, and liveth with him, eateth with him at his table, and is no more a servant of sin, who must fear again, but who is *a son in the house to whom the inheritance belongeth* (Gal. iv. 7), according to the Scriptures.

47. *And when Joseph's steward had brought them into Joseph's house, they were still afraid, and spake to him before the door concerning the money which they had found in their sacks. But he comforted them, and said, I found your money, and have had it: your God hath bestowed treasure in your sacks. And*

he brought Simeon out to them; and brought them into Joseph's house, and gave them water to wash their feet, and gave their asses provender. But they prepared their present against Joseph should come at noon; for they had heard that they should eat bread there (Gen. xliii. 17-25).

48. This now is the figure, and representation of a troubled man, who now entereth into Joseph's house, and giveth again the unrighteous thing; for he had done much unrighteousness and wrong, because he had nothing to give. He giveth it again with his heart before the house of Joseph in true confession and acknowledgement, and would fain give it back again with his hand, if he were but able to do it. To such a one saith Joseph's steward, Fear no more, I have clearly received it in your repentance, Christ hath paid and restored it for you in his blood, so that all is done away, and nothing remaining; and you are in poverty and misery, therefore keep that little which you have, to cherish your life, though indeed you have it of wrong, and should have nothing in this world for your own; yet God hath given you treasure. Take water, and wash your feet; that is, cleanse the conversation of your hands and feet, and do evil no more; keep not that which is unrighteous, but only that little which you have of right, wherewith you cannot repay the wrong.

49. Not so to understand it that he should not restore again that which is of wrong, of his own which he hath rightly gotten besides extortion, if he be able. We speak of the poor, which hath nothing but a piece of bread left to sustain life: no excuse availeth before God, the conscience must become pure, or else thou art a thief. For the figure here addeth that the steward gave their asses provender, which signifieth the earthly body, that Christ will by his steward cause provender and food to be given to it.

50. These stewards here are honest and virtuous people in the world, which shall help to take care of it, that it may live; even though he was formerly a wicked man, if he were now honest from his heart.

51. Not as the false wicked world judgeth, who know a fault in a converted man, which he hath had, and still always upbraid him and condemn him for an unrighteous man, which devilishness the world is full of, that if they see a man who is converted, they cast all failings and infirmities which every one hath in flesh and blood upon him, and judge him for it, and look upon what he hath been, and not upon what he now is. Here saith Christ, *Judge not, and then you shall not be judged* (Matt. vii. 1).

52. *Now when Joseph entered into the house, they brought him the present*

HOW JACOB'S SONS WENT INTO EGYPT

in their hands, and fell down before him to the earth. But he saluted them friendly, and said, Is it well with your father, the old man whom ye told me of? Doth he yet live? And they answered, It is well with thy servant our father, and he yet liveth. And so they bowed and fell down before him (Gen. xliii. 26-28).

53. This now is the state and condition of the soul when it cometh plainly before the eyes of God, and hath wrapt its present up in the sufferings and death of Christ, and beareth it in its hands with the figure of the nail prints of Christ, in the presence of God. That is to say, the will to righteousness, truth, chastity, love, patience, hope, faith, meekness; these are now in the will of the soul, and these the soul giveth to the heavenly Joseph, and falleth down before him in humility.

54. But this Joseph saluteth the soul, that is, he speaketh or inspireth his word of grace into it, and parleyeth friendly in the conscience with it concerning the old Adamical Jacob of its life, and saith, Doth he yet live; that is, if he be still living and not quite dead there shall well be a remedy for him. At which the soul rejoiceth, and saith, It is well with thy servant my father, and he yet liveth.

55. *And Joseph lifted up his eyes, and saw his brother Benjamin, his mother's son, and said, Is that your youngest brother that you have told me of. And said further, God be gracious to thee, my son. And Joseph made haste away; for his heart burnt within him towards his brother: and sought where to weep; so he went into his chamber, and wept there. And when he had washed his face, he went forth, and carried himself boldly, and said, Set bread on the table* (Gen. xliii. 29-31).

56. This now is that excellent type or image, as is above mentioned; when Benjamin, that is the most inward ground, wherein lie the grace-gates of Paradise, is manifested before the eyes of Christ, in whom the great compassion kindleth itself; then God in Christ speaketh in or inspireth the living compassion: as here Joseph into Benjamin, when he said, *God be gracious to thee, my son.* This weeping of the heavenly Joseph kindleth this faded Paradisical image again with this weeping humility of Christ, so that from Christ's weeping into this image the eternal joy riseth up: and then Christ setteth bread upon the table, that this image may eat with him.

57. And Moses saith further, *And they served Joseph apart, and them apart; and the Egyptians that did eat with him, apart also: for the Egyptians dare not eat bread with the Hebrews; for it is an abomination to them. And they placed them before him, the first according to his priority of birth, and the*

youngest according to his youth: and they marvelled amongst themselves. And they carried them food[1] *from his table: but Benjamin's was five times as much as the other. And they drank, and were merry in drinking plentifully with him* (Gen. xliii. 32-34).

58. This figure is now the most secret ground and highest mystery of all between God and man: although it appears outwardly as if Joseph would thus hide himself before his brethren, as if he were not a Hebrew of their progeny, yet the spirit hath here set down so deep a mystery that no reason can discern it.

59. For Joseph in this place standeth in the figure of Christ, who hath food apart, whereof they know nothing: as it is to be seen at Jacob's well, when his disciples called him to eat. Then said he, *I have food which you know nothing of; which is to do the will of him that sent me* (John iv. 32-34): for the heathen woman's faith was his food.

60. Christ, according to the eternal Word of the Deity, eateth not of the substance of heaven, as a creature, but of the human faith and earnest prayer, and the souls of men praising God, are his food, which the eternal Word that became man eateth, as a part; which appertaineth to no man or any other creature, neither can they eat it. And when he eateth the faith and prayer, together with the praise of God, from our souls, then the human faith, together with the prayer and praising God, becomes substantial in the Word of power, and is of one and the same substance with the substance of the heavenly corporeity of Christ, all alike to the only body of Christ, God, and substance, viz. God, man, and substance, all one.

61. This substance, which is one and the same substance with the assumed humanity, from us, wherein he hath shed his blood, which is alike of a divine and human substantiality, viz. supernatural flesh and blood, and then also of the human creature's flesh and blood (except the earthliness of our humanity) he giveth this now to the human faith again to be eaten and drunk.

62. For faith, in the desire of its hunger, is the mouth which sucketh and receiveth it in. In which impression, catching and receiving, faith eateth and drinketh Christ's flesh and blood; which eating and drinking is apprehended and kept in the inward Paradisical image, which faded in Adam and became living again in Christ; wherein the human Paradisical substance, and Christ's flesh and blood, are entirely one substance, and continue so eternally. Which inward man is now no more called Adam, but Christ, viz. [being] a

---

[1] Or, messes.

member of the body and substance of Christ, wherein is the temple of the Holy Ghost; and God's holy Word is therein, substantially. And it is a form or image of the imageless Deity,[1] viz. the imaged Word of God, an express reflex image[2] of God.

63. And this now is the signification of the figure, that they served Joseph apart, and his brethren also apart: that still there is a difference between Christ, and his eating, and man, and his eating. The difference is not as to the creaturely humanity of Christ from us, but between the un-formed eternal Word in him, wherein the total God is operatively and generatively, not shut up and separated, but expressive in full omnipotence; not creaturely, but divine:

64. But in us men (so far as man in his participation hath anything of God and Christ in his own substance) the Word is formed and substantial, and this formed substantial Word eateth again of the formed Word of God, viz. of Christ's flesh and blood, wherein yet also the un-formed Word, together with the whole fullness of the Deity, dwelleth (Col. ii. 9).

65. But the human creature hath it not in his own participation or possession of self, as it is in Christ Jesus, but [the creature hath it] as a vessel and habitation of God. After that manner by way of similitude as fire possesseth iron, and illustrateth it that it come to be all of a fire,[3] and yet it hath not the fire in its own power or authority; for if the fire go out, the iron then remaineth to be dark iron. Or as the sun presseth and penetrateth through a herb, and puts forth itself together in the herb and becometh substantial; and yet the sun's spirit remaineth to be only a power and virtue in the herb, and the corpus or body of the herb doth not come to be sun: thus also is it to be understood between God and man.

66. But that Moses saith, *And they served the Egyptians also apart, for the Egyptians dare not eat bread with the Hebrews*, hath also its figure; though it might well be so outwardly in itself, that they have not dared to eat with them: which we leave unquestionably in its own worth, as also all other things. We leave it standing in a history, but we would only clear and explain the meaning and understanding, wherefore the spirit of God hath caused it to be deciphered so narrowly, curiously, exactly and punctually.

67. Now when we will search out this, we must take into

---

[1] Resemblance of the inconceivable or non-imagible Deity.
[2] Answering exactly as a man's face doth in a glass.
[3] Maketh it all of a light fire.

consideration a natural Adamical man, of what kind, progeny or name soever he is, whether heathen, Turk, verbal or titulary Christian,[1] or Jew; here they are all alike, and no otherwise: all these dare not eat with a right true Christian, as, viz. with Joseph's brethren. But why? Because they have not a mouth to eat such food withal. Their mouth is yet shut up to them, and they cannot eat the food of Christ's body; they are an abomination to it, and have a loathing against it: as we see that it is an abomination to the Jews, Turks and heathen, that a Christian saith, he eateth Christ's flesh, and drinketh his blood (John vi. 53).

68. So also it is an abomination to the titulary Christendom, one part of which believeth not the substantial participation and feeding upon the body of Christ, but will have it merely spiritual. The other part will have the mouth of the Adamical mortal man full of it, and therewith comprehend and receive it. And so there is no right knowledge or understanding in either party; and they sit at table, but without knowing anything as the brethren of Joseph did, who knew not Joseph, where indeed their faith feedeth, but their understanding knoweth not Joseph in his feast or banquet.[2]

69. Now then saith reason, seeing the Jews, Turks, and ignorant unknowing heathen, have no mouth to eat such food with, and that Christ saith, *Whosoever eateth not the flesh of the Son of Man, he hath no life in him* (John vi. 53); therefore they must all of them be damned. O Israel, how blind art thou here, and knowest as little as they, or as Joseph's brethren knew of Joseph.

70. The Turks, Jews, and strange nations, whose desire and prayer goeth to the only God, have indeed a mouth, but not so as a Christian hath: for as the desire, viz. the mouth, is, such is also the food in the mouth. They desire the spirit of God, and such is also their eating: in that manner as before Christ's humanity, in the Father and the Son, viz. in the Word.

71. But a Christian hath an incarnate mouth: for the soul's[3] desire, or much more, the substantial Christ or Christus, viz. the Virgin Sophia, hath a mouth from the substantial Word. But the other have one from the un-substantial Word; they desire the property of God the Father,[4] viz. of the only God, and they do apprehend it also: but here grace is not manifest.

72. But seeing the Father hath given man to his Son Christ

---

[1] Or mouth-Christian.   [2] Or, mess of food.   [3] Or, soulish.
[4] Or, to be like God the Father: our heavenly Father.

(John vi. 37), as Christ saith (John xvii. 6), and hath manifested the grace in Christ, and inviteth them all in Christ, and that there is no salvation without Christ;[1] therefore he giveth to them also the earnest crying prayer, which Christ receiveth from his Father and apprehendeth it in himself, and eateth it, and filleth them with his humanity, suffering, death, and shedding of his blood, and so they are with their spirit in Christ substantially, but in themselves as hidden to them.

73. For they desire not any way the flesh of the Son of Man, and therefore they have not in their selfhood any mouth for Christ's flesh and blood, for they have no desire to it; but with their spirit they are substantially in Christ: but their inward in Adam faded Paradisical humanity (which faded in Adam), wherein the incorporated grace in Paradise lieth, remaineth hidden in them, and without a stirring life.

74. For Christ dwelleth not substantially therein, as in a true Christian. But their faith's substance is hidden in Christ to the day of the restoration of that which is lost in Adam, when their Paradisical image, which is not manifested in this time, will put on their faith's substance, in God's bestowed grace, which proceedeth from one upon all, out of Christ's spirit; for that incorporated grace, viz. the inspoken or inspired Word, standeth also in them, and panteth after Christ's substantiality.

75. But seeing their substantiality is in the Word, without this place, state and condition, in Christ, where Christ in himself fulfilleth their faith to God, therefore also will their substantial faith in God put on that incorporated Word in the Paradisical image, together with the same, at the revelation or manifestation of Jesus Christ; and herewith also the whole man.

76. For the Scripture saith, *Of grace are ye saved, and that not of yourselves* (Eph. ii. 8), not by your knowing, but through God's mercy and compassion [are ye saved].[2] It lieth not in knowing, as if the knowing could receive Christ; but it lieth in the gift, viz. in the grace, which Christ giveth to the unknowing into their faith in God, as well as to the knowing into their desire: it is done to both of grace.

77. For Adam went forth from the only God into self, into ignorance, and led us all with him into that same ignorance. But grace came again from that same only God, and offereth itself to all ignorant unknowing persons, heathen as well as Jews.

---

[1] Or, out of him.   [2] Note how salvation is not of ourselves, but of grace in us.

78. Among the Jews stood the image or type of grace in the figure, signifying how grace would receive man again. But now the fathers of the figure, viz. the Jews, had no more part in the grace, viz. those among whom the image or type had not manifested itself: for the prefiguration and type pointed at Christ. The Jews pressed with their faith and prayer through the prefiguration into the only grace, which was in God, which God bestowed upon Adam and his children. But the heathen, which had not the Law, and yet believed, without circumcision, in the only promised grace of God, they pressed without the type or prefiguration into the grace.

79. For the ability was given to the one people as well as to the other, no people could of themselves; but the grace took the will for the ability, and gave them ability and power alike, the Jews and the faithful heathen. But infidelity and not willing was both with the Jews and heathen their damnation, in that they withheld their wills in self and in hardening, and went awhoring after other gods. Thus the circumcision and the sacrifices were not the Jews' salvation; but grace, which they represented in such figures pointing at the humanity of Christ, when the grace would fulfil the future: the future fulfilling was their salvation.

80. Thus also at present the Christians have the figure of grace under the Gospel in the fulfilling: not that they can receive the fulfilling in self-power and ability, but the fulfilling of the grace tendereth it to them; if they will give up themselves thereinto, then will the mouth be given to them in the grace.

81. But the others bend their wills towards the grace of God, which is even the same grace with the Christians, and no more; but the substantial grace in the image of the fulfilling they know not. But the grace taketh their willing with the desire into it, and giveth the desire in the grace a mouth: which is hidden to the creature, till the day of the revelation of Jesus Christ.

82. Therefore there is no other difference between them but the substantial stirring in the Paradisical image, the Paradisical image not having yet put on Christ in substance, as it is with the true Christians. And yet their faith in the grace of God in Christ is substantial, yet not in the human own possession of self, but in God who fulfilleth all things, and is and dwelleth through all things. Thus the substantial grace is near the faithful or believing Jews and Turks, and in them, but as to the creature not apprehended.

83. They have Christ in them, but they apprehend him not,

HOW JACOB'S SONS WENT INTO EGYPT

unless their will enter into the substantial grace of Christ, and then Christ manifesteth himself in their creature, as well as in Christians. But the grace in Christ is laid by the faithful believing Jews and other people, for it moveth through them, and their will to God is in it, and walketh therein.

84. A titulary Christian without the divine will is further from it than a believing Jew, Turk, and heathen, or whosoever he be that putteth his trust in God, and giveth up his will to God. Such a one is nearer, and will condemn the titulary Christian, in that he boasteth of knowing, and comforteth himself with the grace, but continueth in his evil will and desire without grace, and will set the wicked man up in the grace of God.

85. Thou sayest thus, The strange nations are not baptised into Christ, therefore they are not children to the grace of the Covenant. Answer. If circumcision were alone salvation, then were baptism so also, for the one is as the other, but God requireth that a Jew should be circumcised inwardly in heart. Circumcision was but the type or image, shewing how Christ would cut off sin, which type Christ hath fulfilled. Thus also the spirit of Christ baptiseth with this Covenant in the Paradisical image, in the incorporated grace, and kindleth an ember.[1]

86. But it requireth an ens of faith, which is capable of the baptism,[2] which cometh from the parents, and through the earnest prayer of those who are conversant about the work; else the Covenant is despised, and there is no circumcision of the heart and spirit. For the power and authority wherewith the Holy Ghost baptiseth consisteth not in man, but in God. Whosoever despiseth his Covenant, and manageth it not with earnest and with circumcised hearts, those he baptiseth into his anger: as Saint Paul saith concerning the Supper of Christ, that the wicked receive it to judgment.

87. A wicked priest hath not power and authority to baptise with the Holy Ghost, he hath only the water, and is himself incapable of the office; but the ens of the child, and the believing parents, and those who require and promote the work, their earnestness and prayer reach forth the Covenant with their faith's desire to the baptised infant.

88. But the wicked priest is no more profitable in it than the fontstone that holdeth the water; thus he bringeth only the water and

---

[1] Batheth, steepeth or soaketh into the grace, and quickeneth a sprout.
[2] Or, steeping.

the ceremonies, which a Turk can do, without faith or believing.

89. But a stranger that hath not the baptism, and knoweth nothing thereof, becometh in his faith circumcised in heart, and the Holy Ghost soaketh into his faith's desire, and baptiseth him unto the revelation of Jesus Christ, when his faith shall also put on the substantial Covenant in the grace.

90. O Babel, how blind art thou! How have thy clergy or men ordained and in orders set themselves in Christ's stead! But they all serve not Christ, but themselves to their fleshly honour. O Babel, convert, the door is open, else thou wilt be spewed out. The time is born. Else thou wilt be set before the light and proved, and then thou wilt stand in shame before all people.

91. Further, the spirit of God hath yet a powerful figure in this text, in that Joseph caused his brethren to be set before him according to the order of their birth, and caused his brother Benjamin to be served with five times more than the others. This prefigureth to us, first, the difference in the kingdom of Christ, shewing how they shall be unlike in the regeneration, as St. Paul saith concerning it, *They shall excel one another in glory*,[1] *as the sun, moon, and stars do* (1 Cor. xv. 41).

92. For there it will avail nothing to have been a king, prince, lord, noble or learned, but he that hath had the greatest power and virtue in him, who shall have attained grace, in the name of Jesus, the most clearly in his wrestling of repentance, he will be greatest there. For these orders and degrees signify to us, that they will be unlike in the divine exaltation, viz. in the power and virtue, as the angels excel one another in power, virtue, beauty and brightness.

93. But that Benjamin had five times more food served to him, pointeth in the figure at the inward man, for Benjamin standeth in the figure thereof, seeing he is Joseph's brother; and Joseph here standeth in the figure of Christ: therefore it belongeth to the inward man to eat of his brother Christ's food from his five wounds. This is that which this precious figure signifieth here, as may be seen.

94. But that the spirit saith, They drank, and were all filled with drinking, signifieth that in the kingdom of Christ there is a universal common participation and joy; and in that there is no difference, because in such difference they shall all rejoice in one God. For their drinking fully signifieth here the eternal joy, where, in this joy, we shall be as it were drunk. And then will the inward man drink and eat of

[1] Clarity.

HOW JACOB'S SONS WENT INTO EGYPT

the sweet grace which is manifested in Christ's five wounds; and hereby give it into the fiery soul, which in its fiery essence will, in this sweetness, awaken the triumph of divine joyfulness, and herewith will the noble bride[1] refresh its bridegroom, viz. the soul.

[1] Sophia: the Divine Wisdom.

The Seventy-First Chapter

How *Joseph* caused his Brethren's Sacks to be filled, and the Money to be laid uppermost in their Sacks, as also his Cup in *Benjamin's* Sack, and Caused them to be pursued and charged with Theft: What is thereby to be understood[1]

1. MOSES saith, *And Joseph commanded his steward, and said, Fill the men's sacks with food, as much as they can carry, and lay every one his money uppermost in his sack. And lay my silver cup uppermost in the sack of the youngest, with the money for the corn. And the steward did as Joseph had said unto him. On the morrow, when it was light, he let the men go, with their asses. And when they were not come far out from the city, Joseph said to his steward, Up, and pursue after the men; and when you have overtaken them, say thus unto them, Why have you requited evil for good? Is it not that out of which my lord drinketh, and wherewith he prophesieth;[2] ye have done ill. And when he overtook them, he spake such words to them* (Gen. xliv. 1-6).

2. Now a Christian standeth in this figure, signifying that when he is come to this in right earnestness into the image in the trial on the path of Christ's pilgrimage in this world, how God exerciseth and purgeth him, for this is the way and process on the path of Christ's pilgrimage, and how God carrieth himself, and the world also, towards the creaturely reason of man. For we see in this image how God, when the repentant man is in the true earnestness, filleth his sack, viz. the mind and conscience in the life's properties, with his grace, and layeth the cup of salvation (Psal. cxvi. 13), viz. the true and right silver cup, viz. the cup of Christ (John xviii. 11), out of which he drank in his suffering, uppermost in the sack of the filled grace, out of which a Christian must drink also, and follow Christ in his contempt.

3. For Joseph's cup, out of which he drank, with which he prophesieth or divineth, is in this figure no other but the cup of the Testament of Christ before his suffering, of which he drank with his

---

[1] Gen. xliv.   [2] Or, divineth.

disciples, and whereby he divined or prophesied concerning his eternal kingdom, and that whosoever would drink of this cup should with him divine and prophesy to[1] the eternal life.

4. But this figure sheweth the great earnestness, signifying how this cup should be bestowed upon God's children, and what that *Wine* is which they must drink of out of it; for first Joseph sendeth his steward after them, and bids him tell them they had stolen his cup, and was churlish towards them, when as yet they were not guilty: so also when a Christian hath his sack filled with this food, then will Christ's cup be laid in for him. These now the wrath of God sifteth in the human nature, as to their souls and as to the mortal body, and saith to the conscience, Thou hast not rightly gotten his cup by the right of nature; thou hast stolen it out of God's house from his grace and power. The kingdom of heaven suffereth violence (Matt. xi. 12) herein, and thou hast done violence, and gotten this cup to thee into thy sack; thou hast not grace by the right of nature, thou wilt needs walk back with this cup in peace on these paths.

5. But no, it will not avail thee; if thou wilt take Christ's grace along in thee, then thou must take on thee also his suffering, dying, scorn, persecution and misery, and suffer thyself to be continually reproached in the world for a false wicked man, and to suffer thyself to be accounted a wicked person[2] by the Pharisaical hypocrisy, as one that hath stolen their cup and taken it away by violence; in that he will no more kneel down before the great Babylonish whore, who hath presented a cup full of hypocrisy and blasphemy, and quaff of their cup; and then reproach they him for a wicked person, who hath stolen their cup and authority from them, and run after him and would murder him, and damn him to temporal and eternal death, and reproach him without ceasing for a treacherous person, who hath stolen their cup.

6. That is, when a true Christian obtaineth the cup of Christ, and drinketh out of it, then cometh the anger of God in the fleshly evil nature, as also the devil and the evil world, and set upon him on every side, because he hath this cup in his habitation, and prophesieth or divineth against them, that they have the cup of whoredom and abomination in them, and because he revealeth it, and will not quaff with them in their cup of hypocrisy and blasphemy.

7. And then must a Christian lay down his sack of God's grace at their feet, and suffer himself to be bound and captivated in their

---

[1] Upon, into or concerning. [2] Or, knave.

scorning and contemning; and then they oftentimes bereave him of body and life, honour and welfare, and set him with his cup before their judgment. And there a Christian must drink out of their cup the derision, cross, suffering and death of Christ, and imitate and follow Christ in this cup, and so not go home again in peace, with his filled sack of the grace of Christ, through this world into his eternal country of his Father.[1] He must be conformable to Christ's image (Phil. iii. 10; Rom. viii. 29), and follow him in his way which he hath walked in this world. This is powerfully prefigured in this figure.

8. For Joseph's brethren stood now in the figure of a converted Christian, whom God hath clothed with Christ, and also laid in the cup of the cross, together with grace, and, moreover, uppermost in the sack; to signify that when the grace of Christ, which is bestowed on a Christian, shall work and bring forth fruit, that it is not done in standing still in peace and quietness, but in the strife about this cup, for it lieth uppermost in the sack of grace, and the strife about the cup must always be the forerunner of it.

9. For Christ saith, *The Son of Man is not come to establish peace on the earth, but strife and persecution, that one be against another and persecute him* (Matt. x. 34; Luke xii. 51). Also, *He hath kindled a fire, and desireth it should burn* (Luke xii. 49). And this is it: that a true Christian must always be spoken against, even *those of his own family* in flesh and blood *must be his enemies* (Micah vii. 6), that the sown and planted tree of pearl may stir and bring forth fruit.

10. As an earthly tree must stand in heat, cold and wind, and have great strokes and opposition, whereby the sap is drawn out of the earth into the tree, so that it blossometh and beareth fruit: thus also the poor soul, in such smitings and opposition, in scorn and misery, must draw power and virtue into itself out of the bestowed and entrusted grace, viz. out of [the soil] and field of the Word of God, with earnest prayer and working, and thereby bear the fruit of faith, viz. good doctrine, instruction and conversation.

11. For thereby the soul feedeth the spirit of Christ, and Christ feedeth the soul again out of the sack of the substantial grace, viz. with his flesh of the substantial wisdom of God; and thus they give themselves one to another, to a perpetual working.

12. And we see hereby, how even the wicked must serve God in the working of his grace, for he is its stormy wind; and his cursing and blasphemy against God's children are the heat and cold, wherewith

---

[1] Or, native country.

God stirreth his little plant of pearl in his children, so that it hungereth after heavenly sap, and draweth it into itself and groweth. And this is that which Christ said, He came to set up strife on the earth: for Christ's kingdom is a strife against hell and the devil; Christ striveth without ceasing in his children and members, with Satan, about the kingdom.

13. For in the earthly man lieth yet the ground of the Serpent, viz. a habitation of Satan, wherein Satan withstandeth the kingdom of Christ: So also on the contrary the kingdom of Christ in grace withstandeth the kingdom of Satan, with the cup of Christ; and this strife continueth always while the earthly body continueth.

14. For thus God's anger worketh in the love, that the love (viz. the eternal One and eternal Good) might be distinguishable, perceptible, and discernible; for in strife and opposite will the profundity or abyss, viz. the eternal One, which is without nature and creature, is manifest.

15. And therefore God hath introduced himself with his holy Word of powers into nature and creature, as also into pain and torment, into light and darkness, that the eternal power of his Word in the Wisdom, together with the expressed Word, might be distinguishable and perceptible, that knowledge might be.

16. For without this the knowledge of the eternal One would not be manifest, neither would there be any joy; and though it were in being, yet it would not be manifest to itself. Thus it manifesteth itself through the introduction into nature, through the separability or distinguibility of the speaking; whereby the speaking bringeth itself into properties, and the properties into opposition or contrariety of will, and so through the opposition, the eternal Good, which bringeth itself along in the Word of the speaking, into distinguibility, becometh distinguishable, creaturely and conceivable.[1]

17. Else if the evil in the contrary will were not profitable, God, viz. the eternal only Good, would not endure it, but annihilate it.[2] But thus it serveth to the manifestation of the glory of God, and the kingdom of rejoicing; and it is an instrument of God, whereby he maketh his Good conceivable,[3] that the good may be known: for if there were no evil, then the good would not be known.

18. If there were no anger-fire there could be also no light-fire,

---

[1] Imagible, imaginable, or comprehensible.
[2] Or, make it to be nothing.
[3] Imagible, representable, or discernible.

MYSTERIUM MAGNUM

and the eternal love would be hidden, for there would be nothing that could be loved. Thus the love of God hath an occasion of love, for it loveth the dereliction of that which is forsaken, viz. the weakness; that it[1] also might be great.

19. For God's love cometh only to help the weak, lowly, humble, destitute, forlorn and forsaken, and not those that go on in the might and strength of the fire; not the might of self, but the impotency, and that which is forsaken. Whatsoever is lowly, disregarded, humble and destitute, in that, love worketh and dwelleth therein.

20. For love in its own property is nothing else but the divine humility out of the profundity or ground of the [eternal] One. Love neither seeketh nor desireth any thing but the One, for itself is the One, viz. the eternal Nothing, and yet is through All, and in All; but the appropriation of self-will is a nothing to it.

21. Therefore all is foolish and esteemed evil and base, in the sight of God's Love, whatsoever willeth in its own self-ability: though it may well be profitable, as whereby the willing of nothing manifesteth itself, yet it is, in the sight of the willing of nothing, only a phantasy, viz. a sport of its own driving on, and tormenting itself.

22. For that which willeth nothing, but only that out of which it is proceeded, that hath no torment in itself; for that, to itself, is nothing, but is, only to that out of which it is proceeded. It standeth submissive to its Maker that made it, he may cause it to be something or nothing: and thus it is one and the same thing with the eternal One; for it tormenteth not itself, it loveth not itself, it feeleth not itself in its own will: for it hath no will of its own, but is given up to the total or universal.

23. As we see that the four elements stand in such a will; they are four, and yet but one. For the four stand in one ground, and the ground is neither hot nor cold, neither moist nor dry: it is that one element, an unperceptible life. But thus it would not be manifested to itself; therefore God hath stirred it up, and exhaled and unfolded it out of himself, that there might be opposition to itself, and might perpetually stand in strife, that the One might be manifested in multiplicity.

24. But herein neither of them destroyeth the other that it should cease to be, and be nothing; but that which is overpowered standeth still to that which hath overpowered it, the heat to the cold, or the cold to the heat; and there is no self possession or willing, but one

---

[1] The love itself.

element willeth the other, that the other may be manifest; and when it is manifest, then it giveth itself to the strongest in the stirring, and so there is a strife, and yet the greatest love between them: for in regard of the love struggling it is that the strife and willing or stirring ariseth.

25. Therefore man, in respect of his own willing, is an enemy to himself: if he did give his will to God, and did yield to him, then God would will through him, and with him, and his willing were God's willing. But seeing he loveth his own willing, and not that which hath given him the willing, it is a twofold injury.

26. One, in respect of the own willing, that he will not hold still to the original and ground of his willing, and be one and the same thing with it: as the four elements do all give up their willing into the ground out of which they proceed and move and will according to the same.

27. A second is, that he breaketh off his love from the love of the abyss, and loveth himself, and forsaketh the love that hath given him his love; and himself willeth, goeth, runneth, careth, and looketh after many things, and breaketh himself off from the Unity: therefore he runneth on in his own will in the forms or qualities of nature and the four elements; as also in the multiplicity of the essences of the constellations[1] in mere unquietness.

28. And the unquietness bringeth into anxiety, and the anxiety standeth in the desire of his will, and the desire includeth and over-shadoweth itself, so that it is dark in itself, and cannot see itself. Therefore the self-will runneth on in mere dark anxiety, and vexeth itself in the desire, and seeketh the love in the desire, and yet findeth nothing therein but the image[2] of the four elements which the desire itself maketh. Thus the will serveth its images, and loveth the image in itself: and that is the greatest folly which nature hath brought forth, and yet it is the instrument whereby the highest wisdom is made manifest.

29. O ye men, who count yourselves wise, and receive honour one from another in respect of your self-love and your own will, how mad are ye in the sight of heaven! your own honour which you yourselves seek is a stink in the presence of the only love of God. But he that seeketh another and honoureth and loveth him, he is one thing with the total: For when he seeketh and loveth his brother, then he introduceth his love into the members of his body, and is loved, sought,

---

[1] Or, postures of the stars.   [2] Form, quality or condition.

and found of him who made the first man out of his Word, and is but one man with all men, viz. with the first Adam, but one in all his members; as also with the second Adam, Christ, [he is] but one.

30. For God gave man but one will, that he should will only what God would. God would have the world and the creatures to be, and that would he by and out of his Word. This should man also will through that same Word: as that Word would have it, so should man also will to have it be. God created all things in its own similitude or image, by the Word, and out of the Word, that one should love another; so should man also love his likeness and similitude.

31. For all men are but the one man, Adam. God created only him, and the other creating[1] he left to man, that he should leave his will to God, and with God generate the other men out of himself in that likeness. But when that was not done God cursed the power that was given to man, so that the will of the creatures is opposite to him, seeing he would have them to misuse them, and would no more be a lord of the creatures, but mingleth his love also with them: whereupon the four elements captivated him, and made him also a beast as to the body. And thus now he runneth on in the will of the curse.

32. For he is God's image. But he fashioneth[2] his will into a bestial image, and disturbeth the order of God, from what it was in the word of Creation: He suppresseth the right true will of God, and setteth his own will in the place. He is with his will an enemy to all creatures, and all creatures are his enemies.

33. And therefore must the divine will in man be now born again in such anguish in the opposite will, and the right divine will of the new birth must suffer itself to have the enmity of all creatures; and therefore, because man beareth in his body a bestial will, wherein the bestial opposite will, together with the curse, is manifested, so now the life in the curse is at enmity with the life in the peace, and will not suffer it in itself.

34. But if the bestial will in the flesh could be wholly broken and killed, then the curse would cease, and so no creature could be at enmity more.

35. But seeing this cannot be, therefore must man stand in strife, and endure much evil to will in him from without, and to will much evil out from himself, in and towards that which is without him; and so standeth in strife between evil and good, and in evil and good; and

---

[1] Or, procreating which was further to be done.
[2] Imageth, modelleth, or figureth.

liveth in the strife of the elements, and also in the strife of his own willing that God gave him.

36. For he complaineth always, that wrong is done him, and yet [he] himself is a wrong will, and the right will, which he obtaineth in the regeneration, is not his own natural willing, but it is the willing of the grace of God, which is manifested in his willing; which willing daily killeth his natural willing, and blameth man by God's instrument with the children of the anger openly.

37. Moses speaketh further, and saith, *They answered him, and said, Wherefore speaketh my lord such words? It is far from thy servants to do such a thing: Behold, the money, which we found aloft in the sack, we have brought to thee again out of the land of Canaan: how should we then have stolen out of thy lord's house either silver or gold? He with whom it is found among us thy servants, let him be put to death; and moreover, we will be the servants of my lord. He said, Let it be as ye have spoken: he with whom it is found shall be my servant; but ye shall be quit* (Gen. xliv. 7-10).

38. This figure now sheweth how the conscience desireth to justify itself, when it is apprehended by the wrath of God's anger, that either, when God with his plagues in nature, also many times in the hiding of his graces, or through the evil world, blameth it, and representeth it unrighteous, then it will always justify itself, that wrong is done it.

39. For if it have once turned toward grace, and broken itself off from ungodly courses, then it thinketh no evil at all shall happen: God is bound to protect it, and the world doth it wrong, when it reproacheth it as wicked; it ought no more to be subject to plagues and punishments, and it accounteth that honesty and righteousness, whereby it stealeth grace from God, and reckoneth it for its own, as if it were no more guilty of sins.

40. Also it excuseth itself towards the world, when the world will impute sins and blasphemies to it, as if it were guilty. Then it will needs die, or be put to death, or the like, as Joseph's brethren did who knew nothing of the theft, and did not understand either, that all their unrighteousness, and their stealing of Joseph, when they stole him from their father and sold him, stood in the sacks of Joseph's gifts, viz. were manifest before the eyes of Joseph, so that Joseph knew and understood their theft, and therefore caused them to be held for thieves, and caused them to be pursued as thieves, and fetched them back again, and set them before the judgment.

41. But instead of their thievery of their committed sins, whereby

they had forfeited their lives, Joseph caused his silver cup to be laid to the gift in their sack, and caused them to be blamed for the cup: which they would not confess.

The figure standeth thus:

42. When a man, as is above mentioned, becometh a true Christian, so that God giveth him his grace, then he layeth his grace hiddenly in the sack of his body, in the essences of life. And, moreover, layeth therein the cup of the cross, and blameth it no more in conscience in respect of its manifold committed sins; for he hath utterly destroyed them with the grace of forgiveness, and filled the sack of his sins with grace for the hunger of the poor soul. But it layeth now the cup of Christ to its charge, that it is guilty of that, viz. of Christ's being scorned, also of his suffering and death, that he hath brought Christ to the cross with his sins, that it is verily guilty of the cup of Christ's cross, and not wholly righteous.

43. For when God by his grace forgiveth him the sins unto death,[1] then he causeth this cup of Christ to be laid aloft in the sack; seeing Christ himself hath the guilt of these sins laid upon him, and hath taken them upon him; therefore now this man is guilty of the cup of Christ's cross (in which Christ must taste and drink out the anger of God in man): God's righteousness requires of him to enter into the suffering, scorn, and death of Christ, that he should die with Christ, and give himself up to his scorn, and suffer with Christ.

44. But seeing he cannot do that, and is too weak to enter into such sufferings in the anger of God, therefore hath grace put this cup also into him, that he might drink of Christ's victory, and prophesy or divine of Christ's suffering and death, and make them known.

45. But God's righteousness, which now requireth man to be in the process of Christ, viz. in Christ's sufferings and death, and yet findeth him not always, in his conversation and will, therein, accuseth him for a thief, who carrieth the cup of Christ's cross but as a thief in the sack of his life's essences, and chargeth him of theft, if he walk otherwise than in the process [and imitation] of Christ.

46. For Christ hath received man into his sufferings and death, and turned away the righteousness of God's anger, and introduced him, with his guilt of eternal death, into his innocent death, and is dead from the sins and wickedness in himself; and in this dying of

---

[1] Mortal, deadly, or killing sins.

JOSEPH'S BRETHREN'S SACKS FILLED

Christ God's righteousness, in the anger, requireth a Christian man to be.

47. But if he walk out of this path, and not in it, then saith righteousness, Thou art a thief, and hast wrongfully got this cup of Christ in thy sack, I will set thee before my judgment and sentence, as Joseph did to his brethren, when he caused them to be fetched back to the sentence of his judgment.

48. Therefore hath a Christian, who walketh under the banner of Christ's cross, no excuse, when God by his steward, viz. by the children of this world, causeth him to be laid hold on in the righteousness of his anger, and chargeth him for a thief and an unrighteous person, also for a stranger, innovator or novelist,[1] enthusiast, fool, and the like; when men load him with all his faults, and the infirmities of natural sinful flesh, and without ceasing blame him as wicked and unrighteous, and condemn him to the damnation of the temporal and eternal death; and though he is not, in the sight of the world, nor as to the world, guilty, yet he is liable to bear the scorn, suffering and death of Christ after him, as a Christian, and is liable to take upon him the whole process in the footsteps of Christ, and to follow Christ therein, and to suffer all, in Christ, and wholly to put on Christ in his derision, contempt, suffering and death, and to bear his cross and scorn after him; that he may enter into Christ's kingdom, as a member of the body of Christ that hath suffered with him, and hath daily died to the anger of God in the death of Christ, from his actual sins.

49. For all sins, blasphemies and untruths, which are imputed to him wrongfully from the world, which he is not outwardly guilty of in the fact, that, he suffereth in the process of Christ, as a Christian; and therein drinketh out of the cup of Christ's cross, who hath innocently suffered for his sins.

50. For if he be not guilty of them in his life, yet he is guilty of them in the inherited sin, and hath inherited them also in the seed out of which he is proceeded: they lie in his ground;[2] he cannot excuse himself before God in the process of Christ, he is guilty of all Adamical sins.

51. But this is his comfort: that God manifesteth them by the children of his anger in this world, and so, as a curse, by the children of anger, fasteneth them to the cross of Christ; and in this manifestation drowneth them in him in the blood and death of Christ, in that he still cleaveth to God, as Christ to his Father, and suffered himself to be

---

[1] Novice.   [2] Ground of his nature and heart.

accused of sins which he had not committed, but had only inherited them; and so they were taken from him, and given to the anger of God in his judgment that he might condemn them.

52. For thus also Joseph, in this figure, appeased his just anger towards his brethren: they were all guilty towards him, but he charged them not with their guilt, but charged them only with his cup, for he had clearly forgiven them all their trespasses. But concerning the cup alone he would not hold them guiltless, and yet of right they were not guilty of it: but he had laid it in, as his bounty, and made them guilty of it.

53. Thus also hath God given us his grace of mere love, after that we were clearly guilty of eternal judgment, and hath laid Christ and grace in the sack of our life, with his suffering and death, with his cup of the cross: concerning which he doth not hold us guiltless: we are all guilty thereof, and have not this cup by a natural right, but it is laid into us without our knowledge. Therefore we cannot release ourselves of it, except we cast Christ wholly from us, and give ourselves again to the anger of God; and then death, hell, and the anger of God make us guilty, and hold us captive in them: but at present man may lay hold on which he will.

54. But that Joseph caused the cup to be thrust into his brother Benjamin's sack, it hath this figure: that Christ dwelleth in the inward man, viz. in his Paradisical brother, and hath this cup of the cross in his hand, out of which the guilty soul and the body must drink. He thrusteth it into his brother's sack, for that inward ground is his brother: but the other brethren must drink of it, this brother of Christ holdeth it in him, for he is Christ's member and habitation.

55. Therefore saith Joseph's steward, By whomsoever the cup is found, he shall be my servant, but ye shall be quit; viz. the inward ground, the true Joseph's, viz. Christ's, brother, he is Christ's servant, who serveth his Lord and brother, and must hold the cup in his sack. The other forms[1] of life of nature are free, and cannot hold the cup for Christ.

56. For they are not the right sack to put it in, but the ground of the heavenly world's substance is the sack to which the holy cup of Christ doth belong, which poureth the ground of nature out of it. Therefore must Joseph's brother be made guilty of the cup, because he stood in the figure of the inward man wherein Christ would manifest himself with his cup of the cross: and so the other brethren, viz. the

---

[1] Conditions or qualities.

JOSEPH'S BRETHREN'S SACKS FILLED

poor soul together with the body, be quit and released from the guilt.

57. Therefore saith Joseph's steward, He is my servant who hath the cup, he shall serve me, but ye shall be quit. That is, Christ is, in this inward Benjamin, Joseph's brother, and serveth God with overcoming of death and the anger of God in man. And so all the other brethren, viz. the natural life, shall be quit from guilt and pain: and it standeth excellently in the figure.

58. Moses saith further, *And they hastened, and laid every one his sack off on to the earth; and every one took his sack off, and searched, and began at the eldest, and so to the youngest: and there they found the cup in Benjamin's sack. And then they rent their clothes, and loaded every one his ass, and went again into the city* (Gen. xliv. 11-13).

59. When Adam was fallen into sin, then the law and command fetched him back again, and charged him with the sin and theft, that he had eaten of the wrong fruit with a wicked mouth: therefore must he return again into the city, viz. into the earth, out of which the body was proceeded, and there lay down his sack into the earth. And there God's righteousness searcheth into all the natural properties, viz. truth and righteousness, which availeth before God, viz. the image of heaven; and began from the first form of nature, and so on to the youngest and last, viz. to the incorporated ground of grace after the fall, and cannot find his cup of salvation in any natural property, although the body goes quite to powder in the searching, all but the youngest brother in the inspoken or inspired word of grace; in that lieth the cup of Joseph and of Christ: this the Spirit prefigureth powerfully in this figure.

60. Moses saith further, *And Judah went with his brethren into Joseph's house; for he was there still; and they fell down before him on the earth. But Joseph said to them, How have ye dared to do this thing? know ye not that such a man as I am can find it out? Judah spake and said, What shall we say unto my lord? How shall we speak? and wherein can we justify ourselves? God hath found out the misdeed of thy servants: behold here, we, and he with whom the cup is found, are the servants of my lord. But he said, That be far from me to do such a thing: the man with whom the cup is found, he shall be my servant, but go ye up in peace to your father* (Gen. xliv. 14-17).

The inward figure standeth thus:

61. When God blamed and charged man with guilt by reason of sin, and presented this to him in his anger by the deluge or flood, also

by Sodom and Gomorrah before their eyes, that they had robbed in the house of Joseph, that is, in the Covenant of grace, and transgressed the Covenant, then went Judah with his brethren, that is, Moses, with the children of Judah and Israel in the manifestation of the law, when their sins were manifested, and that God required the cup back again into Joseph's house, that is, the law went back into Joseph's house: Then Judah and Israel could not keep it, and so it went into the grace, and there the Covenant of grace, viz. the right Joseph, presented itself before their eyes, and said, while you are robbers and evil, do you suppose I cannot find you out? But they could not answer him, but must yield themselves to his sentence.

62. For Israel could neither keep the Covenant nor the Law, and therefore must now fall down before him, and yield themselves to his mercy and compassion. Israel would now give up himself to be God's own servant, but he would not have them minister to him with their Law, but would have that to be his servant wherein the cup lay. He would not have only an outward worship and service of God, in the figure of Christ, with the Law, but he would have Benjamin, viz. the inward ground of the heavenly world's substance, for a servant; but the minister or servant of the Law, viz. the natural man, should go home again in peace into his father's country, and take the bestowed grace along with him in his life for food: this the spirit of God sets thus in a figure under these acts, pointing at the future.

63. Under this figure now the spirit intimates, by Judah, who was surety for Benjamin, very secretly and mystically, that the poor soul could not thus with the grace go home again to its father's country, unless it had Benjamin, that is, Christ, in substance in it. For Judah pleaded exceeding hard that he durst not go home, unless he brought Benjamin along with him, or else he would himself remain there a servant.

64. Thus the poor soul giveth itself up to God, when God's righteousness calleth it to go back again home with the Covenant. Then it will by no means go back, except it have Benjamin, that is, Christ substantially with it, else it cannot see God: as here Judah in this image and type excuseth himself, and saith, If he came back and brought not Benjamin with him, then he should bring his father's grey hairs under the earth, seeing his soul clave to Benjamin's soul (Gen. xliv. 30, 31).

65. That is, if the Adamical man should go into Paradise again, without Christ's life and substance, then would he bring his father,

the life's nature, into the eternal divine forgetfulness:[1] for the life of the human nature would not be manifest according to the divine property; that is, it could not live in the kingdom of heaven.

66. Indeed God calleth the soul to go home with the Law into Paradise; but that cannot be, unless it have Christ in life and substance in it, and then it dares go home again into its first native country of its Father.

[1] Or, hiddenness.

The Seventy-Second Chapter

How *Joseph* Manifested himself before his Brethren. And what is to be understood thereby[1]

1. MOSES saith further, *Then Joseph could no longer withhold himself before all those that stood about him; and he cried, Let every one go forth from me. And none were with him, when Joseph made himself known to his brethren. And he wept aloud: so that the Egyptians and Pharaoh's people heard. And he said to his brethren, I am Joseph, doth my father yet live? And his brethren could not answer him, they were so terrified in his presence* (Gen. xlv. 1-3).

The inward figure standeth thus:

2. God gave Israel the Law, and commanded them thereby to go home again into Paradise, even as the figure of the promised land (into which they were to go, but could not for a long time, till Joshua led them in) was as a type and prefiguration of the true leading in by Jesus; and under the Law they had also the Paradisical Covenant of grace, as also the prophets, who lead them to God's mercy and compassion.

3. But they could not by any of these come again into their first Adamical Paradisical country of their Father, to rest. God's righteousness blamed them without ceasing, and required the power and ability, that they should give full obedience to the Law and the Covenant.

4. But seeing that could not be, and that neither the Law nor the Covenant could bring them in, back again, then the heavenly Joseph manifested himself out of the Covenant, for he could no longer withhold, in regard of man's misery, and bringeth his great mercy and compassion through the Covenant into the Law. Which compassion is signified by Joseph's great weeping, when he could no more withhold from his brethren, and he wept so that even the Egyptians and the people of Pharaoh's house heard; which signifieth that this weeping, viz. the mercy and compassion of God through Christ, the Egyptians also, that is, all heathen and people, should hear and receive

[1] Gen. xlv.

it; even as it came to pass, when Christ's weeping and compassion sounded among all nations, so that they all received it into their hearts, and turned themselves to this Joseph, who received them all, and fulfilled the Law, together with the Covenant.

5. But that Joseph cried, *Let every one go forth from me!* when he made himself known to his brethren, that none should stay with him, it signifieth this: When Jesus Christ, viz. the highest mercy and compassion of God, manifested itself out of the Covenant, then must the Law, with all ceremonies, together with the Covenant, cease and be gone, also all man's ability and power, as also all willing, going and running, must go forth and depart.

6. For, that presented itself out of the Covenant and the Law, which, fulfilled both the Covenant and the Law, and set itself in the stead of the Covenant and the Law, in the middle, as a Mediator between and in God and man, as a God-Man, and Man-God, who alone should bring Adam into Paradise, and destroy sin. None should be with him, he alone would and should manifest himself for a Light (*John viii. 12*) and for a new Life to the humanity.

7. And it is the figure which sheweth how the repentant man must come to God: for he must cast away all things from himself; all his works and doings cannot reach the top and point of this, he must wholly enter into resignation and dereliction, and turn himself away from the comfort and help of every creature, that he may stand naked and alone before the most clear and merest mercy and compassion of God in Jesus Christ.

8. No hypocrisy or human comfort, wherewith men please and tickle the heart, will avail in this presence of Joseph, but a total forsaking of every creature, wherein everything is left to the naked soul, and that must in itself sink down in the presence of the heavenly Joseph, in its will and whole desires, and totally leave itself to him, and will nothing without his will, and set no other means or medium aloft in esteem, for all will avail nothing.

9. The whole creaturely life must be resigned and forsake its will and desires, that the creaturely will may be received and purified again by the un-creaturely will, that God's will and man's will may be one will. And then God is all in all in him, according to the inward and the outward world, in each world according to its property, viz. according to the eternal speaking Word in the soul; and according to the animal soul, in *spiritu mundi* [in the spirit of the world], in all, as an instrument of God.

10. Now when this is done, then saith the heavenly Joseph in his mercy and compassion, *I am Jesus in thee*, and openeth the inward eye in the soul, that it knoweth him in a moment; and he speaketh friendly into the soul, and saith, Doth my Father yet live? that is, is the Father's nature yet in the soul, is there yet a breath of the divine life in it?

11. Before this manifestation now the soul's own will is terrified, so that it hath in its own power no word more to speak, nor can it, in self, speak; for in this terror the self of the will goeth to the ground. For with this aspect ariseth the will of God up, and slayeth the soul's own will: as Joseph's brethren were so very much terrified before his face, that they could not speak a word more, all their ability failed them as if they had been dumb. And thus also will the wicked and ungodly at the last judgment be dumb before the face of God, and terrified to eternal death, that his life will be a mere anguish and terror of an evil conscience, which will be an eternal gnawing.

12. *But Joseph said to his brethren, Draw near to me. And they drew near. And he said, I am Joseph your brother, whom ye sold into Egypt. And now be not careful, nor think that I am angry for it, that ye have sold me hither: for to preserve your life hath God sent me hither before you* (Gen. xlv. 4, 5).

The holy figure standeth thus:

13. When Christ with his revelation or manifestation thus terrifieth the soul, that the soul's own will is terrified into the death of its willing and ability, then he speaketh in or inspireth his Word of grace into it, and giveth it power [and virtue], and saith, in the soulish essence, Draw near to me, and raise up thy countenance from the terror of death; go in my power to me and into my will, I am no more angry with thee, that I have been sold into thy death. God hath sent me hither before thee, that I might nourish thee in thy hunger of misery, viz. in the hunger of God's anger, till thou art freed from thy earthly body, in which lieth the great hunger and divine famine in the anger of God.

14. For to preserve thy life hath God sent me into thy humanity and soul, for there will yet be five years of dearth (Gen. xlv. 6) in thy flesh; that is, the divine hunger will yet remain in thy five senses of the earthly reason; therefore hath God sent me before hither, ere this world cease to be, to thee, and into thee, that he might deliver thee in thy earthly five senses with a powerful deliverance, that my power

HOW JOSEPH MANIFESTED HIMSELF

[and virtue] of the famine in the five earthly senses may deliver and feed the poor soul; God hath set me as a lord and prince, and made me a father of thy nature, that I should rule, as Joseph over the land of Egypt. I am become lord over all thy house, and all that thou hast and art, that I should nourish thee in thy famine with the divine food of my flesh and blood: be no more afraid, I am with thee in the necessity of the earthly life, I will deliver thee and bring thee to glory and honour.

15. And Joseph said further, *Make haste now, and go up to my father and to your father, and tell him, Thus saith Joseph thy son, God hath set me as lord over all Egypt: come away to me, delay not. Thou shalt dwell in the land of Goshen, and be near by me, and thy children, and thy children's children, thy small and great cattle, and all that thou hast. I will there provide for thee; for there are still five years of dearth and famine; that thou mayest not perish, with thy house, and all that which thou hast* (Gen. xlv. 9-11).

16. *Behold, your eyes see, and the eyes of my brother Benjamin, that I speak to you with my own mouth. Make known to my father all my glory in Egypt, and all that ye have seen; make haste and come with my father down hither. And he fell about his brother Benjamin's neck, and wept; and Benjamin also wept upon his neck. And he kissed all his brethren, and wept over them: and afterwards his brethren parleyed with him* (Gen. xlv. 12-15).

17. This now is a figure, representing that when the soul hath seen the countenance of the heavenly Joseph, that he hath comforted and refreshed it again. Then saith the divine Word in it, Make haste now and bring also thy father, that is, thy nature and thy whole life, with all thy conversation and doings in thy state and condition, to me, and thou shalt dwell near by me with thy outward life, and I will nourish thee and provide for thee, and all that over which thou art set. Come away with all thy thoughts and works into Egypt, that is, into lowliness and humility, to me; that very land will I give into thee, to dwell in; that is, in lowliness and humility shall thy dwelling be; and there, in thy temporal state and condition, thou mayest with temporal nourishment, in temporal good things, dwell by me. Your eyes shall there see my goodness and bounty, that I will do well to you in the famine of your earthliness.

18. For the land of Goshen signifieth a fatness of the blessing of God in this earthliness; and therein your eyes see, and also the eyes of my brother Benjamin, viz. of the inward new man, that I speak to you with my own mouth, that is, essentially, within you. For if a man cometh to the new birth, then Christ speaketh essentially, that

is, actually or operatively in him; and the eyes of the soul, together with the most inward ground wherein Christ, viz. the Word, is, essentially, see and find the same.

19. But the outward five senses cannot in this earthliness wholly comprehend it, but they dwell near by it. The inward eyes see through the outward senses, as the sun shineth through transparent glass, and the glass remaineth glass still; so also the outward nature of this time of the five following dear years of the earthly essence continue in their right, till the soul forsaketh the body. And then, at the Last Judgment Day, also the right Adamical body of the five senses shall come again to the soul; but the grossness or dross of the earthly body hath no more place: for all temporal things separate themselves in Mysterium Magnum [into the Great Mystery], out of which they proceeded.

20. But that Joseph fell about his brother Benjamin's neck and wept, and kissed them all, it signifieth this in the figure: when Christ in the inward Benjamin, viz. in the image and substance of the heavenly world's substance, which faded in Adam, is manifested again, then the holy name Jesus, viz. God's great love, kisseth the incorporated ground of grace, and penetrateth or presseth through this image, with his weeping love, viz. with God's great sweetness, viz. the temple of Christ, and hereby kisseth the creaturely soul's essences, and presseth also with the weeping love through it, and then it obtaineth its life again, and speaketh with God in Christ Jesus.

21. For in this speech or voice alone the soul is heard of God, for in this kiss the soul hath its hearing given to it again, so that it heareth and teacheth God's word; for the senses or thoughts of the soul stand now in the Word of life, and hear what the Lord speaketh in them through Christ, out of the inward ground; and that is it that Christ said, *He that is of God heareth God's word*; and to the Pharisees he said, *Therefore ye hear not, for ye are not of God* (*John viii. 47*).

22. If the present contending Babel had in it the kiss of Christ, then it would with Joseph's brethren turn to the heavenly Joseph, and in great humility and lowliness speak with Joseph, and would hear God's word in Joseph's love, and speak humbly with him, they would not contend for temporal honour and fat bellies,[1] and about dominion, and waste the land of Goshen in a heathenish[2] manner.

23. O Babel! thy shame and reproach is set in judgment before the

---

[1] Or, benefices.   [2] Or, barbarous.

Most High; thou art that same Antichrist of whom St. Paul hath spoken. Thou boastest of God's word in teaching and hearing, and thy ground is not of God, but from the tower of Babel; thou wilt teach God's word with the letter without the living Word in thee; but the sheep hear not thy voice, for it proceedeth not from Joseph's kiss.

24. And Moses saith further, *And the report came into Pharaoh's house, that Joseph's Brethren were come: and it pleased Pharaoh well, and all his servants. And Pharaoh said to Joseph, Say to thy brethren, do thus, Load your beasts and go up, and when ye come into the land of Canaan, then take your father and your families, and come to me: and I will give you the good of the land of Egypt, that ye shall eat the marrow of the land. And command them to do thus; take you from the land of Egypt chariots for your wives, and for your children, and bring your father, and come. And regard not your household-stuff; for the good of the whole land of Egypt shall be yours* (Gen. xlv. 16-20).

The figure standeth thus:

25. When Joseph's, viz. Christ's, voice soundeth in the soul, then this report presseth into God the Father's property; for the soul in its nature is from the eternal nature in the Word, out of the Father's property of fire; and so is manifest again in the Father, from whom the will had broken off itself; and he speaketh or inspireth himself into its life's essence; for it pleaseth him well that the soul is become manifested in Christ, and biddeth the soul with all its properties, through Joseph's, viz. Christ's, efficiency, to come into Paradise again. He giveth it chariots, and all necessaries, which chariots are his spirit in the Word which bringeth it, and giveth it the whole land of Egypt; that is, the whole Paradise or kingdom of heaven for its own: this the spirit of God powerfully prefigureth under this history.

26. *And the children of Israel did so: and Joseph gave them chariots, according to the command of Pharaoh, and provision to spend by the way. And gave each of them all sumptuous apparel; but to Benjamin he gave three hundred pieces of silver, and five suits of sumptuous apparel. And to his father he sent besides, ten asses laden with the choice good things of the land of Egypt, and ten she asses with corn and bread and food for his father upon the way. Thus he sent his brethren away, and they departed: and he said to them, Contend not upon the way* (Gen. xlv. 21-24).

The figure standeth thus:

27. Christ taketh the provision, as also the chariots, viz. the Holy Ghost from the Father, which he sendeth to his children, as Joseph took the chariots and present from Pharaoh, and giveth them provision to spend upon the way of their pilgrimage, viz. his body and blood for meat and drink.

28. The sumptuous apparel which Joseph gave to every one of his brethren signifies the temple of Christ, wherein the soul feasteth and resteth; and Joseph's five suits of sumptuous apparel, which he gave to his brother Benjamin, are the five wounds of Christ, wherein the inward man feasteth in God's love; but the three hundred pieces of silver, which he gave to Benjamin, are the gifts of the Word out of this great love, wherewith this Benjamin should trade and get increase, and gain much for his Lord and Brother, the heavenly Joseph; for, with money, men trade: so also should the inward Benjamin trade with his gifts of the three hundred pieces of silver, viz. with the gifts of Christ; that is, teach and make known God's wonders, for he is Christ's servant and assistant, yea his true brother.

29. But the ten asses laden with the choice good things of the land of Egypt, which Joseph sent to his father, signify in the figure the ten commandments in the law of nature, which Joseph had laden with good things; that is, Christ hath laden them with his grace, and sent them to God's righteousness in the conscience, whereof poor nature hath to make expenses.

30. But the ten she asses with corn signify the ten forms of the soulish and natural fire-life, upon which Christ loadeth the soul's food, when they go in his process in the imitation of him. The bread and the food upon the way signify the Word of God, of which the poor old Adam must eat, that he may live.

31. These Christ giveth his children and brethren on the way of their pilgrimage, when they go home again in the process of Christ, that they may have provision to spend; and thereon nature, viz. the old father, eateth, and commandeth them that they should not contend one with another upon this way, but in love and peace go home into Paradise.

32. O Israel! where is now thy peace? It seemeth as if thou hast consumed all the provision of Joseph, and must at present want, seeing thou so very much contendest about this food, and hast raised such murdering about it. Truly thou hast murdered thy brother

HOW JOSEPH MANIFESTED HIMSELF

Benjamin by the way, and therefore thou art in strife, and wilt not go home. Thou art afraid, but the famine will drive thee forth, or else thou wilt be hungry and starved.

33. *Thus they went up from Egypt, and came into the land of Canaan to their father Jacob. And made it known to him, and said, Joseph is alive, and is lord of the whole land of Egypt. But his heart thought much otherwise, for he believed them not. Then they told him all the words of Joseph, which he had said to them: and when he saw the chariots which Joseph had sent to bring him, the spirit of Jacob their father revived. And Israel said, I have enough, that my son Joseph yet liveth; I will go down and see him, ere I die* (Gen. xlv. 25-28).

This figure standeth thus:

34. When Christ's Apostles were laden with this present, they went therewith into their father's house, viz. among the brethren in the kingdom of nature in their unbelief, and made known to them the great glory and the present of JESUS Christ, which he had given them, that they should bring it to them. But their heart believed it not, that these simple men, the Apostles of God, laden with such great good things, were sent by Joseph, till they saw the chariots of the Holy Ghost, which brought the present in great power and works of wonder, and heard the powerful word of JESUS Christ, with deeds and wonders out of their mouth. Then said Israel, Now I have enough; now I can believe; I will also go along with you to Christ, that I may see him: as old Jacob said, I have enough that my son Joseph yet liveth, I will go up, that I may see him before I die.

35. Thus also these chariots go out from God's children among the unbelievers, which at first will not believe: but when they feel these chariots, and the present, in them, then they also say, I have enough, I will go along into Egypt into repentance, that I may see and know my Saviour: for their spirit is also revived, as Jacob's spirit was.

36. Where are now these chariots in the teachers' mouths, upon which the Holy Ghost rideth and toucheth the heart of Israel, that his spirit be revived? Indeed, saith Babel, the spirit of Christ at present worketh not so powerfully in our words; we have now the knowledge of the kingdom of Christ: that need not be; we should only believe the word which Christ's Apostles have left behind them, and that is enough.

37. Else if we should teach so powerfully, we must then be also of so simple and poor a life as Christ's Apostles led, and forsake the

world: That needs not be, Christ's kingdom must now be stately, in pomp and glory.

38. O how will poor Christ, who on earth had not whereon to lay his head, reprove this to thee, before thy face: that thou hast taken his Covenant into a false and wicked mouth. Earnestness was never more necessary than at this present, when all the chariots are overthrown, and in great confusion.

The Seventy-Third Chapter

How *Jacob* and all his Children, and all that were belonging to him, and all their Cattle, went into Egypt[1]

1. MOSES saith, *Israel went with all that he had, and when he came to Beer-sheba he offered sacrifice to the God of his father Isaac. And God said to him that night in a vision, Jacob, Jacob. And he answered, Here am I. And he said, I am God, the God of thy father Isaac: fear not to go down into Egypt; for I will there make thee a great people: I will go down with thee into Egypt; and bring thee up hither again: and Joseph shall lay his hand upon thine eyes* (Gen. xlvi. 1–4).

The inward figure standeth thus:

2. Jacob must go into Egypt in the great famine and strait hunger, with all the company he had; and he went up when he heard of Joseph, when Joseph caused him to be fetched by his sons, when he saw the present and the chariots of Joseph, then his spirit was revived, and he went up. Thus it is also in the figure of the new birth: when the Adamical man heareth the voice of the heavenly Joseph sounding in him, and seeth the chariots of the Holy Ghost in him, then he goeth up with all his powers, and goeth into the Egypt of repentance.

3. And when he cometh to Beer-sheba, that is, into the sounding noise of his heart and soul, then he sacrificeth his body and soul, with all that he hath, to the God of his father; that is, he giveth himself up with his life, and all whatsoever he is, into the Word, which created it, in Adam, and made it, out of itself; which is the God of his father: then that divine Word speaketh [or inspireth] into him, that is, it speaketh actually, operatively and powerfully in him. That night in a vision: which is as much as to say here, in the secret hiddenness of man, where God hideth himself from reason and the creature, and out of his principle speaketh or inspireth comfort and power or virtue into the life; and calleth him by his name, as he did Jacob. That is, he compriseth his name in the word of his speaking, which is the Book of Life, wherein the names of the children of God are comprised or written (Rev. xx. 12–15).

[1] Gen. xlvi.

4. And when man perceiveth him in the power, then he speaketh again into the Word, and saith, Here am I, Lord, make me what thou wilt, I stand before thee. And that same inward Word of God saith in power, I am God, the God of thy father; that is, it giveth to man, in this speaking power, divine knowledge, so that man learneth to understand that God worketh in him, and what God is.

5. But seeing the body is a dark valley, and moreover an unrighteous inclination, therefore the Word speaketh into the poor soul thus: Be not afraid when thou enterest into Egypt, viz. into repentance, and goest forth out of the land of Canaan, viz. from the pleasure and voluptuousness of the world, falsehood, wickedness and unrighteousness; although likely they become thy enemies, and persecute thee, yet fear not, I will go along with thee into Egypt, that is, into thy conversion and divine obedience, I will help thee to work repentance, and bless thee in thy Egypt, viz. in thy working of repentance, and make the new birth grow to a great tree, which shall bring forth much good fruit in the kingdom of God: as he said to Jacob, I will make thee a great people in Egypt, and will bring thee out from thence again; that is, thou shalt not remain as one dead or departed from this world; although indeed thou goest into repentance, and in thy mind forsakest the world, yet I will bring thee out of anxiety and trouble again, and leave thee in thy state and condition, if it be right and honest; which is done thus:

6. When man goeth into this Egypt he must leave all his land, viz. all his temporal pleasure and lust of the flesh, and give up all to God, and hold nothing more for his own; but think that it is not his own, but that he is a minister and servant in it, that he should serve God and his fellow members therein, and so regulate his heart as a pilgrim in his journey, who is nowhere at home in this world. He must with Jacob sit in Joseph's, that is, in the Holy Ghost's, chariot, and go whithersoever the same, in this famine, will bring him. Then God goeth in and with him, and blesseth him, so that he worketh and bringeth forth much divine fruit, and his name becometh very great in the word of God.

7. But God doth not for all that cast him out of his temporal possession. He bringeth his spirit up again into the works and labour of his hands, viz. into his worldly state, condition and employment, that therein he may serve God's deeds of wonder, also himself, and the members of his body, viz. his neighbours. Nothing will be taken away from him but only the unrighteousness, falsehood and untruth. God

maketh him now his servant in his state and condition; he may well keep and take along with him his cattle and his goods for his necessity, as Jacob did; but that which is false and wicked he must put away.

8. And when he doth thus, then saith God: Joseph shall lay his hand upon thine eyes, that thou mayest see. That is, Christ shall with his hand of grace lay hold on thy sight, blind as to God, and lay his hand of the divine sun upon thine eyes; and then thou wilt come into divine vision and knowledge in thyself, so that thy reason will wonder whence such light, and [such] deep knowledge, cometh to thee.

9. *Jacob came with seventy souls*[1] *in all, with all his children, and children's children: of which sixty-six were proceeded out of his loins, which went with him, for Joseph had begotten two sons in Egypt* (Gen. xlvi. 6, 7, 26, 27).

10. This number *sixty-six*[2] is a great and mystical number; as also the number *seventy*, which is the number of the great Babel: and the number sixty-six is the number of the beast and of the whore, from which Israel, and every child of God, must go forth.

11. This going forth of Israel is a true figure and image of the last exit and going forth of the children of Israel, viz. the right true Christian, which shall also go forth out of this Canaan, viz. out of Babel, in the end of the beast's and the whore's number: which signal star with the chariot of Joseph are clearly appeared.

12. For the great famine in the time of Jacob (wherein is the great hunger and want of heavenly food) is at hand. And not only a hunger of the soul after the bread of heaven, but also a great vehement (unheard of from the beginning of the world hitherto) impression of desire to selfhood, viz. to covetousness, extortion and pride.

13. The hunger in the wrath of God, after vanity, to devour it, is so great, that at present the powers of heaven do imprint their influence so, that all provision and blessing is consumed, and the mind of man is so hungry after vanity, that there is no rest at all upon earth for this desire.

14. Also the third Principle, viz. the spirit of the world, of the dominion in the four elements, impresseth with its power, from whence all blessing is consumed, and instead thereof an insatiable hunger of covetousness is risen up; so that the beast and the whore, together with their worshippers, are so hungry after pride, covetousness, envy, anger, unchastity, whoredom and bestial voluptuousness, and so hard imprinted or impressed in such desire, that the time is already that this beast together with the whore must burst to pieces.

---

[1] 70 The number of Babel.   [2] 66 Of the Beast and the Whore.

15. And then Jacob's spirit reviveth, and believeth that Joseph is a prince in the land of Egypt, viz. in the conversion: and there will Joseph be manifested to his brethren. And then they must be ashamed of their falsehood and wickedness, that they have suppressed Joseph, and sold him, with lying, into misery.

16. For Joseph's face in the truth shall behold all Israel and Egypt; for Israel must go forth out of Canaan, and leave Babel in the number seventy. But the hunger in Babel saith, I will first fill my sack, that I may have provision in the way: and knoweth not that Joseph hath given Israel provision for expenses; and moreover chariots and apparel; so that they shall take only their cattle along with them, and leave their dwellings and household stuff behind.

17. The provision for expenses, which at present Israel gathereth together in Babel, belongeth all to the wrathful impression of God's anger: which shall devour it all when his fire burneth. God hath beforehand, by Joseph, clearly sent his children provision for expenses; they will have fully enough, if they do not contend upon this way: sumptuous apparel is prepared for them, that they may be at rest from this disquietness of the driver.

18. But Babel thinketh, It is a long time yet; Israel must serve me, I will plague them, sure enough. But the deluge or flood, and the fire of Sodom, falleth suddenly down upon them, so that there is no escaping. He that is awake, let him watch, and take care that he doth not sleep; for the bridegroom calleth everywhere; afterwards the foolish virgins will trim their lamps: but it is too late, the hunger of Babel layeth hold and devoureth them in its jaws.

19. Moses saith further, *And he sent Judah before him to Joseph, that he might direct him to Goshen; and they came into the land of Goshen. And Joseph made ready his chariot, and went up towards Goshen to meet his father Israel. And when he saw him he fell about his neck, and wept a long while upon his neck. Then said Israel to Joseph, I will now readily die, now I have seen thy face, that thou yet livest* (Gen. xlvi. 28–30).

This figure standeth thus:

20. Judah signifieth the incorporated Covenant of God in man, viz. the divine grace in Christ. Israel sends this, that is, the whole man, before to the heavenly Joseph, and uniteth it with him, so that the heavenly Joseph, in the incorporated grace, leadeth the kingdom of nature in man, viz. the old Jacob and Adam into Goshen, viz. on the

HOW JACOB WENT INTO EGYPT

way of conversion, into the rest of Christ; that he cometh to the right goal or mark, where he findeth food for the hungry conscience, viz. the right way to salvation: where there is right teaching and instruction there Goshen is near at hand, where the soul sitteth in fatness, and feedeth in the fat pasture of Christ.

21. And when the heavenly Joseph, viz. Christ, seeth that the old Jacob, that is, the Adamical man, hath sent his Judah to him, and afterwards cometh himself, then he makes ready his chariot; that is, his operation with a powerful affection to entertainment, and goeth to meet the natural man, and when they draw near together, then this Joseph falleth about the neck of this Jacob's Adam, that is, he layeth hold on his desire and longing, and filleth it with his tears, which he shed in his sufferings, and in his victory brought through death into eternal joy.

22. With these tears of joy he kindleth the soul of the old Jacob's Adam, so that Jacob for great joy weepeth a long while on Joseph's neck, viz. in Christ's tears of joy, and mingleth his inward joy with the tears of Christ. With which tears of joy the soul of the old Jacob (Adam) is mightily comforted, quickened and strengthened in himself, in that he findeth that his heavenly Joseph in him yet liveth, that he is not dead in the famine of sins, or quite departed from him.

23. Then saith the natural man: Now I would willingly die and give up all my right and willing; now, having seen and known my loving son Joseph, that is, seeing I find that the new man in Christ is become manifest in me, therefore now I would willingly die to my willing of vanity, in his power of love: as Jacob said to Joseph.

24. *And Joseph said to his brethren, and his father's house, I will go up and tell Pharaoh, My brethren and my father's house are come to me out of the land of Canaan; and are herdsmen,[1] for they are people that are conversant about cattle; and have brought with them their small and great cattle, and all that they have. And now when Pharaoh shall call ye to him, and say, What is your employment and business? then shall ye say, Thy servants are people that are conversant about cattle, from our youth up unto this time, both we, and our father: that you may dwell in the land of Goshen: for those which are herdsmen and keepers of cattle are an abomination to the Egyptians* (Gen. xlvi. 31-34).

The inward figure standeth thus:

25. When the heavenly Joseph, Christ, hath manifested himself to the soul and Adamical man, so that they are come together, and that

---
[1] Shepherds or pastors.

they have received and embraced one another, then that same powerful Word in the spirit of Christ, which hath manifested itself in man, presseth and penetrateth again into the eternal Father's property, viz. into the eternal speaking of the Father. Which here is as much as to say, I will tell Pharaoh, that my brethren, together with all my father's house, are come to me.

26. For Pharaoh standeth here in the figure of God the Father, who is the eternal King, to whom saith Christ, viz. the Word of love and grace, that his brethren, viz. the properties of the human life, from and with all its powers and virtues, are come to him. That is, the Word, Christ, which is come from the Father into our humanity through his power and virtue, speaketh the word of the natural human life into the eternal Word of the Father: which is here called, Telling the king.

27. For Christ is even the Father's Steward over man, as Joseph was Pharaoh's. For man is then manifested again in God when Christ speaketh, telleth and inspireth him into the Word of the Father: else man could not attain God. For the human life is also proceeded from God the Father's Word: for the spirit of God spake and inspired itself from and by the Word of the Father into man (John i. 4).

28. But after it came into a creature, and became natural, it turned itself away from God's love-speaking [or inspiration of love], and manifested itself in the speaking of anger, [and] the power of [the] love-speaking was extinguished in it, viz. the second Principle, the holy generating or working of the divine power; and was not able, in its own power and strength, to enter again into the love-speaking, that it might be able to speak or generate the divine love-power: it had rent itself off from God's love, and brought itself into a natural speaking of self and vanity.

29. And this did move God's pity and compassion, and introduced his love-speaking Word again into the creaturely formed[1] word of the soul and humanity. And that now is this Joseph, whom God hath sent before, that he should inspeak or introduce the human life again into the eternal-speaking Word, and make it manifest therein before the eternal King. He bringeth the human word in the Father's property into the Word of God, and with his love reconcileth the rent and severed human word in the Father's anger-speaking; that is, in his tears of love he changeth the anger in the word of the human life into the divine kingdom of joy, and manifesteth the human life actually,

[1] Imaged, framed, or created.

and working in God: and that here is, as Joseph said, I will tell Pharaoh that my brethren and my father's whole house are come to me out of the land of Canaan.

30. For Christ is become our brother: *The Word of love became man and dwelt in us* (John i. 14). He took Adam's nature upon him; and therefore in this figure it is called his Father's house, viz. the first Adam; and his children he calleth his brethren. So very secretly and mystically the spirit of Moses speaketh, in the figure of Christ: else in this place he had said enough, in saying, My Father is come to me; if he had not had another figure under it.

31. He saith, Out of the land of Canaan, and, they are herdsmen: thus he would tell Pharaoh, that they might dwell in the land of Goshen. That, in the figure, is thus much: Christ sheweth, with his inspeaking of love into the word of his Father, that his brethren are come to him out of the vanity of the Canaanites, out of the wild bestial property; and that they from their youth up, from the time of Adam hitherto, have been only herdsmen. That is, the word of the human life ought to have dwelt in this fleshly Canaan in flesh and blood, and must and ought to have the keeping and ordering of the bestial property of the flesh.

32. For the animal soul *in spiritu mundi* [in the spirit of the world] in man hath many hundred beasts, which it hath awakened and manifested in itself, with the false and wicked lust. These beasts now must the word of the human life keep always, from Adam to this time, and must be conversant with such cattle, and manage these beasts and take care of them. Therefore now said Joseph, That they might dwell with their cattle in the land of Goshen; that is, in a peculiar place by itself, and not with Pharaoh. For herdsmen, saith the spirit, were an abomination to the Egyptians; that is, the bestial property in man is an abomination to God. Therefore Christ bringeth only the inward Paradisical ground (this time of the beast) before the face of God: but he bringeth the beast into Goshen; that is, into the outspoken or expressed creaturely substance of this world, into a place blessed of God.

33. The bestial man cannot dwell with Pharaoh, that is, in God's majesty and holy power and virtue: Joseph, or JESUS, leaveth him in the outward nature, in the kingdom of this world, and setteth him in a blessing, that he should dwell near God; but a Principle is the distinction as between time and eternity.

34. And Joseph said circumspectly, he would say they had brought

along with them their small and great cattle; to signify that the whole man with all his works were brought into the grace and fat blessed habitation before God, that Christ's children with all their earthly works were placed in Goshen, viz. in a state and condition of grace.

35. And he said to his brethren, When Pharaoh shall ask what is your trade and employment, then shall ye say, Thy servants have been herdsmen from our youth up. That is thus much: when God's spirit shall search and try what ye are in mind and thought, whether ye be angels and ministers of God, then humble yourselves before God; and say not concerning yourselves before the face of God, We sit in thy office, and are lords or potentates and rulers of the world, or rich, noble, excellent, learned, understanding persons, or such like. Do not esteem yourselves good in the sight of God; say not, We are thy dear ministers and servants in thy power; but say, We thy servants are herdsmen, from Adam to this time; we keep and manage our bestial property, viz. the works of thy wonders which thou hast made; we cannot subsist before thee, O holy God; for we are unfit, unworthy and ignorant herdsmen of thy wonders; let us but find grace in thy sight, that we may dwell before thee in this Goshen. O Lord, we know not what we shall do before thee; do thou direct and teach us how we shall manage these thy herds, for we are thy servants, and will serve before thee as thy herdsmen.

36. In this glass behold thyself, thou fair world, what thou art in thy high state, places and offices: even all of you, from the emperor to the beggar, and him that is least and lowest of all, are but herdsmen. Every one is but a herdsman, for their authority is but an office of the bestial man, and hath, under his command and management, but to rule over beasts, and no more. For no worldly office can rule over the inward divine man, he must in his office manage only a herd of beasts or cattle, and govern, take care of, and tutor them; and they tutor him again.

37. With these offices of herdsmen the earthly Lucifer now prideth and boasteth himself, as if he had an angelical government: and yet in the presence of God he is but a herdsman or keeper of beasts, and no more.

38. And therefore hath God typified and prefigured his Mysteries by such simple herdsmen, that man should see what man is in his office, state and condition; also that God's wrath may not lift up itself and destroy these shepherds and herdsmen; and so he hath always, in his prefiguration, premodelled them only as herdsmen, that he might

pour out his grace upon man's ignorance and want of understanding.

39. Herein behold yourselves, ye potent, noble, rich, learned people, all of you, one and other, how the spirit of God, in the revelation of his Mysteries, represents you by the dear Patriarchs in the manner of the herdsman's office. Ye are all, one and other, before him no other than his herdsmen; the emperor, as well as his ministers and servants; the noble, as well as his inferior, one as well as another: one in this bestial office ordereth and manageth another in another bestial office.

40. But the Pharisee will say, I keep the sheep of Christ. Woe be to him that committeth his sheep to a wolf: if he teacheth that which is good from the spirit of Christ, then it is not from his own authority and power, but the Arch Shepherd, Christ, doth it through him. But he manageth beasts only, and himself taketh one beast of the herd to himself, which must also be kept and cared for, or else the wolf will devour it.

41. Thus hath God placed all offices in the office of a shepherd, so that one should manage and take care of another; and yet they are all but shepherds before him, which keep beasts and cattle: Christ alone is the Shepherd of souls, and no other.

42. None should trust the sheep of Christ, which he hath in him, to any earthly shepherd, but only to the Shepherd, Christ, for in all the outward offices of shepherds there are wolves, which take and devour the sheep of Christ: He may pass well for one in the office of a shepherd, but let him have a care of the Shepherd's dogs, that they do not bite him.

43. O world, in thy high state and condition! O that thou didst but consider what thou art in thy state and condition in the sight of heaven; and didst not set thy state and condition so aloft in God's love: for it standeth only in his deeds of wonder, in evil and good.

44. When God would have a worldly state and condition prefigured in his love, then he set shepherds in it, or else mean, poor, despised and unesteemed people. See Abel, Seth, Enoch, Noah, Abraham, Isaac, Jacob, Joseph, Moses, David; also the Prophets and Apostles, and all holy men or saints, through whom God once manifested himself; and then thou wilt see that no highness availeth anything before him: that is but a glass of wonders, in evil and good; also a sport of God's love and anger, a premodelling or representation of the angelical dominions in light and darkness, in heaven and hell.

The Seventy-Fourth Chapter

How *Jacob* was set before *Pharaoh* with the five youngest Brothers of *Joseph*, and *Jacob* blessed *Pharaoh*; also how *Joseph* bought all the Land of *Egypt* for *Pharaoh's* own. What is hereby to be understood[1]

1. MOSES saith, *Then came Joseph and told Pharaoh, and said, My father and my brethren, with their small and great cattle, and all that they have, are come to me out of the land of Canaan; and behold they are in the land of Goshen. And he took five of his youngest brethren and set them before Pharaoh. Then said Pharaoh to his brethren, What is your employment and trade? And they answered, Thy servants are herdsmen, we and our father. And said further to Pharaoh, We are come to dwell by you in the land; for thy servants have not pasture for their cattle, the famine doth so hard press the land of Canaan: now therefore let thy servants dwell in the land of Goshen. And Pharaoh said to Joseph, Is this thy father, and are these thy brethren who are come to thee? The land of Egypt standeth open for thee; let them dwell in the best place of the land; let them dwell in the land of Goshen: and if thou knowest any among them that are fit and expert, set them over my beasts and cattle* (Gen. xlvii. 1–6).

The inward figure standeth thus:

2. When Christ manifesteth his brethren, and the old father Adam, in the power and virtue of God, that they are with all their substance come to him, and have wholly given up themselves to him, then he taketh five of the youngest brethren in the properties of life, and setteth them before God; that is, he taketh the five senses of man, which always are and continue to be the youngest in the life's property (for they are continually generated anew), and setteth these, with the power and virtue of their life, before God.

3. For these are they that shall be God's ministers and servants in the love: to these Christ in-giveth his counsel, and saith, When ye come before the face of God, so that the spirit of God in you pro-

---

[1] Gen. xlvii.

ceedeth upon you, and proveth and sifteth what your office and work is in the presence of God, then humble yourselves, and say in the presence of God, Thy servants are but herdsmen, and are come to thee in the famine of misery in our great hunger, to dwell near thee in the land of God; for in our own powers and virtues in the Adamical kingdom of nature we have not pasture and food for the poor miserable life; therefore now, O Lord, suffer thy servants to dwell in the land of Goshen, viz. in thy courts, that we may eat of the dew of heaven, [and live to thee] and serve thee in our office.

4. Then saith the eternal Father to Christ, viz. to his steward, Behold, is that thy father Adam, and are these thy brethren according to the humanity, which are come to thee? The land of Egypt standeth open for thee; that is, the kingdom of heaven, together with the kingdom of nature, standeth open to thee, thou art my steward in the kingdom of grace, and also in the kingdom of the nature of the human property; let them dwell in the best place in the kingdom of grace, and in the kingdom of nature; and if thou seest that there are men among them fit for it, set them over my cattle; that is, those among them that are fit and expert, make them officers in the kingdom of nature, that they may rule over my creatures, that is, set them in the Apostolic office, that they may feed my flock, whom thou leadest inwardly in them with thy staff or crook; let them be outwardly shepherds,[1] and lead and govern the properties of nature, viz. my sheep or beasts.

5. All spiritual shepherds in this world do sit in the office of the Father, as also the worldly shepherds, which are instituted only by Christ, through whom Christ himself inwardly ruleth and governeth; and they are all of them God's officers.

6. But whosoever are instituted in an office without the Chief Shepherd,[2] Christ, they all of them are but in the land of Canaan in the famine of God's anger, and are but devouring wolves, both one and other, be they spiritual or worldly officers, be they noble or ignoble, prince or protector or guardian, priest or sexton, one as well as another. All that ruleth in an office without God's spirit, that ruleth of self, and to the judgment of God; he that thinketh not in his office to serve God, and to manage his office as a shepherd of God, he [is a minister and servant of, and] serveth Lucifer.

[1] Note the true ministers, pastors and teachers in the Church of Christ, *Jure Divino*, who they are.
[2] Or Archbishop.

7. Moses saith further, *Also Joseph brought his father Jacob, and presented him before Pharaoh: and Jacob blessed Pharaoh* (Gen. xlvii. 7). That is, Christ set also the Adamical image before God, not only the five senses but the whole man: and he blesseth God, that is, he thanketh God and bringeth him fruit, to the praise of God, as a blessing. Then saith God, in his acting and working, *How old art thou? And he answereth, One hundred and thirty years is the time of my pilgrimage: few and evil have the days of my life been, and they reach not to the time of my fathers in their pilgrimage. So Jacob blessed Pharaoh, and went forth from him* (Gen. xlvii. 8–10).

8. Thus the Adamical man acknowledgeth and confesseth before God his evil time in the earthly desire, and saith it is but a pilgrimage, viz. a continual wandering and anxiety in continual cares and disquietness, whereby man worketh and effecteth God's wonders.

9. And Moses saith further, *There was no bread in all the land; for the famine was very sore and hard, so that the land of Egypt and Canaan were famished by reason of the famine. And Joseph gathered all the money that was found in Egypt and Canaan, for the corn that they bought: and he put all the money in the house of Pharaoh. Now when the money in Egypt and Canaan was brought, all Egypt came to Joseph, and said, Give us bread: wherefore must we die in thy presence, being without money? And Joseph said, Fetch me your beasts and cattle, and I will give you for them, seeing you are without money. Then they brought their cattle to Joseph: and he gave them bread for their horses and sheep, for their heifers and asses: and so he nourished them with bread this year for all their beasts and cattle* (Gen. xlvii. 13–17).

10. This figure is very powerful, and containeth great and deep understanding: although the bestial man, full of covetousness and extortion, imagineth to himself as if this made for him. Yet the true figure is quite against him; as also is the parable or similitude in the Gospel, of the unjust steward, which saith, *The Lord commended him that he had done so prudently* (Luke xvi. 8).

11. This famine in Egypt and Canaan, when all the land was famished, prefigureth the poor fallen man in body and soul, which the anger of God hath dried up and caused to wither, so that it is famished. For Egypt signifieth the soul's nature, and Canaan the body's nature. The great provision of corn which Joseph gathered together and sold in the famine, signifieth the divine word of grace. The money of the Egyptians and Canaanites, for which they bought corn of Joseph, signifieth God's creaturely word of the human life. The beasts which

they there gave also for bread when there was no more money, signifieth the imagelike[1] property in the life of man.

The figure standeth thus:

12. When man in soul and body in this famine and in this starving hunger cometh into God's anger and withering, then he hath no refreshment nor comfort, for his conscience withereth so quite in God's anger that he must go to the heavenly Joseph and buy this food of grace.

13. First, while the soul together with the body find yet a little power and comfort in them, though indeed the conscience gnaweth, this steward giveth Jesus Christ good words, and prayeth to him, and, for the creaturely framed or conceived[2] word, buyeth food of Joseph. And this now is that which is signified by the money: while these words will in the imagination give the conscience a little virtue and comfort, the nature of the soul and of the body continually buyeth grace for such money, and giveth this Joseph good store of babbling, with an imaginary matter and some framed or figured prayer[3] out of custom; and thus liveth of this food, in hope.

14. But when the anguish of the conscience withereth up this hope, and that such cold prayer and historical faith will no more avail, so that the conscience crieth out that thou must be famished in the anger of God, no prayer more will avail before God; then cometh the poor soul to this Joseph, and saith, Why wilt thou suffer me to perish because I cannot bring my prayer and faith before thee, by which I might attain food for my life; behold, my power is gone, I am able to do nothing,[4] I have no more words wherewith to attain thy grace.

15. Then saith the heavenly Joseph to the soul, Bring thy beasts, viz. horses, oxen and asses, hither to me, and I will give thee food for them; that is, bring to me all thy earthly natural desires and imaginations,[5] and thy false confidence in the creatures, viz. in thy own wit and subtlety, in falsehood and wickedness, and give them up all to me, that thou mayest be quit of them; then I will give thee food, that thou mayest live, and will also feed the imaginations of thy thoughts: And this is the entrance of this figure.

---

[1] Imaged or created.
[2] Imagelike, imaginary, fictitious.
[3] Conceited, contrived or set form of prayer.
[4] Note how man is able to do nothing.
[5] Or images.

16. And Moses saith further, *When that year was ended, they came to him in the second year, and said to him, We will not hide from our lord, that not only the money, but also all the beasts are gone from us to our lord; and there is no more left for our lord, but our bodies and our fields. Why wilt thou suffer us and our fields to die in thy presence? Buy us and our land for bread, that our land and we may be Pharaoh's bondslaves: give us seed, that we may live and not die, and the fields not lie waste* (Gen. xlvii. 18, 19). This is now the true earnestness, when man wholly giveth up all, and quite giveth up himself.

This figure standeth thus:

17. When man standeth thus in the famine of conscience, so that not only the words which he speaketh in the presence of God will no more avail that he might receive comfort, but that in the end those also fail, when he hath beaten down all fictitious[1] desires, and forsaken this world in the desire; then saith the poor soul to the heavenly Joseph, Alas, my lord, what shall I bring before thee that I may attain thy grace? Behold, my prayer findeth no power and virtue, and though I have forsaken the world, and have given up my bestial will, yet I still stand in great hunger before thee; I have no more left, but only my body and soul. My lord, take even this of me, I give myself wholly to be thy own. Give me thy grace, that I may live in thee: I will give myself wholly up to thee with body and life, and will be thy obedient servant. Give thou me but seed only, that is, give thou me but a will, thought, mind and desire, and sow the land of my nature; and let my life be thy servant, that I may be no more without thy will, but that I may be thy servant and thy bondslave.

18. Thus then it is enough, when he hath given up body and soul, will and thoughts, and all that he hath and is, wholly to this Joseph, that he is as it were a bondslave to God, that hopeth and expecteth only what his Lord will give him, when all trust and confidence in his own self is quite yielded up. Then is reason rightly killed, and the devil hath lost his stool [and throne] in man: for in resignation man hath nothing for his own: and the devil can no other way come at man but in the desire of selfhood [in appropriating anything for his own self].

19. And Moses saith further, *Thus Joseph bought the whole land of Egypt for Pharaoh; for the Egyytians sold every one their ground, for the famine was so sore, sharp and strong upon them: and so the land became*

---

[1] Imaged, feigned or imaginary.

HOW JACOB WAS SET BEFORE PHARAOH

Pharaoh's own. And he distributed the people into the cities, from one place of Egypt to the other, except the land of the priests, which he bought not; for it was appointed for the priests by Pharaoh that they should provide for themselves out of that portion which he had given them: therefore they dared not to sell their lands (Gen. xlvii. 20-22).

The figure standeth thus:

20. In such a manner Christ, when man in this pinching hunger draweth near to him, buyeth for his grace his whole nature, with all the forms, conditions and qualities[1] thereof, and bringeth all whatsoever is in man again into the house of the great Pharaoh, that is, of God, and maketh it subject to God his Father again.

21. For in Adam all men are become untrusty and perfidious, and are entered into the selfishness of the will, but Christ hath bought this human own self to be his own again, and giveth this up again to God his Father; and it pointeth directly at Christendom, which Christ hath bought with his grace by the treasure of his precious blood, and made it his own, and hath now distributed his offices, wherein the Christians serve him, and are his own.

22. But that the priests' fields were not sold, and that Pharaoh would not buy them, but leave them for their own, pointeth at the inward man, who is the priestly temple of Christ. This, God buyeth not back again, he willeth that man should have it for his own; he desireth only to have the kingdom of nature for his own servant. But the incorporated ground of grace, viz. the temple of Christ, he leaveth to the soul for a dowry, for it is the place and city of God, wherein God dwelleth in man. No man can sell it again, pawn it, or engage it by oaths, for it belongeth to the eternal One, and not to the possession of the creature: but it is a bestowed ground of grace, wherein Christ manageth his office: it is his habitation and dwelling house.

23. *Then said Joseph unto the people, Behold, I have this day bought you and your fields for Pharaoh: behold, there you have seed, sow your fields. And of your corn you shall give the fifth to Pharaoh; four parts shall be yours: to sow your field, for your food for your house and children. And they said, Now let us live, and find grace before thee, we shall willingly be Pharaoh's bondslaves. Thus Joseph made them a law unto this day concerning the fields: to give the fifth to Pharaoh: except the priests' fields, which were not Pharaoh's own* (Gen. xlvii. 23-26).

[1] Affections, properties or faculties.

24. This figure is a true type and image of Christendom, which Christ hath bought with his love in his blood, having proffered to give Christendom his grace and righteousness for their earthly imaginations,[1] that it should give them only up to him; and when that is done, then saith Christ, Behold, I have this day, that is, from this time forth to eternity, bought all your earthly images,[1] as also body and soul; I have bought you for my eternal bondslaves, servants and ministers, with my grace, from the hunger of God's anger. Behold, there you have seed, that is, there you have my word, wherewith you may sow the ground of your conscience, in body and soul, that this seed may bring forth fruit, and of this fruit you shall return the fifth to Pharaoh, that is, to God: for four parts shall be your food; that is, this seed shall quicken and cherish the four elements of the body, as also the four properties of the soul's fire-life; and ye shall keep this seed of the divine word fourfold, for the cherishing of your life; but the fifth ye shall give to God.

25. The fifth signifieth here very secretly and mystically the fifth form of the natural life, viz. the love-fire in the light, which is born out of the four properties, and manifest, wherein the uncreaturely and supernatural God is manifested. This form generateth now the divine joy, and the praise of God, wherein the soul is an angel, and thanketh and praiseth God, because he hath delivered it out of the fire-source of torment, and hath given himself with this love and grace into its fire-source, and changed it into a love-fire and divine light.

26. This source of love, viz. the fifth property of life, wherein the soul is an angel, it giveth now to God again with great praise and thanksgiving, for it giveth this fifth form to Christ again, for a habitation; for that is the habitation of his word, wherein is[2] the kingdom of God in us (Luke xvii. 21), and wherein we are the temples of the Holy Ghost, who dwelleth in us. And this fifth form, in the praise of God, Christ requireth again from his Christendom, that it should give this to him, that he may gather in the praise of God, that is, the fruit of love, for his Father, into the house of the divine power.

27. But the priests' fields, that is, the inward ground of the heavenly world's substance, he buyeth not with his blood, for that never received the turba of destruction, but in the fall of Adam it went out and faded, and went into the abyss, so that the soul had it no more in its own possession, for it was in the soul as it were dead, although in God nothing dieth; but the soul was blind concerning it, in that

---

[1] Images, or fancies.   [2] Or, consisteth.

HOW JACOB WAS SET BEFORE PHARAOH

manner as God, viz. the eternal One, is in and through all things, and yet nothing apprehendeth it but that which introduceth itself into its substance, wherein he will manifest himself.

28. This faded image or substance is the priestly ground, whereinto God again inspake or did sow his word and seed again in Paradise. That is not bought with Christ's blood, as the averted soul is, but it is filled with the heavenly ens, with Christ's flesh and blood, so that it is or becometh Christ's flesh and blood, wherein the High Priest, Christ, dwelleth. It is his eternal seat and possession, wherein God is manifested in man, for it is the branch on Christ's vine, which is God's proper own, and not man's.

29. It is indeed in man, but not in the possession of the fiery soul's essence; it hath another Principle than the soul, and yet is in the soul, and through the soul, and from the soul, after the manner as the light is from the fire, which is through the fire, and in the fire, and hath its manifestation from the fire, out of which fire and light air proceedeth, and out of which air dewy water proceedeth; and that same dewy water denoteth the substance of this inward ground, which giveth to the fire again nourishment, food, lustre and life.

30. So also it is to be considered and understood concerning the soul. When it extinguished as to the divine light, then this substance was generated no more from it, nor in it, but remained faded, extinguished, or quenched; and then the soul had no divine food more for its source of fire, for it had turned its desire forth into the third Principle, and was overcome by the earthly Lucifer, and by Satan, viz. by the property of the wrath, of the dark world's property in the place of this world.

31. This grace came to help this averted soul, which was bought through Christ's blood; for the buyer entered with his money of grace into this faded image, and took it to himself, and set the soul therein for a high priest and teacher.

32. And this image now was the priests' fields, which he bought not, for it was God's, beforehand. God only set his High Priest, Christ, therein, that he should therein feed and teach the poor soul, that it should not eat of the vanity, and fully darken and again bring to nothing this image.

33. And this is also the same in the figure of Joseph, in that he bought not the priests' fields; and so is the figure concerning Moses and the Levites, that they kept their fields and ground, and yet possessed them as tenants. All which denoteth the inward man of the

heavenly world's substance, which is God's ground, wherein God soweth his word of grace, viz. Christ's spirit. Which ground or substance belongeth only to the High Priest, Christ, for a possession, and not to the creaturely life; but the creaturely life receiveth power and virtue from it: it hath it indeed in itself, but it is not one and the same thing with nature: as the light and the painful source of the fire are not one and the same thing.

34. This figure of Joseph, in that he bought the Egyptians to be Pharaoh's proper own, and made them his own servants, signifieth nothing else but that Christ should buy us from the anger of God in the famine of our destruction, through his grace, to be his obliged servants, through his blood and death, and would give us his word for seed, that we might sow his purchased goods,[1] viz. our natural life, therewith.

35. And for this cause now should we give him again the fifth part of this fruit, viz. the birth of love, the fifth property of life. For in the fifth property standeth faith; and that, his children should give to him again. And this he gathereth into his Father's barns, for an eternal praise, and to the divine manifestation of his wonders.

36. But that earthly men have made such bondage,[2] and keep one another for bondslaves, and vex, torment and misuse one another therein, and squeeze out their sweat for their pomp and pride, this is an image of the anger of God, which representeth itself[3] also according to the heavenly figure.

37. For everything must fashion itself according to the ordinance or appointment of the Word of God: whether a thing fashion itself in evil, viz. in God's anger, according to the property of hell, or in good, in heaven, in the kingdom of Christ; for with the holy, the Word is holy, and with the perverse and froward it is manifest in God's wrath (Ps. xviii. 25, 26): as the people is, such also is their God, saith the Scripture.

38. Earthly men represent the image in the anger of God, in that they vex, torment, squeeze and plague them with bondage, and hold it for just and right: and it is right, in the wrath of nature in God's anger, and it is a figure of hell: and it is also a figure of the kingdom of Christ in the heavenly bondage. For all whatsoever the earthly man doth with pain and torment, that doth Christ in his kingdom with his children, in joy, love, humility, and power.

39. The earthly man taketh away his brother's labour, also his

---

[1] Or possessions.   [2] Or, bond-slavery.   [3] Imageth or modelleth itself.

HOW JACOB WAS SET BEFORE PHARAOH

will [and desires], his sweat and trade, profession and sustenance. Christ also taketh away his children's evil will [and desires], also their labour, working in God, when with great pain and anguish they press thereinto. These labours Christ taketh all from them, and gathereth them into his chest of treasure. He searcheth through and through his children's body and soul, to see whether there be yet a little sparkle that can and will administer to him and work for him; that, he driveth and necessitateth into the divine ministration of God's court, viz. into the vineyard of Christ.

40. He often also withdraweth the food of grace, and letteth them afterwards hunger and lament for it; and letteth them sit in misery, and afflicteth them, so that they must work in great anguish, in lamentation, fear and trembling, before him in divine labour; for the old Adam's ass is unwilling and untoward to labour in that which is divine.

41. And therefore it is often compelled, so that the punishment and threatening is always behind it, where Christ's spirit in the conscience threateneth it with hell and the anger of God; as also the earthly lords upon earth do with their subjects: which stand indeed in the figure of Christ, but the office is altogether unlike.

42. Christ gathereth in, for his Father, by the works of his children, much heavenly fruit, which man will obtain again, and enjoy the same for ever; but a worldly lord gathereth in by the labour and sweat of the poor, only money and goods into his chests, to his own honour, which labour the poor man can no more enjoy in this world: but Christ is his wages, in that he must serve the figure of God's anger here in misery.

43. But in the end, when the earthly offices shall be also gathered into their barns, into the treasure chests of their hearts for whom they have served and ministered, then there will be unlike and different reservatories. Many will have very much gathered into the kingdom of God's anger, and from that will his food be given to him again in eternity, viz. the curse of the oppressed, also the affliction, fear, pain and molestation of the poor, which they have here with their agitation wrought by the inferiors: that will be given them for food also after this time to eternity: for what any soweth here (Gal. vi. 7), that they will find in barns in the eternal life.

44. All offices of this world are God's, and all officers, from the emperor to the least and meanest, are God's officers. But they serve him much unlike and differently: one serveth him in love, as a minister

of Christ, and the other serveth him in his anger, as a minister of hell.

45. All that seek their own in these offices, and do not regard God and his ordinance, and so serve man therein, they serve the anger of God, and gather up, into hell.

46. For all the treasure of princes and potentates should be gathered in for the common profit of brethren, and for the supporting of good orders and offices, also of the miserable and impotent; even as an innkeeper[1] laboureth and worketh with those that are under him, and draweth the profit to himself, and yet therewith he provideth for, feedeth and nourisheth all his servants, ministers and assistants; and the overplus he useth for common necessaries of himself, his wife and children, and what he might else stand in need of, or layeth it by for poor people: such is the officer's gathering together: it should all be gathered together for common benefit, else it is a treasure of the anger of God, and must expect God's judgment.

47. But that the present potentates do thus gather together for their own honour, for voluptuousness and pride, and in that regard do the more hardly oppress and squeeze, that they may only therewith exercise their pride, and keep under the poor as dogs, and say in their hearts, They are bound to do so for me, I have bought or inherited it as a privilege, I have it of right. All this, one and other, is done in the anger of God: they all now in this property serve only Satan, viz. in the figure of God's anger, and no better.

48. All self-owning belongeth to hell, make what thou wilt of it; no seeming rhetoric will avail before God; thou gatherest together into hell: God requireth the ground of the heart, and will have trusty officers.

49. But the miserable is to know, that in such restraint and service, if he endure it without murmuring and grudging, in faithfulness, he serveth even his Lord Christ: for God thereby draweth him away from this world, so that he sets his hope upon that which is to come, and in this servility of his hands he gathereth to him with his prayer into this house of lamentation, his heavenly treasure; whereas if he for this time of his restraint stood in the voluptuousness of the flesh, he would gather no good thing: therefore all things must serve to the best of them that love God (Rom. viii. 28).

50. Thus a man ought to understand the figure under the history and acts of Joseph; for indeed the history is described with great diligence, according to the inward figure, according to the inspiration[2]

---

[1] Or householder. [2] Eingebung, inward suggestion.

HOW JACOB WAS SET BEFORE PHARAOH

of the spirit of God, which always more respects Christ's kingdom than any history of a slight and simple act.

51. For the acts of the Bible are not set down therefore because men should see the life and deeds of the old holy men or saints, as Babel supposeth. No, the kingdom of Christ above all is thereby deciphered, as also the kingdom of hell: the visible figure continually pointeth at the invisible, which shall be manifested in the spiritual man.

52. Moses here finisheth the figure of the new regeneration, under the history of Joseph, and saith further, *Thus Israel dwelt in Egypt, in the land of Goshen; and possessed it, and grew and multiplied very much. And Jacob lived seventeen years in Egypt: so that his whole age was one hundred forty and seven years* (Gen. xlvii. 27, 28).

53. *And when the time was come that Israel was to die, he called his son Joseph, and said to him, If I have found grace before thee, then lay thy hand under my thigh, that thou wilt be loving and faithful to me, and not bury me in Egypt. But I will lie with my fathers, and thou shalt carry me out of the land of Egypt, and bury me in their burying place. He said, I will do as thou hast said. But he answered, and said, Swear to me. And he sware to him. Then Israel bowed himself, sitting up at the head of the bed* (Gen. xlvii. 29-31).

54. This now is a very mystical figure, and pointeth at the resurrection of the dead, when the soul shall come to the body again; and the body will be pure and holy. For the land of Canaan, which was also full of the abominations of the heathen, signifieth the earthly body; and Egypt, where Pharaoh dwelt, and Joseph was steward, signifieth the soul, which dwelleth in God's Word, viz. by or near the eternal King.

55. And we see it very finely portrayed in this figure how Adam's soul turned itself with lust into the earthly Canaan of the earthly body, and turned away from God; therefore now the soul must go again into Egypt, into repentance to Joseph, viz. to Christ, and to King Pharaoh, viz. to God; and there it will be received as a child of grace, to be a bondservant, so that it will be obedient to God, and be his servant and minister, and must forsake the earthly Canaan, viz. the evil body, with its will and contrivances, as Israel must leave and forsake Canaan.

56. But after he should be dead, he would then have his body into the land of Canaan, that it should be buried there. Which signifieth that the earthly body must be buried in its mother the earth, and come into its first mother again; and it signifieth that the soul shall come

again out of Egypt, viz. out of the bondage of the affliction of repentance, to the body into rest: for the heathen must be driven out of Canaan, when Israel entereth thereinto. So also must the abominations in the property and condition of the body be consumed, and all false and wicked desires be killed, ere the soul come to the body again, and dwell therein.

57. And it is powerfully represented how the will of the soul shall and must in this lifetime break off from the earthly Canaan, viz. from the lusts of the body, and press into God again by earnest repentance, where then the soul must rightly be in Egypt, viz. a poor bond-servant, in much anxiety and affliction; but in the end, when the body shall die, then it also desireth to go along out of the house of bondage, viz. out of the torment of repentance, and will go again into the first Adamical pure image which God created: as Jacob would lie by his fathers, when as he might have lain as well in Egypt. But the spirit stood in the figure of the resurrection, shewing how the whole man should go again into the first image created by God.

58. But that Jacob required an oath from Joseph, that he would bury him in Canaan with his fathers; it denoteth the oath which God in Christ made with man, that God hath with his Word of love incorporated himself with man, and engaged as by an eternal oath to him. Jacob requireth this oath from Joseph, as from the figure of Christ, and desireth he should lay his hand under his thigh and swear.

59. This is a figure signifying how Christ should lay his hand, that is, his power and might, viz. the eternal Word, which is the hand that hath made all things, into the human essence in body and soul; and not only into that, but under the thigh, as under the human power, and to give himself to man for his own; and swear therein, that is, bind himself to it, that he will bring the whole man, when he is here dead in the temporal death, again into the first land of inheritance wherein Adam in innocency dwelt, viz. into Paradise, and bury the body and soul, with his oath, in God, as in the divine rest.

60. This is signified by the figure of Jacob, where the text saith, *Israel dwelt a long time in Egypt, and multiplied there.* And when Jacob was to die, he had a desire to be carried, after his death, again into the land of Canaan, to his fathers. This [I say] signifieth that a Christian or child of God must go into this Egypt, viz. into repentance, and into the exit from the earthly will, and continue therein the whole time of his temporal life, and bring forth much good fruit in that land. And then Christ, viz. the heavenly Joseph, shall bring him into the right

HOW JACOB WAS SET BEFORE PHARAOH

country of his father to rest again, viz. into the right promised land, wherein the milk and honey of divine power floweth (Exod. iii. 8).

61. And the whole history of all the five books of Moses is even this in the figure: the exit out of Canaan, and the going into Canaan again, is only this; representing how the right Adamical man should with great hosts and armies, and much purchased goods effected in the divine operation, enter again into the eternal promised land; and how in this lifetime he must be a bondservant of God's anger in this Egypt, which would, through its ministers and servants, afflict, persecute and torment him in his office of anger, and continually keep him for a bondslave, till the right Joseph shall bring him through the temporal death, again into Paradise into rest.

The Seventy-Fifth Chapter

How *Jacob*, before his End, blessed the two sons of *Joseph*, and preferred the Youngest before the Eldest. And what is thereby to be understood[1]

1. MOSES saith, *Afterwards it was told Joseph, Behold, thy father is sick: and he took with him both his sons, Manasseh and Ephraim. And then it was told Jacob, Behold thy son Joseph cometh to thee: and Israel strengthened himself and sat up in the bed, and said to Joseph, The Almighty God appeared to me at Luz in the land of Canaan, and blessed me. And said to me, Behold, I will cause thee to increase and multiply, and will make thee a multitude of people; and will give this land for a possession to thy seed after thee for ever. And now thy two sons, Ephraim and Manasseh, which were born unto thee in the land of Egypt before I came in hither to thee, shall be mine, as Reuben and Simeon. But those which thou shalt beget after them, shall be thine, and shall be named according to their brethren in their inheritance* (Gen. xlviii. 1–6).

2. In this figure now the patriarch Jacob standeth again in the limit of the Covenant, whereto God had ordained him in the mother's womb. When he had finished his course in the world with the figure of the kingdom of Christ and his Christendom, then his spirit figureth[2] itself again in the limit of the Covenant, and through the limit of the Covenant blesseth his children and his children's children, and pointeth at the future time, how it would go with them. That is, he speaketh from the root, and intimateth concerning the branches and twigs of this tree, which God in Paradise planted again after the defection and fall, and had made it manifest in Abraham: and so Jacob stood in the same stock, and intimateth from the spirit of this tree concerning his branches and twigs, but especially in both Joseph's sons, both which he grafted back again into his root, that they should be his sons, as Reuben and Simeon.

This figure standeth thus:

3. And Jacob said to Joseph, *The Almighty God appeared to me at Luz in the land of Canaan, and blessed me; and said to me, Behold, I will cause thee*

---

[1] Gen. xlviii.   [2] Frameth, modelleth or imageth.

HOW JACOB BLESSED JOSEPH'S TWO SONS

to increase and multiply, and will make thee a great people, and will give this land for a possession to thy seed for ever. In this figure the spirit speaketh not only of the inheritance of the outward land of Canaan, but also of the inheritance of the kingdom of Christ, [which is] understood and signified under this Canaan; for he saith God hath given him and his children this land for an eternal possession, in which for a long time after that they had no inheritance; therefore then in this [figure] the Kingdom of Christ is understood, which shall endure for ever.

4. Thus Jacob took the two sons of Joseph and set them in his root in the inheritance of this kingdom, and, moreover, in his first power and virtue, as Reuben and Simeon his first sons. Which signifieth how Joseph's, that is, Christ's, children in the faith and spirit (whose nature yet is come from the seed of corrupted Adam) shall be through faith planted again in the first root of God's Covenant. For Adam hath set his twigs and children with himself in the kingdom of God's anger; but the Covenant and grace taketh these Adamical twigs and puts them back again into the image of God: whose figure Jacob here represents with Joseph's sons.

5. *And Israel saw the sons of Joseph and said, Who are these? Joseph answered his father, and said, They are my sons, which God hath given me* (Gen. xlviii. 8, 9). That is, the Covenant of grace was strange to the corrupt nature, and said, Who are these children of nature in self, have they not broken themselves off from God. But Joseph, in the figure of Christ's humanity, said, They are my children, which God hath given me in the kingdom of this world. And the Covenant of grace in Jacob said, *Bring them to me that I may bless them* (Gen. xlviii. 9), that is, that I may anoint them with grace, that is, Christ shall bring them to God, that he may bless them again.

6. And Moses saith, *For the eyes of Israel were dim with age* (Gen. xlviii. 10). That is, nature, in the Father's property in the soulish creature, was grown dim and old, and that, because the soul's ens had modelled[1] itself in the time,[2] for all that liveth in the time[2] groweth old and dim. But the Covenant in Jacob groweth not old. The Covenant was that which should bless the sons of Joseph with the future revelation or manifestation of the power in the name *Jesus*; and Joseph, who stood in the image or type of the humanity of Christ, should bring them to this blessing; for the humanity of Christ bringeth Adam's children to the blessing of God: as here Joseph bringeth his sons to the Covenant of God, in Jacob.

[1] Imaged or framed.   [2] Temporariness.

7. Moses saith further, *But he kissed them, and encouraged them, and said to Joseph, Behold, I have seen thy face, which I had not thought to have done; and behold, God hath let me see thy seed. And Joseph took them from his[1] bosom, and bowed himself towards the earth before his countenance* (Gen. xlviii. 10–12): Which is as much as to say, in the figure, thus: When Joseph, in the image or type of the humanity of Christ, brought his sons to his father, viz. before the Covenant of God, then the Covenant took them in the arms, or into the bosom, of his desire, viz. into God's essence, and kissed them with the kiss of love, which God would manifest in Christ: and the father's righteousness in the Word of might and power saith to the soul's essences, Behold, thou art dim to my sight, and now I have seen thy countenance again, through the love and grace of God, which I thought not to have done; for I thought to have kept the soul in the strong and severe might of God's anger, for God's eye was departed in it, with its turning away from him, and so, as to God's righteousness, it was rent off from God: But now I have seen the countenance of the soul again, through God's love in the grace of God, and God's love hath let me see them[2] in the seed of the Covenant of grace.

8. And the spirit of Moses saith, And Joseph took them from his father's bosom, and bowed himself to the earth before his face. That is, when the Word became man, then Christ took the soul from the Father's bosom, viz. from the Father's nature, into himself, and in a creaturely manner presented himself with the assumed humanity before God the Father; and bowed, that is, humbled himself with the assumed soul, viz. God and man in one person, to the earth, that is, even into death, and entered before the face of God with our assumed soul, that is, he brought the soul's will through the introduced power of the Deity back again into the resigned humility before the eyes of God.

9. And Moses saith further, *Then Joseph took them both, Ephraim in his right hand towards Israel's left hand, and Manasseh in his left hand towards Israel's right hand, and brought them to him* (Gen. xlviii. 13). This now is the precious figure of the great earnestness of God, shewing how man is blessed again. For Ephraim was not the firstborn, but Manasseh: and Jacob laid his right hand upon the head of the youngest. But Joseph took Ephraim in his right hand, and Manasseh, in his left hand, that he might stand with the firstborn before Jacob's right hand, and

---
[1] Jacob's.
[2] The soul's essences, powers or faculties.

with the other before Jacob's left hand: but Jacob inverted the will of Joseph.

The figure standeth thus:

10. *The Word became man* (John i. 14), understand, the not-natural, un-creaturely Word of God manifested itself in God's creaturely word of man's soul, and took on him the faded light's image, and quickened or made it living in itself, and put it into God's left hand, viz. into the Father's anger: which is here expressed by setting the youngest son, viz. Ephraim, before Jacob's, viz. God's, left hand, but took it in his right hand.

11. For Christ took the incorporated Covenant of grace in the faded heavenly image (which incorporated Covenant of grace in man was the youngest, viz. the new man) in his right hand, viz. into the highest love in the name *Jesus*, and entered with this new man from the Covenant of grace before God's left hand, viz. before God's strict righteousness in the anger, that he might atone the soul, viz. the first birth; and the soul, viz. the firstborn, Christ took in his left hand, that is, he took the first Principle (which beforehand had the superior jurisdiction, authority and power) and put it under, that its power, viz. the self-will, should go back and enter into humility before God's right hand.

12. For these two sons of Joseph here rightly signify the inward spiritual man, viz. the fiery soul, which is the eldest son; also the spirit of the soul, viz. the light's power, which signifieth the other or second son, viz. the two Principles. These did Joseph, that is, Christ, set before God, and took the spirit, viz. the second Principle, in his right hand, viz. in his love, and set it with his love before God's left hand, viz. before his anger, for he should break the Serpent's head; and the soul he setteth before God's right hand, that it should receive the blessing from God, that is, that God's love should manifest itself out of the soul: but that might not be. For Moses saith, *But Israel stretched forth his right hand, and laid it upon the head of Ephraim the youngest, and his left hand upon Manasseh's head; and did so with his hands knowingly, for Manasseh was the firstborn* (Gen. xlviii. 14).

13. That is thus much in the figure: God would no more give the dominion or government to the first birth, viz. to the fiery soul, seeing it had turned away its will from God, but laid his hand of power and omnipotency upon the second, viz. upon the image of the light, which in Christ in his love became living again. To this he gave now the

power of the divine virtue, that the soul might be under Christ; for in the light's image is Christ understood, and upon it God laid the hand of his omnipotence and grace; and upon the soul, he laid his left hand, that it should be a servant and a minister of grace.

14. Thus the first birth was set behind, viz. in subjection, and the second birth foremost and uppermost in the dominion. And here is that figure concerning which Christ saith, *Father, the men were thine,* that is, they were of thy nature's property, *but thou hast given them to me*; for the Father gave to Christ the highest blessing and power, whereby the fiery soul lost its dominion of self-will (John xvii. 6).

15. And Moses saith Jacob did thus knowingly, that is, the Covenant of God knew it in Jacob that God would have it so. Jacob could not with his bodily eyes for age well know these two lads, but with the eyes of God's Covenant he saw and knew them, for God's spirit in him did this.

16. *And he blessed Joseph and said, God, before whom my fathers Abraham and Isaac have walked, the God who hath preserved me all my life long even to this day, the Angel that hath released me from all evil, bless these lads; that they may be called after my name, and after the names of my fathers Abraham and Isaac; that they may increase and multiply on earth* (Gen. xlviii. 15, 16).

This figure standeth thus:

17. The God of love blessed the incorporated Covenant of grace out of which should come Christ, viz. the heavenly Joseph: as here Jacob with his blessing began at Joseph, and blessed Joseph's sons through Joseph. Thus God also through the name of *Jesus* blesseth the soul and the spirit, for God hath appointed the name *Jesus* to be a throne of grace; and through that throne of grace he blesseth Christ's children and members according to the humanity; and here in the words of the blessing maketh no difference between the children, to signify that the soul and the spirit shall in Christ enjoy like graces and gifts; only the power he gave to the new regeneration out of the faded heavenly image, that the soul should through the power of the new regeneration work and flourish, spread forth and be great therewith, that is, that the soulish tree with its branches should grow out of this blessing.

18. In the words of this blessing there is this understanding or meaning: The incorporated ground of grace in the power and virtue of the Word spake forth the power, and comprised in Jacob his body,

HOW JACOB BLESSED JOSEPH'S TWO SONS

soul and spirit, in one, and thereby spake itself forth upon the children of Joseph: God, before whom my fathers Abraham and Isaac have walked, that is, through the wills and desires which my fathers have inclined to God, with which they have walked before God: also, through the power of God who hath sustained me my life long, even unto this day: also, the Angel who hath delivered me from all evil, bless these lads. That is, he blesseth them through the divine and [through the] human power, through the Angel of the great counsel in Christ Jesus, which Angel hath delivered men from all evil, that they should according to these names be called children of the Covenant, and in this power increase and grow great.

19. *But when Joseph saw that his father laid his right hand upon Ephraim's head, it pleased him not well: and he laid hold of his father's hand, that he should turn it from Ephraim's head upon Manasseh's head. And said to him, Not so, my father: this is the firstborn; lay thy right hand upon his head. But his father refused, and said, I know it well my son, I know it well: this shall also be a people, and be great: but his younger brother shall be greater than he, and his seed shall be a multitude of people* (Gen. xlviii. 17–19).

20. By the outward figure the spirit pointeth at their offsprings, which stock or tribe should excel the other in greatness and might; but by the inward figure of man's conversion and new birth it pointeth at the inward ground; signifying how the inward and youngest ground of the incorporated grace in Christ would be greater than the ground of the first created Adamical man.

21. But that Joseph disliked it, and would not willingly that the youngest should be preferred before the eldest, in the figure it signifieth this: Joseph stood in the figure of the new regeneration, signifying how the inward ground, viz. the eternal-speaking Word in the humanity of Christ, should turn itself forth through our soul, and take away the power of self-will from the soul, and that the creaturely soul would not that it should lose its power: it would not willingly die to its own will, but would keep its first natural right.

22. As we see in Christ's humanity, viz. in the human soul, when it was to die to self and yield up its natural right, then said Christ on the Mount of Olives, *Father, if it be possible*, that is, the human soul in him from the Father's property in the Word, said, *Father, if it be possible, let this cup pass from me*; but if it be not possible, and that I must drink it, *Thy will be done* (Matt. xxvi. 39; Luke xxii. 42): as Joseph here in this figure was loath to come to it, and would not willingly that the last should be preferred before the first.

23. The text saith it pleased him not well. The natural man is not well pleased to give up his natural right and let the kingdom of humility reign in him: he would rather be lord himself. But his own will hath squandered that away, so that he is set behind, for it is not possible that he should become the child of God unless he drink the cup whereby he dieth to his own natural will. Therefore saith Christ, *Father, thy will be done, and not my* natural Adamical human *will*, but let God's will in my inward ground be done, and not my Adamical soul's will: It shall and must be resigned into God, the first natural right must go behind, and Christ forward, else there is no salvation.

24. In this type and image the spirit of God sporteth with the children of the saints; signifying how the new incorporated kingdom of grace would spread itself forth aloft, and how the kingdom of nature should be set behind: for if Christ arise and be born in man then must Adam be servant and minister.

25. And it declareth besides that the kingdom of nature would also be great, but the kingdom of grace yet greater. Of which we have a similitude in a great tree of many branches, which through nature generateth many twigs and branches, and wherein nature is powerful; but the virtue and power of the sun is much more powerful. For if this doth not co-operate then the tree cannot grow nor bear any fruit; and we clearly see thereby that the virtue and power of the sun must get aloft, if the tree grow and its fruit come to be ripe and profitable. So also is it in man.

26. Man is nature: and nature begetteth him that he may come into the forms and conditions of the creatures. But the understanding must come forth in him, which governeth and taketh care of nature. Nature willeth indeed that its desire be fulfilled, but the understanding ruleth over nature.

27. But now nature is sooner and earlier than the understanding. Nature goeth foremost; but when the understanding cometh, then it must follow behind. Thus it is to be understood also in this figure of Jacob and Joseph, concerning the new regeneration, that when the divine understanding shall again be manifested in man, then shall nature follow behind.

28. *Thus he blessed them that day, and said, He that will bless any in Israel, let him say, God set thee as Ephraim and Manasseh* (Gen. xlviii. 20). In this text what the spirit declareth in this figure is as clear as the sun. For Ephraim and Manasseh were re-inoculated back into the root of Jacob, that is, into the Covenant of grace which God had manifested

HOW JACOB BLESSED JOSEPH'S TWO SONS

in him, and were transplanted with the birth of the natural right, when the youngest was preferred before the eldest. Thus also should all blessing and wishing be, among the children of God, that God would set them back from the evil Adamical will of self, and set them into the Paradisical Covenant again, and make them grow therein and bring forth the kingdom of grace in them, and set it above the kingdom of nature of the first Adamical birth. When this is done in man then he is a child of God again in Christ, and standeth in the blessing of God.

29. Courteous rabbis and masters of criticisms upon every letter,[1] learn, I pray, to understand the figures of the Old and New Testament, and dispute not about the outward shell of words; look upon the chief ground, why the spirit of God thus speaketh, and why it sets down such types and images. And consider what this signifieth: that the Holy Ghost, in all the figures of Christ, always sets the youngest before the eldest. Begin at Cain and Abel, and go quite through: and then you will come to rest, and your strife have an end.

30. The time of strife is at an end: Ephraim shall rule over Manasseh. If you do not so, then will the sun dazzle and blind you with its rising, that ye must for ever be blind. Ye would verily see with the eye of the kingdom of nature, and yet ye contemn the eye of grace. But Ephraim attaineth the natural right of the first birth. Why will ye strive against your father Jacob as if he did not rightly bless? For ye set Manasseh before, and Ephraim following behind. It is made manifest before the eyes of the Most High, who hath set Ephraim foremost again: the kingdom of nature in human self should be the servant: and that, ye would not. But the purpose of the Most High goeth forward, and ye are all therefore like to go to the ground: there is no preventing of it more.

31. Now when Jacob had blessed Joseph and his sons, then he represented a very secret type or image of Christendom upon earth: For thus saith Moses, *And Israel said to Joseph, Behold, I die: and God will be with you, and will bring you again into the land of your fathers. I have given thee a piece of land beyond thy brethren, that I took with my sword and with my bow out of the hand of the Amorites* (Gen. xlviii. 21, 22).

32. Although there may well be an outward figure herein, which indeed is always so, yet this is much more an inward figure of Christendom. For what could Jacob give away of that which he had not in his possession? He had not Shechem in possession, as the glosses upon this text will have it expounded, which look only at some

---
[1] Literature.

outward thing. So he could not give it severally to Joseph, for Joseph dwelt not there, but he and all his children and children's children died in Egypt.

33. Besides, Jacob said he had taken it with his sword and with his bow out of the hand of the Amorites, which is nowhere to be shewn; and yet may well be outwardly done so, seeing he saith he hath given it to Joseph (as to the type of Christendom), and took it with the sword, therefore it is a figure and secret speech.

34. For Jacob saith, Behold, I die, and ye shall come again into this land: God will bring you thereinto. This first pointeth at Christ, who should come out of Jacob's Covenant which God had in him. When that should die according to our humanity then would God bring Israel again into the land of God's Covenant, and the Covenant hath a piece of land in this world that at all times would be a dwelling for Christendom upon earth; although that piece of land would be often turned with Manasseh and Ephraim from one place to another.

35. That same piece of land or Christian habitation hath Christ taken with his bow and sword of the spirit, and subdued the princes of this world in his victory, that Christendom should have this at all times upon earth. Whereby then we see that Christendom should have the smallest victory upon earth, so that its kingdom is like a remaining overplus piece of land; that so the name of Christ might therein be outwardly known and acknowledged.

36. Further, it is the most excellent figure concerning Israel, which with Jacob, that is, with the rising of the kingdom of Christ, would die. That is, the Jewish polity and government would be suppressed, but God would in the last time bring them into this land, viz. into the true Covenant in Christ; for he hath reserved this piece of land beforehand, that they should possess the same again; which Babel believeth not. But their time is near, for the fullness of the heathen is at an end.

The Seventy-Sixth Chapter

How *Jacob* called all his Sons before his End, and signified and prophesied to them how their Generations would rise up, and what each of their State and Condition would be, whereby he expressed the Root of *Abraham's* Tree, together with its Branches and Fruit; what the State and Office of each of them would be, and how they would behave themselves, and how Christ would be born of the Stock of *Judah*: also how long their Kingdom would continue under the Law[1]

1. MOSES saith, *And Jacob called his sons, and said, Gather yourselves together, that I may make known unto you what will happen to you in the future times. Come together, and hearken, ye children of Jacob, and hear your father Israel* (Gen. xlix. 1, 2). In this chapter lieth the whole understanding and knowledge, how it would go with the children of Israel in the future time under the Law, as also afterwards with Christendom. For in this chapter the spirit hath expressed and figuratively represented the tree of Israel, with its branches, twigs and fruit, both according to the kingdom of nature, and according to the kingdom of grace; and under that signifieth concerning all states, conditions, orders and officers, among both Jews and Christians; especially the Antichristian kingdom among Jews and Christians is powerfully prefigured under it, whence it ariseth, and how it must fall to the ground again, and yet would continue a long time, even till the manifestation or revelation of Jesus Christ.

2. For Israel here under this exposition declareth concerning the whole Adamical tree, how it was good in the beginning, and how it perished; also how it would be helped again; and how the kingdom of

[1] Gen. xlix.

nature would outwardly govern in God's wrath, and yet the kingdom of grace co-operate through the wrath; whereby the natural evil man would outwardly seem as if he would serve God and minister to him, but would only be a false flattery and show of hypocrisy, so long till Christ would break forth out of God's Covenant, and destroy Satan's hypocritical kingdom.

3. And he beginneth at Reuben, viz. from the first power of the human life, and reacheth to Benjamin, the last, under whom Christendom is powerfully prefigured, and what its properties would be; so also are the times and ages of the world powerfully portrayed under it. If the Reader will observe it, and gather the sense thereof, then he will find our exposition in the true and right ground.

I

THE TESTAMENT OF REUBEN

4. He began at Reuben, and said, *Reuben, my first son, thou art my power and virtue, and my first might and strength, the chiefest in the sacrifice, and the chiefest in the kingdom and government: He was vain and fickle therein as water: thou shalt not be the chiefest, thou didst climb up into thy father's couch, and there hast defiled my bed with thy climbing up* (Gen. xlix. 3, 4).

In the figure it standeth thus:

5. The spirit in the Covenant speaketh forth the human nature of Adam, viz. the first power of the first seed to a re-propagation, as indeed Reuben also was the first power of Jacob; and signifieth that the natural first Adamical man should be the chiefest in God's sacrifice; that is, he should bring forth right fruit to him, which might be to the praise of God, and in the virtue thereof increase the heavenly joy. He should generate virtue to him, and a re-expression through the implanted Word of God. And that is called sacrificing to God, when the creaturely human word, which God formed into a creature, viz. the human understanding life, re-expresseth God's word out of itself, and formeth itself in holy images [thoughts or imaginations].

6. Which formation is effected in the generating of the heavenly mercurial harmony, viz. after that manner as when the implanted word in man imageth or frameth itself into a song of divine joyfulness, and sporteth in the holy pure element before God; in which modelling[1]

[1] Framing, figuring or imaging.

HOW JACOB CALLED ALL HIS SONS BEFORE HIS END

or holy desire the holy wisdom of God co-modelleth, and becometh figured in wonders; whereby the eternal One becometh formable and distinct, viz. is known in different varieties. This is called sacrificing to God, in that manner as twigs and branches bear fair fruit to the tree, whereby the tree is known and manifested to be good: thus also the creaturely formed word, viz. man, should, to the eternal-speaking holy Word of God, which Word is the stock, generate or bear to the stock good fruit, viz. the praise of God.

7. This is as much as to say: Adam was the chiefest in the sacrifice, for he was the first out-spoken or expressed word that God spake in his image, and was also the chiefest in the kingdom or government; for to him belonged the eternal dominion: he was created out of the eternal, in and to the eternal, he was the image of God, wherein the word of God according to time and eternity was imaged or framed.

8. Therefore now the spirit in the Covenant representeth this before him by the stock of Israel, out of which the new tree should spring out of the old, and pointeth at both the Adamical and also the new tree of regeneration, and speaketh further concerning the first power in Adam and Jacob, viz. concerning the kingdom of nature, of the first image.

9. He was unstable or fickle therein as water, as we experience that in Adam and all natural men as Adam suddenly and unstably therein departed from his glory, both from the divine kingdom and also from the sacrifice of God, and entered into self-will, and forsook God's will, and brought himself from the divine formation[1] into an earthly formation, with the desire and lust, whence he became bestial and evil.

10. Whence now the spirit in the Covenant saith through Jacob: Thou shalt not be the chiefest; that is, the first image shall not keep the government, neither in the dominion of the kingdom, viz. of the natural power and authority, nor in the sacrifice of God; but the second Adam, Christ, out of Judah, shall be he; and therefore, because thou hast climbed up upon thy father's couch, and there hast defiled my bed with thy climbing up.

This figure standeth thus:

11. Adam had his Father's chaste marriage-bed in him, when his Eve was yet unmade. He was man and woman, and yet neither of them, but a true and right marriage-bed of God, wherein God's Word

---
[1] Imaging or modelling.

in his marriage in both tinctures, viz. of the fire and light, worketh in power; for he stood in the image of God, in which God wrought, as in the holy angels. The propagation stood in one single image. As God is in one eternal substance, so also was he, who was out of that same substance of all substances, created in one only image; for the spermatic nature and kind was in him the *Verbum Fiat* [the Word *Fiat*], which had formed him into the image of God, wherein the self-love lay, viz. in the perpetual conjunction of both properties of the only tincture, viz. the power of the holy magic fire and light, which is spiritual, and the true life.

12. In this image he was the chiefest in the sacrifice, and in the kingdom; for he could sacrifice to God both spiritually and creaturely, in that manner as a tree, without the interposition or supply from another, doth itself bring forth its branches and fruit, and thrusteth forth from itself the fair blossoms in a lovely smell and virtue, with fair colours according to its kind, and that, as God's Word had ejected and generated it out of itself: all this power lay also in him.

13. But the self will was unstable and fickle therein, and brought itself into a bestial property, into false and wicked lust and desire, and climbed with the bestial lust and desire into this holy marriage-bed of God. Into which lust Satan brought it, viz. the ground of the dark world according to the imaging or representation of fancy, as also the devil with the holding forth of the monstrous bestial property, together with the subtlety and wit of the Serpent, viz. of the ground of the first Principle. So that the self-will plunged itself therein, and was infected therewith, and made its power of imaging or thinking, according to soul and body, monstrous, whence the bestial imagination in Adam awaked and began.

14. And here he climbed up upon his Father's, viz. upon God's, marriage-bed, and defiled it with bestial, as also devilish, false and wicked, imaginations. Which lust he introduced into God's concubine, viz. into the heavenly sperm or seed of the heavenly world's substance. Upon which God's spirit, viz. the holy Word in this heavenly substance, departed from him. That is, the self-will of man rent itself off from the will of the Word; and now it was unstable in the devil's poison, and lost the kingdom and the priesthood, viz. the princely throne, and was thereupon weak and blind as to God, and fell down into sleep, and lay, between God and the kingdom of this world, in impotency and weakness.

15. Now thus saith Moses, And God suffered or caused him to fall

into a deep sleep, and framed a wife[1] out of him (Gen. ii. 21, 22), and brought her to him, and gave him a bestial marriage-bed for a heavenly: where he may now copulate in self lust, which, in the presence of heaven, is but a defiled marriage-bed, but is born withal under God's mercy in divine patience, seeing that the vessel of this marriage-bed must consume, rot and die. And Christ hath given in himself in this marriage-bed into the middle, as a Mediator and Redeemer from this monstrous image, which he will regenerate anew in himself.

16. This powerful type or image the spirit of God also represents by Reuben, who was Jacob's first virtue and power, wherein the desire of Reuben also modelled itself in the Adamical image, and went back and lay with his father's concubine, and in falsehood and wickedness copulated with her: as the free will of the soul in Adam copulated with God's concubine in him, by false and wicked lust, and became a breaker of wedlock to God, as Reuben did.

17. And for the sake of this hath Adam, viz. the first power of the natural man, in all men, lost the kingly priesthood, so that the natural man in his own power and virtue can no more offer sacrifice to God; also he understandeth nothing more of God's word or kingdom, It is foolishness unto him (1 Cor. ii. 14), and he cannot apprehend it any more: For he standeth in a poisonous monstrous image, which in this Adamical property cannot inherit the kingdom of God, and hath lost the kingdom of God, and is now but a figure or similitude of this world and of hell; a monster [instead] of the image of God, and shall no more be the chief in the sacrifice and kingdom, but Christ in the new birth in him hath attained the kingdom in the sacrifice and government.

18. The natural man, viz. the first power and virtue, must be servant, and lay off the monstrous whorish image, and be new born again: the soul, through the spirit of Christ, and the body, through the putrefaction of the earth, from which, at the end of the day,[2] he shall be severed and be formed again into the image of God.

II and III

THE TESTAMENT OF SIMEON AND LEVI

19. *The brethren, Simeon and Levi, their swords are murdering weapons. My soul, come not into their counsel, and my honour, be not thou in their churches,*

[1] Or, woman.   [2] Last Judgment Day.

assemblies or congregations; for in their anger they have slain a man, and in their stubborn self-willedness, they have destroyed oxen. Cursed be their anger, because it was so vehement and fierce; and their wrath, because it was so raging: I will divide them in Jacob, and scatter them abroad in Israel (Gen. xlix. 5–7).

20. In this testament the spirit very wonderfully taketh the two brethren together, and represents their figure accordingly, which ought well to be observed; as also the spirit of Moses, in the thirty-fourth chapter, taketh them together; where he saith, *Simeon and Levi took their swords, and went boisterously into the city, and slew Shechem, together with Hamor his father, and all the males that were in the whole city, and took the women and children captive, and spoiled all* (Gen. xxxiv. 25–29); which might indeed be the action and robbery of two stout young men. But the spirit hath in that place, as also in this, its figure, according as Jacob saith, He would tell them how it would go with them in after times.

21. In Reuben the spirit representeth before the Adamical corrupt nature, that the first virtue and power of man squandered away God's priesthood and kingdom, viz. the kingdom of heaven, and defiled God's marriage-bed, and made a bed of whoredom thereof. But now in this figure the spirit of God representeth a powerful figure, signifying how the first power of man would nevertheless desire to keep its priesthood and dominion, and what kind of priests and rulers would be in this world, in the kingdom of self nature.

22. For out of the stock of Levi came the priesthood under the Law; and of this the spirit here speaketh, and joineth Simeon to him, viz. the worldly dominion, and saith of them both, as of one, *Your swords are murdering weapons. My soul, come thou not into their counsel; and my honour, be not thou in their Churches.* That is, God's living Word, which he calleth his soul, shall not be in the dominion of this earthly world, viz. in man's first natural self-power, his holy Word shall not be in their counsels and determinations, wherein they seek only temporal voluptuousness and riches. Neither shall it be in their Churches and priesthood, because they do but flatter with the mouth; for he saith, *My honour, be not thou in their Churches.*

23. But his Church is the true image of God from the heavenly world's substance, which, in their murder, by the introduced poison of the Serpent, faded in Adam, and is born again in Christ. But seeing they would only play the hypocrite before God in the monster of the Serpent, and had not the Church of God in them, therefore saith the spirit, *My honour, be not thou therein.*

HOW JACOB CALLED ALL HIS SONS BEFORE HIS END

24. For God's honour, together with Christ Jesus, shall not come from the natural Adam, but from God and his holy Word. These should be the holy Church of God in man, viz. the image of the heavenly world's substance, which died in Adam, and budded forth again in Christ; in this should God's honour appear; as when life buddeth forth through death: this was God's honour. But the Adamical self-will, which was a murderer, and murdered the heavenly image in him, shall not have this honour: this honour shall not appear in his murderous will.

25. In this image the figure standeth clearly, which is portrayed in the *Apocalypse* (Rev. xvii.) of the great seven-headed dragon, upon which the Babylonish whore rideth, where the dragon and whore are prefigured as one image: and it is even the same with this of Simeon and Levi, and it signifieth, in the Adamical corrupt power in the monstrous image, the government of nature in self-will, together with the sectarian hypocritical priesthood.

26. The seven heads of the beast are the seven properties of nature, which are departed from the temperature, and have attained seven heads, viz. a sevenfold will, whence the life is come to be in strife, misery, sickness and corruption; and the whore upon this beast is the soul, which is defiled as a whore, and entereth before God with this whore's image, and playeth the hypocrite in his presence.

27. But the will of the seven-headed beast giveth its power and strength to the whore, viz. to the soul, so that the soul sticketh full of murder, pride, whorish lust, and self-honour; and in this Church and den of murder God's honour will not be.

28. This figure and magic exposition concerning Simeon and Levi prefigureth to us the spiritual, and the worldly, dominion. First, in every man, whereby he governeth himself both in spiritual and in natural things; and secondly, the management and authority of spiritual and of worldly offices, both in the Church and in worldly matters; whatsoever ruleth therein in Adamical self-power, without the new regeneration, that beareth this image in it, viz. the murdering sword, where men condemn and slay one another with words.

29. All scurrilous, slanderous, libellous books, wherein men reproach and kill one another with words for the sake of the divine gift and knowledge, are the murderous swords of Simeon and Levi. Also all unrighteous sentences of worldly judgment are the same, and God's honour and will is not therein.

30. The spirit taketh them both together in one figure, because both these offices govern the Adamical nature. They govern the world, viz. the formed outspoken word of God, [and] to them is given the power and authority of the kingdom of nature: but they shall give an account of this government. For the judgment of God is set in this figure, and the *Apocalypse* (Rev. xix. 20) casteth the falsehood and wickedness of this image down into the fiery lake that burneth with brimstone, and sealeth up the beast and the whore in eternity, and giveth the kingdom, the power and authority, together with the priesthood, to Christ, and [to] his children born of him.

31. The spirit of Moses saith, *In their anger they have slain a man, and in their self will they have destroyed oxen* (Gen. xlix. 6). The man signifieth the inward spiritual man, viz. the true image of God, which Adam murdered, in all his children, through his anger, viz. through the first Principle (the kingdom of God's anger, which Adam awakened with his desire and lust); and it signifieth further, Christ that should come, whom the Levites, with the Simeonites, viz. worldly dominion, viz. the Pharisees and heathenish government, would kill. For Jacob said he would make known to them what would befall them in the future times.

32. Therefore this figure looketh at the future man, Christ, whom the Levites would slay in their envy and anger, as is also come to pass: and for that cause shall his honour be no more in their Churches. For after such slaying of Christ their Church was taken from them, and the temple destroyed, and their sacrifices ceased, in which formerly the figure of Christ, viz. God's honour, stood.

33. But the oxen, which they have caused to perish in their self-will, signifieth the outward man from the limus of the earth, which they have caused to perish with the desire of vanity, so that it is become so grossly bestial and miserable that it is turned from a heavenly Paradisical image into a corruptible one, which is done out of self-will.

34. Further, it pointeth at the future self-will of the Levites, with their worldly dominion, signifying how they would slay and kill with their murdering swords: whereas they can destroy no more of God's children but the oxen, viz. the bestial man. Which murdering swords have ever been among this generation, both with the Jews and [with the] Christians: which the children of God ought well to observe, that the spirit of God in the Covenant saith, *his soul shall not be in their murderous counsel, nor his honour in their Churches*; for the sake of which

they murder and destroy many that will not believe their sects and self-willed conclusions and determinations.

35. Especially at this present time, when men strive only about the Churches and Church matters, and murder one another for such things, and destroy land and people in their self-will; men living only in self-will, and do not intend to seek God's honour thereby, but only their own honour, might, authority and power, and thereby fatten the ox, viz. the belly-god. The honour of God and his word is not among all these; but as Jacob saith, *Cursed be their anger, for it is vehement and fierce, and their wrath, for it is raging*; for they do all out of self-will and anger; and therein the anger of God driveth them on: and therefore they run on into the curse, in the murderous swords.

36. And it saith further, *I will divide them in Jacob, and scatter them in Israel*; which is indeed befallen them, so that they are divided and scattered among all people, and have now no city, country or principality more. Also the spirit intimateth the dividing of the earthly life, wherein this anger and self-will must be quite divided from it, and the body be scattered like ashes. For the curse breaketh in pieces and scattereth both its dominion and priesthood, together with its body and outward senses and life; for in the presence of God it is all only a curse and vanity.

37. For the spirit of Jacob saith, *I will divide them in Jacob*, that is, through the Covenant of Jacob, viz. through Christ; *and will scatter them in Israel*, that is, through the new sprout out of the Covenant the Adamical tree shall be destroyed and divided, and its works, together with its body and thoughts, be scattered, and the works of the devil be brought to nothing. Also this their priesthood and dominion shall be yet so destroyed, divided and scattered as the chaff is by the wind, when the kingdom of Christ and his priesthood shall spring up, where Christ alone shall reign: and then all this will have an end, which seems strange to Babel.

IV

THE TESTAMENT OF JUDAH

38. *Judah, thou art he, thy brethren will praise thee: Thy hand will be upon the neck of thy enemies; thy father's children will bow down before thee. Judah is a young lion: thou art come aloft, my son, through great victory: He hath stooped down and couched, as a lion, and as a lioness: Who will set upon him to rouse him up? The sceptre will not be removed from Judah, nor a master from*

his feet, till the Saviour come; and to him will the people cleave. He will bind his foal to the vine, and his she-ass's colt to the precious branch: He will wash his garment in wine, and his mantle in the blood of grapes: His eyes are redder than wine, and his teeth whiter than milk (Gen. xlix. 8-12).

39. By the first three sons of Jacob, the spirit intimates concerning the corrupted lost Adam and his children, signifying how they were in the sight of God, and what their kingdom upon earth would be. But here, with Judah, he beginneth to intimate concerning the kingdom of Christ, viz. concerning Christ's person and office, and setteth Christ in the fourth line, which is a great mystery; for in the fourth property of the generating of nature is understood the fire, viz. the original of the fire, out of which the light taketh its original, whereby the abyss becometh majestic: wherein then also the original of life is understood, before the soul is therein understood according to its property.

40. Seeing then this soul's ground in Adam was fallen and perished, therefore hath God also set his figure of the new life therein, and in this testament of the twelve patriarchs the figure standeth, signifying how the beginning of life is, and how the new birth springeth forth in the light again, through the perished fire-life in the light. Also in the Testament of Judah all circumstances are declared, shewing how the new life in Christ would spring forth through the soul, and rule over the sting of death.

41. Jacob saith, *Thou art he: thy brethren will praise thee*. In this he looketh outwardly upon the earthly kingdom, which should arise in the future time: and inwardly he looketh upon the kingdom of Christ, which both Jews and heathen would embrace, and praise and honour Christ as God and Man.

42. And he saith further, *For thy hand will be upon the neck of thy enemies*. By this he understandeth and meaneth, not only the Jews' outward enemies; but that the hand, viz. the power of Christ's grace, would essentially, actually and effectually be upon the neck of Satan, and the Serpent's poison and will, in flesh and blood, and evermore trample upon that Serpent's head in his children of faith.

43. Also, *Thy father's children will bow before thee*. That is, before this Christ of the stock or tribe of Judah will all the children of God stoop, bow, and pray to, as a God-Man and Man-God.

44. Also, *Judah is a young lion*. That is, one roaring against the devil, and a destroyer of death and hell, as a fresh, young nimble lion, mighty in strength and power.

45. Also, *Thou art come aloft, my son, exalted, by a great victory*. That

is, after he had the victory over God's anger, over death, sin, the devil and hell, he was placed at the right hand of God's power, as a Man-God, and ruleth over all his enemies.

46. Also, *He stooped and couched down, as a lion, and as a lioness, Who will set upon him to rouse him up?* That is, he hath so deeply humbled himself with his highest love, and rendered himself in our assumed humanity into the scorn and contempt of the fallen man, and stooped into God's anger, and suffered the natural life to break in pieces, and very patiently given his strong lion's might thereinto.

47. But that the text saith, *as a lion and as a lioness,* it signifieth the young lion of the divine Word in the soul, and the lioness signifieth the name *Jesus,* in the most inward ground of the heavenly world's substance, viz. the noble lioness of *Sophia,* that is, the right seed of the woman from the Adamical light's tincture, which faded in Adam, and in this lion was made living again in divine power, and associated itself again to the lion, viz. to the soul.

48. Also, *Who will set upon him to rouse him up?* That is, who can set himself against this lion and heavenly holy lioness to rouse them up, which are God over all and through all? Who will take away his power, Who is the beginning of all power, strength and might? Where is the champion that can strive when there is no higher power to be had?

49. Also, *The sceptre shall not be removed from Judah, nor a master from under his feet, till the Champion or Saviour come; and to him will the people cleave.* The understanding or meaning of this is twofold, viz. outwardly concerning the kingdom of Judah, that the Jewish sceptre of its kingdom should continue, and they be a kingdom, till this Champion or Saviour, viz. the lion with the lioness, viz. Christ, that is, this Covenant, should become man; which is so come to pass that they held their kingdom, though it seemed often as it were quite overthrown, till Christ. And then it quite ceased, and there was another Master or Governor that ruled it, for since that time they must be servile people; for the Champion or Saviour hath taken to himself their kingdom, and is therewith entered in among the heathen, and hath called them also to himself.

50. But the inward ground is this: that the kingdom of Christ, and his dominion over sin, death, the devil and hell, will not cease, nor any other ruler or master come from between his feet, that is, from the Covenant of God, till this Saviour, Christ, should come again to judgment, and sever his enemies: then shall he deliver up the kingdom

again to his Father, and then God shall be All in All. Therefore do the Jews in vain hope for another master or ruler: although indeed he will come to them also in the time of his revelation, manifestation or appearing, which time is near, wherein the kingdom of Christ will be manifested to all people.

51. Also, *To him will the people cleave.* This is done already according to his humanity, and will much more be done in his last manifestation, that all people will cleave to him and acknowledge him. When Babel taketh its end then will this be first perfectly fulfilled, which dependence and cleaving to him at present the images, imaginations or fictions of opinions and sects in Babel, do keep back, in that the strange and foreign people and nations stumble, and are scandalised at the contentions and disputations of confounded speeches,[1] and withhold from it.

52. But when the tower of Babel falleth on every side, then shall all people cleave to him, honour and serve him, which dependence and cleaving to him supposed Christendom hath hindered by the Antichrist, which hath a long time sat in the seat of Christ as an earthly god. When this ceaseth, then will the kingdom of Christ be wholly manifest, which men at present behold only in images:[2] This is understood by those of our society.

53. Also, *He will bind his foal to the vine, and his she-ass's colt to the noble branch.* O thou poor, sick, old, miserable Adam, if thou didst understand this rightly, then thou wouldst be delivered from all strife. What is the foal and the she-ass's colt? The foal is the human soul: for the young lion signifieth the power of the divine Word in the soul; but the foal is the natural soul, which Christ should bind to the vine of the sweet-tasted divine love, viz. the eternal-speaking Word would bind this foal, the creaturely soul's word of the soul's essence and substance, to itself, and be married to it; and the she-ass is the inward Paradisical man, viz. the divine man, from the ens of the inward ground, from the heavenly world's light's substance, viz. the Virgin Sophia.

54. This she-ass, which must bear the outward burden of the bestial man upon it, should Christ, that is, the Word, bind to the name *Jesus*, viz. to God's own self-subsisting substance, viz. to the most noble branch, which beareth the sweet wine of the love of God.

[1] Or, words of jarring contention.
[2] Or opinions, without certain knowledge.

55. And this she-ass is the temple of God, wherein the kingdom of God is again manifested in us; it is Christ in us (Col. i. 27 and iii. 11), which, as a she-ass in man, himself taketh upon him the burden and sin of man, and slayeth it through the young lion.

56. This inward new spiritual holy man is rightly the she-ass's colt, for it must be manifested through the soul, as light is manifested through fire. Thus a man is to understand that the light is the fire's colt, and is manifested through the fire from the dying of the candle: thus also it is to be understood in the ground of the soul, which is also a fire-spirit.

57. O thou poor Christendom! if thou didst understand this rightly, and didst press into it, so that thou also, with this she-ass which faded in Adam, stoodest bound to the foal's noble branch, what need of striving then? Is it not now a simple she-ass which beareth Christ and Adam upon it, viz. Christ in it, which is its noble branch, viz. its sap and power, and Adam upon it as a burden?

58. O thou Babylonish whore! thou keepest off this she-ass with thy dragon-beast, so that poor Christendom must bear thy evil beast; whereon thou, whore, ridest: but thy time is near, that thou art to go into the abyss of hell-fire, saith the spirit of wonders.

59. Also, *He will wash his garment in wine, and his mantle in the blood of the grape.* That is, Christ will wash our humanity, viz. the garment of the soul, in the wine of his love, and with the love wash away from the defiled Adamical flesh the earthly dross and spawn of the Serpent, that Adam had received with his desire and lust, from which the earthly man became a beast; and leave the spawn of the Serpent to the earth, and in the end burn it up with the fire of God.

60. *And his mantle in the blood of the grape.* The mantle is the cover which covereth the washed garment, and is even the precious purple mantle of Christ, viz. the scorn, affliction, torment and suffering; when he thereby washed our sins in his blood, that is, the right blood of the grape, wherein he washed his mantle, which now he casteth over our garment and covereth it, viz. over our humanity, that God's anger and the devil may not touch it.

61. O man! consider this. This mantle will not be cast over the beast and the whore, to cover them, as Babel teacheth, but over the washed garment that is washed in right true repentance with God's love: this garment of the soul will be covered with the mantle of Christ, which is once washed in his blood of the grape; and not whores, panders, unclean persons, covetous extortioners, unrighteous,

cruel, raging, stern and proud; so long as they are such they have only the mantle of the Babylonish whore about them, and get not this holy washed mantle of Christ upon them; flatter and play the hypocrite as much as thou wilt, yet thou wilt not get it, except thou art washed beforehand; thy comforting thyself will not avail thee, thou must set upon it in earnest, that thy she-ass may live, and thy foal be essentially bound to the vine, Christ, else thou art a member of the whore sitting upon the seven-headed dragon; and if thou couldst pass through the thrones of heaven, yet thou wouldst be but a child of the dragon.

62. O Babel, Babel, what hast thou done, in covering the beast with this mantle, and thyself remaining under it, a wolf?

63. Also, *His eyes are redder than wine, and his teeth whiter than milk*. His eyes are now the fire-flaming love, which pierce and press through the Father's anger, and look through the fiery soul, wherein the Father's anger in the fiery soul becometh a light-flaming love-fire; and so the soul's essence is thereby become a sweet, pleasant tasted, divine, red love-wine; one property in the soulish essence tasting the other in great desire of love, and the Father's property of anger flowing forth in a clear, good, pleasant relish.

64. *And his teeth are whiter than milk*. These white teeth are the desire of the inward spiritual man, where the holy word is together in the desire of these teeth, which white teeth of heavenly desire apprehend, eat and drink, the grape of Christ's blood; for it is the spiritual mouth, for which Christ hath ordained his testament, that it should with these white teeth, *eat his flesh and drink his blood* (John vi. 53). This the spirit of the Covenant declareth clearly and plainly by Jacob.

65. For the testament of Judah pointeth throughout at Christ, at his person, office and kingdom. For of Judah Christ should come according to the humanity; outwardly the figure of the type standeth, and inwardly, in the spiritual figure, Christ standeth clearly.

The Seventy-Seventh Chapter

A Further Exposition of *Jacob*'s Testament, Concerning the other Eight Sons, how both the Jewish Government or Kingdom on Earth, and also Christendom, is typified under it. Shewing how it would go with them[1]

1. BY the first three sons of Jacob is typified in the figure the kingdom of perished or corrupt nature, viz. the Adamical man, what it is; and by Judah, Christ is typified, who should come and bring the Adamical man into his kingdom; but by the other eight sons of Jacob is typified only the figure of worldly offices, states and governments; signifying how the Adamical man would manage the superior dominion, and how also the inward figure of the kingdom of Christ would stand close by it.

2. For here in the outward figure is first typified where each tribe or stock would have their dwelling and habitation, and what their office in Israel would be. But near to it standeth always the figure representing how the outward and the inward man would stand close by one another; and how the kingdom of nature and the kingdom of grace would dwell one by another; also how the seven properties of nature in God's anger, according to the first Principle, would also put forth or explicate themselves, and introduce themselves into figure, to the divine manifestation: Which the Reader should well observe and consider, for we will explain both the inward and the outward figure.

V

THE TESTAMENT OF ZEBULUN

3. *Zebulun will dwell at the haven of the sea, and at the haven of ships, and reach to Zidon* (Gen. xlix. 13). This first is the outward figure, shewing where this tribe or stock will dwell in the promised land: but the spirit also hath its figure to which it pointeth.

4. For Zebulun, in the Language of Nature, in sense, is called a desire or longing that goeth to God, which longing resides with good

[1] Gen. xlix.

people; and it signifieth here that the Adamical man would dwell near God, and that he would have delight and refreshment from the divine co-habitation.[1] For Jacob begat Zebulun of Leah, who otherwise was not esteemed, because she was tender-sighted and blear-eyed, and not so fair as Rachel was; which Leah, put her hope in God, that he would bless her, that she should be fruitful and bear children to her husband Jacob.

5. Now when she bare Zebulun, she said, God hath pleaded well for me (Gen. xxx. 20); that is, I turned my desire to him, and he hath fulfilled it for me. Now his will dwelleth with mine, and she called him [Zebulun][2] a near dwelling or co-habitation, that is, God dwelleth with me, and now also will my husband dwell with me in love; and it signifieth that the grace of God in his mercy and compassion shall still dwell with the poor Adamical perished or corrupt children of flesh, and not forsake them in their misery.

6. But it hath more respect to the Covenant, that the children of the Covenant in their Adamical nature would be a near co-habitation in hope, and that the outward man would not apprehend the kingdom of Christ, but would be a near co-habitation with it, where Christ should dwell in the inward ground, viz. in the spiritual world, and Adam in this time [of the life],[3] and yet be a co-habitation.

7. For as the spirit hath by Judah declared Christ in the flesh, so now here he declareth that our outward man would not be Christ, but be a co-habitation of Christ; Christ would possess the inward ground; as he also saith, *My kingdom is not of this world.* Therefore the outward mortal man should not say of itself, I am Christ; for he is only a co-habitation of Christ, as the outward world is only a co-habitation or near neighbourhood to the kingdom of Christ; for Christ is the inward spiritual world, hidden in the outward visible world; as the day is hidden in the night, and yet they dwell one by, near and with the other.

VI

THE TESTAMENT OF ISSACHAR

8. *Issachar is a strong-boned ass, and he lodgeth in valleys, between the borders or hills of the country. And he saw rest, that it was good, and the land, that it was pleasant and fruitful; but he hath bowed his shoulders to bear, and is become a tribute servant* (Gen. xlix. 14, 15). In this testament of Issachar

---

[1] Neighbourhood. [2] זְבֻלוּן [3] World or outward life.

FURTHER EXPOSITION OF JACOB'S TESTAMENT

the spirit pointeth, first, at the outward figure of this tribe or stock, shewing where they should dwell, viz. in the midst of the land, in good ease and rest, but yet be tributary: but the powerful figure looketh upon the inward ground, viz. upon the human nature.

9. For when Leah bare Issachar, she said, *God hath rewarded me, in that I gave my maid to my husband: and she called him Issachar* (Gen. xxx. 18), that is, a divine wages or reward: for she had given Rachel her son's mandrakes, that she suffered Jacob to sleep with her this night, upon which she conceived this son, therefore she called him a recompense from God.

10. But the spirit saith in this figure he would be a strong-boned ass, and lodge between the borders; which outwardly in its habitation was just so. But in the inward figure, he saith, the man which is obtained from God by prayer is indeed a gift and wages, but his Adamical nature is only a strong-boned ass for the burden, who beareth the Adamical sack. But he dwelleth with his mind between the borders; viz. between God and the kingdom of this world: his mind presseth into the borders of God, and the body dwelleth in the world.

11. Therefore the mind must be as a boned, servile, slavish ass, which, though it sitteth at ease and rest in a good habitation in the borders of God, yet it must bear the burden of sins and of death in the earthly sack, and there is no buying it off with the mandrakes before the death of the earthly man; also no praying to God for it availeth that thereby the strong-boned ass might come to divine liberty: it must remain an ass, till Christ in himself bringeth it into the eternal rest. The Adamical hurt and loss is so great that the ass must leave the sack in the death of Christ, else he will not be rid of it.

12. But he addeth the cause why he must remain a strong-boned ass, for he saith, *He saw the rest, that it was good, and the land, that it was pleasant.* That is, that the mind would always desire to rest in the lust and pleasure of the flesh, and would desire to take care of the earthly lust; and in that regard the mind must be a servile ass, and servant of God's anger; and so separateth the natural Adamical man from the seed of the Covenant, viz. from the person of Christ, so that the natural Adamical man, in its inbred nature, is but this ass with the sack, till Christ possesseth his kingdom in him; no Covenant or praying availeth, but that Adam must in this world remain an ass till the sack be gone. And then he is called a new child in Christ, which new child in this life is the inward ground: but the strong-boned ass is the

new child's instrument, upon which the sack is carried, for the servility to God's anger continueth so long as the sack lasteth.

VII

THE TESTAMENT OF DAN

13. *Dan will be a judge among his people, as any other generation in Israel. Dan will be a serpent by the way, and an adder in the path, and will bite the horse in the heels, that his rider shall fall back. O Lord, I wait for thy salvation* (Gen. xlix. 16-18). This is a powerful figure of the outward power and authority of human offices in the kingdom of this world, and is so strongly prefigured that it is terrible to read, if a man rightly discern the figure. And yet in the presence of God it standeth in its own proper figure, thus: The spirit saith, *Dan will be a judge among his people, as one of the generations or tribes in Israel.*

In the figure it standeth thus:

14. Dan standeth in the figure of all outward offices, from those of highest authority and power, even to the government of the human life itself;[1] therefore the spirit saith of him, he shall be in his own might and power as one man is to another. In the presence of God he is not esteemed greater in his own nature than a servant or minister, for he serveth God in his office as another servant doth his lord and master; the office is God's, wherein he sitteth as a judge. The office is the authority and power, and he himself is, before God, as another man.

15. But the spirit saith, *Dan will be a serpent by the way, and an adder in the path.* That is, this judge in God's office would draw poison out of the power and authority, viz. self-will, and say of himself, *The authority is mine, the office is mine.* That is called, *in the way*; for the way which they should go is God's, viz. true righteousness. Then saith Dan, *That land and country, this city, that village, those goods, that money, is mine; it is my own. I will use it to my own profit, advantage and honour, and live in this office as I will.*

16. And this very selfhood is the serpent and venomous adder on the way, for it walketh very dangerous steps upon the paths of

---

[1] Ordering of a man's own private affairs or employment.

FURTHER EXPOSITION OF JACOB'S TESTAMENT

righteousness; it turneth righteousness into selfhood, to do what it will. It saith, I am a lord, the city, land and country, the village or authority and power is mine, I may do with the people what I will, they are mine. And so sucketh poison out of God's office of a judge, and thereby afflicteth the miserable, and stingeth with this poison round about in the way of the office, as an adder and serpent.

17. For the spirit saith, *He will bite the horse in the heels, so that his rider will fall backward.* That is, he will bite the horse, that is, the office whereon he rideth, in the heels, viz. in the just right, that the righteousness, viz. God's rider which he shall bring, may fall backward, and that he may govern as God's rider instead of the righteousness. Whereupon the rider, God's righteousness in his office, saith, *O Lord, I wait for thy salvation,* that is, till thou sendest the right rider, Christ, who shall ride over this adder and serpent again.

18. *When Rachel could bear no children to Jacob, she was troubled at Jacob, and said to him, Procure me children, if not, I die. But Jacob was wrath with Rachel, and said, I am not God, that I should give thee fruit of thy body. But she said, Behold, there is my maid-servant Bilhah, lie thou with her, that she may bring forth on my lap, and I shall be built up by her. And thus she gave him Bilhah her maid-servant to wife: and Jacob lay with her. So Bilhah conceived, and bare Jacob a son. Then said Rachel, God hath judged my cause, and heard my voice, and hath given me a son: therefore she called him Dan* (Gen. xxx. 1–6).

19. This now is the powerful figure of Jacob's testament, wherein he prophesieth so terribly concerning Dan, that he would be a serpent; and in the right figure it signifieth, man's own will, which will not suffer God to judge and lead it, but always murmureth against God, as Rachel murmured against Jacob, because it went not with her as she would, and was implacable with pressing Jacob, that he would give her children, or else she would die, at which Jacob was wrath.

20. So now the spirit represents the figure by Bilhah, Rachel's maid-servant, whom she gave to Jacob for a wife, who bare this Dan, who should be a judge and determiner of the anger and strife between Jacob and Rachel, when the self-will of Rachel would have children by force.

21. And it prefigureth this to us, that the worldly office of a judge hath its original from God's maid-servant, that is, from the kingdom and dominion of nature, and that God created man under no office of a judge; but the murmuring, stubborn and opposite self-will of man, which will not be obedient to God, nor endure to be judged and led by

his spirit, that hath caused, that Dan, viz. the power and authority to judge, is born in the lap of Rachel, viz. in the liberty of nature.

22. Therefore the spirit in the Covenant by Jacob pronounceth so sharp and severe a sentence upon it, and saith, this Dan, that is, this office of a judge, would be a serpent and adder in the way of righteousness, and would bite the just right, viz. the heels of his horse, that his rider, viz. justice and righteousness, might fall to the ground; and then nature shall wait for the salvation of God, viz. for the justice and right of Christ, by and through love: and then Dan's office shall cease.

23. Which ought well to be considered by thee, Babel, seeing thou boastest of Christ, whether thy salvation be in thee or no; that thou mightest judge thyself, and not need to have judges who must judge thy unrighteousness, wherein thou art no Christian, seeing thou continually murmurest with Rachel, and seekest thy will, therefore also the adder and serpent of Dan may well sting thee; for thy evil malice and wickedness causeth that, viz. thy own wilfulness. Therefore also hath God given thee up under Dan's fallen rider, so that thou must go along as a slave and ridden horse, whom the serpent stingeth with his venomous sting, viz. with the power and authority of usurping self.

24. But that Dan's rider must fall backward, signifieth that this Dan with his office shall fall backward in the conscience of a Christian, when he turneth to Christ and worketh repentance; for in repentance Dan's government ceaseth, the rider, God's anger, falleth backward. Therefore also every Christian is bound to forgive every one from his heart, when repentance and confession and acknowledgment of sins cometh, and so cast the office of a judge behind his back, for the office of a judge is the office concerning sin, that severeth right from wrong, and always falleth heavy upon that which is false and wicked; but the serpent often biteth the horse in the heels, viz. favour, greatness, reward, gifts and bribes: these make Dan an adder and serpent.

25. And we see clearly that Dan, viz. the office of a judge in Israel, hath its original from the murmuring, stubborn and opposite will, and that Dan is only a determiner of strife, and not, as he supposeth to be his own lord in his office, but a divider, as Rachel saith: *God hath judged my cause*, viz. by this Dan, her maid-servant's son, and not her own son; to signify that a child of God needeth no judge: he judgeth himself, and suffers with patience.

FURTHER EXPOSITION OF JACOB'S TESTAMENT

VIII

THE TESTAMENT OF GAD

26. *Gad stands prepared, he will lead a host, and retreat back again* (Gen. xlix. 19). This figure doth not prefigure that the children of Gad shall be captains of troops, as also Dan's children shall not be mere judges, but it represents the spiritual figure, which is to be seen by Leah, who gave her maid-servant also to Jacob, when she ceased to bear, and would make haste to prevent Rachel. For Gad was born of Zilpah, and should prevent Dan, for she said, readily, *Turn thee before him, and turn about to me again* (Gen. xxx. 9–11). And it denoteth human forecasting and carefulness, subtlety, policy and wicked craft and cunningness, that do with all subtlety prevent the right and justice, and would elevate themselves above all right and truth.

27. For Gad and Dan are both from the maid-servants, and are in the figure as a strife, for Rachel and Leah would one prevent the other, and therefore their ways were merely opposite: so this figure standeth thus: When Dan will judge, then cometh Gad with his subtle agility and readiness,[1] and worketh him out of his office with flattering speeches and specious pretences; with lying and perverting prevarication, for it windeth all truth about, and setteth his agile nimble subtlety in the right of truth, and so the judge is blinded by his agile nimble pragmaticalness.

28. This the spirit intimates strongly concerning Israel, signifying how they would live one among another, and how the self-power and authority with Dan, and the agility with Gad, would govern the world: But these are both of them but children of the maid-servants, and not of the free women, and their offices shall have an end.

IX

THE TESTAMENT OF ASHER

29. *From Asher cometh his fat bread,[2] and he will act to please kings* (Gen. xlix. 20). When Zilpah, Leah's maid-servant, had born Gad, prepared, subtle, crafty, always ready at every subtle assault against the right, justice and judgment of Dan, then saith Moses, *Zilpah bare Jacob the second son. And then said Leah, It is well with me, for the daughters will praise*

---

[1] Officiousness to undermine and insinuate himself.
[2] Or, finest of flour.

me and call me blessed: and she called him Asher (Gen. xxx. 12, 13). And Jacob said in the testament, *From Asher cometh his fat bread, and he will live to please kings.* Here Jacob, viz. the spirit in the Covenant, compriseth these two brethren together in a figure: for Gad hath the agility, and Asher taketh his fat bread from the king, and Leah saith at his birth, *The daughters will praise me and call me blessed.*

30. Here now standeth the figure. But what explanation may this have? Gad ordereth his ways with subtlety, and Asher with flattery and hypocrisy, among the kings and potentates in authority and power, whereby he attaineth prosperous fat days of plenty, pleasure and voluptuousness: and such are everyone that shall sit in offices; and as judges and magistrates they do all to please their lord and king; that they may be reputed, honoured, applauded and rewarded by him, and that they may have their fat bread from him. And the spirit by these three sons signifieth powerfully what kind of people would rule the world; viz. by Dan, the serpent, viz. self-will; and by Gad, subtlety, treachery, and undermining deceit; and by Asher, false and wicked flattery, and sycophanting hypocrisy, who always sit in the courts of kings, and serve them for their fat bread, and only hunt after the applause and honour of men.

31. Therefore saith the spirit, From Asher cometh his fat bread. From whom cometh the fat bread? Answer, from the nimble subtle heads, who make the cause of flatterers and hypocrites seem right. The flatterers sit near kings, and applaud them in their selfhood, and say, Do what thou wilt, it is all good and right: and when the king would fain have it in the appearance of right, that it also may be applauded, then cometh Gad with his nimble, subtle, perverted, far-fetched argumentative prerogative right, and setteth the king's own self-will in the right of nature, so that it seemeth to be right: to these Asher giveth the king's fat bread. Thus they all three live in the serpent, and so it biteth the horse in the heels, and they are all three the maid-servants' children, viz. ministers and servants of self-will.

32. Dan is the manager of the superior[1] office, Gad is his counsellor at law in matters of right, justice and judgment, such as the lawyers and jurists[2] are; and Asher is the nobility and councillors of state. These the spirit hath foreseen in their testament in these things, which they would hereafter practise; for the testator saith not, ye shall be such, but ye will be such; and sheweth excellently what the government on earth in the self-will of the human nature would be.

---

[1] Or, supreme.   [2] Advocates, proctors, pleaders and attorneys.

FURTHER EXPOSITION OF JACOB'S TESTAMENT

X

THE TESTAMENT OF NAPHTALI

33. *Naphtali is a swift hind, and giveth fair words* (Gen. xlix. 21). Naphtali is the second son of Bilhah, Rachel's maid-servant, which she bare after Dan, and is a right brother of Dan. These brethren of Naphtali are now among kings and judges, and denote the earthly wisdom from the constellation[1] or stars, which with eloquent fair speeches adorn the office of judicature, so that, Dan, Gad and Asher are called able, wise, understanding and learned lords and masters.

34. But he also proceedeth only from the strife between Rachel and Jacob. For Rachel said, when Bilhah her maid-servant bare him, *God hath decided between me and my sister, and I shall prevail over her* (Gen. xxx. 8). This signifieth in the figure, that these wise and learned speeches of Naphtali in this office of judicature would be able to bow, bend and turn about all causes, so that self-will would remain still a judge in all causes, so that none would be able to object anything in the least against these four rulers, the sons of the maid-servants, but they would have the government in Israel, and rule the world, and prevail over all men.

35. But they are all four the sons of the maid-servants. And Sarah said to Abraham, *Thrust out the son of the maid-servant, for he shall not inherit with my son Isaac.* And God was pleased with it, and commanded Abraham to do it: to signify that these offices shall not inherit nor possess the kingdom of heaven, but shall have an end, when Christ, the son of the free woman, shall receive the kingdom. All these states and governments shall [then] be thrust out, and he alone in his children and members shall govern.

36. Behold thyself in this looking-glass, thou politic, cunning, very wise and understanding world, in thy subtle policy, eloquence of speech, favour, might, potency and honour, and see where it is thou sittest, and whom thou servest; behold thy fat bread, also the applause from the king whom thou servest, and what thou purposest, designest and doest, and how thou standest in thy figure before God and the kingdom of Christ. Thy eloquence availeth nothing in the presence of God; thy prudence, policy, subtlety and cunning, availeth nothing. If thou wilt not give right counsel, and say and do according to truth, and persuade and inform thy superior lord and master rightly, then

[1] Or configuration.

thou helpest to generate this adder and serpent in the testament of Dan for thy superior; and thou thyself art that adder and serpent, who biteth judgment, justice and right in the heel: and therefore thou also shalt attain the end, wages and recompense of the serpent in hell fire for it.

XI

THE TESTAMENT OF JOSEPH

37. *Joseph will spring forth: he will spring as by a fountain, the [sprouts or] daughters pass on to the government; and although the archers be angry, and fight against him and persecute him, yet his bow holdeth strong, and his arms and hands in strength, through the hands of the mighty in Jacob; from whom have proceeded the shepherds and stone in Israel. Thou art helped by thy father's God, and from the Almighty thou art blessed with blessings from heaven above, and with blessings from the deep that lieth beneath, with blessings of the breasts and womb: the blessings of thy father have prevailed more than the blessings of my ancestors, according to the desire of the lofty in the world; and shall come upon the head of Joseph, and upon the crown of his head that was separate from his brethren* (Gen. xlix. 22-26).

38. In this testament of Joseph the spirit in the Covenant represents the figure of a right divine governor, in whom the spirit of God ruleth, who is not the son of the maid-servant, but of the free woman, who serveth God and his brethren, in his office, who governeth in truth and righteousness, who suffereth not tale-bearers, sycophants and flatterers about him, who seeketh not his own profit, credit and honour, but God's honour, and his brethren's profit: This the spirit hath powerfully prefigured by Joseph.

39. For Joseph was not an intruding governor, but one rightly called, not out of policy, subtlety and plausible speeches and pretences, so that he can draw and turn the horse about by the tail and yet persuade the simple people that he turns him about by the head: and the flattering hypocrite also saith of such governors and rulers, they are the head; and they do this only that they may eat their fat bread from the court. He sat not with adorned, eloquent, acute speeches in the office of judicature, but by divine understanding: if he would have flattered and have been a lascivious adulterer he could well have been a governor with Potiphar: but that ought not to be. For in him stood the figure of a true Christian man, shewing how such a one would regulate his life, and also his office, and how the good well-spring,

FURTHER EXPOSITION OF JACOB'S TESTAMENT

Christ, would flow forth through him, and judge and rule through him.

40. For Jacob began that testament and said: Joseph will spring, he will spring as by a fountain; that is, his wisdom will spring in God's power, and flow forth from him; so that he will find wise counsel; also the [sprouts or] daughters pass on to the government, that is, his wise words, counsels and determinations go forth, as a fair daughter in her virgin chastity and virtue.

41. Also, *though the archers be enraged, and fight against him and persecute him, yet his bow remaineth strong, and his arms and hands in strength, by the hands of the mighty one in Jacob*; that is, though the devil with his crew set upon him and despise him, so that he seeketh not his own honour and profit, and though wicked people shoot their arrows upon him, who bring forth lies under the specious pretence of truth, against him, yet his wisdom remaineth under the divine arms, and his will to righteousness standeth as a strong bow, through the co-habitation of the mighty God.

42. Also, *from him are proceeded shepherds and the stone in Israel*; that is, from him, from his wisdom, are proceeded other wise, righteous, understanding rulers, viz. faithful counsellors who are near him, shepherds and pillars in the government: for such as the prince is, such are his counsellors, as the proverb is. When the council seeth that the prince loveth righteousness, and that he will not be served with hypocrisy and flattery, and that only honest, trusty and understanding wise people bear sway with him, then they diligently labour for wisdom and righteousness, that they may please him therein: and then that land and country hath good shepherds.

43. Also, *Thou art helped from thy father's God, and thou art blessed from the Almighty*, that is, from the God[1] of Abraham, which helped Abraham, thou hast gotten wisdom and understanding, and that helpeth thee against thy enemies, and against their arrows. And thou art blessed from the Almighty, with blessings from heaven above, and with blessings from the deep beneath; with blessings of the breasts and womb; that is, from waiting on the Lord thou shalt receive good things, honour and sustenance, he will bless thee in body and soul, in goods and estate, and in all thy ways, and give thee sufficient, so that thou wilt not need nor dare to use subtle cunning deceit to pervert that which is right; thou wilt not dare to say of anything it is thy own to use as thou wilt, and yet thou wilt have sufficient and plenty.

[1] Or, faith.

44. For one that feareth God, and leaveth selfhood or appropriating anything for his own, he getteth instead thereof, all, in the kingdom of Christ; the heaven and the world is his; whereas, on the contrary, the wicked must supply himself with a piece of that which he hath stolen in subtlety and acquired to himself with deceit, and take nothing of it away with him but the hell only, and his wicked unrighteousness, and the curse of miserable people whom he hath tormented upon earth; they have kindled hell fire with their curse in him, and that he taketh along with him.

45. Also, *The blessing of thy father hath prevailed more than the blessing of my ancestors according to the desire of the lofty in the world; and it shall come upon the head of Joseph, and upon the crown of his head that was separated from his brethren*: That is, Jacob's blessing hath therefore prevailed more than his ancestors', because in him the ens of faith was sprouted forth and come into many boughs and branches: for the fruit did shew forth itself more than by Abraham and Isaac. For Abraham generated but one twig out of the line of the Covenant, viz. Isaac; so also Isaac generated but one twig out of the line of the Covenant, viz. Jacob, on whom the spirit looked. Seeing Jacob generated twelve sons, which all stood in the root of the line of the Covenant, and grew out of it as twigs (but in Judah stood the stock), therefore he said, *his blessing prevailed more*; as a tree which is grown into branches from the stock.

46. But that he saith, *According to the desire of the lofty in the world*, he signifieth under it the prosperity of the blessing to those that are blessed; for as the rich of the world desire only highness and good things, so these in the blessing of God receive temporal and eternal good things; these shall from the blessing of Jacob come upon the head of Joseph, that is, upon his children, so that they shall in this sprouting bear good fruit: for the head signifieth the blossoms and fruit of this tree.

47. Also, *Upon the crown of his head that was separated from his brethren*: that is, the blessing shall not press forth alone out of the line of the Covenant, so that it alone among Jacob's children stood in the blessing, viz. the stock of Judah, but upon the crown of his head that was separated, viz. upon the ground of the natural root of the Adamical tree in them all; that they all of them together should be as a fruitful tree. But concerning their states and worldly offices, wherein they would live wickedly in the future, he representeth the figure in Dan, and the four brethren from Jacob's wives' maid-servants, signifying how in the end the Serpent would manage the government in the

FURTHER EXPOSITION OF JACOB'S TESTAMENT

Adamical nature, and how their successors would live in their offices, and what kind of world would rise up therein: as it hath come to pass among the Jews and the Christians.

XII

THE TESTAMENT OF BENJAMIN

48. *Benjamin is a ravening wolf: in the morning he will devour the prey, but in the evening he will divide the spoil* (Gen. xlix. 27). Benjamin was Joseph's nearest own dear brother, and yet the spirit saith of him: he is a ravening wolf, who in the morning would devour the prey. In this testament of Benjamin is couched the most hidden secret figure of the whole Scripture, and yet in its type, in the unfolding in the effect and work, it is the most manifest and open figure, which is clear in the fulfilling, so that men may see it with bodily eyes, and yet in their reason are quite blind concerning it.

49. This figure is fulfilled, and yet is in action, and shall be yet also further fulfilled: it is very secret, and yet as manifest as a sunshiny day, and yet is not understood. But it is known to the Magi and Wisemen, who indeed have written much concerning it, but it hath not been yet rightly explicated, while the time of the evening (when Benjamin's spoil shall be divided) was far off; but now it is near. Therefore we shall offer somewhat concerning it, and hint the sense and meaning for those of our society to consider of, and yet remain as it were dumb to the unwise, seeing they sit in the dark, and open their jaws only after the spoil.

50. The two brethren, Joseph and Benjamin, are the image or type of Christendom, and of a Christian man, which in their figure is twofold, viz. the Adamical man in his nature is signified by Benjamin, and the new man out of the Covenant in the spirit of Christ is signified by Joseph; and the figure representeth how Christ hath assumed the Adamical man, and that this man is half Adamical and half heavenly, and that entirely in one person which cannot be divided.

51. So also in this image or type he prefigureth Christendom, and how they would receive Christ and become Christians, viz. that in them Christ, and also the evil wolf Adam, would govern; that is, when they would receive the faith, they would be so ravenous raving and zealous as a wolf, and would draw the heathen to them with power and compulsion, and yet would devour them; that is, whosoever will not above all hold the same opinion with them, they would

presently fall on to condemn that other opinion, and persecute it with wars and the sword; as a raging lion or wolf biteth and devoureth, thus in zeal they would devour round about them with excommunication and the sword; and that therefore, not because they are zealous in the spirit of Christ, but from the wolf of the evil Adam, which would always set itself in spiritual and worldly states and polities above the spirit of Christ.

52. Thus their zeal would be only from the devouring wolf, men being more zealous under the name of Christ for temporal goods, fat livings, good days and worldly honour, than for love, truth and salvation. They will not be zealous in the power of Christ's love, but in the power of the devouring wolf; also in the zeal of their accustomed exercises and worship, wherein yet they would but play the hypocrites before God, they themselves would devour one another as covetous greedy wolves; and so outwardly the wolf would govern. But yet inwardly, in the true children, Christ would govern: Outwardly Benjamin, viz. the natural Adam, which indeed is also a Christian, but it is first, after his resurrection, when he is quit of the wolf; and inwardly Joseph, who is hidden under the wolf.

53. And now the spirit of Jacob in the Covenant of God pointeth at the time, shewing how it would be; viz. in the first time of Christianity they would be zealous, and hunger after God in the spirit of Christ, and yet must hide themselves from their enemies, as [from] a wolf that men hunt as an enemy.

54. But when they shall be great and possess kingdoms, that is, when Christ's name shall come under the power and authority of Dan, so that laws and ordinances shall be made out of pretence of Christian liberty, and its orders and exercises shall come under worldly authority and dominion, then will this Christendom be a wolf, which will no more judge and proceed in the love of Christ, but whosoever will not call all their belly-orders good and right, those they would devour with the sword of excommunication, with fire and vengeance,[1] and would raise wars for Christ's name, and for their superstitions; and compel the people with power to the acknowledgment of Christ, and devour round about them as a wolf, and always hunt after the spoil, and yet for the most part intend to get the goods and authority of strange and foreign people to themselves.

55. Thus would Benjamin, in the morning, viz. in his rising up, devour the prey, and towards the evening he would again divide this

[1] Racha.

FURTHER EXPOSITION OF JACOB'S TESTAMENT

devoured spoil; that is, towards the end of the world, when Joseph's government will get aloft again, so that Christ shall be wholly manifest, and that this wolf shall cease, then will Benjamin, viz. the holy true Christendom, divide the spoil of Christ, wherewith Christ hath suppressed death and hell.

56. This dividing or distribution of the spoil shall come, and is already come, and yet is not, though it is, really, in truth, and the whole world is blind concerning it, except the children of the Mystery. The time is, and is not, and yet truly is, when this prey and spoil of Christ, and also the wolf's prey, shall, through Joseph's hand, be given into Benjamin's hand, and be divided and distributed.

57. O Babel, let this be a wonder to thee, and yet no wonder, either; for thou hast nothing, and seest nothing at which thou canst wonder: as a young plant groweth from a seed, and becometh a great tree which bringeth forth much fair fruit; so that a man would wonder at the grain of seed, how so excellent a tree, and so much good fruit, hath lain hid in one only grain or seed, which men neither knew of nor saw before. But, because men have knowledge and experience thereof, that it is possible that a tree should come out of one grain or seed, men wonder not at it; yet men see not how it comes to pass, or where that great power and virtue was. So also at present, men see the grain or seed of the tree well enough, but reason contemneth that, and believeth not that such a tree lieth therein, whence such good fruit should come, that thereby the kingdom of Benjamin, at the end of time, shall be called a dividing or distribution of the prey and spoil.

58. But Joseph must first be a governor in Egypt, and then Benjamin cometh to him; and then Joseph giveth him five garments of sumptuous apparel, and five times more food from his table than the others. When the famine famisheth the land, and the soul of Jacob hungereth, then know that God will thereby draw Israel into Egypt, viz. into repentance: and then is the time of visitation, and Benjamin carrieth his spoiling sword in his mouth. But Joseph's countenance smiteth him, so that he cometh into great terror, and fear of death, because the silver cup of Joseph was found in his sack, at which he is ashamed, and letteth his spoiling sword and wolves' teeth fall from him. And then Joseph manifesteth himself to him, together with all his brethren, at which there will be such joy that the wolf Benjamin will become a lamb, and yield his wool patiently. This is the end of that speech.

59. *The Testament of Jacob is a figure of the whole time of the world, from Adam to the end: of which we will set down a short figure for the Reader that knoweth the vision or histories to consider of.*

60. I. *Reuben*, in this place, being the first son, is set in the figure of the first world, which lived in the right of nature without law, that hath the priesthood and the kingdom in the right of nature, and should be in the chiefest sacrifice, and in the greatest dominion: but he was fickle therein as water, and was thrust out.

61. II. *Simeon* beginneth with Noah, after the flood, and keepeth Levi with him; that was Shem. But the sword of Ham and Japhet was Simeon: so there went two in one substance, viz. the spiritual will and the fleshly will, till Moses, and then the worldly and the spiritual were divided into two several states.

62. III. *Levi* beginneth under Moses, who with the priesthood managed the sword of Simeon and Levi in the Law, and cut very sharply therewith.

63. IV. *Judah* beginneth under the Prophets, and manifesteth himself with the Incarnation of Christ, at which time this sceptre began.

64. V. *Zebulun*, with his co-habitation, setteth himself in the midst, viz. in the kingdom of Christ: and that was the beginning of Christendom, who dwelleth on the coasts of the sea, viz. among the heathen, and sat pleasantly, for it was a new love.

65. VI. *Issachar* is the time when Christendom was settled in rest, viz. in power, might and dominions, which must yet always bear the burden of the heathen, and be servile, and be as a bound ass for the burden, for they still bear the cross of Christ, and were still conformable to the image of Christ, about three hundred years after Christ.

66. VII. With *Dan* did the potent kingdom and government of Christendom begin, when they set up kings, popes, archbishops and potent pompous churches, chapels and other consecrated places, and then was the adder and serpent by the way of Christ in human honour generated in the kingdom of Christ; when men began to dispute about the pomp, state and glory of churches, and to exalt men into the kingdom and offices of Christ, and set them in the place of Christ, and to honour them in Christ's stead; then was Christ suppressed, and the adder and serpent sat in Christ's office of judicature, and then the Holy Ghost was rejected, and councils were set in the place thereof, and then was Antichrist born. At that time the spirit of Christ said, Lord, I wait now for thy salvation, for here now my name must be the

cloak of Antichrist, till thou shalt deliver me in Joseph's time. In this time is truth strongly bitten in the heels, so that the rider in the spirit of Christ must fall backward.

67. VIII. With *Gad*, who should be the leader of a host, beginneth the time of the universities and schools among Christians, about eight hundred years ago, when men readily set Antichrist with power and might of armies in the chair of Christ, and with babbling, disputing, and perverting prevarication, maintained him against all opposition; when men made the tail to be the head, and forced the power of Christ into human traditions and canons, and made a worldly kingdom of Christ's kingdom.

68. IX. With *Asher* began the time when men lived to please King Antichrist, when he was God on earth. Then came the flattering hypocrites from the universities and schools, who flattered this king for fat bread, viz. for good offices, benefices, prebendaries and bishoprics, and applauded his doings and cause, and did all to please him, and set Christ with Antichrist upon a soft cushion, and so worshipped the image in the *Apocalypse*;[1] about six hundred years ago and nearer.

69. X. With *Naphtali* beginneth the time of the great Wonder, when man went on with high sermons and deep searching disputes about the council[2] of God, so that men have seen that these in Christ's chair were not Christ in power; yet men sought deep, that they might cover themselves with a mantle, with fair and plausible maxims, conclusions and determinations, then came the knotty acute logic, whereby men dispute. One part of them saith he is Christ, in power and authority; the other part contradicteth and opposeth it, that part setting his followers and dependents with his pretences into the blood of Christ, and buildeth all authority and holy sermons upon it; and so the spirit of Christ in the inward ground set itself against it, and saith, *He is the Antichrist*: This time hath continued to our time wherein we live.[3]

70. XI. With *Joseph* beginneth the time when Christ will be manifested again, when he shall cast to the ground the adder and serpent, Dan, with the chair of Antichrist, with all might and power of selfhood in the kingdom of Christ upon earth, and terrify it with his countenance, when Joseph's brethren must be ashamed of their great unfaithfulness which they have committed against Joseph, in that they cast him into the pit, and moreover sold him for money. And then

[1] *Revelation.*   [2] Predestination.   [3] Anno 1623.

will all subtlety, craft, flattery, hypocrisy and deceit be made manifest, and will, by the aspect of Joseph's countenance, be cast to the ground. And it is that time wherein it will be said, *Babylon, she is fallen, she is fallen, and is become a habitation of all devils and abominable beasts and fowls* (Rev. xviii. 2). And then Joseph springeth up in his own power and virtue, and his daughters pass on in their ornament, and his blessing beginneth.

71. XII. With *Benjamin* beginneth the time of the evening, under Joseph's time, for then he shall again divide and distribute the spoil of the first Christendom. He belongeth to the first and last time, especially to the first time of Joseph, when Christ beginneth to be manifested; and then he is first eager as a wolf, and devoureth far and wide, when he beginneth to bite and devour Antichrist; yet all that while he is but a wolf. But when Joseph's countenance shall be unveiled, then he is ashamed, as a wolf that is taken in a gin, and beginneth to be a lamb, and to yield his fat and plenty of wool.

72. This is the testament of Jacob, in its true figure, wherein the spirit hath pointed at the times; and the spirit of Moses saith, *When Jacob had finished all these sayings he drew his feet up together upon the bed, and departed,* to signify that when these his prophecies would be all fulfilled, then God would call again the unfolded nature in the strife of time into himself, and draw it together into the temperature; and then would this time have an end, and strife cease. This we desired a little to delineate for the lover of truth. Let him search further in the spirit of God, which searcheth all things, even the deep things of the Deity, and then he will see our ground in the truth.

The Seventy-Eighth Chapter

Of the Holy Patriarch *Jacob*'s Burial in the land of *Canaan*. What is thereby to be understood[1]

1. THE burial of Jacob, that Joseph should carry him again into the land of Canaan, after his death, and bury him with his fathers, and that Joseph went thither with a great company, with all the children of Israel, and many Egyptians, it prefigureth to us Christ's powerful exit out of this world, when the Adamical man, after its death, should again be carried from this Egypt and house of torment into its father's first country, into Paradise, into which Christ will bring it.

2. But that also many Egyptians went along with Joseph thither, and accompanied him, signifieth that Christ, when he shall bring home his bride into Paradise, will have many strangers with him, who in the time of this life knew him not as to his person or office, and yet are sprung up in him, in his love, which will all go with Christ into Paradise, and dwell and co-habit with him.

3. Their weeping and mourning signifieth the eternal joy, which they should receive in Paradise, as the Magi always by weeping and mourning prefigure joy. This funeral solemnity, and what is to be understood thereby, is declared before concerning Abraham.[2]

4. Moses saith further in this chapter: *Joseph's brethren feared, after their father was dead, and said, Joseph surely is wrath with us, and will requite all the evil which we have done unto him. Therefore they caused it to be told him: Thy father commanded before his death, and said, Thus shall ye say to Joseph, Forgive, I pray thee now, the misdeeds of thy brethren, and their sin, that they have done so evil to thee: therefore forgive the misdeeds of us the servants of the God of thy father. But Joseph wept when it was told him: and his brethren went in and fell down before him, and said, Behold, we are thy servants. But Joseph said to them, Fear not, for I am under the presence of God. You thought to do evil by me, but God turned it unto good, so that he hath done as it is at this day, to preserve much people. Therefore be not afraid, I will provide for you and your children. So he comforted them, and spake friendly to them* (Gen. l. 15–21).

[1] Genesis l.   [2] *Gen.* xxiii and *Mysterium Magnum*, ch. 51.

5. This figure is a mighty comfort to the brethren of Joseph. But seeing Joseph standeth in the image and type of Christ, and his brethren in the figure of a poor converted sinner, therefore we must expound this figure thus: that is, when poor sinful man, who hath committed great sins, and hath turned to repentance and attained grace, and committed some fault again, then he is always in fear and trembling before the grace of God, and thinketh God will impute his first committed sins to him again, and take an occasion against him by this fault; and in that regard standeth in great anguish, and beginneth to confess his first committed sins again, and falleth anew at the Lord's feet and entereth again into earnest sincere repentance, and bewaileth his first misdeeds, as David did when he said: *Lord, impute not to me the sins of my youth* (Ps. xxv. 7).

6. But by this new repentance and earnest lamentation, when the poor man appeareth again so very earnestly and humbly before God, the heavenly Joseph is brought into such great pity and compassion (as here Joseph was), that he comforteth the poor soul in its conscience, saying, it should not be afraid, all its committed sins should not only not be imputed, but they shall also turn to the best: as Joseph said, *Ye thought to do me evil, but God intended good thereby.* Thus God in Christ not only forgiveth the by-past sins to the humble converted man, but he also addeth to him provision for him and his children, with temporal blessing and maintenance, and turneth all to the best: as Joseph did to his brethren.

7. In the end, Joseph desireth an oath, that when he shall die, that they will carry his bones along with them out of Egypt to his fathers (Gen. l. 25); which signifieth to us the oath of God in Paradise, that Christ, God and Man, would come again to his brethren, and stay for ever with them, and be their High Priest and King, and nourish them with his power of love, and dwell by and in them, as Joseph by his brethren, and provide for them, as his branches and members, eternally, with his power and sap. Amen.

8. This is a brief summary exposition of the first book[1] of Moses, from a right true ground and divine gift, which we have very faithfully imparted, in a co-operating member-like love and care, to our dear fellow brethren, that shall read and understand this.

9. And we admonish the Reader of this, that when he findeth somewhat in any place of our deep sense to be obscure, that he do not contemn it according to the manner of the evil world, but dili-

---

[1] Genesis.

OF JACOB'S BURIAL IN LAND OF CANAAN

gently read, and pray to God, who will surely open the door of his heart, so that he will apprehend and be able to make use of it to the profit and salvation of his soul, which we wish to the Reader and Hearer, in the love of Christ from the gift of this talent in the ground of the soul, and commit him into the working meek love of JESUS CHRIST. Dated 11 September 1623, and then finished.

Praise the LORD *in* Sion, *and praise him all people, for his might and power goeth through, and is over, Heaven and Earth: Ha le lu jah.*

A TABLE

OF THE CHIEF MATTERS TO BE
FOUND IN THIS BOOK OF THE

MYSTERIUM MAGNUM

A

Abel

CHAP.		VERSE
27. Why Abel offered sacrifice		9
29. What the name Abel or Habel signifieth in the Language of Nature		20
30. Why Abel must be slain		16

Ability

| 61. How the soul may attain ability to receive grace | | 39, 40 |
| 69. How man's ability to receive grace is lost | | 17, 18 |

Abimelech

46. What the names of Abimelech and Gerar signify		2, 3
47. How Abimelech made a covenant with Abraham. What that signifieth in the spiritual figure; and what Moses here signifieth under the veil thereof		1–27
47. The holy figure of Abimelech and Pichol		6, *et seq.*

Above

| 43. What is called above and beneath in the text | | 9, 11, 12 |

Abraham

37. Of Abraham and his seed, and of the line of the Covenant in its propagation		1–61
37. Why the Spirit called Abraham out of his father's country		21, *et seq.*
37. How God appeared to Abraham		45–49
39. How God appeared to Abraham		1
38. How the ens of the Serpent as well as the line of Christ lay in Abraham		13
39. Of Abraham's sacrifice		13–25
39. How God established the Covenant with Abraham, and how the faith of Abraham laid hold of the Covenant, which was accounted to him for righteousness, and how God called Abraham to sacrifice		1–32

THE TABLE OF THE MYSTERIUM MAGNUM

CHAP.	Abraham	VERSE
40.	What is represented under the history of Abraham, Isaac and Jacob	1
40.	How two lines sprang out of Abraham	2–6
40.	From what property of Abraham Isaac and Ishmael were	13
40.	How Abraham in his seed had the land for an eternal possession	50–58
42.	How the Trinity appeared to Abraham	1
42.	What Abraham signifieth in the Language of Nature	1
42.	What Abraham's washing of their feet that came to him signifieth	11
43.	What Abraham's praying to the men for Sodom and Gomorrah signifieth	16–21
45.	How Abraham's pilgrimage was a type of Christendom	1–13
45.	How Abraham, Sarah and Abimelech were a powerful figure of Christendom	15, 16
45.	How God led Abraham so wonderfully, and how he was always in trial, and how the Lord preserved him	1–20
46.	Of Abraham's unwillingness to thrust out the maid-servant with her son	24–28
47.	Of the richness of the figure of Abraham's actions	1
47.	Of Abimelech's covenant with Abraham	2 27
48.	How God tried Abraham, and represented the figure of Christ's sacrifice in his sufferings and death	1–34
48.	How Abraham saw Christ's sacrifice afar off, even 2000 years before it was done	10
48.	How Abraham went up with Isaac to sacrifice	8–13
48.	Of Isaac's carrying the wood, and Abraham's carrying the fire and the knife	14, 15
48.	Why God said: Abraham, Abraham	25
48.	How men should look upon Abraham's figure	37–43
49.	How Abraham would not have the field of the children of Heth for nothing	11
50.	How Abraham sent his servant to take a wife for Isaac	1–57
51.	How Abraham had six sons by another wife, to whom he gave gifts, but all his goods he gave to Isaac; and how he died	1–55

CHAP.	Adam	VERSE
17.	How Adam did eat before the Fall	13, 14
17.	Whence Adam's imagination and longing proceeded	37
18.	How Adam was before the Fall	2–9
18.	Of two fixed substances in Adam	7, 8
18.	How the propagation should have been if Adam had stood	9–14
18.	How long Adam stood in Paradise before Eve was made	19–27
18.	How Adam before his sleep had eaten of the forbidden fruit	30–33
19.	Adam was not created in a bestial image	20–25

CHAP.	Adam	VERSE
23.	At what Adam was afraid	17, et seq.
25.	How God drove Adam out of Paradise, and set the Cherubim before the Garden	1–41
25.	How Adam getteth his bride again that was taken from him in his sleep	14, 15
25.	Why Adam and Eve were brought into Paradise	17
25.	What provoked Adam that he lusted against God's command	18
25.	Why God created Adam	19
25.	Why the Tree of Temptation was set before Adam	23
25.	Why Adam was tempted and driven out of Paradise	38
37.	Of God's Covenant with Adam	3
76.	How Adam was, before his Eve was, and became monstrous	11–18

All

3.	How a particular is the sport of the universal total All	21

Altar

27.	Where the altar of God is	48

Angels

8.	Of the creation of angels, and their dominion in all their worlds	1–34
8.	Why we see not the angels	19
8.	Where the angels dwell	16, et seq.
17.	How the holy angels live	35
25.	What the angel with the sword is	2
42.	For what God created the angels and man	24, 25
43.	Of the two angels that came into Sodom	22–64
43.	How the angels did eat with Lot	38
59.	How the angel met Jacob, and what that signifieth	24

Antichrist. Antichristian

27.	Of the wicked Antichristian Church, also of the true holy Church	41–60
28.	Of Cain's murdering of his brother, viz. of the proud Antichristian seeming Church upon earth, as also of the true Christianity	1–71
36.	What the Antichrist is	17
43.	The Antichristian whore doth as the Sodomites did	47–52
51.	What Antichrist is both among Jews and Christians	44
70.	How Antichrist hath deceived poor Christendom	38, 39
77.	When Antichrist will fall	70

Ararat

32.	Of the name Ararat in the Language of Nature	33–37

THE TABLE OF THE MYSTERIUM MAGNUM

CHAP.   Ark   VERSE

32. There is a very great mystery in the Ark of Noah . . 10, *et seq.*

Asher

77. The Testament of Asher, and the figure thereof . . . 29–32

As I live

42. An exposition of these words: As I live . . . . 27, *et seq.*

Author

5. From what sight and vision the Author hath written . . 15
12. The Author had a glass to see even beyond Moses . . . 34
18. From what knowledge the Author hath written . . . 1
21. The scope of the Author's writing 17

B

Babel

22. Out of what Babel is generated 54
25. How Babel shall end by the fiery sword 26
27. How Babel entereth into the presence of God . . . 52–60
29. How Babel speaketh out . . . . 7, 65, *et seq.*, and 77
30. Of the fall of the city Babel 43
31. How God will at present drown Babel with the fire of his anger 27
36. How the city Babel and Christ are one by the other . 60, 61
36. Why so much is written concerning the beast and whore in Babel 68
36. What the city Babel is 56
43. The time of the judgment upon Babel 52
44. How the figure of the destruction of Sodom is applied to Babel 5, *et seq.*
59. How it is that Babel will have the children of Christ go to God . 19, 20
59. How it is that Babel cannot hinder or hurt the children of Christ 21, 22
69. How Babel is a spy as to the grace of God . . . 19
70. The time is born, that Babel shall be spewed out . . 90
72. How Babel's reproach is set in judgment before the Most High . 23
73. The number of Babel and of the beast 9, 10
73. How Babel at present filleth its sack with provision . . 16, 17
73. How the deluge and the fire of Sodom falleth upon Babel unawares 18

Babylon

41. A warning to Antichristian Babylon 66–71

CHAP.	Baptism	VERSE
31.	How the deluge signifieth the baptism of Christ	38
41.	Of the seals of the Covenant, circumcision of the foreskin and baptism	1–41
41.	Of Christian baptism	10–14
41.	How the Jews and the Christians have but one and the same baptism	15–17

Beast

31.	How abomination may be imputed to a beast	31–38
36.	What the Antichristian Babylonish beast is	18, 19
36.	What the beast and whore is	64
36.	Where the beast, the whore, and Christ in us, is	49–51
73.	What the number of Babel and of the beast is	9, 10
73.	Wherefore the time is at hand that the beast and the whore must break in pieces	14, *et seq.*
76.	How Simeon and Levi prefigure the beast and the whore	29, 30

Beersheba

47.	What the city Beersheba or Bersaba signifieth	20, *et seq.*

Benjamin

77.	The Testament of Benjamin, and the signification thereof	48–58

Benoni

63.	What the name Benoni signifieth	26, 27

Bestial Man

21.	Of the bestial man's original, and of his sickness and mortality	1–17
21.	Of the government of the bestial man	11, 12

Bethel

63.	What Bethel signifieth	19

Bible

74.	How the kingdom of Christ and the kingdom of hell are portrayed by the histories in the Bible	50, 51

Blessing

41.	What in man shall possess the eternal blessing	1

Boasting

2.	We come short of that boasting or glory that we ought to have in God	3

THE TABLE OF THE MYSTERIUM MAGNUM

CHAP.   Bodies. Body   VERSE

11. Of two outward bodies 22
11. How all things of this world have a twofold body . . . 19
11. Man hath a threefold body 20
40. The heavenly body of the soul dieth not 44, 45

Bondage

39. What the figure is of the bondage in Egypt . . . 26, *et seq.*

Book

43. How a man must understand the first Book of Moses . . 57
52. How the first Book of Moses is a figure of the Spirit of God . 51
76. How all slanderous books and libels are the murdering swords of Simeon and Levi 29

Breath

15. Of a threefold breath in man, which is a threefold soul . . 14, 15

C

Cain

26. Of the propagation of man in this world, and of Cain the first-born and murderer 1–76
27. What is to be understood by Cain's sacrifice 41
27. Why the will of the Serpent and Devil in Cain would kill the body of Abel 9, 10
28. What was the cause that Cain murdered Abel . . . 4–25
29. What the name Cain signifieth in the Language of Nature . 18
29. How Cain and Abel were the two branches, and the image of the whole tree 23
29. What mark God had set upon Cain 53
29. Of Cain's fears 54
29. Wherefore grace came upon Cain 56
29. Cain was not born to perdition 57
29. What should be avenged in Cain sevenfold 58
37. What in Cain is cursed 35
40. Cain, Ham, Ishmael and Esau are an image of the Turks and heathens 71

Cainan, *see* Kenan

Calf

42. What Abraham's fatted calf signifieth . . . . 19, *et seq.*

CHAP.	Camels	VERSE
50.	What the ten camels which Abraham's servant took with him signify	14, *et seq.*

Canaan

49.	What Moses understandeth by Canaan	12

Care for the Belly

24.	What a man doth effect by pride and care for the belly	21, *et seq.*

Cave

49.	What the twofold cave signifieth	13, *et seq.*

Changed

11.	How all things may be changed	11

Chaos

1.	What the eternal Chaos is wherein all things lie hid	7, 8

Chariots

72.	What the chariots, provision, and sumptuous apparel signify, that Joseph gave to his brethren	24–38

Cherubim

25.	Of the Cherubim, that drove the evil Adam out of Paradise	38, *et seq.*

Child of Perdition

46.	How the child of perdition shall be revealed, and the beast and whore put to shame	33, 34

Children of God or Christ

31.	How the children of God saw the daughters of men	12–16
37.	How the line of the children of God is as a tree	1, 2
38.	How God delivereth his children through the might of his anger	14
44.	How the children of God do often keep back great plagues from God	19–21
46.	How it is that men see no more in the children of God than in others	4–6
55.	Of the misery and ignorance of the children of God	35, 36
55.	Why the true children of Christ are persecuted by the children in the kingdom of nature	47–50
56.	How the children of Christ instantly after the blessing enter upon Christ's pilgrimage	1, 2
56.	How God so wonderfully leadeth and preserveth his children	3

THE TABLE OF THE MYSTERIUM MAGNUM

CHAP.	Children of God or Christ	VERSE
56.	How the Lord standeth aloft on Jacob's ladder, calling and comforting the children of God	11, 12
64.	How the despising of the children of Christ is good for them	12
66.	The type and image of the children of God in chaste Joseph	32–40
66.	How the children of God have the greatest danger in worldly honour	53
66.	The final and last trial of the children of God	61–63 and 68

Christ

19.	Wherefore Christ became a man on the woman's part	17
23.	Why Christ sweat drops of blood in the Garden	4
23.	Why Christ must drink gall and vinegar	5, 6
23.	Why Christ must be scorned, killed, etc.	8, 9
23.	How Christ assumed a masculine fire-soul in the woman's property	43, *et seq.*
25.	Why Christ must be tempted	24
29.	What was Christ's office	25
34.	Why Christ would not be generated of man's, or the masculine, seed	28
37.	How Christ should become a God-man, and Adam and Abraham a man-God	28–32
37.	Of Christ's Person	42, *et seq.*
40.	How Christ and his subjects must be twofold persons	11, 12
40.	How Christ was generated out of the Covenant made with Abraham	15
40.	How the humanity of Christ anointeth his branches	14
40.	Wherefore Christ came	48–70
41.	What Christ's, viz. God's, corporeity is	19, *et seq.*
48.	How Christ will certainly come to us again	13
50.	How Christ is a masculine virgin and God	26
51.	How Christ is a grape-gatherer that gleaneth	53
56.	A firm ground and assurance that Christ assumed our Adamical soul and humanity in the body and womb of Mary	14–20
56.	From what property Christ became man	20
56.	Why Christ took his soul from woman and became a man	21, 22
69.	Where a man must seek Christ	22
76.	How the time is near, that the kingdom of Christ will be manifested to all people	50, *et seq.*

Christendom

27.	How verbal Christendom partakes of the sacrifice of Christ	42
68.	How at present Christendom standeth in God's presence	32–42
68.	What the four elements of hunger in Christendom are	35–39

Christian

CHAP.		VERSE
27.	What a Christian is, and how he is a Christian	46
63.	What a Christian is, and how he is a Christian	51, *et seq.*
40.	How a Christian must be a Christian	97
51.	How a Christian in his faith worketh in the flesh of Christ	31
51.	When any is a Christian	43
64.	How a Christian must not account the hate from his brother to be grievous	26, 27
64.	What the wish of a Christian to his enemies should be	27
64.	How a true Christian should present the misery and sins of the people where he liveth, daily before God	37, 38
66.	What officer is a Christian, and what no Christian	20
66.	How a Christian must be armed, in worldly offices	65, *et seq.*
68.	The most excellent figure in the whole Bible, of a tried Christian	48, *et seq.*
70.	How a man beginneth to be a Christian	24, 25
70.	What the difference is between a Christian and other strange heathen people	80, *et seq.*

Church

63.	What the greatest whoredom is in the churches of stone	39–43
63.	How at present men are ready to storm the Church, or house of whoredom	45
63.	How churches were erected out of a good intention	46
63.	What holiness is in the Church	47
63.	What a man must do that he may enter into the Church worthily	50

Circumcision

41.	Why God commanded circumcision to Abraham	2, *et seq.*
41.	Why the males must be circumcised on the eighth day	35, *et seq.*
41.	What circumcision is	3, *et seq.*

Clod

2.	The whole world lieth in one clod of earth	6

Coat

64.	What Joseph's particoloured coat which his father made him signifieth	39
64.	What it signifieth that Jacob was deceived by Joseph's coat	49, *et seq.*

Concubines

63.	How Jacob's concubines signify the stone churches	36

Conditions. *See* Forms

THE TABLE OF THE MYSTERIUM MAGNUM

CHAP.	Configuration	VERSE
13.	A whole configuration or constellation lieth in each element	12

Contention

17.	The contention of the high schools or universities about the Tree of Knowledge	16
28.	What the cause of contention about religion is	26–43
35.	Whence contention doth arise	61, *et seq.*
36.	Of the contention at the Tower of the confusion of tongues in Babel	12, 13
40.	How contentious preachers embitter the ears of the hearers	98
51.	How the false cold love of titulary Christendom contendeth about knowledge	46, *et seq.*
65.	What the contentious opinions in Babel are	49, 50

Copulation

41.	How the bestial copulation is borne withal under divine patience	2, 3

Councils

77.	When councils were set in the place of the Holy Ghost	66

Counsel

66.	To whom there is no more counsel or remedy to eternity	47

Covenant

30.	Of the line of the Covenant	1–54
32.	Of the Covenant between God and Noah	1
33.	Of the Covenant of God with Noah, and all creatures	1–40

Covering

22.	The covering for our nakedness is ours and no more	77, *et seq.*

Covetousness

24.	Whence the great covetousness doth arise	10

Cradle

63.	What the cradle of the child Jesus is	48

Creation

10.	Of the creation of heaven and the outward world	1–62
11.	Of the mysticalness of the creation	1

Creature

32.	How the image of the creature shall not pass away	16

| CHAP. | Cup | VERSE |

17. What Joseph's cup in Benjamin's sack signifieth . 1–13; 41–57

Curse

10. Of the curse of the earth 8
24. Of the curse, and of the body of sickness, whence that ariseth . 1–35
24. What the curse is 2

D

Damn. Damned

41. An excellent figure against those that, according to their conclusions in reason by the letter, damn some children from the womb 41
66. What the torment of all the damned is 67

Dan

77. The Testament of Dan, and the figure thereof 13–25
77. How it is signified by Dan, Gad and Asher, what kind of people would govern the world . . . . 30, *et seq.*

Darkness

3. Of the eternal original of the darkness 5
5. Of the enmity in the darkness 6

Day. Days

12. Of the six Days' work of the Creation 1–39
12. Of the first Day . . . . 13, *et seq.*
12. Of the second Day . . . . 19, *et seq.*
12. Of the third Day . . . . 32, *et seq.*
13. Of the fourth Day 1–20
14. Of the fifth Day 1–13
15. Of the sixth Day's work of Creation 1–31
16. Of the creation of the seventh Day 16–18
16. How the seventh Day hath been from eternity . . . 28

Death

4. The original of the eternal death 12
11. What the death and misery of man and all creatures is . . 17
23. Why the rocks clave in sunder at the death of Christ . . 3
33. Why God's anger often putteth one man to death by another . 21, 22

Decrees

61. How the decrees in Scripture point only at two kingdoms . 55

THE TABLE OF THE MYSTERIUM MAGNUM

CHAP.   Deity   VERSE

52. How the Deity manifesteth itself through the soul's nature . 7, 8

Delight
3. The delight or longing is the property of the Son . . . 7

Deluge
32. Why the Deluge, or Noah's flood, came after seven days . 20, 21, 22
32. Wherefore the fountains of water opened themselves in the Deluge . . . . 26, *et seq.*

Desire
3. The desire ariseth from the longing or delight, and is the Father's property 6, 7
3. The desire coagulateth itself 5

Devil. Devils. *See* Lucifer
8. That which is pain and torment to the devils, is joy to the angels   21
10. How the Devil is the most despicable poor creature of all . . 31
17. How Lucifer became a devil 28
22. Where the Devil's council-chamber and school is . . 17, *et seq.*
37. How the heathen had not their answers from the Devil . . 12, 13
38. How the Devil is a prince of this world 5, 6
38. What those four elements are wherein the Devil and all evil creatures live 7
66. Where the Devil is a frolick guest 54
70. What the Devil's fishhook is 41
74. How the Devil lost his seat and stool in man . . . 17, 18

Dinah
58. The figure of Dinah 39–45
62. How Dinah was deflowered, and Sichem and the city slain and spoiled: the gate of Christians' wars and the Babylonish whoredom, to be well considered of 1–40
62. How Dinah went forth to see the daughters of the land, and, what is prefigured thereby . . . . . 3, *et seq.*
62. How Dinah's whoredom and Simeon and Levi's murder is a figure of Christendom 9–18

Doctors
35. What understanding the doctors have in their contention about God's habitation and being 66

CHAP.	Dominion	VERSE
39. Whence dominion ariseth		32

Dove

32. What Noah's first dove signifieth		40
42. What the three doves and the raven signify . . .		42–46

Dragon

76. What the dragon's seven heads are		25, 26

Drank plentifully

70. What that signifieth, that Joseph and his brethren drank plentifully		94

Dreams

67. What it is to expound dreams		1, 2
67. Whence it is that a beast dreameth		5
68. Of King Pharaoh's dreams		1, *et seq.*
68. Wherefore the natural Magi could not expound Pharaoh's dreams		2, 10, 18, 19

Driver. *See* Hunter

Dying

20. Of Adam and Eve's dying		26, *et seq.*

E

Earth

10. Whence the grossness of the Earth proceeds		30
10. Out of what the Earth is proceeded		61
12. How the glove of the Earth is extruded		7
22. What the Earth is		45
25. Why God created the Earth		29, *et seq.*
25. When God set the time for the Earth to endure . . .		19

Eden

17. What Eden is		6

Edom

53. What Edom is, and signifieth, in the High Tongue . . .		5
64. What Edom is, and signifieth, in the High Tongue . . .		3

THE TABLE OF THE MYSTERIUM MAGNUM

| CHAP. | Egyptians | VERSE |

78. What it signifieth that many Egyptians went along when Jacob was buried 2

Elected. Election

25. Of that saying of St Paul, We were elected in Christ Jesus ere the foundation of the world was laid 20
48. How God elected not only the natural line of Christ, but also the line of nature 35, 36
51. An excellent figure, against the wise rationalists, concerning election or predestination 4–24
26. Of election or predestination 1–76
32. A curious example, how God hath predestinated no election in nature 3, 4
46. How God's election passeth only upon the figure . . . 30
61. Of God's election, or predestination, or decree concerning Jacob and Esau . . . . 1–3 and 23

Elements

10. That the four elements are but properties 49

Ember

23. How, in many there is an ember glowing towards the virgin's child of the new birth 41, 42

Enos. Enoch

30. What Enos signifieth in the Language of Nature . . . 11
30. What Enoch is in the Language of Nature . . . 27, et seq.
30. How long Enoch's voice must be silent 49, 50
31. Of the line of wonders, issuing from Enoch . . . 1–45

Envy

24. Whence the great envy ariseth 11

Ephraim

75. The figure of Israel's laying his right hand upon Ephraim's head . . . . 12, et seq.

Esau

52. What Esau signifieth in the Language of Nature . . . 36
53. How Esau despised his being first-born, and sold it for a mess of pottage 1–28
54. The figure of Esau's forty years, and of his two wives . 18, et seq.

CHAP.	Esau	VERSE
55.	How the figure of Isaac's blessing, and of Esau and Jacob is to be understood	1–5
55.	Why Esau was blessed with the word of strife	11
55.	Why Esau was all over rough and hairy	21, 22
55.	What that signifieth, that Esau attained not the blessing	39
55.	What figure Esau is, in his blessing	40, et seq.
56.	The figure of Esau's being a grief to his parents	9, 10
60.	What Esau the first-born signifieth	3
60.	What Esau's four hundred men signify	6
60.	How Esau went to meet Jacob, and how Jacob sent Esau presents	1
61.	The figure, of Esau's saying to Jacob: Whose are these with thee	10, et seq.
61.	How Esau's curse and malice was turned into love	18, 19, 53
61.	A plain exposition of the Scriptures, saying, Esau sought repentance with tears and yet found it not	20, et seq.
64.	How Esau standeth in the figure of the kingdom of nature	2

Esdras, or Ezra

38.	How Esdras, in the knowledge of the Spirit, had the lost Bible dictated to him	24
52.	How Ezra hath briefly written the figure and history	52

Eve

18.	Why Eve's will was subject to her husband's	11
20.	Why Eve so suddenly lusted after vanity	2–8
20.	How Eve gazed on the Serpent	22

Evil

10.	How the evilest must be the cause of the best	62
11.	What the great evil of this world is	15
22.	What the greatest evil is	25
28.	How the evil causeth that the good is manifest to itself	67, et seq.
29.	How nothing is created evil, or to the dominion of evil	11
61.	Whence evil and good proceed	61, 63, 68

F

Faith

27.	What that is which is called faith	35
39.	What it is rightly, to believe God, with Abraham. Which is the right ground of our Christian faith	8, 9
48.	What faith in God's children is able to do	33, 34
56.	How the faithful, or believers, put on Christ	32, et seq.

THE TABLE OF THE MYSTERIUM MAGNUM

CHAP.	Fall	VERSE
9.	Of the Fall of Lucifer, and his legions	1–25
11.	What the Fall of Lucifer, and the heathen idols, were	6
17.	Whence the desire to fall in Lucifer proceeded	22–43
17.	Of the Fall of Lucifer	25, et seq.
17.	How man came to fall	31
17.	How God saw the Fall	33
20.	Of the lamentable and miserable Fall of man	1–38

Famine

73.	How the great famine and hunger after heavenly food is near at hand	12–14

Favour

66.	How the children of God must not set their hope in the favour of man	50–56
67.	How the children of God must not set their hope in the favour of man	15, et seq.

Fear

70.	What Jacob's fear, that he would not let his son go to Joseph, signifieth	28, 29

Fiat

11.	How the Verbum Fiat, the Word of Creation, is still creating to this day	9

Figure

52.	When the figure shall wholly be manifested in substance	52
54.	Of the figure of the Old and New Testament	17

Fire

3.	Of a twofold fire	23, 24
24.	Wherefore all things shall be tried in the fire	4–9
27.	With what fire the sacrifices of Abel and Moses were kindled	8, 23
27.	How man in the Resurrection shall pass through the fire of anger	21, 22
27.	The eternal fire, and also the love-fire is magical	31
37.	What fire at the end of the Day shall purge the floor	20

Food

70.	What is the food of the eternal Word that became man	60

CHAP.	Fool	VERSE
22.	What the word fool meaneth	65, 66
24.	What is the greatest foolishness	16–30

Form. Forms *or* Properties of Nature

28.	The Spirit of Christ in his children is bound to no certain form	51–55
3.	What the first form, condition, property or Fiat is	8, 9
3.	What the second form is	10, 11
3.	What the third form is	12, *et seq.*
3.	What the fourth form is	18
5.	What the fifth form is	1, *et seq.*
5.	What the sixth form is	11, *et seq.*
6.	What the seventh form is	1–13
6.	Of the seven forms, conditions or properties of the eternal nature	14, *et seq.*
6.	Of the out-birth or manifestation of the seven forms, conditions or properties	21–24
7.	How seven forms or properties are in all things	18
20.	Of four forms or properties in man	33, *et seq.*
40.	How in the moving of nature two forms or properties divided themselves	7, 8

Free Longing

3.	The free longing or lubet is no property	6

Fruits

70.	What the fruits signify, which Jacob commanded his children to carry along with them	33, *et seq.*

G

Gad

77.	The Testament of Gad, and the figure thereof	26, *et seq.*

Germany

45.	How Germany shall be blinded by a star shining from east to west	12–14

Globe

18.	Moses' Tables written on a globe	20, 21

God

1.	What God is	2
2.	Where God dwelleth	8
3.	Where God is called Father and Son	7

THE TABLE OF THE MYSTERIUM MAGNUM

| CHAP. | God | VERSE |

God

5. How God is in the darkness and in the light 10
8. How God willeth good and evil 24
19. It is idolatrous to portray God as a man 27
36. Why God became man 65, 66
43. How reason thinketh that God dwelleth only above the stars and firmament 2, 3
43. Where God dwelleth according to love and anger . . . 4
43. How God seeth in the devils and in the wicked soul . 5, *et seq.*
43. How that is understood where it is said, The cry was come before God 6
60. How God is manifested in the thrones of the holy angels, and of the devils 45, 46

Good

2. Of what God made the good and the evil . . . 4, *et seq.*
3. How out of the eternal Good evil is come to be . . 1, *et seq.*
3. By what good is known 22
22. To whom we must do good, to whom not . . . 81, 82
71. How the eternal Good became creaturely . . . 14, *et seq.*

Goshen

72. What the land of Goshen signifieth 18
73. Of the figure typified by Goshen . . . . . 31, *et seq.*

Government

22. Whence the earthly government ariseth 74
66. How the governor in the office of Joseph governeth in Christendom . . . . 12, *et seq.*

Gulf

8. The gulf between darkness and light, and between the holy world and the dark world 22, 23

Guts

19. How the guts and entrails were added to Adam and Eve . . 19

H

Hagar

40. Of the history and most wonderful prefiguration of the Spirit of God, by Hagar, Sarah's maid-servant, and her son Ishmael, of his casting out from the inheritance, and of Isaac's inheritance 1–100
46. The figure of Hagar's casting out, and the birth of Isaac . . 8–15
46. A noble figure concerning forsaken nature, by Hagar and her son 16–23

MYSTERIUM MAGNUM

CHAP.	Ham	VERSE
31.	What Ham is in the Language of Nature	7
32.	Why Ham's image was cursed by his father	9
34.	How Ham's spirit at present hath the government in Christendom	37, *et seq.*
37.	What in Ham and Cain is cursed	35

Hanoch

29.	What Hanoch signifieth in the Language of Nature	28, 29

Hardened. Hardening

61.	Why man continueth hardened	23, 42
61.	How the hardening is not from the purpose of God	66, *et seq.*

Head

23.	What it is to tread upon or break the head of the Serpent	32, 37

Heaven

5.	Of the fullness of joy in heaven	5
8.	Heaven is in hell and hell in heaven	28
10.	What we are to understand by the two words, *Himmel* and *Erde*, heaven and earth	47, *et seq.*

Heels

23.	What the stinging in the heels is	33, 34

Hell

3.	The true original of the dark world or hell, into which the devils are thrust	2
4.	Whence hell hath its name	16
5.	What and where hell and the dark world is	9
8.	How heaven is in hell and hell in heaven	28

Herdsmen

73.	The figure of this, that Joseph's brethren must say before Pharaoh that they were herdsmen	35, *et seq.*

Hirah

65.	What Hirah of Odollam is in the figure	21

Honest

66.	How all things must serve to the best for those that are honest or virtuous and fear God	68, *et seq.*

THE TABLE OF THE MYSTERIUM MAGNUM

CHAP.	Hunter	VERSE
35.	Of the hunter or driver and his office	36

I
Idols

37.	The original of the heathenish idols, and their oracles	7–12
59.	Of Rachel's idol-gods	9–18

Image. Images

21.	How the heavenly image that God created in Adam, is capable of the kingdom of God	14
68.	How the makers of images are threatened by the anger of God	26–31

Infidelity

51.	How infidelity is as great in one people as in another	42, 43

Interpretations. Interpreter

37.	By what understanding interpretations are made	10, et seq.
69.	What the interpreter, by whom Joseph speaketh, signifieth	35

Isaac

40.	Why Isaac was chosen and appointed to the inheritance	39, 40
46.	Of Isaac's birth, and Ishmael's casting out with his mother Hagar: what is thereby signified	1–37
48.	Concerning Isaac's saying to his father, Here is fire and wood, etc.	16, 17
48.	Why Isaac must not be slain	20
50.	The figure of Isaac's meeting Rebecca in the field	54, et seq.
52.	How Esau and Jacob were born to Isaac, and what happened to them	19, et seq.
52.	Why Isaac loved Esau more than Jacob	44, et seq.
54.	How Isaac in the famine went to Abimelech, and how the Lord appeared to him	1–17

Ishmael

40.	God did not reject the whole person of Ishmael	19
40.	The figure of Ishmael's rejection or casting out	36, et seq.
52.	Of the twelve princes from Ishmael, and of his falling before his brethren	16, et seq.

Issachar

77.	The Testament of Issachar, and the figure thereof	8, et seq.

MYSTERIUM MAGNUM

J

CHAP.	Jacob	VERSE
52.	That Jacob cometh after Esau, and holdeth him by the heel: what that signifieth	37
52.	What Jacob is in the Language of Nature	41
53.	Why God called Jacob Israel	23, *et seq.*
55.	How Jacob was blessed by Isaac unknowingly in the stead of Esau; and what is signified thereby	1–50
55.	Why Jacob must take upon him the rough hairy beast's skin	23, *et seq.*
55.	The figure of Jacob's being smooth under the skin	29
55.	How the figure of Jacob points at Christ	30
56.	How Jacob must wander away, and how the Lord appeared to him	1–39
57.	How Jacob came to Laban and served him in keeping his sheep fourteen years for his two daughters: what the spiritual figure thereof concerning the bride of Christ signifieth	1–34
58.	How Jacob served Laban twenty years, and begat twelve sons and one daughter, and how God blessed him, and how Laban often changed his wages	1–53
58.	How Jacob's subtlety was a figure of Adam's subtlety	16, 17, 19, 24, *et seq.*
58.	How the twelve children of Jacob signify the line from Adam to Noah and his children	38
59.	The figure of the sayings of Laban's children that came to Jacob's ear	1, *et seq.*
59.	The figure that Jacob fled from Laban, and that Laban pursued him	1–25
59.	What that signifieth, that God said to Jacob: Get thee up, and go to Bethel	14, 15
59.	How Jacob stole away Laban's heart: what is thereby to be understood	16
60.	What it signifieth, that Jacob divided his flocks into two parts because of Esau's wrath	4
60.	What it signifieth, that Jacob humbled himself before God and his brother Esau	7, 8
60.	What the present that Jacob sent to Esau signifieth	9–13
60.	How Jacob arose in the night and led his wives and eleven children over the water: what is thereby to be understood	14–16
60.	How a man wrestled with Jacob	17–23
60.	How Jacob's sinew was displaced: what that signifieth	24–27
60.	The figure of Jacob's saying: I will not let thee go except thou bless me	28–35
60.	The inward holy figure of Jacob's saying: What is thy name	37–50

THE TABLE OF THE MYSTERIUM MAGNUM

Jacob

CHAP.		VERSE
61.	The wonderful figure, how Jacob and Esau met, and all mischief and evil will was turned into great joy and compassion: what is thereby to be understood	1–22
61.	The figure how Jacob divided his wives and children, and went himself before them, and bowed seven times before Esau	4–9
61.	The figure, how Jacob would not go along with Esau	69–71
61.	The figure, that Jacob pitched his tents before the city of Shechem	73
63.	How Jacob went to Bethel, how Benjamin was born, and Rachel and Isaac died: what is thereby to be understood	1–53
63.	The figure of Jacob's coming to his father before his end	53
64.	How Jacob and Esau departed one from the other: what that signifieth	4
69.	How Jacob's sons came before Joseph: what is thereby to be understood	1–35
73.	How Jacob sacrificed at Beersheba to the God of his fathers, and spake with him: what the signification is	1–8
73.	The figure of Jacob's going forth out of Canaan into Egypt	11
73.	The figure of Jacob's sending Judah before him to Joseph, and his weeping upon Joseph's neck	19, et seq.
74.	How Jacob and the five youngest brethren of Joseph were set before Pharaoh, and how Jacob blessed Pharaoh	1, et seq.
74.	The very mystical figure, that Jacob would be buried in the land of Canaan	53, et seq.
75.	How Jacob before his end blessed the two sons of Joseph	1–30
76.	How Jacob called for all his sons, and told them what the state and condition of every one of them would be	1, et seq.
76.	What Jacob in the Spirit calleth his honour	24, 25
77.	A short figure of the whole world in Jacob's Testament	59–72
78.	Of Jacob's burial	1

Japhet

31.	What Japhet is in the Language of Nature	9

Jared

30.	What Jared is in the Language of Nature	19, 20
30.	How Jared's office is twofold	21, et seq.

JEOVA

35.	Of the name JEOVA	49, et seq.

Jewel as a Present

50.	What the jewel and present sent by Abraham's servant signifieth	22–47

CHAP.	Jews	VERSE
37.	How the time of recalling the Jews is near at hand	36
51.	How the time of recalling the Jews is near at hand	42
37.	How the Jews are rejected, and shall be grafted in again	59, et seq.
41.	The cause of the Jews' and Christians' blindness	47, et seq.
41.	Advice to the Christians, Jews, Turks and heathen	53–71
51.	Why the Jews did not all turn to Christ when he manifested himself in the flesh	25, 26
51.	What a Jew is	27, 28
51.	How a Jew in his faith worketh in Christ's office	28, et seq.
51.	How the Jew and Christian come to salvation	44, 45
65.	Wherefore the Jews oftentimes slew the Prophets	28
70.	How to eat Christ's flesh is an abomination to Jews, Turks and heathens	66
70.	How the Jews, Turks and strange nations do eat Christ's flesh	69–77
70.	How the Fathers, viz. the Jews, had no more a part in grace than the strangers had	78
75.	A figure, shewing that God would bring the Jews into the true Covenant into Christ	1–36
76.	How the Jews do in vain look after another Master, Ruler or Messiah	50

Joseph

58.	How Joseph signifieth Christ	50, et seq.
64.	The beginning of the most excellent figure of Joseph	6–61
64.	How Joseph was sold and carried into a strange land	53, et seq.
64.	How Joseph is taxed for unchastity by Potiphar's wife	56, et seq.
64.	How Joseph was sold for twenty pieces of silver, and Christ for thirty pieces of silver	59, 60
66.	How Joseph was sold for twenty pieces of silver, and Christ for thirty pieces of silver	1, et seq.
64.	What the whole history of Joseph drives at	61
66.	Of Joseph's chastity and fear of God	1–72
66.	How Joseph fled from the whore, and what is signified thereby	45, et seq.
67.	How Joseph interpreted the dreams of Pharaoh's butler and his baker, and what is thereby to be understood	1–18
68.	The figure of Joseph's putting on other clothes and shaving himself	22
69.	The figure of Joseph's letting his nine brethren out of prison and keeping Simeon prisoner	24–29
69.	The lovely figure of Joseph's causing his brethren's sacks to be filled, and their money to be given them again	36, et seq.

THE TABLE OF THE MYSTERIUM MAGNUM

CHAP. Joseph VERSE

70. How Jacob's sons go again into Egypt to Joseph, and take Benjamin with them: how Joseph caused them to be brought to his house, and to eat at his table: how Joseph caused his brethren to be set in their order, and how Joseph was served by himself, and his brethren and the Egyptians also by themselves 1–94
71. How Joseph caused his brethren's sacks to be filled, and the money to be laid in the top of the sack, and his cup in Benjamin's sack, and caused them to be pursued and challenged for thieves 1, 66
72. How Joseph manifested himself before his brethren . . . 1–38
72. How Joseph kissed his brethren . . . . . 20, *et seq.*
73. How the countenance of Joseph was manifested to his brethren again, and how they must be ashamed 15, 16
73. The figure of Joseph's saying: I will tell Pharaoh: My brethren and all my father's house is come to me . . . 24, *et seq.*
74. The very potent figure of Joseph's gathering all the money together in the famine 9–15
74. The figure of Joseph's buying all the land of Egypt for Pharaoh 19–21
74. Wherefore Joseph bought not the priests' fields: what is the signification thereof 22, 27–33
74. The figure of Joseph's law concerning the Egyptians' fields to give the fifth part to Pharaoh 23–35
77. The Testament of Joseph, and the signification thereof . 37, *et seq.*

Judah

65. What the three sons that Judah begat signify . . . 6, *et seq.*
65. Why the history of Judah and Tamar is put between in the history of Joseph . . . . 64, *et seq.*
76. Of the Testament of Judah . . . . . . 38, *et seq.*

Judging

70. What the speech of Christ concerning judging signifieth: Judge not that ye be not judged 51

K

Kenan, *or* Cainan

30. What Kenan signifieth in the Language of Nature . . . 17

Keturah

51. What Keturah signifieth in the Language of Nature . . . 2

CHAP.	Kine	VERSE
68.	What Pharaoh's seven fat kine and seven lean kine signify	. 11–17

Kingdom

49.	How the outward kingdom remaineth eternally	. 17, 18
76.	How the time is near that the kingdom of Christ will be manifested to all people	50, *et seq.*

Kings

66.	For what kings and princes are served by the nobility	. 18, 19

Knowledge

45.	What knowledge the outward man hath of the kingdom of Christ	17, *et seq.*

L

Laban

58.	The figure of Laban's changing Jacob's wages ten times	. 28, *et seq.*
59.	How Laban chid with Jacob, and what is thereby to be understood	19

Ladder

56.	What the ladder of Jacob was, and what the angels descending and ascending signify	. 4–8

Lamb

37.	What the wedding of the Lamb is, at which God and man is espoused, and Christ born	. 12, *et seq.*

Lamech

29.	What Lamech is in the Language of Nature	. 37, 38
31.	What Lamech is in the Language of Nature	. 2
29.	Of Lamech's two wives and their children	. 39–46, 49
29.	What the man and the young man which he slew are	. 48
29.	What as to Lamech shall be avenged seventy-seven times	. 59–64

Land

75.	Of the piece of land that Jacob gave to Joseph severally from the rest of his children, and the signification thereof	. 31, *et seq.*

Language

35.	Of the ground of the Head Language, when all people spake but one language	. 54–59
35.	What language the spirits use	. 60
37.	How long the undivided language continued	. 4, *et seq.*

THE TABLE OF THE MYSTERIUM MAGNUM

CHAP.	Life	VERSE
11.	Whence the true rational life in the elements is	27
35.	The cause of the long life of the patriarchs before the flood	11, *et seq.*

Light

3.	The eternal light, and the eternal darkness, are not created	2–5
10.	Without light the elements had been unmoveable	44, 45

Logic

77.	When the acute logic came up	69

Lord

33.	How a lord, prince, or magistrate hath no authority to shed blood	15, *et seq.*

Lot

43.	Why the two angels lingered in going in to Lot	34, *et seq.*
43.	What is signified by Lot's wife	37
43.	The figure of Lot in that he would give his two daughters to the Sodomites	53, *et seq.*
43.	Why Lot's kinsfolk would not follow him	65, 66
44.	How Lot went out of Sodom, and of the terrible destruction of that whole country of Ham's generations, and what happened upon it; also how it was done	1–47
44.	Why Lot's daughters made their father drunk with wine	3
44.	To what end Lot's wife was turned into a pillar of salt	28, *et seq.*
44.	Lot's wife is a figure of the present Babylonish Christendom	33, *et seq.*
44.	Why Lot's daughters did lie with their father	38–47

Love

71.	How God's love cometh only to help the weak	19

Lucifer

12.	Wherefore and from what Lucifer was thrust out	4
12.	Where Lucifer lieth captive	35
22.	Wherefore Lucifer was swallowed up into the wrath	30, 31
25.	Where Lucifer sat before the creation of the earth	18
44.	How Lucifer desired to see the wrath of nature	17
60.	How the pride of Lucifer by the masters of the letter doth shut God up into a peculiar heaven apart	41, 42

M

Magistrate

22.	How the magistrate is good, and how not	74, 75

MYSTERIUM MAGNUM

CHAP.	Magia. Magus	VERSE
11.	The Reader is admonished not to misuse the Magia or Magic	8
11.	How man is hurt by the wicked Magus or Magician	12, et seq.
68.	Of the Magi or Magicians, which titulary Christendom is full of	4, et seq.
68.	Of the Magia or Magic art, among the Egyptians and heathens, till the kingdom of Christ	3
68.	How man is a true divine Magus or Magician	23, et seq.

Mahalaleel

30. What Mahalaleel is in the Language of Nature 18

Maid-servant

40. What it is that the son of the maid-servant shall not inherit with the son of the free-woman 16–70

Man

15.	Man is threefold	27, et seq.
16.	Of the distinction between the heavenly and the earthly man	1–15
16.	How man was while he stood in Paradise	8, et seq.
18.	How man shall be after the Resurrection	3
19.	How man was ordained to the outward natural life	1–16
21.	Why God created man of the heavenly essence	16
22.	How man deceived himself	27
23.	How the Word in the seed of Eve was propagated from man to man	31
24.	How man hath a cure, and the Devil not	13, et seq.
24.	How a divine man must have enmity in himself	31, 32
27.	How man presseth into God	14, 15
29.	How man was in the beginning, in his properties	12, 13
29.	How man is become a striving dominion	14

Mary

37.	How Mary is not the mother that hath generated God	37, et seq.
56.	What is the blessing belonging to Mary	30

Māusim

36. What that god *Māusim* is 32

Meal

42. What the three measures of fine meal signify . . . 17, 18

Melchisedek

38.	What Melchisedek was	19, et seq.
38.	Why Melchisedek blessed Abraham	21

THE TABLE OF THE MYSTERIUM MAGNUM

CHAP.   Mercifulness   VERSE

70. How mercifulness hideth its countenance from the repenting soul   3, *et seq.*

Mercurius
17. What Mercurius is 18

Metals
10. What the metals are 17
10. Of the seven properties in the metals 18–29
16. How in the earth, stones and metals lieth a twofold substance . 10

Methusael
29. What Methusael is in the Language of Nature 35, 36

Michael
12. When Michael strove with the dragon 10

Midianites
64. How the Midianites will bring Joseph with them to Pharaoh; the time is near . . . . 30, *et seq.*

Money
70. The figure of the wrong money that Jacob commanded them to take with them again . . . . . . 36, *et seq.*, 48, 49

Moon
23. What the moon and the woman in the Apocalypse signify . . 34, 35

Moses
11. The time is born that Moses casteth away his veil . . . 4
30. When Moses will keep the sheep . . . . . 53, *et seq.*

Motion
29. Of God's eternal motion, moving and forming 4

Mouth
29. What the mouth of the eternal understanding is . . . 3

Murderer
19. Why Eve brought forth a murderer the first time . . . 10
62. The figure of Simeon and Levi's murder 31–40

N

Naamah

CHAP.		VERSE
29.	Of Naamah	43, *et seq.*
29.	How Naamah shall be manifested to all people	68

Names

| 17. | What the great names are that God called Abraham by | 23, *et seq.* |

Naphtali

| 77. | The Testament of Naphtali, and the signification thereof | 33, *et seq.* |

Nature

3.	The description of the eternal nature	1–26
35.	How the Language of Nature is extinguished	12, *et seq.*
40.	Whereto God useth the temporary nature	31
40.	What the condemnation of the temporary nature is	32

Night

| 12. | Where there is no night | 1 |

Nimrod

| 35. | Of the name Nimrod | 29, *et seq.* |

Noah

31.	What Noah is in the Language of Nature	3
32.	What Noah is in the Language of Nature	2
32.	Why Noah was accounted righteous before God	13, 14
34.	What Noah's drunkenness signifieth	27
34.	How Noah cursed Ham	1–40
35.	The names of the children of Noah are seventy-two	15–48
43.	Where Noah's curse came into judgment	29

Nothing

| 3. | The nothing hungereth after the something | 5 |

O

Oak

| 63. | What the oak signifieth under which Jacob buried the idol-gods and the earrings | 4–15 |

THE TABLE OF THE MYSTERIUM MAGNUM

CHAP.   Office. Officer. Officers   VERSE

22. How the office is good, and how not good 72
66. How the potent in the office of God are great trees without fruit . 16, 17
66. How the offices and officers are God's, and are God's servants . 22
66. How a man in an office must serve either God or the Devil . . 59
66. How this world hath two sorts of officers 37–59
77. Where the worldly office of a judge hath its original . . . 21–25
66. How an officer becometh a Lucifer; also how he is free from the commandment of death 23–27
66. How all officers are set in the kingdom of this world . . . 28, 29
66. How at present is the time of the coming of the Lord to burn the city of these wicked evil officers with the fire of God's anger . 30, 31

Oracle

37. How the first holy oracle after the flood manifested itself . . 15

P

Paradise

17. Of Paradise 1–43
18. Of the Paradisical government 1–34
25. How Paradise is one certain place 16

Pastors

74. Of all spiritual pastors or shepherds, who sit without Christ in that office 6

Pearl

22. How the pearl of the whole world is trodden underfoot . . 35

Philistine

47. What Philistine is 23, 24

Physician

21. Whence the physician doth arise 7–9

Plants

12. Whence it is that some plants are poison 36

Potiphar

64. What the figure of Potiphar's wife is 10, 11

Pottage

53. What the lentil pottage was 4

Prayer

CHAP.		VERSE
38.	How man with his prayer and will awakeneth the sword of anger	11

Predestinated

30.	What is predestinated to condemnation	8, 9
40.	Ishmael is not predestinated to condemnation	35–54

Present

70.	What the present was that Joseph's brethren brought him in their hands	52, 53

Pride

24.	What men erect with their great pride and care for the belly	21, *et seq.*

Prince

33.	How a prince or lord hath no power to shed blood	15, *et seq.*

Principles

4.	Of the two Principles, God's love and anger	1–21
32.	How Shem, Ham and Japhet are an image of the three Principles	5, *et seq.*

Prosperity

66.	Man in temporal prosperity, and in favour and good will of many men, ought not to be secure	50–56

Prophet

67.	How the Prophet is the mouth of the kingdom	9, *et seq.*

Purgatory

25.	Of the purgatory of souls	13, 14

Purple Mantle

70.	To whom the purple mantle of Christ is available	42, 43

Purpose

61.	How in God there is no purpose	60, 61 and 64

Q

Qualities. *See* Forms

THE TABLE OF THE MYSTERIUM MAGNUM

R

CHAP.	Rachel	VERSE
58.	Why Rachel said: Give me children.	1, 2
58.	Why Rachel must be barren.	47
63.	What it signifieth that Rachel died and was buried at the city Bethel	28
63.	How Rachel was big with child when Jacob went from Laban	30
63.	How Rachel bare Benjamin and died: what the signification of it is.	20, *et seq.*

Rained. Rainbow

32.	Why it rained forty days and forty nights.	23, *et seq.*
33.	Of the rainbow and its colours	25–40

Ram

48.	How the killing and dying falleth not upon the right man, but upon the ram.	28, *et seq.*

Raven

32.	What the raven signifieth	38, 39, 41

Reason

41.	How reason introduceth everything into God's will	53–71

Rebecca

50.	Rebecca signifieth Sophia	48
50.	The figure of the glorious banquet of Abraham's servant with Rebecca.	49, *et seq.*
52.	How in Rebecca two kingdoms strove one with another	20–30
52.	Wherefore Rebecca loved Jacob	54
53.	Why the strife arose in Rebecca	27
55.	Why Rebecca must set Jacob in the place of the blessing	17, *et seq.*
55.	Of Rebecca's subtlety and deceit with Jacob	19, 20

Religion

36.	Whence the contempt of religion proceeds	14

Remedy

66.	To whom there is no more counsel or remedy, to eternity	47

Repentance

31.	Of God's repentance, where he saith: It repenteth me.	17–45
70.	It is a figure of repentance, that Jacob's children must go into Egypt for food twice	15–23

CHAP.	Respect	VERSE
51.	How in God's presence there is no respect of name or person	34-41

Reuben

63.	What Reuben signifieth	44
63.	How Reuben lay with his father's concubine, and what the signification thereof is	31-45
76.	The Testament of Reuben, and the figure thereof	4-18

Revenge

22.	Whence in man the wrath and vengeance to be revenged ariseth	58-64

Rib

19.	What the rib and dividing of Adam signifieth	2, 6

Riches

58.	How the riches of the outward man belong to the new man	21, *et seq.*

Right

66.	How right is God and wrong is the Devil	60

Rocks

23.	Why at Christ's death the rocks clave asunder	3

Ring

65.	What the ring, bracelet and staff of Judah signify	32

S

Saba or Sheba

54.	What the fountain Saba or Sheba signifieth	15, 16

Sacrifice

27.	Of Cain's and Abel's sacrifice	1-40
27.	Why an earthly sacrifice must be	18, *et seq.*
27.	Why the sacrifice without faith is loathsome to God	13

Sarah

40.	Why God made Sarah unfruitful	27, 28
42.	How God asked for Sarah	26, 27
42.	What Sarah's laughing and lying signify	30, *et seq.*
49.	Of Sarah's death and Abraham's purchased burying place: what is signified thereby	1-18
51.	Why Sarah brought forth but one son	3

THE TABLE OF THE MYSTERIUM MAGNUM

CHAP.	Schools	VERSE
51.	Of what profit the knowledge of the high schools or universities, and the Devil's knowledge, is	49, 50
64.	Whence the confused languages of the high schools or universities come	24
69.	The spying and prying of the high schools or universities helpeth not into the kingdom of God	20, 21
77.	When the time of the high schools or universities began . .	67

Scorner

40.	Why God must have the scorner also, in this time of life	23, *et seq.*

Sea

16.	What the glassy sea is	27

Serah or Zerah

65.	The powerful figure of the birth of Peres and Serah or Zerah .	58, *et seq.*

Serpent

20.	Of the creation and subtlety of the Serpent	9–19
22.	Of the creation and subtlety of the Serpent	29
20.	In the Serpent lieth excellent art	17, 18
22.	The Devil hath infected the ens of the Serpent . . .	33
22.	Why the Serpent is said to be a virgin	34
23.	Wherefore God cursed the Serpent	23–29
27.	Where the Serpent's head was first trod upon and broken .	11, 12
38.	How the Serpent's ens and also the line of Christ lay in Abraham .	13

Seth

29.	What the name Seth signifieth in the Language of Nature . .	24

Shechem

61.	What the name Shechem signifieth	75

Shekel

49.	An exposition of the four hundred shekels of silver that Abraham gave for the field	8, 9

Shem

31.	What Shem is in the Language of Nature	6
34.	How Shem and Japhet took a garment upon their shoulders .	20–26

CHAP.	Shepherd	VERSE

58. How a shepherd is more highly esteemed before God than the highly learned worldly wise man . . . . . 32, *et seq.*
60. Why God's Spirit hath so exactly described the slight actions of mean shepherds 49, 50

Signal Star

70. How the signal star or ascendant appeared . . . 32, *et seq.*

Simeon

76. The Testament of Simeon and Levi, and the figure thereof . . 19–37

Sin. Sinner

22. Of the original of actual sin, and of the awakening of God's anger in the human property 1–82
22. What sin is, and what is not sin . . . . . 39, *et seq.*
22. What the sin against the Holy Ghost is 43, 44
27. What it is that attaineth the forgiveness of sins 45
48. How far it must go with the repenting sinner . . . 21, *et seq.*
78. The figure of a converted sinner 5, 6

Sinew

60. What it signifieth, that the children of Israel eat not that sinew of the ham . . . . 51, *et seq.*

Sleep

19. What Adam's sleep signifieth 5

Sodom

42. Of the three men, which appeared to Abraham in the plain of Mamre and went towards Sodom, and burnt the city of the children of Ham with fire from the Lord 1–35
43. Of the destruction of Sodom and Gomorrah: how God shewed it to Abraham before 1–71
43. How Sodom is a looking-glass for the present world . . 67, *et seq.*
43. What figure the judgment upon Sodom is 14
44. What fire was rained down upon Sodom . . . 24, *et seq.*

Sophia

25. Sophia is the tincture of the light 14
25. The fire-soul is the man or husband of the noble Sophia, and it is of the fire's tincture 14
37. How Sophia generateth the true Joseph 14, 15
52. What is called Sophia 6
52. When the magic fire of the soul is bridegroom to the noble Sophia . 11–14

THE TABLE OF THE MYSTERIUM MAGNUM

CHAP.	Soul	VERSE
10.	True understanding lieth in the soul	3
11.	What the soul is	20, 25
15.	How the soul standeth in three kingdoms	15, 18–24
15.	There are not three souls but one	24
17.	Of the soul's great power	43
22.	Whither the soul must go after the judgment	47
23.	How the soul of Adam and Eve were ashamed	1
25.	How the soul may go through the judgment, or how not	2, 3, 26
25.	How the virgin child must not flee from the fire-soul	9
34.	Of the animal soul in the regeneration	17
37.	Wherefore God bringeth the soul into trouble	8, 9
52.	How the soul may see God	10
56.	When God's grace entereth into the soul	36
69.	The first condition of the poor soul when it turneth to Christ	7, *et seq.*
70.	How the soul standeth in three Principles	5

Sound

5.	How the sound or tune in heaven is	19
5.	How the sound or tune in the darkness or hell is	19

Speak

35.	Whence it cometh originally that man can speak	73
36.	From what it is that man can speak and understand	85

Spirit

4.	Of the original of the multitude of spirits, good and evil	11
8.	Of the spirits of the outward world, from time, that pass away	13
29.	How the Spirit of God hath from eternity sported with itself in the spiritual world	4
36.	From what the false spiritual persons or clergy have spoken	30, *et seq.*

Steward

70.	What Joseph's steward signifieth	50

Strife

25.	Of the strife between the seed of the woman and the seed of the Serpent	10, *et seq.*
36.	Wherefore men do strive	62, 63
52.	When the strife in man is manifested, and Christ breaketh the Serpent's head	31, *et seq.*
60.	What the strife about the letter is	47, 48
62.	Wherefore the strife in Christendom must be	19

Strife

CHAP.		VERSE
62.	With what strife a true Christian striveth	21, *et seq.*
64.	How all strife cometh from the Tower of Babel	28
75.	How the time of strife is at an end	29, 30

Substance

53.	How the divine substance giveth itself into Nature	18

Succoth

61.	The figure of Jacob's going to Succoth	72

Sun

11.	From what power the sun shineth	35
13.	Whence the sun taketh its lustre	16

Supper

70.	What that supper is (Revelation iii)	44–46

Swearing

53.	What swearing by God is called	9

Sword

25.	Of the Cherubim angel's sword	4–13
25.	The original of the flaming sword of fire	25

T

Teachers

28.	What teachers the children of this world will have	44
36.	By what a man shall know whether a teacher come from God or from the letter	54, *et seq.*
41.	How the unfitted teachers will needs preach the Holy Ghost into the self-will	46

Temple

15.	What the temple of God is	28
36.	What the temple of God is	16
52.	What the temple of God is	8
27.	How the temple of Christ must be brought along into the material church of clay	49

Temptation

48.	How man without God's grace cannot stand in temptation	2

THE TABLE OF THE MYSTERIUM MAGNUM

CHAP.   Testament   VERSE

46. What a man must do if he would read and understand the Old Testament 29, 30
46. Wherefore the figures of the Old Testament have remained silent to this last time and now shall be made manifest . . . 31, 32
54. Of the figure of the Old and New Testaments 17

Tetragrammaton

35. Of the name Tetragrammaton 53

Tamar

65. Of Judah and Tamar: A mystical figure of Adam and Christ, wherein the new birth is excellently prefigured . . . 1–65

Time

30. Of the seven appointed times 34–46
30. When the sixth number of time is 44
31. Of the seven times from Adam to the end of the world . . 38–45
69. How the time of redemption draweth near 23

Timnath

65. What Timnath signifieth 22

Torment

71. What it is that hath no torment 21, 22

Tower

35. Wherefore the children of Noah purposed to build a tower . . 64, 65
35. How the time is born that we shall be led away from the Tower of Babel 67
35. What the mystery is of the Tower, and of the divided languages . 68–75
36. What the Tower of Babel is 15
36. What the figure of Babel's Tower is 5–11
36. What the Babylonish Tower was under Moses and among the heathen, and now is among Christians, Jews and Turks . . 33
36. How a man ought to consider of the Tower and city, Babel . . 58
36. How we must go out from all Babylonish master-builders of that Tower . . . . 50, *et seq.*
66. How worldly judges ought not to rely upon the Tower of Babel . 60

| CHAP. | Tree. Tree of Life | VERSE |

35. How the human tree hath by Noah's children spread itself abroad in its properties, and how at the Tower of Babel they were divided in the properties by the confusion of languages into several and different people and nations 1–75
36. How the Jews, Christians, Turks and heathens are but one only tree 37–40
36. How we may again, one with another, be one people, one tree, one man, with soul and body 43, 44
17. Why God set the Tree of Life before Adam . . . 38–43
17. The Tree of Life and the Tree of the Knowledge of Good and Evil are but one . . . . 10, *et seq.*

Trinity. Threefoldness

1. Of the Trinity 3, 4, 5
7. Of the Holy Trinity or Threefoldness of the divine essence or substance 1–19

Tubalcain

29. Of Tubalcain 44–46

Turks

40. How the Turks lie under the veil of Christ, and are born in the house . . . . 72, *et seq.*
40. How God heareth the Turks in the Son . . . 74, *et seq.*
40. How the Turks do not blaspheme the Holy Ghost . . 78, *et seq.*
40. Wherefore God hath taken away the candlesticks from the Turks . . . . 82, *et seq.*
40. How the holy voice of Christ is not departed from the Turks, to forget them eternally . . . . 87, *et seq.*
40. Of the difference between the Turks and the Christians . .92–100

U

Understanding

3. Why the divine understanding bringeth itself into spiritual properties 13
3. The divine understanding receiveth no source into itself . . 21
29. What the eternal divine understanding is 1, 2

Unquietness

66. What the unquietness is 65

THE TABLE OF THE MYSTERIUM MAGNUM

V

CHAP.	Venus	VERSE
10.	How the inward and the outward Venus are step-sisters	53
13.	Venus is the substance of all metals	18

Verbum Fiat

11.	How the Verbum Fiat is still at this day creating	9

Visions

67.	What the right visions are	7

Voice

23.	Of the voice that was in the Garden	11–16
55.	The figure of Isaac's saying: The voice is Jacob's voice, but the hands are the hands of Esau	27, 28

W

War. Warrior

22.	How war is good, and how not good	73
38.	Whence all war and strife hath its original	7–10
33.	Whence all war and strife hath its original	22, et seq.
38.	Of the beginning of the heathenish wars: how Abraham delivered Lot; and of Melchisedek to whom Abraham gave tithes	1–26
55.	How it is not God, but the kingdom of nature in the anger of God that will make war	45, 46
38.	How it is not God, but the kingdom of nature in the anger of God that will make war	16, 17
30.	What the Christians' wars are	42
38.	No Christian warreth	15, 16
62.	What the outward war that Christians make is	24
33.	What every warrior or soldier is	19, 20

Washing the Feet

42.	What Abraham's washing the feet signifieth	11

Water

4.	Of the water of eternal life	15
10.	Of the water which Christ will give us to drink	57

Wedding

70.	Where the assured wedding of the Lamb is	25, et seq.
70.	What a man must do, when he will enter into the wedding of Christ	38

CHAP.	Whore	VERSE
30.	Whence the mother of the Babylonish whoredom is arisen	22, 23
36.	What the Babylonish whore and the dragon beast are	20, *et seq.*, 37
36.	Of the Antichristian Babylonish whore, of all tongues, nations and languages, and what lieth hid under the languages and Tower of Babel	1–85
36.	Of the Babylonish whore's child or bastard, which is predestinated to damnation	23, *et seq.*
36.	What the whore's beast is	41
36.	How the whore hopeth for a golden temple or time	70, *et seq.*
36.	How the whore must fall	69
36.	What is meant by the whoredom committed with the letter	44, *et seq.*
37.	How the unchastity of the Babylonish whore is come up before the Most High	61
62.	What is whoredom in the sight of God	30, *et seq.*
65.	What the whoredom of Judah with Tamar signifieth	38, *et seq.*
65.	What David's whoredom with Bathsheba signifieth	41
65.	What Solomon's whoredom signifieth	45, *et seq.*
66.	What the powerful figure of the whorish unchaste world is: which vermin the world is at present full of	41, *et seq.*

Wicked

60.	How God dwelleth even in the abyss of the wicked soul	44

Wife

41.	How a man must leave wife, children, etc. to be a true Christian	54, 65

Will. Willing

26.	Wherefore the fire-soul hath free will	7
27.	What the will must do that it may with its desire go to God	4, 5
27.	The human free will is become sinful	16
29.	Why there is a contrary opposite will	6, 7
61.	What the ability of the will is	57, 58
61.	The cause why the false wicked or evil will turneth not itself towards grace	59
66.	How in this time [of life] all things pass in free will	21
66.	How knowing nothing is better than willing for self	66
71.	Of the divine willing and of the human willing	25–36

Wisdom

1.	What the eternal wisdom is	6
29.	How the eternal wisdom hath introduced itself into a formed visibility	1–70
41.	A speech to the reason-wise	42, *et seq.*

THE TABLE OF THE MYSTERIUM MAGNUM

CHAP.	Woman	VERSE
19.	Of the building or framing of the woman	1–27
41.	How the woman is saved through bearing of children	29, *et seq.*
66.	What the woman upon the moon in the Revelation is	34, 35

Word

2.	Of the Word or Heart of God	1–11
2.	Of the outspoken word	7
28.	What the literal word is	56, 57
36.	How man should try himself in the framing of his words	81, *et seq.*
40.	What God's Word assumed	10
56.	Why our soul and the Word that became man, are compared together	23, *et seq.*
61.	What the Word is	43, 44

World

2.	The whole world lieth in a clod of earth	6
2.	Of the inward world	9
2.	How one world is in another	10
4.	Of the three worlds	12
17.	That same world, wherein Adam was before his Eve was, must come again	9
29.	What the invisible spiritual world is	4, 5
31.	How Shem, Ham and Japhet are an image of the three worlds	10, 11

Wrong

71.	How man doth a twofold wrong	25, *et seq.*

Z

Zebulun

77.	The Testament of Zebulun, and the figure thereof	3–7

www.ingramcontent.com/pod-product-compliance
Lightning Source LLC
Chambersburg PA
CBHW031610160426
43196CB00006B/82